Lesley Lyle is a certified Laughter Yoga teacher who uses laughter therapeutically in her work as a coach, facilitator trainer and consultant. She has a DipHe in Clinical Hypnosis and was trained in Laughter Yoga by its founder, Dr Kataria. Lesley is also a qualified NLP Practitioner and Stress Management Trainer. It was Lesley's insistence on focusing on people's solutions instead of their problems that led her to learn about Positive Psychology Training and enrol on MAPP (Master in Applied Positive Psychology) to become a Positive Psychologist herself. Lesley now practices hypnotherapy and happiness consultations in clinics in Harley Street and the New Forest.

'The key to happiness is to start where you are right now, today. From there we can learn to adopt the habits that make us feel happier and more resilient. Whether you laugh because you are happy or laugh to become happy really doesn't matter, the outcome is still the same.'

Laugh Your Way To HAPPINESS

Use the Science of Laughter for Total Well-being

Lesley Lyle

WATKINS PUBLISHING
LONDON

This edition first published in the UK and USA 2014 by
Watkins Publishing Limited
PO Box 883
Oxford, OX1 9PL
UK

A member of Osprey Group

For enquiries in the USA and Canada:
Osprey Publishing
PO Box 3985
New York, NY 10185-3985
Tel: (001) 212 753 4402
Email: info@ospreypublishing.com

10 9 8 7 6 5 4 3 2 1

Designed and typeset by Gail Jones
Printed and bound by CPI Group (UK) Ltd, Croydon, CR0 4YY

A CIP record for this book is available from the British Library

ISBN: 978-1-78028-674-7

Watkins Publishing is supporting the Woodland Trust, the UK's leading woodland conservation charity, by funding tree-planting initiatives and woodland maintenance.

www.watkinspublishing.co.uk

DEDICATION

To all members of the New Forest Laughter Club, thank you for sharing the laughter and the joy. To Dr Kataria and all those who continue to spread the sound of laughter around the world. And especially for Iain.

ACKNOWLEDGEMENT

I'd like to thank the people who have helped me to find my way to 'here' and provided me with support and encouragement. My family (Iain, Bernard, June, Tim, Ben, Katy) and the 'family' I have come to know at Watkins Publishing (in particular, Sandra, Francesca, Deborah, Lydia, Vicky and Stephen) and the people who inspire me through their work of NLP, Stress Management, Clinical Hypnosis, Laughter Yoga and Positive Psychology.

Contents

Foreword 11

Introduction 15

Chapter 1: Discovering the Power of Laughter 23

Chapter 2: The Science of Laughter 39

Chapter 3: The Spirit of Laughter 61

Chapter 4: Laughter at Home 97

Chapter 5: Rediscovering the Laughter of Children 125

Chapter 6: Laughter Games and Activities 143

Chapter 7: The Power of the Smile 163

Chapter 8: Stress-busting 185

Chapter 9: How to be Happy 211

Resources 235

Foreword

It has become a rarity today to see someone smile and laugh with gay abandon. It seems as if people have forgotten how to laugh. In this competitive high-pressure and high-tension world, laughter is fast disappearing and people are succumbing to daily stressors that relentlessly rob them of the ability to laugh.

In my quest to find a solution to put the smile back on people's faces, I walked different paths before creating Laughter Yoga. Laughter Yoga proved to be a panacea for all negativity. It is indeed the best prescription for good health and happiness. A daily dose of laughter is the one solution that has the power to unwind stress and uplift joy; the power to slow down a racing heart and strengthen the mind; the power to raise the spirit and fend off pessimism … and all this in an instant. Sounds crazy, but works like magic! It is, in fact, nature's most creative and complete way to keep healthy and safe.

For centuries, laughter was referred to as the best medicine for body and mind, but never was there a reliable delivery system. Laughter was simply the end result of entertainment or amusement, but Laughter Yoga has taken laughter to a new level. It is a complete delivery system, allowing laughter to actually be prescribed as part of a daily routine in order to realize all of its health benefits. It enables everyone to laugh, even those who are serious, introverted and uncomfortable being funny. Never in my wildest dreams could I have imagined that laughter could be as simple as that – just laugh, because we can!

The benefits of laughter are numerous in all facets of life – personal, professional and social. Laughter, backed by countless evidence-based studies, is being practised not only as a fitness exercise but also as a therapeutic tool to control chronic diseases such as depression, hypertension, heart disease, cancer, diabetes, arthritis and migraines.

This wonderful book by Lesley is not just about learning Laughter Yoga: it will teach you how to bring laughter fully into your life and use it optimally to enhance your well-being. But remember, the secret is to share your laughter with everyone around you. If you are happy, but people around you are not happy, they will not allow you to stay happy. Therefore, it is imperative to bring happiness to others in order to become happy yourself.

Lesley is doing a great job of sharing her joy and laughter with everyone she meets. An airline professional, she travels around the world spreading the word of love and laughter and connecting with other laughter leaders to generate awareness about the significance and value of laughter in people's life.

This book will help you understand how unconditional laughter helps you get in touch with your true self and spiritual nature. The narration of Lesley's personal experiences is inspiring and will help you keep your spirits high despite the challenges of life. This book will teach you to shift your perspective through laughter so that you can navigate your life in a better way and discover the benefits of laughter for body, mind and spirit.

I thank Lesley for her inspired contribution to bringing more laughter into people's lives.

And remember: keep laughing and smiling – it really can change your life … ha ha ha!

Dr Madan Kataria

Bangalore, 2013

Introduction

A day without laughter is a day wasted.
Charlie Chaplin

If there is a route to increased health and happiness, then I believe that laughter is the superhighway!

This has been my experience and one I have shared with countless people around the world who have also discovered that the power of laughter brings about positive change. Research has shown that people who frequently laugh and smile are likely to enjoy a higher income, have better relationships and better health, live longer and are regarded as more attractive by others. They feel happy. The aim of this book is to show you how you too can discover the power of laughter to change your life.

My starting point and inspiration has been the work of Dr Madan Kataria, the Indian GP who founded Laughter Yoga and invented the concept of 'laughing for no reason'. Rather than relying on humour and comedy for laughter, which we may not encounter every day,

Dr Kataria found that laughing as an exercise is just as effective – and may actually be even more effective than mere humour. This is because participants are able to engage in extended, hearty laughter that provides maximum health benefits. The most important element of Laughter Yoga is that it is based on the scientific fact that the body does not know the difference between fake and real laughter. As long as you do laughter exercises with willingness, they will provide the same physiological and psychological benefits as a real laugh. In practice, as laughter exercises are carried out in a group where there is lots of eye contact, authentic laughter is almost guaranteed because laughter is so infectious.

This book is about laughter, not about humour. The distinction between the two is that humour requires something or somebody to make you laugh, like a joke, comedy or a funny situation. I do not dismiss the value of therapeutic humour and there is some wonderful work being done across the world where humour is used as an intervention to promote health and wellness – for example, therapeutic clowns working in hospitals and other organizations. However, in this book I look at what is often called *unconditional* laughter. It is the sort of laughter that is always available for you to access as long as you are willing to allow yourself to 'laugh for no reason', whether you are with others or on your own. Of course, once you get into the habit of laughing for no reason, you may find that you are more easily amused and your sense of humour develops, but to begin with, you just need to be willing to 'fake it till you make it'.

Discovering the benefits of laughter

Laughter is a resource that is available to you in a never-ending supply, but first you need to access it and allow it to flow so that you can utilize its full potential. You may have forgotten, but during your early childhood, laughter was your *only* means to communicate pleasure, joy and happiness! Now you may have become one of the majority of adults who are estimated to laugh an average of 15 times a day, unlike children who laugh and giggle between 300–500 times each day.

When we are happy, we laugh, but did you know that when we laugh, we become happy? This is the simple principle that lies at the foundation of Laughter Yoga.

Dr Kataria's principle of 'fake it till you make it' applies not just to Laughter Yoga but to other mind and body connections as well, as our mind influences our body and our body influences our mind. You can often tell how someone is feeling by watching the way they move their body: for example, a happy person walking down the street is likely to walk energetically, with a spring in their step and their chin tilted upward. A person who feels depressed may walk slowly, with shoulders slumped and looking down. We now understand that if we adopt the posture and behaviour of a happy person, we will start to feel like that because our brain produces the biochemicals to match the actions of our body. Social psychologist Amy Cuddy, Associate Professor at Harvard Business School, has shown that standing in a posture of confidence, even for as little as two minutes, can increase testosterone and decrease cortisol levels in the brain. The same is true of a happy posture.

If you have previously tried to improve your health and happiness through self-help methods, but failed to adopt the suggested health regimes because you found them too time-consuming or difficult to maintain, you will love the fact that you can gain so much by simply laughing. This book is for you if you want to live proactively and enjoy your best life, rather than passively leaving positive experiences to chance. By simply making some small changes, you will learn how you can bring more laughter into your life, increase your 'happiness ratio' and improve your relationships with family, friends and colleagues.

You may be one of the many people who struggle to deal with stress and anxieties effectively, and frequently find yourself reacting automatically in ways that do not help or even make you feel worse. This book will explain how laughter is one of nature's ways of helping us cope in difficult times, as well as allowing us to express joy and happiness when things go well. You will gain the knowledge and information you need to create a happier and healthier lifestyle so that you will feel better physically and psychologically, socially and emotionally. Research shows that when our health and happiness improve, we also have a positive influence on the happiness and health of those around us.

I will share with you my own personal experience of finding happiness and health through laughter to provide you with a participant's perspective of the laughter experience, although nothing will inform you more than trying it for yourself, of course!

My story is not a rags-to-riches, tragedy-to-success type of story that some authors of self-help books like to describe. I have not gone from the depths of depression to experiencing euphoric, everlasting joy. But the results I have experienced have been profound in a subtle way, and I have found that each small change has lasted and become a permanent feature of how I feel. The compound effect of this has led me to experience the upward spiral of positive emotion that is described by positive psychologists (I will explain more about positive psychology later in the book). I have had the pleasure of working with numerous people who have achieved incredible acts of courage such as climbing Everest, overcoming addiction or rebuilding their life after a devastating incident. I respect and admire them very much, but I can only offer a story of someone who is ordinary and average. Still, I hope that you can relate to my life experience.

I share some of the knowledge I have gained through my training in Laughter Yoga, Neuro-Linguistic Programming (NLP), Clinical Hypnosis, Stress Management and Positive Psychology, and I include research results that show how laughter increases our positive emotions and promotes good health. You will find plenty of tips and techniques, along with practical exercises, so that you can try out some of these proven strategies for yourself. There are also links to numerous resources where you can gain further information and support. I have deliberately excluded a detailed bibliography as I have not written a reference book as such; however, I have included enough information for you to be able to find the relevant research. In addition, all the available scientific studies are listed on my website and are regularly updated.

When I first started to look for ways to increase my health and happiness over a decade ago, I wanted to find a book that would provide me with lots of reliable information from various sources; instead, I found that most authors presented their own work and opinion and offered a 'one size fits all' approach. You only have to look at siblings brought up in the same house, with the same parents, going to the same school, eating the same food and having the same opportunities to realize that every choice we make takes us on a different path. I think that no one is more qualified than you yourself to know what your needs are. Back then, I bought and studied lots of books and cherry-picked what I considered to be the most pertinent points from them. I hope this book fulfils your needs by providing a broad range of information gathered from the most respected and up-to-date sources, presented in one place. If this can speed up your progress from gaining knowledge to putting it into practice that, consequently, leads to an improvement in your health and happiness, then I will have achieved my aim.

There are many theories and concepts about what makes us healthy and happy, but the truth is that reading about them will be useless unless you take action. People can guide, support and advise you, inform, direct and help you, but ultimately you are the only person who can decide whether to create change or not. If you believe in the 'no pain, no gain' principle and think we have to suffer in order to get healthier and happier, I can categorically state that this particular statement is untrue and unhelpful! You do not need to buy expensive equipment, join a club or radically change your lifestyle to reap the benefits of increased health and well-being. With practice, we can all incorporate more laughter into our lives, whether we do so as an exercise or as a response to our increasing happiness. A one-hour session of Laughter Yoga will provide a thorough workout with an abundance of laughter that you are extremely unlikely to experience in a gym!

I am so grateful that I now have so much more laughter in my life, and I feel much more relaxed, joyful, optimistic and energetic. I hope you find, as I did, that opening up yourself to laughter allows you to be more open in other ways, too, such as being able to express love, kindness and gratitude.

Being healthy and happy is a choice and a consequence of the decisions you make each day. If you choose to make laughter a habit in your life, you will find that health and happiness follow naturally.

Chapter 1

Discovering the Power of Laughter

Against the assault of laughter nothing can stand.

Mark Twain

In some ways, it may seem obvious that we would all want more laughter in our lives – so what, you might ask, is so special about what I have discovered? In this chapter, I want to share with you my own journey to uncovering the power of laughter. I hope you will share the joy of my awakening to a different view on life and experience my breakthrough when I joined Dr Kataria in enjoying the power of laughing for no reason. It is the story of an ordinary person discovering something extraordinary – something that we all have access to.

So, if every journey has a beginning, where did my journey to discovering the joy of laughter begin? That is a difficult question to answer because I was never looking for laughter in the first place – I was looking for something else. Had you told you me that the answer could be as simple as 'laughing for no reason', I would have laughed, but for the wrong reason! Yet, the answer to so many of the things I wanted to manifest in my life, and subsequently in the life of others, turned out to be so childishly simple: laughter.

In the beginning

From my earliest recollections, I have been labelled several things such as 'dreamer', 'chatterbox' and 'rebel'. At school I was known as someone who would do anything for a laugh, and I often got involved in classroom pranks that resulted in detention. Even at junior school the teachers told my mother at parents' evening, 'Lesley may not always start the trouble, but she'll always be found at the scene.' I do not think that I was particularly naughty; I just wanted to enjoy myself, and reading, writing and mathematics did not quite do it for me!

I used to deny that my labels were truly representative of me, but, in hindsight, I can see that they were an accurate description of aspects of my personality. The difference is that I now see them as parts that serve me well, as long as I choose my environment carefully.

By a stroke of luck, one of my first jobs in 1975 was as a temporary cabin crew for Laker Airways. Obviously, I cannot exactly say that it suited me down to the ground – after all, I spent the majority of my time above 9,000 metres. It turned out to be a good choice for me, though. The 'dreamer' who dreamt of travelling to different countries got to go to them; the 'chatterbox' was provided with the opportunity (and even encouraged) to talk to lots of people; and the 'rebel' was satisfied with a job that had irregular hours, a lack of routine and provided lots of fun, even if it did mean conforming and wearing a uniform. Thirty-nine years later, I am still doing the same job, but I am now working for British Airways, and I can honestly say that I have never lost my enthusiasm for this job that I love so much.

Nowadays, I work part-time so that I can fit in the other jobs I do as a Clinical Hypnotherapist, NLP Practitioner, Stress Management Trainer and, of course, Laughter Coach/Teacher/Trainer. And being accepted as a student on the Masters Applied Positive Psychology in 2012 felt like a dream come true.

My working life has been full of smiling; I suppose you could call me a professional smiler. It is a significant part of the job as cabin crew, and unless your smiles are authentic and natural, they will look fake. You can smile throughout a ten-hour night flight if you love your job and work with people who enjoy their job, too. Fortunately, most cabin crew fall into the latter category, and there are always plenty of opportunities to tease each other and have a laugh. This playful attitude spills over and positively affects the social interaction between crew and the customers on board. When I fly as a passenger on holiday, I can always spot the crew who get on together, and if they do, I know that I can expect good customer service.

I have had a lot to smile about in my personal life during my career: I married and had three children, and after a brief break I was able to return to my cabin-crew job. The flexible working hours meant that I could often attend school events like Sports Day and be at home for much of the school holidays. I suppose I was one of those women who appeared to have it all, yet I still did not feel completely fulfilled.

The missing link

As I got older, I frequently had the feeling that something was missing. I could not put a name to it, and I had no idea how to look for something that had no name, no identity and that maybe did not even exist. At times, I just felt a little empty, with an underlying feeling of dissatisfaction. I had a yearning for something, but I could not pinpoint it. It would manifest itself in several ways. Sometimes, it felt like a certain type of hunger, but despite looking in a well-stocked fridge and cupboards, there would be nothing there to satisfy me. Or I would feel the need to be busy, to take up a hobby, to go shopping or to chat on the phone. It was pre-Internet days, but I am sure I would have spent my time on-line either trying to distract myself from these feelings or googling for an answer.

Most of the time I would ignore, deny and bury these feelings as I resented them; they seemed inappropriate and intrusive, and although I could go for weeks or even months without experiencing them consciously, they would always return, the spoilsport of an otherwise contented life. In the years that I have been involved in therapeutic practice, I have spoken to many people who described exactly the same sort of thing in their own way. I have come to the conclusion that these feelings are prevalent in our modern society and that they are one of the many symptoms we can experience when we do not spend enough time resting, recovering and recuperating. Even when we enjoy our lives and what we do, we still need time just 'to be' and not 'be doing'. Many of us have been brought up with an attitude of 'the devil makes work for idle hands' and that we are wasting time and are being lazy if we are not constantly busy.

Even worse, we may believe that things like drinking a cup of coffee, eating a doughnut, smoking a cigarette and flipping through the pages of the daily newspaper will provide us with an adequate break. In fact, these activities are more likely to stimulate and stress us and make a rest even more essential.

Now that I have studied Positive Psychology, I recognize that what I was experiencing is something called 'languishing'. This is a description of people who, while not suffering from depression or mental illness, are nevertheless lacking the character traits that enable them to flourish and feel happy.

For many years, I was one of those people searching for something, and even when I read the words of wisdom 'to look within', I still did not understand. I thought that this meant that the answer was in my heart or in my mind, but I now believe that the answer was there all the time in my body, and I discovered this truth when I discovered the power of laughter.

What makes us tick?

If you were the sort of person who likes to watch people, then you would love my job as cabin crew. I could not possibly estimate how many people I have seen over the years. I find it fascinating that everyone is so different, and yet, in so many ways, we are all the same. Eventually, my curiosity got the better of me. I wanted to know more about psychology so that I could understand how and why we behave in certain ways and what makes us tick. Although my conscious intention was to understand other people, I wonder whether another, unconscious motive was to understand myself better.

First, I studied psychology, then Neuro-Linguistic Programming (NLP), and, in 2009, I became an NLP Practitioner. NLP helps us understand the different ways we communicate with each other and with ourselves. Much of our communication is outside of our conscious awareness, and unless your thoughts and actions are congruent, people will soon realize that you are not being authentic. This is another reason why only real smiles work in the customer service industry. NLP showed me that what we know consciously is such a tiny proportion of what we know unconsciously. Everything we have ever experienced since our birth is stored as memory in our brain, but the percentage amount we can consciously access is minuscule.

Much of NLP is based on the work of Milton Erickson, a renowned psychiatrist, psychologist and hypnotherapist. I was really interested in his work and his ability to help people within a short period of time. Erickson believed that everyone has the resources to solve their own problems. Through his extremely intuitive style of therapy, usually of a conversational nature, he was able to facilitate his patients' unconscious search so that they could find their own unique solutions to feel better.

In 2010, I heard about a Diploma of Higher Education in Clinical Hypnosis course at St Mary's University in London, and I seized this opportunity to learn about the scientific application of Clinical Hypnosis and Brief Strategic Therapy, a rapid, solution-based therapeutic practice. As I learnt about psychosomatic illness and how our thoughts and beliefs can affect our biology and everyday experiences, I realized how I had been affecting my own health and happiness in ways I had not imagined. It was disconcerting at first, but also empowering because this new knowledge provided me with information about ways in which I could make a significant and positive impact on my mental and physical health. I became fascinated as I learnt about psychoneuroimmunology, something that I could barely say and struggled to spell! This is the science that looks at how our psychological processes affect our nervous system and our immune system. I was astounded by the implication that what we think, what we believe and how we behave can affect our quality of life and also influence whether we get ill, suffer from the negative effects of stress – and even influence the amount of pain we experience. This had incredible implications not just for my well-being but for my clients, too, and I was eager to pass on all this useful and potentially life-changing information.

Around this time I was introduced to Positive Psychology, the scientific study of the things that help us thrive and feel good. Rather than focusing on what is not going right, it encourages us to look at what is going well and to do more of it. Owing to Positive Psychology and the work of its founder, Professor Martin Seligman, I learnt how to accept my previously perceived character weaknesses (dreamer, chatterbox, rebel) and reframe them into positives. In particular, I am thankful to Dr Barbara Fredrickson, Positive Psychology expert and author of the book *Positivity*. It was reading this book that would have such a profound and far-reaching effect on my life and later lead me to applying for a place on the Masters of Applied Positive Psychology course. For, in an obscure and convoluted way, it would be the catalyst for a series of events that would lead me to discover the wonderful experience of 'laughing for no reason'.

I can be bothered!

I was only a couple of chapters into reading *Positivity* when I made a rather impulsive and rash decision. From that moment onward, I would never use the excuse 'I can't be bothered'. I would continue to refuse to do things if I did not want to or was not able to do them, but no longer was 'can't be bothered' going to be an acceptable reason not to do things. Going forward, I *would* be bothered! Before long I would discover the extent this small change would have in my life. It *is* amazing how making tiny changes in your life can result in far-reaching ones ...

I am lucky that I am still able to fly as part-time cabin crew. I am even luckier that my partner, Iain, does the same job and we are able to work on 'joint rosters'. This arrangement allows us to work together on the same flight and enjoy the same days off. At times, we feel like 'professional tourists' and feel privileged to enjoy this occupation. The day after making my 'pledge to be bothered', we both travelled to Mumbai, India, on a rostered trip as cabin crew. During the drive to the airport I told Iain about my new resolution. He did not say much, but judging by his raised eyebrows, he did not seem totally convinced.

The flight was full and busy, and we arrived at Mumbai airport in the early hours of the morning, tired and looking forward to getting to the hotel for a good rest. As I left the aircraft, I noticed some discarded magazines and newspapers. I picked up *Saga* magazine, the magazine for the over 50s, and took it with me for a little light reading.

The next morning I made us a cup of tea and glanced through the magazine. One particular article caught my eye. It was about Laughter Yoga and its founder, Dr Kataria, who had invented the idea of combining laughter and exercise as a way to promote good health. I was fascinated with the concept, which sounded mildly preposterous and yet intriguingly enticing.

Later, over lunch, I told Iain about it, adding that, by coincidence, we were in Mumbai, the very place where the idea had been conceived. 'Maybe the concierge knows about it,' I said. 'I suppose I could go and ask him, but then again, oh, I can't be bothered!' As I uttered the words, I remembered with dismay my prior commitment to ditch this excuse. I was irritated; I really could not be bothered. Iain was amused – less than 24 hours and I was already being challenged. Surely I could not give up so easily, especially with a witness who would relentlessly remind me if I failed? Reluctantly, I went to see the concierge after lunch.

At the concierge's desk, I tried a throwaway leading question with the intention of a quick getaway: 'I don't suppose you've heard of something called laughter yoga, have you?'

I was prepared for a negative response, but the concierge was delighted to tell me that not only had he heard of it, but he informed me there was a laughter yoga club nearby that met up each morning in the local park. I asked him if he could write down the name and address of the club so that I could go and see what a laughter yoga session looked like the next time I was in Mumbai. He checked something on the Internet and then picked up the phone to make some enquiries on my behalf. After a brief conversation, he handed over the telephone. I had no idea who I was going to speak to or that as I held that phone to my ear, it would turn out to be a defining moment in my life.

The laughter doctor

I took the phone and said, 'Hello.' No one responded with a 'Hello' in reply to mine. Instead, I heard a slow, deep, melodious 'Ha, ha, ha'. Rather bemused at this unusual greeting, I instinctively smiled as the soft and reassuring laughter continued. This was my introduction to Dr Madan Kataria, the Indian GP who started Laughter Yoga in 1995 to see whether he could help people gain health benefits

Navajo first laugh ceremony

Navajo Indians traditionally celebrate a baby's first laugh. A baby is not considered to have become fully human until its first laugh. This usually occurs around the age of three months and is believed to signify the last stage of moving from the spirit world to the world of humans.

The baby is thought to assume some of the personal characteristics of the person who makes it laugh, and therefore parents tend to be careful to keep the baby away from those with unfavourable dispositions. It is a great honour to be the person who facilitates the baby's first laugh, and he or she is responsible for throwing a party to celebrate the event.

from laughter. He started out with just five people, and now tens of thousands of people in over 60 countries around the world enjoy the benefits of laughter every day.

When Dr Kataria stopped chuckling, he asked how he could help. He told me about Laughter Yoga, what it does and why it matters. Although Dr K (as I will call him from now on) gave me a lot of information about the scientific evidence that validates Laughter Yoga, he explained that the most important factor is the way that it makes people feel. Indeed, I came off the phone feeling elated, laughing and happy after just a few minutes of talking with him and sharing his giggles. Curiously enough, I was not the only one to be affected: the concierge was laughing, too – evidence of the infectious nature of laughter. Suddenly, the concept of 'laughing for no reason' sounded like a sensible idea.

Meeting Dr Kataria

My next work trip to India took me to Bangalore without Iain as he was on leave. On an impulse I decided to email Dr K to say that I was going to be in the country very soon. Much to my astonishment he replied that he had relocated to Bangalore from Mumbai and would be delighted to meet me. I rang Dr K once I arrived in Bangalore, and he explained that a blessing ceremony of his new house had been arranged for that afternoon and that I was welcome to join in. I arranged for a hotel car to take me there at the appointed time, 2 pm.

As I got out of the car, Dr K, instantly recognizable by the sound of his laughter, met me in front of his house. With outstretched arms he laughed, 'Ha, ha, ha! You've made it, you've arrived!' As I look back, I see how significant these words would become.

Monkeys, a turtle, fire and laughter

If you are wondering what Dr K looks like, think about the actor Yul Brynner in the film *The King and I*. Add a beaming, happy face and imagine being in the company of someone who just makes you feel comfortable and at ease. Inside Dr K's house we settled down with a cup of *chai*, sweet Indian tea, prepared by one of his assistants. He told me a little of his life history and how he came to be a medical doctor and subsequently the founder of Laughter Yoga. His story is remarkable, and I was spellbound as he described being brought up in a remote village, the youngest of eight children. Despite the fact that neither of his parents had been to school, young Madan Kataria was encouraged to get an education and become a doctor. The odds against this happening must have been enormous. The nearest doctor to his village was nearly 15 miles away, and few children, including his brothers and sisters, had the opportunity to have a full education.

As Dr K talked, the time flew past, and despite the fact that I had only just met him, I felt completely relaxed and comfortable in his company. It was like being with an old friend or a favourite uncle, and, of course, the conversation was frequently punctuated with gentle laughter, now from both of us.

Meanwhile, Dr K's pet turtle took a stroll around the large and mainly unfurnished room. He walked across the marble floor exploring his new surroundings, and I watched as he negotiated the step that divided the living room from the corridor. Compared to the turtle's size, the step was huge, and yet he seemed determined to make it. Arranging first one front leg and then the other, I wondered if he would end up doing a handstand (or flipper stand?!) and end up on his shell, but he just about managed the manoeuvre. Almost immediately, the turtle turned around to make the return journey, but going up the step, against gravity, defeated him. Dr K gave him a helping hand and continued to talk. This was to happen several times, although it never interfered with the conversation or appeared to wear Dr K's patience.

I was invited to view the house, set over three floors. The marble flooring throughout felt smooth and comfortable underfoot, and upstairs there was a wide veranda framed by tall trees on all sides. To my delight, I later heard monkeys chattering, swinging down from the trees and scampering across the veranda floor.

Downstairs, a man in robes arrived to perform the house blessing. He set up his equipment in the middle of the room. A large sheet, metal bowls, various boxes and containers were strategically placed and positioned close to him. As people arrived, they seated themselves in a circle around what appeared to be a brazier. A bundle of sandalwood twigs was lit and fragrant smoke filled the room. From time to time a spoonful of oil was put on the fire and more sticks were added to keep it going. Everyone seemed familiar with the procedure as they joined together chanting in unison, their faces lit with the glow from the fire.

Although, in truth, I had little idea what was being said or what would happen next, I felt completely relaxed while watching and listening and far from excluded even though I was literally on the edge of the circle. A bowl containing flower petals was passed to me, and with simple hand gestures I was encouraged to throw the petals around. I felt extremely honoured. Later, the red powder spot, *bindi*, was placed on our foreheads between our eyebrows, and, like everyone else, I also received a red sacred ribbon that was tied to my left wrist. It has remained there ever since, and as I write these words, I am aware of it, still here, literally tying to me to these past events. The ribbon only consists of a few fragile strands now, and the red colour has faded to the palest pink. I know that one day soon it will break and be lost, but until then it acts as a constant reminder of the importance of laughter.

After the ceremony, my driver who had been waiting patiently (or rather snoozing in the back of the car) drove me back to the hotel where I managed to have a few hours' sleep before my flight back home. It had been a most interesting day. I sent a message to Iain to tell him of my experience. It read: 'Monkeys, turtle, a fire and laughter – tell you all about it later.' It did not occur to me how absurd this text message must have appeared until later when I got home and tried to describe my experience to Iain, who recognized the look on my face as one he had seen before. It was a look that told him that he would be hearing a lot more about Laughter Yoga in the future – and he was absolutely right!

The next day I received an email from Dr Kataria: *Thanks for coming and meeting me yesterday. In India, we say God comes to your house in the form of a guest. Your presence in the ceremony was important for me. Keep laughing, ho, ho, ha, ha. Dr K.*

Over the course of this book, I want to explain exactly how laughter will help you and how to bring more laughter into your life. But the enduring message is actually as simple as Dr K's: 'Keep laughing!'

Chapter 2

The Science of Laughter

Laughter is the sun that drives winter from the human face.

Victor Hugo

As soon as I got back from meeting Dr K in India, I could hardly wait to start researching Laughter Yoga. Although I did not doubt Dr K's integrity and passion, it is in my nature to question things and, in this case, look for supporting scientific evidence. My mind was racing with questions. Why had I never heard of Laughter Yoga? If it was so therapeutic, why was it not happening everywhere? Surely, laughing away your troubles must be better than taking medication or remaining in pain? What made better sense – laughing for no reason or feeling unwell or depressed for no reason? Or, was this all a matter of belief, a placebo effect? In other words, if you thought the claims about Laughter Yoga were true, would you get the results you were expecting?

Although I had been impressed with Dr K's explanations, I had no personal experience of laughter as an exercise. In order to accept these claims about the benefits of laughter, I needed to find the scientific evidence that validated them. I could not see how laughing could do you any harm, but could it really do you so much good? Was it actually true that 'laughter is the best medicine'?

In this chapter, I want to explain in more detail the scientific evidence that supports the benefits of laughter for us in every aspect of our life – physical, emotional and spiritual. As you will see, the evidence is compelling. But perhaps the best place to start is by looking at what laughter is and why it matters.

What is laughter?

One thing I know for sure is that everyone knows how to laugh because we are born with this ability that manifests itself around three to four months after birth. Babies learn to laugh at this age, and, along with crying, this is the way they communicate their emotional state. When we are happy, it is natural to laugh, and yet, somewhere between infancy and adulthood, we seem to stop or severely reduce the amount of natural, spontaneous laughter in our lives. I am not just talking about laughing at humour or laughing about something funny: I am talking about laughing from sheer joy and happiness.

This is more noticeable in some cultures than in others, and it seems that countries that are rich in terms of wealth are often poor in terms of laughter. A great example of this is Bhutan: it is the only country in the world that puts happiness at the heart of government policy because they value happiness as being far more important than being rich. I am sure most people would like to be wealthy and happy, but if you could only choose one, which would your prioritize? This question may reveal some important information for you.

We may speak a different language or come from a different culture, but all humans understand different sorts of laughter. In a study conducted at University College London, researchers compared the behaviour of people living in remote settlements, where they had no formal education, no electricity, no running water or contact with anyone from outside their group, with people from modern societies. Despite the disparity between the groups, they both had an equal understanding and recognition of laughter. At an elementary level, laughter is an immediate way to communicate to someone that we are not a threat or danger to them, and when we join in with the laughter of others, it demonstrates that we are sociable and accepting. Laughter connects us with each other.

The purpose of laughter

There are several theories on the purpose of laughter and although there are differences of opinion, one thing is certain: laughter has an important evolutionary purpose. We know this because humans learn to laugh long before they learn to talk. Smiling between mother and baby increases the bonding process, whereas laughter is associated with play, an extremely important part of healthy childhood development. Both smiling and laughter result in increased levels of oxytocin, the 'love hormone', and our brains respond more to the sound of children's' laughter than that of adults. Babies tend to laugh in response to playful behaviour: for instance, when we blow raspberries and make funny noises. So, when we try to get infants and children to laugh, we automatically engage in the play behaviour needed; they reward us with the sound of their laughter and we enjoy our interaction with them.

In adulthood, laughter can be shared between a group to increase a sense of trust and community. However, group laughter that excludes an individual can have the opposite effect and be used as a weapon to isolate and ostracize.

Another important purpose of laughter is to relieve tension. Even when we laugh at a joke, it is because we have experienced a type of stress. Jokes are told like stories, so as we listen, we follow the logic of what we are being told and anticipate what will happen next. The skill of the joke-teller is to unbalance us: what we expect to happen does not take place, and at the last moment, with the punch line, the story goes in a completely different direction. The effect of this is to cause momentary confusion of our thoughts and emotions, causing stress, but our laughter relieves this stress and leads to us feeling amused.

I believe this is the way we get young children and babies to laugh. Traditionally, we tell stories like 'Round and round the garden, like a teddy bear' and 'This little piggy went to market'. Each has a repetitive story, but just when everything feels predictable and safe, the teddy bear suddenly runs from the hand, up the arm and tickles, or the little piggy unexpectedly runs all the way home! Even when the rhyme is repeated and the child understands what is going to happen, the tension is still present, and perhaps, in a way, it is even worse. Every time the rhyme is repeated, there is the anticipation that anytime soon the tickling is going to happen. To add to the effect, we adults insert a long and deliberate pause: 'One step … two steps … and …. … … tickly under there!' Or: 'And this little piggy w e e e n t … … … all the way home!' Another example is 'Peek-a-boo' where the adult disappears from view, causing a little bit of anxiety, then suddenly reappears and says, 'Boo!' The child jumps with surprise, but it is the laughter that causes the relief and the relief that causes the amusement. If you ever had a 'jack-in-the-box' as a child, can you remember the feeling of waiting as the key was turned, listening to the music 'Half a pound of tuppenny rice … and POP! goes the weasel!' Even though we knew that the POP! was coming, we still jumped.

Whether it is a joke told to an adult or a game for a young child, the elements are the same. The person at the receiving end of the joke/game experiences the thoughts and feelings associated with 'For a moment I felt unsure, but it's OK now'. There is a video that demonstrates this beautifully. A baby first shows fear when his mother blows her nose and then laughs heartily when she stops. The mother repeats her action a few times, and it is amusing to see the extreme reaction as the baby shifts back and forward between what looks like abject terror and convulsive laughter. We laugh at what stresses us, and this makes us feel better.

Laughter with others

Laughter is something that often happens naturally when we are in company, but it is far less likely to happen when we are alone. It is the reason we have 'canned laughter' in comedy shows, because if you hear someone laugh, you are more likely to laugh as well. Even so, if you watch your favourite comedy TV programme on your own, even with canned laughter, you will not laugh as freely and easily as you would if you were in company. When there is laughter in a group, it spreads rapidly, not necessarily because we choose to join in, but because it triggers a reaction in our brain that is outside of our conscious awareness. This phenomenon is exploited in activities like Laughter Yoga, where the sound of laughter as exercise causes natural, spontaneous laughter. These 'flash mob' videos show how groups of people can deliberately induce the spread of laughter in large crowds. You will find wonderful examples on my website: www.laughyourwaytohappiness.com.

Mirror neurons

Another reason that laughing is contagious is because of the activity of mirror neurons. When we see people laugh or yawn, we tend to react by displaying the same behaviour. It is possible to resist, but it takes effort to overcome this automatic response. As soon as we see or hear someone laugh, our neurons are stimulated and they 'fire off' so that we have an automatic response and laugh, too. There is a school of thought that says that this is a form of empathy. When you see someone displaying an emotion, you have a similar emotional response, and, consequently, you understand how this person feels and are able to empathize with him or her. When we watch a film and see someone who is upset or distressed, we too may cry. We know that it is only a film with actors and actresses playing a role, but it does not stop us empathizing with them and matching their emotion. We know that Bambi is just an animated drawing, but I challenge anyone not to feel upset when Bambi's mother is shot and killed. Apparently, the more empathetic you are, the more you will respond to Laughter Yoga or laughter exercises, but I am unaware of any research that has been done to support this.

When I was about ten years old, I was in the church choir, and I often used to get the giggles. The more I tried to stop, the more I wanted to laugh! My friend used to encourage me by making funny faces because she could control her laughter a lot better than I. It caused me equal amounts of pleasure and pain; I enjoyed the laughter, but I was worried about getting into trouble or upsetting someone. Even when I did not look at my friend, I could feel the pew shake with the vibrations of her silent laughter and see her shoulders go up and down in my peripheral vision. That was enough to set me off, so maybe I could take this opportunity to apologize to anyone who was ever upset or disturbed by a giggly choir girl at

Laughter names

Many cultures around the world recognize the importance of laughter by naming their children accordingly. Below is a list of boy's names signifying laughter from around the world.

Ahanu *(Native American)* – he will laugh
Carino *(Greek)* – smiley, friendly
Chebona-Bula *(Native American)* – laughing boy
Gelasius *(Greek)* – laughter
Gelon *(Greek)* – laughter
Hasan (Gujarati) – handsome, good, laughter,
Hotei (Japanese) – God of happiness

St Michael's and All Angels Church, Winterbourne Earls, during the 1960s! Funerals and weddings were the worst because as soon as the thought 'Wouldn't it be awful if I started laughing?' came into my mind, I would feel a smile appear on my face, and I knew that I was in the danger zone of inappropriate, spontaneous laughter.

I have noticed that when people attend laughter sessions for the first time, some of them often apologize for getting the giggles and find it difficult to make eye contact with other people when laughing. I believe this often affects those who have been told off for laughing during their childhood, maybe in school or at home during meal times. Some people struggle to enjoy unrestrained laughter at first, but after a while it begins to feel natural, and this inhibition usually disappears and does not return. In this way, laughter sessions can have a profoundly positive impact on people's relationships and their social life.

We are not the only ones ...

Smiling and laughing has been observed in monkeys, chimpanzees and apes and is often present when they play. Although the laughter of apes sounds more like panting than laughing, their rhythmic change in breathing patterns is similar to human laughter. For many years I have been following the progress of Koko, a beautiful lowland gorilla, who has been brought up to understand sign language and spoken English. She is absolutely amazing and can sign over 1,000 words and understands 2,000 spoken words. On my website you will find a video that shows her inviting the actor Robin Williams to play with her. She introduces him to her favourite games of chase and tickling. Not only does she love it, but you can see that she finds it funny, and she laughs a lot!

Helpless with laughter

It takes a lot of muscles to produce laughter. First, you need all the ones that make a smile, plus many more facial muscles besides, but it does not stop there. If we are engaged in hearty laughter, muscles from all over our body are affected. Some of them, like the diaphragm, have to work extra hard, but laughter relaxes us, too. This is why it is such a good way to relieve stress. This relaxation also affects our muscles so that they temporarily lose their strength to support us: you have probably seen people lean forward and hold on to their knees when laughing. This braces the arms, supports the legs and stops the person laughing from toppling over. It is also a good position to assist breathing and to help the diaphragm go up and down.

Although it may not be socially acceptable, lying down on the floor when laughing is probably a good idea and will certainly save you from falling down by accident. If you have ever had a really intense bout of laughing when you cannot stop, even though you want to, you may have felt 'helpless with laughter' and felt the need to hold on to something. I can vouch for the fact that laughing is much easier when you lie down (and we usually do this in our laughter sessions). If you also put your feet up in the air, your laughter will increase because it releases the diaphragm (it also looks and feels particularly silly!).

Trauma release

There may be other explanations as to why laughter is so therapeutic. Recently I have learnt about the psoas, a large muscle that draws the knees toward the hips and torso, and its apparent involvement with trauma and trapped emotion. The theory is that all mammals are genetically encoded so that this muscle is activated when the stress response is triggered, as this enables a creature to fight or flee. Afterwards, the animal will shake or tremble in order to release the psoas, which clears tension and allows the autonomic nervous system to bring the body back into a state of relaxation.

Humans have exactly the same response to perceived stress, but although we may shake and shiver in childhood, we inhibit this natural response in adulthood because of the social conditioning that regards trembling and shaking as a sign of weakness. We may sometimes witness this effect when someone shakes after experiencing extreme emotional shock, or see a trembling jaw in someone who is on the verge of tears. There is a theory that we store trauma in contracted muscles if it is not released. Perhaps this explains why many of my hypnotherapy clients with emotional problems have backache and some also have the chronic pain disorder, fibromyalgia.

The psoas is directly attached to the diaphragm; so it gets a lot of shaking when we engage in hearty laughter, which could explain why occasionally people find themselves inexplicably crying after they have laughed for an extended period and why many people describe feeling more emotionally balanced after regular attendance at laughter sessions.

The specialist in this area is Dr David Berceli, creator of Tension and Trauma-Releasing Exercise (TRE), who has worked with many people who have suffered deep trauma in wars or natural disasters, as well as people who have suffered what he refers to as 'soft traumas' such as the stress associated with work or relationships. You can find further info on the Laughter Business website (*see* Resources, page 235).

Laughter as a workout

Many people are surprised to discover that laughter as an exercise can be hard work. It exercises the diaphragm and muscles in the abdomen, face, legs and back, and also has a huge impact on the respiratory system, leading to increased oxygenation of the blood. Laughter Yoga has been described as an internal massage that affects the internal organs and the digestive tract. Yes, laughing *is* hard work! Unless you have had a really good laughter session recently, you may have forgotten this, but trust me, it is definitely an intense exercise, and it is different to other exercise pain.

If you partake in vigorous exercise during sport or at the gym, you may choose to stop when you start to feel your muscles getting tired. By the time you get to this stage through laughter, very often you find you cannot stop at all! When we think we have stopped laughing, we may groan and say, 'Oooh, my stomach', or take a deep breath and sigh, and this frequently turns out to be the trigger that sets us off again. We may complain, 'Oh, stop it!' and 'Oh, it hurts!', but part of us is reluctant to stop. You think you have stopped until it starts all over again. This is caused by the combination of the infectious laughter in a group, the feelings of mental and physical relief and the effect of endorphins in the blood stream.

Endorphins are neurotransmitters that are produced in the brain when our bodies experience pain. When we laugh intensely, we use a lot of muscles that we are not used to using and this stretching causes pain. Endorphins block the pain signals to our brain so that we feel sensations of calm, relaxation, happiness, contentment and even euphoria.

So now, perhaps, we understand a little more about the purpose of laughter. But what evidence is there for its benefits?

Inuit laughing competition

Inuit women traditionally play a throat-singing game aimed at causing their competitor to laugh. Throat singing, Katjjaq, *is not really singing at all but a combination of rhythmic deep breathing and vocal noises. The 'songs' are improvised and involve complex harmonizing between the two competitors. The women stand close to each other, face to face, and hold each other by the arms. One of them begins a pattern of rhythmic humming and the guttural sounds of throat singing, leaving a gap, which is filled by the other competitor in a sort of call-and-answer style of singing. The object of the game is to make your partner laugh, miss a beat or run out of breath.*

Multiple benefits

Laughter comes with many more benefits than just looking and feeling happier. Although researchers try to look at the effects of laughing in isolation, it is difficult because laughter affects us physically, psychologically, emotionally and socially, too, and each one of these benefits can facilitate others. For example, through laughter we can also gain the positive effects of better health, smiling, happiness, exercise, social connection, play and catharsis, and we gain the advantages of less stress, pain reduction and increased positive emotions. These are not exclusively connected to laughter as they can be facilitated in a number of ways, but I know of few activities that offer such a simple way of accessing them all. Let us look more specifically at the particular benefits.

Improved immune system

Laughter boosts the immune system so that we are less likely to get ill, and if we do get ill, we can recover quicker. In 2003, a study conducted by Western Kentucky University looked at whether laughter could increase Natural Killer (NK) cell activity. NK cells are a type of white blood cell that can kill tumour cells and virally infected cells. Thirty-three women (the study had already been carried out on men) were allowed to pick one of three comedy videos, and their NK cell level was measured while they watched.

Those who displayed overt laughter had increased NK cells, but there was no change in the women who watched the videos, but did not laugh, although they still benefitted from a decrease in stress levels, which also has a positive effect on the immune system.

To recap: Overt laughter can increase NK cells and watching comedy can make you less stressed. So, doing both is a double whammy!

At the time of writing, I have not had a cold since participating in laughter as a form of exercise, and I have not had a day's illness either. I cannot prove that this is because laughter has improved the efficiency of my immune system and increased my level of natural antibodies, but I suspect it is so. It could be the result of a placebo effect: that because I believe laughter makes me healthier and happier, it does, but I feel that I am much more resilient and healthy now, and this makes me feel happy and grateful.

Laughter and increased blood flow

In 2005, in a study at Maryland Medical Center, researchers worked with a group of 20 non-smoking, healthy volunteers – ten men, ten women – and measured the effects of their watching two films, one designed to cause mental stress and the other to induce laughter.

Each person watched 15-minute segments of each film while lying in a temperature-controlled room and was tested before and after each segment. Although there was little change while watching either film, there were significant alternations to the volunteers' blood flow afterwards. The results indicated that stress caused blood vessels to constrict and reduce blood flow, whereas laughter had the opposite effect and caused blood vessels to dilate and increase blood flow.

This means that laughter could be an important factor in maintaining a healthy endothelium. The endothelium is the thin layer of cells that lines the surface of the blood vessels. It plays a crucial role in blood flow, coagulation and secretion of chemicals that help battle infection.

Apart from helping battle infection, I think increased blood flow would have other positive effects on cardiac and circulatory health.

Anticipation of laughter

In 2006, Dr Lee Berk and a group of American researchers carried out a study that showed that even anticipating laughter could reduce stress hormones.

In the first experiment, Dr Berk used two groups. The first group anticipated watching a humorous film; the second group did not.

The first group showed an increase of 27 per cent in beta-endorphins and of 87 per cent HGH (human growth hormone); the second group showed no increase in either hormone. Beta-endorphins are the chemicals that alleviate depression; HGH helps with immunity.

Further tests showed that the same anticipation of laughter reduced the levels of three stress hormones: cortisol (the stress hormone), epinephrine (also known as adrenaline) and dopamine (which assists the brain to produce adrenaline). After testing, it was shown that the hormones of the first group reduced by 39 per cent, 70 per cent and 38 per cent respectively, with a decrease in the control group.

This study seems to show that laughter can reduce depression, improve immunity and prevent stress, but best of all, it suggests that even anticipating laughter can have a positive physiological effect. Good news if you look forward to going to a Laughter Club!

Improved tolerance to pain

Researchers at Oxford University found that tolerance to pain is a wonderful side effect of laughter. People who suffer from pain can get a lot of relief from indulging in prolonged laughter. Famously, Norman Cousins, author of *Anatomy of an Illness*, used laughter as a way of relieving his intense pain during his illness. He found that the pain relief experienced after ten minutes of intense laughter would allow him to enjoy a few hours of undisturbed sleep. He would watch the comedy films of the Marx Brothers to facilitate his laughter and then sleep. If he woke up in pain during the night, he repeated the process.

When we suffer pain, our bodies become tense, and it causes

Healing laughter

The BBC programme South Today *came to one of our laughter sessions to make a short film about the therapeutic benefits of laughter. On that particular day, a lady joined us who suffered from a range of medical conditions. She was interested to find out whether laughter could actually relieve the pain that she experienced almost constantly. Within minutes of participating, she felt her mood improving, and during the session she was unaware of any discomfort. In fact, afterwards she was concerned that anyone seeing the film would think that she was not as disabled as she claimed to be. Laughter is not a cure for medical conditions, but it can create periods of respite for those who suffer from physical and emotional pain.*

stress, but laughter changes our physical response by making us relaxed, reducing our levels of stress and producing endorphins. Natural endorphins are more powerful than synthetic painkillers and do not have negative side effects.

Laughter and bereavement

In 1997, a study conducted at the University of California, Berkeley suggested that genuine laughter has a positive impact on people

Laughter and grieving

Several of the people who attend laughter sessions and workshops have suffered bereavement and find laughter to be helpful. One person told me that it was a relief to laugh and have fun in a safe environment because he feared his friends and family would think it was 'too early' to sound so happy while still in the grieving process.

A bereaved woman said that she had been sad for so long that she thought she had forgotten how to laugh. Being in a laughter session and laughing as an exercise meant that she could laugh unconditionally 'for no reason' and did not have to wait for a reason to feel jolly.

Lots of happy memories are built around the sound of laughter, and it is quite common for people to suddenly recall an incident from their childhood or from many years ago. One particular lady said it helped her remember the good times during her marriage because when her husband was alive, he was always laughing and making her laugh.

In this way, we can celebrate past relationships with smiles and laughter, whereas we often tend to feel sad when we remember those no longer with us.

who have been bereaved. In the study, a bereavement group consisting of individuals who had each lost a spouse was studied over an 18-month period. The researchers differentiated between genuine laughter and 'polite' or 'forced laughter'.

They discovered that the participants who displayed the most genuine laughter experienced less anger and had increased enjoyment and better social interactions.

The researchers' findings showed that laughter creates an emotional dissociation from stress and can dissemble negativity to allow for a more positive outlook. This resulted in the subject being able to cope better and aiding his or her recovery. Laughter was responsible for a positive psychological shift.

This seems to show that laughter relieves stress and can improve emotional resilience.

Laughter and breastfeeding

In a 2007 study in Osaka, Japan, researchers looked at 48 breastfed babies who suffered from Atopic Eczema (AE), a common skin disease. Apart from causing irritation to the skin, AE causes allergic responses to latex allergies and dust mites, and can cause sleep problems.

Half of the mothers had AE themselves, but the others were healthy. They were asked to watch either a humorous Charlie Chaplin film or a non-humorous film about the weather. Afterwards, their breast milk was sampled at various intervals.

The study concluded that the mothers who watched the comedy film had increased levels of breast milk melatonin regardless of whether they had AE or not, and their infants subsequently had a reduced allergic response. There was no difference in the breast milk of the other mothers. The study concluded that the laughter of breastfeeding mothers may be helpful in the treatment of infants with AE.

Health benefits of laughter

A study published in 2009 looked at the long-term health benefits of laughter and compared two groups of individuals aged 18–39, one living in Canada and the other in India.

The results showed that moderate levels of laughter produced benefits to both psychological and physical health, but low levels of laughter had little impact. The researchers also found a correlation between well-being and disease. One outcome of the experiment was that they thought it would be useful to incorporate patients' laughter habits into their medical assessment.

These researchers suggested that well-being can be a positive influence against disease and even suggested collecting this information in medical assessments. Therefore, if laughter raises positive emotion, then good physical and mental health may follow on as a consequence.

The end result

Laughter has been shown to reduce the levels of epinephrine (adrenaline) and cortisol, the hormones that the body creates when we are stressed. These stress hormones suppress the immune system and increase the number of blood platelets that can cause obstructions in the arteries and raise blood pressure. However, laughter reduces our blood pressure and improves both our cardiovascular and immune systems by increasing our level of antibodies. When you take all these benefits into account, it is possible to see where the claims come from that laughter can improve your longevity. If we have less chance of getting heart disease or cancer and if we are happy, healthy and resistant to disease, we are far more likely to live a longer and happier life. After all, laughter is naturally available and free to everyone.

I have learnt many techniques and strategies from my training in Positive Psychology, NLP, Clinical Hypnosis and Stress Management, and I have applied them to myself, but what has brought me more joy and more happiness than anything else is laughter. Even on the days when things do not seem to be going well, I know how important it is to ensure that I bring more laughter into my day. I do not need to find a reason to laugh, or to necessarily have authentic laughter, because laughter as an exercise works just as well since my body cannot tell the difference (more on this in Chapter 3, *The Spirit of Laughter*).

Of course, if we are stressed, unhappy, anxious or feeling miserable, authentic laughter is not likely to occur. This is why laughter as an exercise is so valuable because anyone can do it and you do not have to rely on a sense of humour or being in a good mood. Your body provides you with the chemical match of your laughter, and very quickly you can start to feel happy and positive. When I am happy, I laugh, and when I laugh, I become happier. It is simple and effective.

Laughter changes us. It changes our brain chemistry and our body, our perceptions, emotions and attitudes. Laughter changes the people around us, too, whether they are family and friends or complete strangers. No one is immune to the sound of laughter and how it makes you feel. Laughter opens us up, it makes us more receptive and more accepting, more grateful and more forgiving, and these are the qualities that research has identified as the ones that make us feel happy.

Happiness and laughter are wonderful companions, each complementing the other and both contributing to an uplifting feeling of well-being. Laughter makes us happy and healthy, and happiness makes us healthier and happier. It is a beautiful arrangement.

Chapter 3

The Spirit of Laughter

When you realize how perfect everything is, you will tilt your head back and laugh at the sky.

The Buddha

Understanding the theory and science of laughter is one thing, but there is nothing like experience to really change your attitudes and behaviour. This chapter explores in depth my experience of Laughter Yoga sessions with Dr K. I want to give you a sense of the breakthrough I discovered in learning to 'laugh for no reason' and how profound its effects can be.

Every experience teaches us something. For me, simply the experience of trying to enter India in order to visit Dr K's Laughter Yoga sessions was to teach me much about laughter and my attitudes to problems and challenges. That is the reason why I want to share the story.

I had three full days off between work trips to prepare for my Laughter Yoga training visit to India. I thought that would be plenty of time, but I soon discovered it would take that time alone to process the visa itself, putting the whole trip into jeopardy.

With time ticking away, I received a text message from the Indian Embassy to say that my visa had been processed. I was hopeful that I would receive a message to pick it up the following day, Thursday. This, I had been told, would happen in the morning, and the passport could be picked up in the early afternoon.

Thursday came and went with no message, and at 10 am on Friday, I sat looking at my phone, willing a text message to appear, but an hour passed and nothing happened. By 12, I was feeling desperate. I knew my visa had been processed, but had it left the embassy? If so, why had no one sent me a text? By 12:30, panic set in, and I decided to call them. The only telephone number I had – an emergency number – had an unobtainable tone. I discussed my options with my partner, Iain. Should I drive to the visa office in Uxbridge to pick it up as maybe it was there already, but what if it was still at the embassy in London? The visa office closed at 4 and was a two-hour drive away, but it would take three hours to drive to London. If only I knew where my passport was, I could make an informed decision where to go.

I emailed Dr K; perhaps he had experienced this sort of thing and maybe he would know what to do? He replied quickly: *Just visualize yourself laughing with me in India. Go to the Consulate and make a strong request. I am already seeing you in India, ha, ha, ha. Everything will work out fine.* I wanted to share Dr K's sentiment that it would all be OK, but I could not and was convinced that he did not understand. I decided to ring the embassy, but the lady on the switchboard was determined that I would not be put through to anyone. I begged and pleaded with her to let me speak with someone who could tell me where my passport was. Unless I could pick it up, it would be too late to travel. I needed to know where to go – to London or to Uxbridge. If I did not leave soon, it would be too late to pick up my passport from anywhere. I decided that, at least, driving was taking action.

Iain drove as I was way too agitated to drive safely. Being in the passenger seat meant that I could continue to make phone calls. I rang the embassy again, this time attempting to sound like someone else making a casual enquiry. It seemed that I had managed to convince the receptionist, and she agreed to put me through. The phone rang for ages, but eventually someone picked it up and said, 'Hello, maintenance department.' I was talking to a janitor working in the basement of the building; perhaps I had not fooled her after all!

I persuaded Iain to ring back and see if he could get past this persistent and determined woman, and he stopped the car at the next service station and made a phone call on my behalf. This time, it *did* work, and the call was put through to a helpful lady. I explained my dilemma. What did she think I should do: drive to the embassy or go to the visa office? She confirmed that my visa had been processed and had left her department; she did not know where it was now, but gave me a telephone number that I could call.

Relieved that I did not have to try and bypass the tenacious receptionist for a third time, I rang the number. It was engaged. I tried the number continually for the next 15 minutes as we continued driving along the motorway. At last, a man who sounded as if he had been running answered the phone. Breathlessly, he gasped, 'Hello, yes, how can I help you?' I told my story as slowly and as calmly as I could, assuring him that I did understand the protocol of visa applications, but needed help to find out where to collect my visa from so that I could travel to India on Sunday.

He listened without interrupting me, and then he replied, 'I do understand your situation, and I would really like to help you, but your phone call has come through to a dry cleaner's, and I don't know anything at all about visa procedures. If it is any consolation, if I did work at the embassy, I would help you.'

Strangely enough, it did help, although I did not know why at the time. Did I think it was funny? Not in the slightest! With hindsight, I realize how much I have changed since, because if this happened now, I know I would laugh like a drain! However, this was before I knew that laughter could be a resource to use in situations like this. I was feeling stressed, frustrated, irritated and on the verge of tears. I had *so* looked forward to travelling to India to learn about Laughter Yoga, and it felt as if the world was conspiring against me to prevent me from going.

All day long I had been subjected to the physiological effects of stress on my body: rapid shallow breathing, increased heart rate, a churning stomach and feelings of anxiety. I was exhausted. I reluctantly sent a message to Dr K, telling him that it was unlikely that I would make it. Dr K replied: *I understand this, but life is a challenge. I know you will be there laughing with me. To me, this kind of thing happens all the time. Nothing can dampen the spirit. Don't worry, everything will be okay. Ho, ho, ha, ha. Dr K.*

I surrender

His words did little to reassure and comfort me, and I decided then and there that I was defeated. I felt powerless in the situation, and I could see no alternative but to accept that things were not going to work out. Dr K was right: these things happen all the time, although I did not agree with his statement that 'nothing can dampen the spirit'; I was feeling saturated with disappointment. I asked Iain to turn the car around and take us back home. I had given up.

Iain could not have been more understanding or sympathetic, and it was now that I started to truly appreciate how kind and supportive he had been. I started to look beyond my self-centred feelings of frustration and disappointment and viewed the situation more objectively. Nothing in the world had changed apart from the fact that I was not able to get what I wanted, when I wanted. No catastrophe had occurred, no one was hurt; very little, if indeed anything, had changed. I had been overreacting and caught up in my own self-made drama.

I was not going to be able to go India, but I could still enjoy time at home, with a loving partner in the beautiful countryside of the New Forest. I wondered how many people would be glad to swap their real problems with my inconvenience. I felt a huge relief at giving in, and for the first time in days, I relaxed and started to feel much better. I was getting things back into perspective. The details of my visa application were not as important as the lesson I learnt that day, and Dr K's words have stayed with me ever since.

Things go wrong all the time, or rather, they don't go the way we expect or anticipate they will. How we react determines how we feel. External events have no power over us, and how we respond is down to our own choice. I do not always get it right, but nowadays, most of the time, I choose to feel happy. I no longer try to be in control and realize that most of the time being in control is an illusion anyway. Does my new attitude change what happens? Maybe. Does it change how I feel? Undoubtedly.

I see it like being on the edge of a cliff holding a rope while in front of you is a huge ravine. On the other side of the ravine a powerful force is holding the other end of the rope, drawing you nearer and nearer to the edge. It takes all your energy to keep yourself from being pulled over the edge and into the abyss below. This is how it sometimes feels when you feel overloaded, overwhelmed and powerless. Yet, rather than struggling, you can choose to do something else: let go of the rope! The simple action of letting go can make such a difference.

A lesson learnt

It was a powerful lesson I learnt that day, and it was made even more memorable by an event that happened almost simultaneously. As we

More laughter names for boys

I love the idea of naming a child for laughter. Perhaps these names will inspire you.

Ikka *(Finnish)* – he will laugh

Itzaak *(Hebrew)* – laughter, the laughing one

Isaac *(Hebrew)* – he laughs/he will laugh

Itzik *(Hebrew)* – laughter, the laughing one

Sahak *(Armenian)* – he will laugh

Yitzak *(Hebrew)* – laughter, the laughing one

Ochi *(African)* – laughter

Sekan *(Zimbabwean)* – laughter

Teshi *(African)* – cheerful, full of laughter

Timke *(Aboriginal)* – laughter, joy

were approaching the next motorway exit, my phone 'dinged' with the sound of a text message. It was from the visa office, and it read: *Your visa application has been processed. Your passport is ready to be picked up at the visa office*. Did my previous text message get lost? I will never know.

In the end, the situation resolved itself, and my involvement was not required. In fact, by interfering and attempting to control the situation, I had exhausted myself and almost jeopardized being in the right place to pick up my visa. Doing nothing and allowing things to change around you may seem difficult at times, but sometimes this is what is required. I believe that what happened was meant to teach me something and that once I listened and accepted the truth of it, things began to run smoothly. A few hours later, I was home with my Indian visa in my passport.

Laughter Yoga

Once I arrived in India, students and members of Dr K's team met me at the airport. It was still dark as I travelled with my fellow Laughter Yoga initiates along Bangalore's streets toward our destination: the School of Ancient Wisdom. After about 15 minutes, we turned off the main road and headed down what appeared to be a long track full of potholes. We bounced along the road, swerving to miss some of the bigger holes and large stones, and eventually arrived at some tall and imposing wrought-iron gates that were opened by a guard. As we drove through, I noticed a sign that read: *As you enter these gates, leave your small self outside so that your HIGHER SELF may unfold inside*. It was too profound a comment to consider in such a short space of time; yet, with hindsight, it was a good hint of what was to come later.

It was close to dawn when I lay down on my bed and closed my eyes, and I don't think I had been asleep long when I woke up to the sound of birdsong. It was so loud, so persistent and so beautiful that I could only imagine that there was an aviary nearby. I decided to abandon the idea of going back to sleep and went to see my surroundings for the first time.

First Impressions

As I walked out of my ground-floor room, I realized that the birdsong was coming from all around me, from the trees and the bushes. For someone who loves birds and goes to a lot of trouble to feed the garden birds at home, this was a real treat. Even though I live in the New Forest and have frequently got up early enough to hear the dawn chorus, I had never heard anything as intense and robust as this. It was as if there were amplifiers in the trees, and I went back to my room to get my voice recorder so that I could capture the sound of birds that literally filled the air. I have heard that expression before, but never actually experienced it like this. I walked along the winding paths bordered by dense shrubs and bushes, listening to the many different birds, each with its own particular call and trill. Then I saw another large sign attached to the branch of a tree: *Listen to the Song of Life*. Suddenly, the birds singing took on a new meaning, and as the sun came up and I felt its warmth, I felt so happy and content. At that moment, there was nothing more I could have wanted or needed. I did not realize it at the time, but I had already fallen under the spell of living in the tranquillity and the beauty of the School of Ancient Wisdom.

It was peaceful, gentle and calm everywhere, and the three dogs that lived at the school were frequently asleep or just awake enough to move places, sometimes only a few feet away, before resuming their slumber. I found my way back to the centre of the complex where we had been dropped off the night before and discovered that this was where our food would be cooked and served to us three times a day. The food was delicious, vegetarian and served by the lovely, friendly staff. They did not speak English, but they did not need to as they communicated with smiles and gestures. Most, if not all, of the food we ate was grown on the property and picked fresh each morning. I spent the rest of the day meeting my fellow Laughter Yoga group and becoming familiar with our surroundings. There was just one other person from the UK there; the other 24 members of our group were from a wonderful mixture of countries: Japan, China, Thailand, Germany, South Africa, Korea, Hong Kong, South America, Egypt, Denmark, India, Italy, New Zealand and more. We were all here with the same aim: to learn about Laughter Yoga from the Master himself, Dr K, so that we could return home and teach others the art of laughing for no reason.

That night, as I went to sleep, I had a happy and content feeling, as though I had already been there for a long time. The next day would be my first experience of Laughter Yoga, and although I would be slightly anxious under normal circumstances, I simply closed my eyes and fell into deep and restful sleep.

First day at Laughter School

So what do you wear for a Laughter Yoga session? I decided that something loose and comfortable would be the best bet and settled for linen trousers and a blouse. The arrangements for the morning were to meet in the large hall for our first session before breakfast. I had brought a collection of notebooks, my camera, recording equipment and some textbooks. I was thinking like a scientist and intending to be both a participant and an observer of the experience of Laughter Yoga, not yet realizing the impossibility of this task.

We went up the steps to the large hall, left our shoes outside and found that Dr K was already there, waiting. He asked us to bring a chair and sit with him in the corner of the room. When we were settled, he told us that he would like us to introduce ourselves, not in the normal way but in the Laughter Yoga way. He explained that we would take it in turns to stand up and introduce ourselves by saying our name, then we would laugh, and everybody would join in. The others would not be laughing *at* us, he explained, but *with* us. After this, we would say where we came from, and, again, we would all laugh together. Then we would say what job we did, and, once again, we would all laugh. Finally, after the last laughter, we would all clap our hands and say loudly, 'Very good, very good', then raise our hands in the air and shout, 'YEAH!' He demonstrated: 'My name is Dr Kataria, ha, ha, ha, ha, ha, ha (we all laughed), I live in Bangalore, ha, ha, ha, ha, ha, ha (we laughed again), and I am a doctor, ha, ha, ha, ha, ha, ha, ha, ha, ha!' (More laughter; for some reason, when Dr K said this, it seemed really funny!) Then we clapped, and finally we joined in with 'Very good, very good, YEAH!'

Now, I am sure this sounds a little mad, and I admit it did seem rather odd, but the experience of participating and doing this in a group was interesting. First of all, it was enormously enjoyable, and by the second or third time that we did our 'Very good, very good, YEAH!', we were all chanting the words in a sing-song sort of way, with the emphasis on the first word – '*Very* good, *very* good, YEAH!' I for one was actually starting to *feel* very good, too. As each of us went through the ritual, the group supported them by clapping, chanting and laughing, and I could feel my energy, and the group's energy, getting higher and higher.

It was unlike my previous experiences of being asked to introduce myself in a group setting. Everyone here was eager for it to be his or her turn, myself included. The combination of laughing, clapping, chanting and cheering felt relaxing and slightly hypnotic. When it was my turn, I stood up, and all around me I saw a sea of smiling faces. When I said, 'My name is Lesley', we all laughed together and it felt great. It was warm, gentle, welcoming and inclusive – and something else had happened, too. I realized that I could remember everyone's name.

Often, when people think they have forgotten someone's name, the real problem is that they did not actually hear it in the first place. So, it is less a case of forgetting the name and more a case of forgetting to hear the name. This is especially likely to happen to us on occasions when we are nervous, meeting people for the first time, for instance. On those occasions when everyone is expected to stand up in turn and talk about themselves, sometimes called the 'creeping death' as you wait for your turn, is it any wonder that your attention turns inward? You tend to think about what you will say, rather than listening attentively so that you actually hear and remember someone's name. You may not have noticed this, but I would hazard a guess that you are more likely to remember the names of the people who speak *after* your turn, when you start to relax, than the ones of those who spoke before you. If you ever have to facilitate a warm-up or arrange a group introduction, I highly recommend Dr K's welcoming method.

This was my introduction to the pleasure of unconditional laughter, and it seemed perfectly natural. This was because I had been so involved in doing it that I had not spent time thinking about it. Activities like clapping, cheering and laughing tend to cause the right-hand side of our brain to become more dominant than the left. Consequently, our critical, logical 'voice', associated with the left side of the brain, cannot be heard so easily. If you have ever had the experience of the same thoughts going over in your mind, time and time again because of worry or stress, Laughter Yoga can provide almost instant relief from this.

After the exercise Dr K invited us to discuss how it had felt, and we all reported how lovely it was to laugh in a group together, *especially* for no reason. We agreed that we already felt comfortable and relaxed with each other and also in a very good mood. Several people explained that they had long held a fear of being laughed at in front of a group, and this had prevented them from ever doing any sort of public speaking. For some, it was an irrational fear, but a couple of people had stories of being humiliated in front of their class at school and openly mocked by their classmates. For them,

Hotei, god of contentment and happiness

On my desk sits a statuette of Hotei, one of Japan's seven lucky gods. Rather like the laughing Buddha, he has a big belly and a very cheerful face. He carries with him a cloth bag that contains an inexhaustible amount of treasures, including food and drink, that he gives away to the poor and needy. The size of his protruding stomach is a symbol of the extent of his inner power, vitality and resourcefulness, something to bear in mind if anyone ever suggests that you have put on weight!

Hotei always wears an expression of cheerful happiness and represents the essence of a jolly person. When I sit at my desk, struggling to find the right word or the right phrase, or just feeling stuck, I simply look at Hotei. He reminds me to stop taking myself so seriously and to relax, and as soon as I do, I find that all of a sudden I can move on. Hotei is a giver, and the more he gives away, the more he receives, as is proved by his never-emptying bag of gifts. I like to think that this is the same with the gift of laughter. The more you facilitate laughter for others, the more laughter you will receive in return.

this had been a cathartic and positive experience, as well as being great fun.

Dr K went on to explain about how he conceived the idea of laughter as an exercise in 1995 when he realized the potential benefits that laughter contributes to people's health, happiness and well-being. For years, people have said that 'laughter is the best medicine' and scientific research has validated this. However, the assumption was that it had to be 'real' laughter – that is, laughter caused by humour. Studying the research material, Dr K realized that *any* sort of laughter works, including 'laughing for no reason', or laughing exercises.

Of course, it would be great if we all had so much natural laughter in our lives that we did not need any more, but ask yourself when you last laughed so long and so hard that it hurt. When asked this question, most people find themselves describing odd occasions here and there, and many say that they have not laughed like this for years. When we laugh, it is usually only for a few seconds. In a Laughter Yoga session, we will get about 15–20 minutes of hearty laughter!

Dr K believes it is best to arrange for laughter to happen through Laughter Yoga rather than just hope it will occur through chance. Laughter Yoga has a few advantages over 'normal' everyday laughter, too. For a start, your laughter is guaranteed: all you have to do is decide to laugh, and you do not have to rely on someone else making you laugh or to find something funny. You laugh for yourself, and you laugh with the knowledge that it is doing you good, whether it is spontaneous or whether you are just making the sound of laughter.

He emphasized that the most important thing about Laughter Yoga is that *your body does not know the difference between laughing spontaneously and laughing as an exercise*. This is the reason why Laughter Yoga is so effective.

It all made perfectly good sense to me, and I thought this was a lovely start to our course.

We then stopped as it was time for breakfast. As we crossed the courtyard, we were greeted with wonderful aromas from the food that had been prepared for us: there were fresh *dhosas*, bananas and *chai*, along with a few things that I did not recognize. I felt ravenous, and everything I tasted was delicious. There is nothing as good as eating when you are really hungry, and I soon discovered that laughter, like any exercise, gives you an appetite.

Taking notes

After breakfast we returned to continue our day's lesson. I realized that I had forgotten to take notes, and so I got out my new notebook and pen, determined that I would not forget again. Dr K said that he would explain Laughter Yoga to us as though we were completely new to the concept; after all, we would have to teach this to beginners when we got home. This was a relief to me and allowed me to relax a little, knowing that I would not have to rely on any prior knowledge. Although we would go into a great amount of detail of every aspect of Laughter Yoga during the next few days, Dr K gave a simple overview of it, to begin with.

He described Laughter Yoga as a unique exercise routine that combines unconditional laughter with yoga-type breathing.

Unconditional laughter is when you laugh for yourself without relying on comedy or humour. Laughter is simulated as a physical exercise, but by maintaining eye contact with members of the group, and incorporating childlike playfulness, this frequently leads to authentic, contagious laughter. Laughter Yoga helps people participate in hearty laughter without involving any intellectual processes.

Sessions begin with gentle warm-up exercises, stretches, chanting and clapping. Breathing exercises are also introduced, to help prepare the lungs for laughter. Simple laughter exercises involving role play are interspersed with breathing exercises, and the session usually ends with laughter meditation, sometimes called 'free flow laughter', followed by some guided relaxation. During laughter meditation/free flow laughter, the participants sit or lie down, and laughter is 'allowed' to flow freely, but only if it occurs naturally. In this segment of the session, only genuine laughter is expressed, and in this respect it is unlike the rest of the session.

The 'yoga' part of Laughter Yoga refers to the type of breathing that is incorporated; there are no formal yoga poses. Anyone who is reasonably fit and healthy can participate in Laughter Yoga without having any previous experience, equipment or physical skill. I was thankful for this, too, as I have never practised yoga; however, several of the people on the course were advanced yoga teachers. When Dr K founded Laughter Yoga, he noticed that when we laugh heartily, we breathe out more air than we breathe in: this is similar to *pranayama*, a specific type of breathing carried out in yoga.

This kind of breathing has a powerful effect on our bodies; it changes our physiology and helps us relax deeply. Extended exhalation pushes out residual air from the lungs and replaces it with air containing more oxygen. Of course, this is exactly what happens when you indulge in hearty laughter, the sort of laughter where, eventually, you have to gasp for a lungful of air. The combination of breath work with laughter exercises ensures that participants get lots more oxygen than they would normally, and this has many health benefits.

Forgetting notes

Once again, I realized that I had not taken any notes and decided to make time to write some later. There was no time now, because we were about to do some Laughter Yoga. I was pleased and nervous at the same time. This would not be a full Laughter Yoga session but a demonstration of how to introduce the first part of a session. So first, Dr K checked that everybody was fit and healthy enough to participate. There are only a few contraindications. If you have had surgery, have a hernia or suffer from high blood pressure, Laughter Yoga may not be suitable for you. People who are on medication, have a condition such as epilepsy or consider themselves in any way unwell should check with their doctor first. In general, though, if you are able to take part in aerobic exercise without suffering any problems and consider yourself to be reasonably fit, you will probably be fine. The best advice is that if you feel any new pain when you begin, feel uncomfortable or experience anything unusual or worrying, stop!

We all confirmed that we were fit and well, and Dr K began the introduction. We started with rhythmic clapping, ensuring we held our hands parallel to each other and achieved a full, finger-to-finger and palm-to-palm contact. This stimulates acupressure points in the hands and increases energy levels (I had already experienced this before breakfast with the 'Very good, very good, YEAH!' exercise). We began to clap in a 1–2, 1–2–3 rhythm, to which we then added the words ho, ho, ha, ha, ha. Once we had the hang of this, we added movements, clapping one side and then the other, stretching up and down. Finally, we began to move randomly in the group, smiling and making eye contact with each other.

It is this eye contact that facilitates the phenomenon of mirror neurons. When we see an emotion displayed by someone else, our brains recognize it and we mirror that emotion, although this often happens outside of our awareness. If you have ever been in the company of somebody yawning and find yourself yawning, too, even if you are not tired, then you have already experienced this. Likewise, if you have ever been in the company of people laughing and found yourself laughing without understanding why, this, again, is the effect of mirror neurons.

It was obvious that the others in the group had done this many times as they put a lot of energy into it and were already laughing and smiling. Once more, we did the 'Very good, very good, YEAH!' exercise, and by now, not only was I an expert at doing it, but it felt really good every time I did it as well.

And breathe ...

Next, we did some breathing exercises, all of them designed to bring more oxygen into our bodies. The exercises were gentle stretches with deep breathing, the emphasis being on breathing out. Breathing in, we stretched our arms up high and held our breath for a few seconds, before bending forward, dropping our arms and bending over, while laughing gently. I found the exercises quite enjoyable, although this was nothing like laughing for real. Dr K encouraged us to regard the noises we made as just 'noises' and not to associate them with laughter. Therefore, ho, ho, ha, ha, hee, hee could just be regarded as ways of exhalation. In fact, we tried something called 'Calcutta laughter'. This involves putting your hands out in front of you, elbows at your side, palms facing down, and then forcefully saying ho, ho, while pushing your hand downward the ground. Then you place your hands in front of you, palms away, and push forward, while saying ha, ha. We did this for a minute or two and I found it invigorating and a very good exercise for the diaphragm.

The diaphragm gets utilized when we laugh, along with the intercostal muscles attached, causing this area to ache. The most common complaints are my 'ribs are hurting' or 'my sides are splitting'.

Laughter exercises

Next we were told we would do some laughter exercises. Laughter exercises are short, active and fun. They are intended to connect us with the childlike part within us, the part that really enjoys laughter. Dr K informed us that we were to start with five exercises, learn more during the day and that by the time we went home, we would have learnt over 50 of them. It sounded a lot, but, in fact, we not only learnt these, we created dozens more ourselves!

We began with a greeting laughter exercise that is commonly used at the beginning of a Laughter Yoga session. In this exercise, we greeted the others in the group by shaking their hand enthusiastically, while looking into their eyes and, most importantly, laughing. It probably sounds a little odd, and I did feel quite self-conscious at first, but I soon found myself responding as the absurdity of what we were doing was somehow appealing. However, the exercise only lasted a few moments before Dr K started the now familiar 'ho, ho, ha, ha, ha' exercise, and we stopped what we were doing and joined in with him. This is the way the leader of the session communicates that the exercise has ended.

I soon learnt that, apart from the leader who introduces and explains the exercises, there is no talking in Laughter Yoga sessions, just laughter. When you stop talking, it is much easier to stop thinking, and when you stop thinking, you lose inhibiting thoughts – the thoughts that tell you, this is mad and you are crazy! Laughter Yoga is based on unconditional laughter and laughing for no reason. Eventually, you can learn to disengage from the left-hand critical, logical side of your brain and allow the right-hand side of your brain to become dominant. It is the right-hand side of your brain that connects you to creativity, fun, joy and relaxation, but getting from one to the other can be difficult, especially at first.

Talking

Although I have said that there is no talking in Laughter Yoga, there is one exception and that is when we speak Gibberish. Gibberish is the name given to the practice of making language sounds that have no meaning. Gibberish is very expressive, though, and we can use it to communicate by adding body language and varying our tonality,

The power of Gibberish

Although I have always enjoyed Gibberish as a fun activity, it was only recently that I appreciated how therapeutic it can be after hearing this story from a friend. After an acrimonious divorce she was left feeling depressed and suffering from low esteem. She felt that she had never really stood up to her husband who was a dominant figure, and she also had lots of unspoken thoughts. One weekend when her ex-husband came to pick up their three children for an outing, she rather impulsively asked him whether he would allow her to talk to him in Gibberish. Although it may have sounded bizarre, he agreed, and for a full five minutes she expressed everything she had ever wanted to say to him about her feelings. She spoke of anger, disappointment and regret as well as some loving feelings that she could never have said in any other language. He, of course, had no idea exactly what her words meant, although the tone of her voice and the tears in her eyes would have communicated a lot. There were no words to trigger his anger or denial, justification or hurt, so he simply listened and for the first time she felt heard. Afterwards, she says, she felt relief and closure that have enabled her to be more forgiving of him and accepting of the past.

speed and punctuation. Children are excellent at speaking Gibberish, and there is a wonderful example of this on my website. Dr K showed us how we could use Gibberish as a warm-up exercise that can often help people overcome their shyness or inhibition. It was fascinating to realize that we can express so much without the need of words, and we told jokes, had debates and sang songs (great when you forget the words), all in Gibberish. I am pretty sure that if we gave directions to someone who did not understand English or our native language, they would understand if we used Gibberish.

Multitasking doesn't work!

So far, so good, I thought. I was enjoying myself, but at the same time I was trying to be analytical and understand what was going on. In order to do this successfully, I would need to be engaged with logical thinking, while having my attention completely focused on my body. This is not difficult: it is impossible! However, I had yet to find that out, the hard way! I may not have had my notebook with me, but in my mind I was scribbling notes, making references and trying to understand things from an intellectual perspective. But as I would soon discover, I was sabotaging my chances of ever having a wonderful experience.

Some things are not meant to be rationalized or examined, because if you do that, you simply strip away the joy. For instance, imagine that you and your partner are making love for the first time. You have been looking forward to it, you have anticipated it, and you want it to be memorable. Now imagine that in the middle of a passionate embrace you whisper, 'Just a minute, darling', as you open the bedside drawer. Wondering what you were going to get, your partner would probably be curious and perhaps get even more excited. However, in this scenario you pull out a notepad and pen and say, 'Hang on a second, I just need to make a note of that. Right, OK, carry on!' Apart from possibly traumatizing your partner and ruining any future experience, you would have ruined it for yourself, too. The idea of trying to 'measure' (no pun intended!) such a thing is ludicrous, and yet it is an analogy for what I was trying to do in Laughter Yoga. I would not realize this until later, though.

We tried another exercise called *namaste* laughter, where we greeted each other in the Indian fashion, with palms together in front of our face, and bowed to each other, laughing. I was still analyzing things, but I had no resistance. I was not actively 'not' enjoying it, but I was not getting much from it either. We did more laughter exercises and more breathing, and this short session ended. I remember thinking, 'Is that it? Is that why I came to India? There must be more than this, surely?' I looked at my fellow students: they were smiling and their eyes were shining with obvious energy and excitement, but I was not feeling whatever it was that they were feeling. I was smiling, too, but my smile seemed lacking somehow, and I remember thinking that I would have to try harder and work harder to 'get' Laughter Yoga.

This was counterproductive. I did not realize that when it comes to laughter, all you have to do is allow it to happen, and while you are waiting for it to happen, you can just pretend or, as Dr K says, 'Fake it till you make it!' The thing is, it does not matter either way. You cannot fail! Whether your laughter is real and spontaneous or whether it is laughter as an exercise, it has the same value in your body and you will have the same beneficial response. Have you ever felt that you were going to sneeze and got a tissue, held it in front of your nose and waited in anticipation? Maybe you felt the beginning of a sneeze as you breathed in slowly, lifted your head back slightly, breathed out, waited and then – nothing! Suddenly, the same tickly feeling comes back and you repeat the process. You may even say 'Ahh ...', but the 'choo' bit eludes you. You try some technique to help, like looking up at the light or holding your breath, but still no sneeze. Eventually, you give up and you may even put your tissue away – and often it is at this very moment that you spontaneously sneeze! It seems that the moment you give up, the moment you give in, the moment when you stop trying and surrender is when you give your sneeze the space it needs to just happen. Well, I think it is the same with laughter! By definition, being spontaneous means 'performed or occurring without premeditation or external stimulus', so therefore we can never have control over spontaneity.

Inner critic

So, all the time when I could have been laughing freely and enjoying the moment, I chose, instead, to evaluate, criticize and compare myself to everybody else, which led me to feeling that I was lacking. I felt shameful about it and a failure as it brought up similar feelings from my past when I felt that I had failed and let people down. 'You need to try harder!' repeated the voice in my head over and over again. But now, thank goodness, it was time for *chai* and a change of scenery, and I was grateful for the distraction.

This could have been a great opportunity to talk to some of my group and tell them how I felt. I have no doubt that they would have assured me that they too had had similar feelings in the past when they first experienced Laughter Yoga. However, I kept all these thoughts and feelings to myself, presuming that no one else would understand.

As I mentioned before, many of the people on my course came from all over the world, and we were a diverse and interesting group. Between us, we represented a teacher, a bank manager, a retired businessman, a doctor, a magician, healers, life coaches, professional clowns and many more, but we had one thing in common: the desire to enjoy and facilitate laughter for others. Yet, at the time, I felt that I was the cuckoo in the group, the one who did not quite fit in.

The value of silliness

After our break, we returned to the large hall to continue with our Laughter Yoga exercises – and I was dreading it! The exercises in the morning had been connected to greetings, but now we were going to do something more active.

I found these new exercises rather silly. I still regard them as silly, but the difference is that I now value silliness as a wonderful commodity that helps us take ourselves less seriously. We started with milkshake laughter. Following Dr K's lead, we tipped an imaginary milkshake from one imaginary glass to another, and then, throwing back our heads, we poured this imaginary milkshake into our mouths, while laughing heartily. It is a clever laughter exercise because it puts you in the prime position for joyous laughter: head back, chin up, arms (or one arm) raised. We did this several times, followed by the usual chorus of ho, ho, ha, ha, ha.

You may possibly be able to imagine what we looked like as we pretended to have runaway lawnmowers, drink hot soup and act like lions. I certainly did and spent a considerable amount of time imagining what I would look like and what an observer would think of me. I was judgemental, self-critical and disparaging; yet, at the same time, I was thinking, 'This isn't real, this isn't funny, I don't feel comfortable with this.' I was consumed with the thought: 'If I feel like this on Day 1, what will I feel like at the end of the week? Maybe it's not for me, maybe I should go home.' Had I known what lay ahead, I would have felt reassured, but it was early days …

The saving grace to all of this, though, was that of being in the company of such lovely people as my wonderful fellow students, the inspiring Dr K and his marvellous team, and the splendid people who not only cooked and served our meals, but took pleasure watching us enjoy them. Appreciating the food with its enticing aromas wafting invitingly across the courtyard was not difficult, and I briefly allowed myself to forget my anxieties. After lunch, we had time to ourselves. Some of us had a rest; others read, meditated or went for a stroll around the grounds. I returned to my room and made some notes which I have not kept, but I remember that they were notes of despondency and disappointment about my lacking of ability, peppered with positive comments about everything else.

Multilingual

A few hours later, we went back to the hall to continue our training. We practised introducing the laughter exercise we had done in the morning just as we would do in a teaching environment. Then we each took turns to do a presentation of our teaching skills to Dr K and the rest of the students. Dr K invited everyone to do their presentations in their own language, and so we got to listen to an explanation of Laughter Yoga and a few Laughter Yoga exercises in Japanese, Chinese, Korean, German, Italian and several other languages. It was an excellent lesson in how much of our communication is through body language, and at the end I felt almost multilingual!

Afterwards, Dr K informed us that we were ready to learn another five laughter exercises. Again, I had that sinking feeling in my tummy and a slight resistance to the idea of participation. I went through the motions of doing each exercise, but I could not get rid of the thoughts that were going round and round in my mind like a mantra, telling me 'This isn't real, this isn't funny, this isn't real, this isn't funny.' It seemed that the more I tried not to think these thoughts, the more persistent they became. Some members of the group had really loud laughs, and I began to find this type of laughter intrusive; it felt inappropriate, artificial and unwelcome, and it only served to remind me that I was not 'getting it' at all. I was glad when the exercises stopped and Dr K suggested that we go on to laughter meditation, 'free-flow laughter'.

Turning on the laughter tap

Laughter meditation, 'free-flow laughter', is not necessarily a passive experience. It describes the process of focusing on laughter and on your body. Unconditional laughter manifests itself everywhere in the body, *except* the head and the mind. By sitting quietly and focusing on laughter and noticing the body, a strange phenomenon occurs, which is difficult to explain unless you have experienced it, but I will try.

It is important to make the distinction that this is completely separate from laughter exercises when laughter is contrived as an exercise and not necessarily authentic. This *is* natural laughter that is released; it is not forced, false or contrived. The analogy that comes to mind here is burping! It is possible to force a burp – you would know if you did that – but it's also possible for a burp to 'just occur' naturally. You can, of course, suppress it, and most of us do when we are in company, but you can also, in the appropriate surroundings, just let it out. Sometimes, a burp comes out unexpectedly and surprises you – 'Oops, pardon!' And this is what laughter meditation is like, allowing the body to express something that is outside of your conscious awareness.

The room was quiet. Some people had their eyes closed. I sat there, not knowing what to expect, but as I looked around, I saw that most people were smiling, and I became aware that I was smiling, too. After a few moments, someone behind me began to giggle, very gently, very quietly. Another person let out a ripple of laughter and then stopped. I found myself responding to this, and my smile widened. Someone else started to laugh a little longer than the other person, and then more joined in and the laughter began to be ever-present, with pockets of laughter becoming louder, then quieter, around the room. Suddenly, I laughed out loud, too. It came as a surprise, and it felt as though it had come from nowhere. By now, the laughter level had risen considerably, and some were laughing continually. I joined in, and all of a sudden, the room was full of the most incredible sound of uninhibited, joyous laughter.

Have you ever watched a pan of water as it comes to the boil? The first sign of it getting hot is the steam, then you see a few bubbles at the edge of the pan, a few more, then some in the middle, and in a mere fraction of a second the water starts rapidly bubbling and boiling away. The water becomes alive with frenetic activity, and so it was with this laughter meditation.

And it hurt! I had not laughed like this for years, or maybe I had never laughed as much as this before at all. In between my laughter, I groaned and held my sides, and I was so pleased that we were sat down, because I knew I could not have remained standing and laughing like that. I noticed some people were lying down, with their knees held against their chest, and I did the same, hoping it would bring some comfort to my aching sides. It just made the laughter come louder and harder, and I had tears running from my eyes. Around me, I could hear others groaning, too, as they felt the accompanying aches. I was exhausted, but exhilarated at the same time.

I was laughing for no reason! There was this wonderful moment where it felt as if someone had found a switch inside me and turned laughter on to 'full flow'. Once my laughter started, it built in intensity. It felt like a different part of me was being expressed, and I was just a witness to it. I could not stop laughing, but, most importantly, I did not *want* to. Within seconds I felt euphoric. As I was laughing, I looked around, and sometimes I would look at someone who had stopped laughing and my laughter would make them start to laugh again. I stopped for a few moments, and others stopped as well, but then I would feel a wave of happiness pass through me and once more my laughter would erupt. Gradually, the laughter started to ebb and there was a moment of calm and quiet. This provided some relief because this is such an energetic and tiring experience, and diaphragms like mine, unused to such robust activity, were aching, along with facial muscles and jaw. Then, just when it seemed that it was all over, someone let out a snort of laughter, and almost everyone started laughing again, and so it continued, like a rollercoaster of laughter going up and down.

Euphoria

I can say without hesitation that this was probably one of the most incredible moments of my life. I did not think about whether this was funny or not, or judge the laughter; I did not think about anything at all. For those moments, I thought of nothing. I was incapable of thought, incapable of doing anything other than being in the moment of simple joy and unconditional laughter. And from that moment, I have changed because I learnt that the laughter that I had looked for, and hoped to create, had been there all the time, inside me, waiting to emerge. And *that* was the lesson I needed to learn and understand because after this I knew that my job as a Laughter Yoga teacher would be to help other people come to the same understanding.

There was a lot to learn, of course – the exercises, the breathing, the principles, and so on – but these were the tools for sharing some innate wisdom that we all seem to have lost in our modern world. We *are* laughter. We always have been, and we always will be, but we cannot realize it until we know it. Reading this book will only tell you about it, and you will never truly understand until you experience it and *become* laughter yourself. Then you will have the choice of how you live the rest of your life, whether you continue to live as you are now, or to keep connected to the joy and laughter that is within you and share it with others. But you never need worry about finding it because it is part of you, and always has been. Some of us just need a little help to get reconnected.

My notebooks went in the bin! In the days that followed, I laughed and I laughed and I laughed. It was the most therapeutic, cathartic and fantastic experience that I have ever had. I am not saying that all the laughter from then onward was real, far from it, but I knew better than to worry about what sort of laughter it was. I accepted and enjoyed the fact that any laughter that comes from a place of willingness is just as valuable and beneficial as what some might call 'real' laughter. I truly believe that I laughed more in that week than I had done in my entire childhood, and my childhood was not an unhappy one.

For a few days, I found that I often apologized when I was laughing, and it took a while to lose this habit. I think that this sort of extended laughter reminded me of being at school, when young girls were told off for laughing in class and on the school bus. In fact, I had a particular moment of clarity when I suddenly remembered being told off by my teacher for having a dirty laugh; although, at the time, I had no idea what a dirty laugh was, I still remember feeling shameful and embarrassed. I wonder whether this had the effect of making me inhibited about freely laughing in company? I no longer worry about it, though, and it certainly does not matter now.

I have more than made up for it by significantly improving my laughter factor since my visit to Bangalore, and I have realized that people who appreciate the value of laughter never judge somebody else's laugh. In fact, the snorters, chucklers, chortlers and titterers often have the most infectious laughs of all, and they are always welcome at laughter clubs around the world.

I am not going to give any more details on what we learnt on the course. You may decide to do the course yourself (I recommend you do), and you should enjoy some of the many surprises. I will share this, though: whether you call it meditation, contemplation, mindfulness, self-hypnosis or visualization, there is something empowering about taking time every day to be still and quiet and just 'be'. There is plenty of time for rushing, multitasking, worrying, working, eating, shopping, speaking, and so on, but I invite you to find some time just to 'be' still and quiet.

This is something I have grown to value, and every day I take time, just a few moments, when I wash my hands or travel to work, to bring some serenity and calm into what can sometimes be the most hectic and manic of days. If you can do this each day, together with some laughter of whatever kind, I have no doubt that you will feel happier, healthier and more resilient. After all, we are human *beings*, not human *doings*!

Bittersweet goodbye

My time at the School of Ancient Wisdom was one of the most amazing experiences of my life. I learnt far more than just Laughter Yoga: I learnt a lot about myself, too. Spending time in a place of such serenity, being in wonderful company and spending long days laughing and playing was like being a child in a big, happy family. We had nothing to worry about; our days were structured, our meals lovingly cooked and prepared for us; and the sun shone every day. We were cut off from the modern world, cut off from telephones, emails, deadlines, traffic queues, shopping malls, household chores and bill paying. We did not watch television or read newspapers, and so there were no negative influences to cloud our thoughts or cause worry. When we felt the need for entertainment, we made our own, and as you may expect, laughter was always present. At the end of the course, I felt that I had learnt enough about Laughter Yoga to be able to teach it to others, but I also felt that I had learnt much more about myself and what matters in life.

On the last night, we dressed up and each of us took it in turn to sing or dance or tell a story. Riccardo, the Italian magician, performed some magic tricks, and we danced and celebrated both the end of something and the beginning of something new. And even though we left and went back to different places all over the world, we promised to keep in touch, and I am pleased to say that we have. Each of us, in our own unique ways, have continued to spread the sound of laughter. You will find links to my friends on my website.

We all had our plans and dreams and that included Dr K, who told us about his ambitious plan to open a 'Laughter University'. I suggested that if everyone in the world who has been touched by 'laughing for no reason' were to buy just one brick, his university could be built overnight. He laughed as he always does, but he promised that he would allow me to lay the first brick when the building work starts, and I intend to hold him to that promise!

Your own joyous laughter, as I hope you will discover, grows and multiplies in volume and magnitude every time you express it. It is as though every time you allow laughter to flow, you make room for more to come in and replace it. In this way, it is similar to sharing love. The two, I believe, are a perfect match.

As I left the School of Ancient Wisdom, I saw the sign again that had welcomed me a week earlier, but now the words *As you enter these gates, leave your small self outside so that your HIGHER SELF may unfold inside* made perfect sense. It had been my small self that had created the only barrier between laughter and me. Now I had found a way to allow the natural expression of joy to emerge from deep within my very being, and I knew that I would be able to facilitate a similar experience for others.

Chapter 4

Laughter at Home

Most folks are as happy as they make up their minds to be.

Abraham Lincoln

During my time in the wonderful surroundings of the School of Ancient Wisdom, I had no contact with the outside world. No Internet, telephone or newspapers, and although I did not notice it at the time, this was one of the elements that led to me feeling relaxed, serene and happy. I believe we underestimate the negative influence of the news fed to us by the media, whether it is the television, radio or press. When I came home, I realized how emotionally debilitating it was to listen and read the news each day, and so the first thing I did was to stop – and I have never returned to it. I will return to this subject in Chapter 8.

How else do we translate breakthrough experiences into our daily routine? That was my challenge after my experiences with Laughter Yoga. I knew that I wanted to share my insights with others and wondered if there was a unique way I could work with laughter, inspired by Dr K, but also utilizing my other interests in positive psychology, NLP and hypnotherapy. This chapter explores my development of the principles of working with laughter into my own approach, and I hope it may inspire you to consider how you might adopt laughing for no reason for your own particular needs.

To get the full therapeutic benefits of laughter, we need to laugh regularly. As the laughter needs to be prolonged, most of us can only experience this if we laugh as an exercise. Even if I was lucky enough to have a laughter club located nearby, unless I was able to attend at least once a week, I would still need to laugh on my own to get the full therapeutic benefits.

I was glad to be back home, but immediately I missed the abundance of laughter that I had enjoyed in Bangalore. I desperately wanted to join a Laughter Yoga club, but the nearest one was 90km away. The only solution was to start laughing on my own and to form my own club as soon as I could.

Laughing on your own

This is a different experience to laughing in a group. You have to take full responsibility for your laughter as you cannot rely on the energy of group laughter or the infectiousness of hearing others laugh. Consequently, laughing on your own can be more meditative and reflective, which was my experience, especially when I first started, and I found it very soothing. I began a routine where, each morning, I would get up, wash and dress, and then spend a minimum of 20 minutes practising breathing exercises, mindfulness and laughing for no reason. Dr K had encouraged us all to try this every day for 40 days. I really wanted to do this, knowing that the repetition would develop new neural pathways in my brain so that this daily practice would become an ingrained habit.

It was easy at home, but it was more difficult when I was away on trips. Ideally, I wanted to have a routine where I practised at the same time every day, but often I would be on an aircraft or staying in a hotel. Although it was 7 am at home, it might only be 2 am where I was, and I feared that security would arrive at the door of my hotel room after receiving complaints of a manic laughing woman. Dr K encountered a similar problem when travelling or staying as a guest in someone else's house, so his solution was silent laughter. I found silent laughter to be really enjoyable, and it frequently caused me to get the giggles. There is something deliciously wonderful about laughing in a fashion that suggests that you really should not be laughing at all! Dr K actually filmed one of his silent laughing sessions while he was staying with guests and you will find this on my website.

The best way to laugh on your own is to experiment and find what works for you. I tried a variety of different methods, and the most effective for me was using observation and appreciation. After doing some breathing exercises I would look around, and whenever I saw something pleasing or something that I appreciated, I would laugh. The laugh would be quiet and gentle, and when I had paid enough attention to one object, I would switch my attention to another. It was not like laughing *at* something, but more like laughing *for* something. I would laugh at the sun rising, the birds hopping around the garden and the leaves moving in the wind. This laughter could never replace the laughter I love sharing in a group, but it proved to be a great addition and had the added benefit of always being available. Over the next few weeks, I tried out different sorts of laughter exercises, some as a planned morning routine and others as impromptu laughter exercises, as I went about my day.

Laughing on your own as a daily routine

Morning practice is preferable because it sets you up to have a great day. At first, you may not find laughing alone to be as much fun as laughing in a group, but as your body does not know the difference between real and fake laughter, you will still get the same therapeutic benefits. If you persist, you will find it gets easier, and you will discover what works best for you. There is no right or wrong way to practise: you can make up your own exercises or, if you attend a laughter club, you can utilize some of the ones you enjoy doing in a group. As long as you are laughing, you will be benefitting.

In her book *Meet Your Happy Chemicals*, American author Loretta Graziano Breuning explains that with repetition we can build new neural pathways in our brain. To do this, she says we must practise for a minimum of 10 minutes every day for 45 days consecutively, whether it feels good or not. Every time we complete our goal, we should celebrate because eventually, as we succeed, we will be rewarded with a release of dopamine that makes us feel good so we begin to look forward to repeating our habit. What starts out as a chore or something we have to make ourselves do soon becomes something that makes us feel happy and joyous. When we laugh, we also benefit from another 'happy chemical', endorphin. Laughing on your own every day is a habit that will bring you both feelings of health and happiness. Eventually, laughter will become something that is hardwired in your brain: even thinking about laughing will be enough to improve your mood

Breathing

Start by taking a nice deep breath and just letting it go. If you say 'Ahhh' as you breathe out, it can add to your feelings of relaxation. You can do this sitting or standing, whichever you prefer. In between laughter exercises, take a few moments to practise deep breathing, making sure that you exhale fully so that you are able to maximize the amount of oxygen you breathe in.

Warm-up

Shaking is a great way to warm up the body, and it feels like laughter, especially in the shoulder and belly area. Stand with your feet shoulder width apart, knees slightly bent, and gently shake in an up-and-down motion. You will find that there is a natural bounce that accompanies your shaking. Allow your arms to dangle loosely and move around as you shake and bounce. Your feet keep you firmly planted on the ground, while the rest of your body is like a ragdoll. This action forces pockets of air out of your mouth and by adding different sounds you will get different effects. There is no right or wrong way to do this – just experiment. Some noises and actions 'feel right', so follow your instincts and do what feels best for you. After a minute or two of this, you will be relaxed and energized, and your body will feel tingly. Apart from feeling wonderful, this exercise is said to enhance lymph flow and improve immune function.

Gibberish warm-up

Gibberish enables you to express yourself without engaging the conscious mind. Just allow noises and sounds to emerge without thinking about it too much. It is impossible to do this wrong! If you have a problem or irritation on your mind, express it in Gibberish. Speaking loudly and fast in one breath feels really good and releases tension and anxiety. If you are feeling happy and relaxed, then you can allow more serene and relaxed noises to be released. Use your face expressively, using your cheeks, your eyebrows, tongue and jaw. You may look a little silly, but as you are on your own, it does not matter!

Next, warm up your vocal chords. Imagine you are in an orchestra or a choir and go up and down the scales using the laughter sounds of ho, ha and hee. Do this for a minute or two, or longer if you are enjoying it.

Take a deep breath and then exhale as you repeat each of the vowel sounds a, e, i, o, u. You will find that the 'e' sound will put your mouth in the shape of a smile, and it is easy to progress to tee and hee sounds, which sound more like laughter.

Whenever you do laughter exercises, on your own or with a group, open your mouth a little wider and tilt your chin up. Try this for yourself to see the difference it makes in the resonance of your laughter.

Some simple exercises

Breathe in, stretch your arms up high and relax as you breathe out and lower your arms. Repeat and, on the third time, breathe out with laughter.

Try repeating ho, ho, ha, ha. You will find that this will automatically regulate your breathing. You do not have to think about breathing in and out: it will happen naturally.

Different types of laughter

Experiment with different sorts of laughter. Imagine you are an actor/actress who has been asked to portray different types of laugh – dramatic, posh, snorting, shy, evil, manic, high pitched, like Father Christmas, like a small child.

Mirror laughter

Some people find it helpful to laugh in front of a mirror. This is probably because of the effect of mirror neurons, and you will never find a better match of body language and facial expressions than your own reflection. Imagine that you are sharing a joke with yourself and laugh. If you find making faces at yourself makes you laugh, then do that. Finding out what works for you is the most important part of beginning laughing alone exercises.

Aloha laughter

This is a favourite in our house. Raise your arms above your head and stretch. Say 'Aloooo' in a loud voice for an extended time before lowering your arms and laughing ha, ha, ha. It should sound like the Hawaiian greeting 'Aloha', just much longer and with lots of ha, ha laughter. There is something anticipatory about waiting for the ha, ha, ha.

Iain and I use this greeting form just like other people say 'Yoo-hoo' to indicate that they are back home. We say 'Aloooo' as we come through the front door, and we try to keep it going until we get eye contact to join in the ha, ha, ha together. It is the nicest way of saying 'Hi, I'm home' that I have experienced! Once you start practising these laughter exercises, little things like this begin to creep into your everyday life. It might sound a bit eccentric, but when you consider that these moments of laughter add up to increase our experiences of positive emotions and ultimately make us feel happier, who cares?!

Here are some more ideas for laughter exercises, but try creating your own as well.

Swimming laughter

Pretend you are swimming and laughing at the same time. Try the breaststroke, front and back crawl.

Singing laughter

Singing can be a good way of incorporating laughter exercises. Just choose any song and change the words to ho, ho, ha, ha, hee, hee or Gibberish if you prefer. You may be surprised to find that at some stage it makes you laugh authentically, although, of course, 'fake' laughter is fine. Remember that your body does not know the difference.

One of my favourite singing laughter exercises is to laugh to the tune of the Can-Can. If you remember the tune, my words are haa, ha-ha, ha-ha, haa, haa, ha-ha, ha-ha, haa, haa, ha-ha, ha-ha, haa, oh ho, ho, ho, ho, and so on. I sing it louder and quicker as I go, using big breaths and making sure I empty all lungs full of air all the way through. Afterwards, I need to breathe and rest because it is really hard work, but it is guaranteed to tip me into authentic laughter because it is so absurd, especially when I pretend I am wearing a Can-Can skirt to swing and shake.

Surprise laughter

Take a big gasp of air as if you have had a big shock or surprise. Hold it for a second and let it out with laughter. Keep exhaling until you cannot get out any more breath.

Machine gun laughter

My friend and I devised this exercise when we both had a lot of frustrations to deal with. Instead of getting irritated, we lined up our problems and then obliterated them with machine gun fire of laughter. With the staccato sound of a machine gun ha-ha-ha-ha-ha-ha, we pulverized them and we were soon in fits of giggles. It is a very effective exercise and one that I do any time I feel stressed.

Silent laughter

You do not have to save silent laughter for the times when you cannot laugh out loud – it is fun to do anytime. Imagine you are laughing, but use no sound. This can be an effective way of starting spontaneous laughter. Shake your shoulders up and down and make sure you feel the laugh in your belly.

Telephone and Skype laughter

Many Laughter Yoga teachers around the world have organized laughter sessions by telephone so that people can laugh with others even though they are at home alone. There are links to several of these on my website and in the Resources section on page 235. Most are available for free, and they are great fun. This is a great addition to laughter clubs and means that it is possible to laugh with others practically every day.

Animal laughter

Try laughing as if you were a dog, cow, cat, chicken or any other animal you can think of.

Laughter on the line

I first talked to Christine on the telephone when she enquired about Clinical Hypnotherapy for her symptoms of anxiety and insomnia. During the course of the conversation she expressed an interest in my laughter session and joined us on the following Saturday. Christine became a regular at our sessions and also joined a daily telephone laughter club. She told me that starting the day with telephone laughter gave her a reason to get up, and she enjoyed connecting with people even though there was no conversation. Until she started laughing, she explained that the only company she enjoyed had been her two cats. Laughing with others gave her something to look forward to every day and helped her become sociable, where, previously, she had lived a reclusive life. She started sleeping better and became less anxious, and we felt that there was no need for hypnotherapy sessions.

Crying/Happy laughter

Starting with your hands in the air, lower them while making a crying sound with matching expression. Then lift up your hands while smiling and laughing.

Body part laughter

Discover what laughs match different parts of your body by scanning your body as you laugh.

Occasional laughter exercises

Occasional laughter exercises are those that you can do whenever you think about it or have the opportunity. It is a good idea to have some exercises that you do whenever you perform a particular task or when you are in a particular place. Once you have developed the habit of laughing in these circumstances, you will find yourself doing it without really thinking about it. A few seconds here and a few seconds there add up and will add to the effectiveness of your daily routine.

In the bathroom

The bathroom is a good place to practise laughter exercises because it is somewhere you go every day, and it is normally a place where you have some privacy (when my children were young, it was the only place where I could be on my own!). Make it a habit to laugh while you are in the bathroom.

I started with laughing in the shower. People often sing in the shower presumably because the acoustics are good which makes people's voices sound more resonate and tuneful. It felt quite natural to sing a little song made up of ho, ho, ho and ha, ha, ha. Over time, I have developed this further, and I now have specific laughter sounds for different activities. There is 'shampoo my hair laughter' where the bubbles burst into giggles and 'soap laughter' when the sound of laughter changes depending upon which area is being washed: feet are tickly 'hee, hee' laughter, tummy is deep 'ho, ho' laughter, and there is other laughter for other places.

If you feel adventurous, the bathroom is also good for 'chimpanzee laughter', a loud laughter using the mouth to make the sounds of 'ooo, ooo, ooo, haah, haah, haah' sound like an excited primate. It makes a good facial exercise, and if you enjoy role play, you can add some chimpanzee body language, too.

Dropping things laughter

I have developed the habit of laughing whenever I drop something, whereas before I would tut, sigh or complain. If I am in a situation where I feel it would be inappropriate to laugh, then I smile. I also laugh when I walk into a room and forget the reason I was going there (I think most of us do this at least occasionally!). Learning to laugh at yourself with kindness and taking yourself less seriously relieves unnecessary stress. If you learn to laugh at the silly mistakes we all make each day, you will probably never run out of laughter exercise opportunities either!

In the car laughter

Being in the car is a great place to laugh. When I am on my own, I use traffic lights as my laughter beacon. If they are green, I smile because I have not had to stop and maybe give a little chuckle. An amber light means I start to laugh as a warm up to 'red light laughter', or if I have already started to go past the lights, I do 'just made it laughter'. Red light laughter has become one of my favourite driving experiences. Whenever I stop at a red light (with my windows closed), I laugh as loud and as heartedly as I can until the lights turn to green. Since I have been doing this, I have surprised myself with the volume and power of some of the laughter I produce. I laugh in a way that I have never done in company, and this totally uninhibited laughter can make me feel positively euphoric. If it is a long journey where I stop at lots of red traffic lights, I often arrive at my destination feeling full of energy, enthusiasm and excitement, which is far better than arriving stressed and anxious. Try this car laughter for yourself. Some people describe this type of laughter as 'like being on top of a cliff and screaming for all you're worth'. I have never tried that, but it sounds like a good comparison. I recommend this as a much better alternative to using road rage as a way of venting to feel better.

Other car exercises

- Indicator laughter – right indicators: go 'ho, ho, ho'; left indicators: go 'ha, ha, ha'.
- Gear stick laughter matches the gear changes and speed of the car.
- 'After you laughter' involves leaving home in plenty of time and allowing everyone to filter into your traffic lane or join your carriageway from a side road. It could also be called 'random act of kindness laughter' as it generates feelings of well-being for you and sometimes the other driver. If they fail to notice or appreciate your gesture, then you should immediately go into 'they didn't even notice' laughter.

There are limitless variations of this laughter whether you are alone or with other passengers. It is a great way to make a car journey fun and interesting for children. You can introduce different laughs for whenever you see a particular colour of car or type of vehicle. Children are natural and spontaneous laughter experts, and a car full of laughter is better than a car full of bickering siblings demanding to know, 'Are we nearly there yet?'

Of course, it is important to maintain your concentration while you are driving, but you may find that you are much less stressed and less prone to aggressive driving if you find opportunities for laughter at the wheel.

Housework laughter

You can incorporate laughter with any household chore (as you are probably realizing, you can incorporate laughter with almost anything!), and although it may not make cleaning windows, ironing or sweeping the floor more enjoyable, you can at least take comfort from the fact that adding laughter brings about more benefits than just domestic tidiness. Just as we sometimes hum or whistle when we are doing an activity, we can learn to laugh instead.

Taking laughter to the people

I told my friends and family about my adventure to Bangalore, and most of them were interested, some were intrigued and others were a little sceptical. I often found myself in situations where people would say, 'Go on then, make me laugh!' I had encountered a similar reaction when I was on my Clinical Hypnosis course at university, and some friends and family would say, 'Go on then, hypnotize me!' People often mistakenly believe that hypnosis is something that is 'done to them', whereas, in fact, hypnosis is a naturally occurring state that we enter at regular intervals during the day. So a hypnotherapist does not *make* somebody hypnotized: they facilitate the conditions that help a person enter into natural hypnosis more easily. This is just the same with Laughter Yoga, where you facilitate laughter by providing the ideal environment and some laughter exercises so that laughter can occur more easily. Both require the willingness of the participant to allow a natural process to happen, and neither can be forced on you (regardless of what stage hypnotists may make you think).

Laughter in the community

I really wanted to introduce Laughter Yoga into my community, but my job as cabin crew presented me with several practical problems. My timetable meant that I could be flying on any day of the week, and that made it difficult to make a regular commitment. I knew I would be able to find a free day off each week, but I suspected that most people want to know in advance so that they could plan. I also needed to find a suitable venue, and I felt sure that I would only be able to rent a room for a set time each week.

I wanted to follow in Dr K's philosophy of not charging for Laughter Yoga so that it could be free and available to everybody. These problems appeared to have no solution, but I stayed with the philosophy of Dr K that everything would work out in its own time and in its own way. I just needed to stay alert to pick up the clues as they came along and take action when the time was right. Once you adopt this attitude, it is really difficult to experience worry, stress and concern because you are open to all possible solutions rather than being focused solely on problems.

I decided that I could facilitate one-off laughter sessions and give talks about Laughter Yoga, and I began to contact local clubs and organizations. I also gave some talks at local Toastmasters clubs where I was already an active member. I discovered that when I gave a talk about Laughter Yoga, everyone wanted to experience it for themselves, but not many people were prepared to commit themselves to joining a pre-planned session. Eventually, I found that the best method was to combine the two, explaining the concept first and then asking the audience, 'Would you like to try a few exercises now to see what it's like?'

Generally, the majority of people joined in and enjoyed their experience, but some had a strong resistance to laughter as an exercise. Typically, they would insist that unless laughter was spontaneous, it was false and inappropriate, and a lot of older people said laughter should only be expressed in 'appropriate company'; otherwise, it was vulgar. Someone even told me that they associated uninhibited laughter with places of ill repute where there was drunkenness and loose women! I accepted that someone holding such a strong view might not change because of anything that I would say. Laughter Yoga can only ever work when people are open and willing to consider the idea, and the very nature of it encourages experience, but only if you are ready for it.

The power of the moment

I met groups of people who would believe they were incapable of laughter because they were suffering from pain or depression or had a serious illness. Regardless of the science to show how laughter could help, it seemed to me they felt that appearing to be happy, carefree and untroubled would be incongruent with their circumstances. I could sympathize and understand their concern. After all, if I were a carer for someone who had been dependent on me, maybe I would question how they could suddenly become happy and energetic.

After giving this some thought, I began to incorporate some new material into my explanation of Laughter Yoga, pointing out that no one can be in any one state constantly. Whether it is happiness, unhappiness, pain, depression, euphoria or anxiety, we always have moments, no matter how brief, where we notice a change in how we feel. No matter how much pain you were in, if something dramatic and unexpected happened, you would be distracted from that pain even if it were only for a moment. For instance, imagine you had won the lottery, had seen an escaped lion in your garden or opened your front door to see your favourite film star. You do not consciously choose how to react; your brain does it for you by prioritizing what is more important in that moment. If you have got a headache and someone stands on your foot, for a moment your headache will go and be replaced by foot pain. The same effect can be created by something much more acceptable than pain – laughter.

Once we understand this, we can accept that laughter can become a distraction as well. Not a cure from problems and illnesses but a break from them. When we laugh, we can temporarily change

The man who had no sense of humour

Martin came to our laughter sessions because he felt that he had no sense of humour and rarely laughed. Many people feel this way and just 'don't get' jokes. Martin said that he hated it when people started to tell jokes because he would laugh along, but feel like a fake. For this reason, he did not enjoy being at parties or meeting people in pubs and bars, although he said he envied people who could enjoy a good laugh.

Our laughter sessions were great for him because he could laugh and join in without any social pressure, and he did not have to face the anxiety of trying to understand a joke. He enjoyed 'laughing for no reason' and pointed out to me that he had probably had more experience of 'fake laughter' than anyone, but this was the first time he had been able to laugh and feel relaxed. He soon discovered that he had a very infectious laugh that would often make others in the group laugh spontaneously, and for once he was able to feel fully integrated in a group of people laughing. Once he was less anxious about laughing in company, he found that his sense of humour developed to the stage where he even told jokes himself.

our state and enjoy the experience of being free from all thoughts and feelings. We literally *become* laughter and experience nothing else other than being in the present moment. When we stop, we go back to what was there before: circumstances have not changed, but the wonderful thing is, we may have.

It is impossible to be anxious and relaxed at the same time, and after a laughter session you become very relaxed. Your blood pressure is lower, and you have all those wonderful endorphins rushing around your body, so you feel much more positive and happy. The effects do wear off, but even if you only experience this once a week, it is something to look forward to and the more you do it, the more effective it becomes. Even if you discover that you can only feel free when you laugh, is it not worthwhile making sure that you laugh more often? All problems have a beginning, middle and an end. When you feel stuck in the middle, you may not be able to see the end and feel that 'this' is forever. I think that laughter opens you up to the realization that 'this' is now and that things can and will change.

Laughing with depression

I remember working with a support group for people with chronic depression and meeting a young woman. I will call her Elaine. She was quite confrontational as she asked questions about Laughter Yoga. Elaine challenged everything I said regarding its benefits, its effectiveness and its purpose and told me that she thought I was delusional and naive. Owing to my training in Clinical Hypnosis, I did not regard this resistance as negative but as a reaction and a release of emotion. Rather than argue, I agreed that this was her view and that she could, indeed, be right. She told me that no one could understand how she felt and I agreed. She said that laughing was the last thing she would want to do and I agreed. Eventually, when she had run out of things to object to I asked her whether she wanted to join in and infuriated her by suggesting that she would still get benefits from hearing other people laugh. She eventually agreed if only to prove how pointless it was.

When we did the laughter exercises, she managed to produce a really loud, slow, false and sarcastic-sounding ha, ha, ho, ho response, and her body language was similar to that you would expect from a moody teenager. When everyone smiled, she went to a great effort to make her mouth turn downward, and she also added some dramatic sighing, a demonstration of how pathetic and boring she found everything. Some people in the group seemed embarrassed by her behaviour, and I think they were worried about how I might feel. Someone broke out in a nervous laugh, but tried to cover it up. The next time Elaine demonstrated her unwillingness to join in, a few more people giggled. Then the floodgates opened and the whole group started to laugh spontaneously, unable and unwilling to stop. Elaine got really annoyed at this because the purpose of her behaviour was to prove that Laughter Yoga did not work with depressed people. But here were depressed people proving the opposite, and she was the person who had facilitated it, not me! Then the laughter got to her and she started to laugh, too. At first, she tried to pretend it was false, but she could not keep this up for long. In the end, the only way to save face was to join in and go along with the group, and this she did with good grace.

Mountain Goddess Festival, Japan

I have read about this festival and been greatly intrigued, although I have never had the chance to see it. It is traditionally held on 7 February and is also known as the stonefish festival. People gather at a shrine in the mountain area of Nodaji and form a circle passing sake between them. In the centre of the circle sits the man in charge of the proceedings, and inside his clothes he hides a stonefish. A ritual dialogue then takes place, where the leader is asked, 'What have you got hidden inside your clothes?' and he responds, 'I'll show you, but you must promise not to laugh.' The participants duly promise and the leader reveals the fish for a second or two. Despite their promises, the participants all laugh heartily. The leader pretends to be upset at their reaction and drinks more sake to cheer himself up. The routine is repeated several times as the laughter becomes more natural and spontaneous. The joyous laughter is said to entertain the mountain goddess, and as an act of gratitude, she protects the villagers during the following 12 months, until the next laughter festival.

It was a superb icebreaker that helped me, and to her credit, Elaine really entered into the spirit of it once she started to join in. When it came to free flow laughter, she laughed longer and louder than anyone, and afterwards she turned out to be the most enthusiastic of the group. She shared with the group that she had not realized that she was capable of such laughter and had rediscovered something that she had long forgotten. This gave her the recognition that laughter was something that was still accessible to her and offered her a glimpse of what it felt like to be in the moment, connected to positive emotions.

Now she had something to work toward, with her focus not on the absence of depression but on the presence of positivity. For me, this was a clear validation of the 'fake it till you make it' principle. Her body responded to her actions and matched them with the release of the chemicals associated with joy and happiness. It was a privilege to witness this transformation and to have been part of its facilitation along with the group. Everyone present, even those who did not have such an intense response, were able to appreciate what had occurred, and I felt that this one event alone was reward enough for having trained in Laughter Yoga.

Laughing nearer home

I still wanted to do something in my own community, and one day I rang to see whether it would be possible to book our local village hall for just one session. A friendly gentleman answered my call and explained that he was dealing with bookings for his wife, while she was away visiting relatives. I am not sure that she would have approved, but he told me that the main hall would be free the following Wednesday at 10 am and agreed to let me have it free of charge. I printed a few posters, put them up around the village and waited to see what happened.

On the day, Iain and I turned up at 9.30 am and began to arrange the room which could easily have accommodated 30–40 people, but we had no idea of knowing whether anyone would come or not. In the end, five people arrived – one of them was a friend of mine, Liz, who brought two friends with her, and two people had seen the posters and come out of curiosity. It was not the big turnout I had hoped for, but it seemed a lucky number as Dr K also had had five people at his first Laughter Yoga session.

I do not think that any of these people had ever heard of Laughter Yoga, but they listened to my explanation and watched me demonstrate the exercises. Everyone joined in as best they could, but it felt a bit strange and uncomfortable to be in such a huge, empty space, and I was unable to reproduce the relaxed and happy atmosphere that I had experienced in Bangalore. Rather than struggle on, I thought it would be a better idea if we sat down and talked about how we felt about laughing as an exercise. After a while, when I could see that everyone seemed settled, I suggested that we tried again with some seated Laughter Yoga, and it did not take long before there was spontaneous laughter as well. I like seated Laughter Yoga as well as moving around and my preference is a session that involves both. Although we were a small group not in the best of surroundings, I treasure the memory of this first laughter session and feel grateful to those who made the effort to attend.

Iain set up a website – www.laughyourwaytohappiness.com – for me which was a task that I could never have completed on my own. I added information about the benefits of laughter and included lots of funny videos so that anyone visiting the site could enjoy a good laugh if they had the time. There was little more that I could do than just follow Dr K's advice and trust that things would work out on their own – which they did, and in the most unlikely of circumstances at that.

The Laugh-Inn

Truly the best opportunities seem to come by chance. I found the perfect venue for my laughter club in a chance discovery of a pub on a wet and rainy evening. The Rose & Crown proved to be cosy, friendly and had a conference room I thought might be suitable for holding a Laughter Yoga session. I explained the concept of Laughter Yoga to Ann, the landlady, and it became apparent that we both believed in the importance of providing services for our community. The Rose & Crown is at the very heart of village life and was already regarded as a place where people can meet together, and it has lots of great facilities, especially for families. Ann was enthusiastic about the idea of having a 'Laugh-Inn', and she offered the pub as the venue for a new laughter club, free of charge. I could not have hoped for anything more, and the New Forest Laughter Club was born in February 2012.

Together with Gill, a local yoga teacher also qualified in Laughter Yoga, we held our first meeting, which proved to be a great success. I have been running a free laughter club at The Rose & Crown ever since. On the second of our laughter sessions, we arranged for some of the staff to join in. They threw themselves into it wholeheartedly, and one of them could not stop laughing for the rest of the day: every time he looked at one of his colleagues, he would start giggling.

During our time there, we have often created chaos, moving tables, getting in the way and, of course, raising the roof with the sound of laughter, but we have always been welcomed and supported. In the summer, we use the beautiful gardens and passers-by and customers must wonder what is going on to create such a cacophony of laughter. It is not unusual to get the order 'I'll have whatever they are drinking'! Thanks to The Rose & Crown, we can have a really authentic 'happy hour' and stay afterwards for coffee and cake or one of their great pub lunches.

Learning through experience

I remember when I passed my driving test (on the third attempt!), my father remarked that I would really have to learn to drive now. I thought it was an odd remark at the time because surely I had just got a driving test certificate that 'proved' that I had learnt how to drive? I now understand perfectly what he meant. Passing the driving test is the first stage of a long process. It is the same with most skills that we learn. We first need to learn the basics, and then we need to build upon them until we are proficient. It is the same with running a laughter club.

The most important element I wanted to bring into our laughter sessions was fun, and to achieve that, each week would have to be different. There are hundreds of Laughter Yoga exercises and no end to the amount you can make up. *What* you do is never really as important as *why* you are doing it. The group dynamic is different every week, and we often include other elements that complement Laughter Yoga. Over the years, Dr K has adapted his Laughter

Yoga style slightly, incorporating elements of play, singing, dancing and using Gibberish that were not included originally. Through his website, Laughter Yoga teachers around the world are able to share their knowledge and findings, and, in this way, Laughter Yoga continues to grow and evolve, which has probably contributed to its increasing popularity.

Although the laughter sessions in Brockenhurst are deeply rooted in the concept of Laughter Yoga, I made a conscious decision early on to exclude the reference to yoga. Although the yoga reference is to the yoga-type breathing only, I found that, in the UK, people are less familiar with this idea, and most presume that Laughter Yoga will include yoga-type poses. Rather than risk disappointing people who wanted the yoga experience and alienating those who did not, I have always referred to our activities as a laughter session.

As the weeks and months passed, we all got to know what worked best, and I began to know intuitively what was going to work and learnt to be flexible with the session plan. I began to include some NLP techniques, and others began to share some of their skills like Chi Kung and Circle Dancing.

After our sessions it became customary to stay and chat. Our conversations were frequently about health and happiness, and we shared our views and experiences with each other. I discovered that for some, this was one of the few opportunities to socialize, and I think that Laughter Yoga clubs all over the world provide a valuable social benefit in addition to the physical and psychological ones.

Dr K's excellent training course had enabled me to start facilitating Laughter Yoga sessions, but it was only when I started to work with a variety of different people in different situations that I would extend the skills that I had been taught, all the time not only learning valuable lessons from the members but also new things about myself.

Chapter 5

Rediscovering the Laughter of Children

With mirth and laughter let old wrinkles come.

William Shakespeare

One of the most profound things I learnt in my Laughter Yoga sessions with Dr K was that laughter constantly lies within us, waiting to be released. This is something that is difficult for adults to accept and embrace, but recognizing this truth is the secret to releasing the potential for joy in your life.

In the summer of 2012, I experienced another reminder of the power of this inner laughter – a reminder that the joy we experienced as young children still lies waiting within us all to be tapped once more.

You may not have heard of Elliotology, but if you are interested in finding more joy, happiness and laughter in your life, then I would recommend that you become acquainted with this philosophy. Learning to apply Elliotology in your life is simple, highly effective and can lead you to experience the world in an entirely new way. For me, discovering Elliotology was a life-changing experience. Before I explain what it is, let me tell you the story that precedes my knowledge of it.

Plan A

August 2012 was a very busy month for me. Unexpectedly, Tim, my eldest son, came to stay, and my studying, writing and hypnotherapy sessions were all put on hold. I wanted to spend precious time with him, and yet I was aware of deadlines I had to meet and jobs that needed to be attended to. In particular, I needed to work on the proposal for the writing of this book. However, I knew better than to put routine and chores before my family, and I intended to enjoy every minute with Tim. In any event, I had a plan to manage the situation so that I could get my work done *and* spend time on holiday with my son.

I am an early riser, especially in the summer, so my idea was to get up before 6 am and do a couple of hours' work before anyone else was awake. This would have been a great idea had my son not lived in the Middle East, where the time is a couple of hours ahead of the UK. Consequently, he was up every morning before 6.30, sometimes even before me. So, with my devilishly clever idea dashed on Day 1, I gave in to the fact that I was having time off, and perhaps there was a reason why I should not work. I decided that I probably needed a complete break anyway. This 'reframe' was helpful, and we had a lovely time together walking and riding in the beautiful surroundings of the New Forest area where I live. When Tim left the following week, I felt refreshed and energized and was positive that I would finish my work in half the time.

Plan B

Two days before the end of my son's stay I got an email from a dear friend, Simon, who had an open invitation to 'come and stay, anytime'. The time was right (for him), and he asked whether it would be convenient. To be honest, the 'old me', pre Laughter Yoga and Positive Psychology days, would have put him off, but I recognize that people are more important than tasks, and apart from that, I was really looking forward to seeing him. How was I going to manage these deadlines, though? I had no idea. Time was running short and another three days had just disappeared from my working schedule.

My original Plan A, getting up early in the morning before everyone else, seemed even less likely a solution, as Simon did not come to stay alone. He brought with him his two-year-old son.

Although my children are all grown up, I did recall that small children are not particularly fond of lie-ins and tend to wake up earlier than most adults. There was nothing I could do but accept the situation and hope that, perhaps, after they left, I could work all day and most of the night, too.

Since my self-created drama over my visa and the lesson I had learnt from Dr K about accepting things rather than resisting them, I had become more pragmatic in my life and tried to see the benefits of new situations. Rather than considering that things had 'gone wrong', I acknowledged that things had just 'gone different' and looked for reasons why this might be a good thing. However, I failed to see the advantage of running out of time for work, but still accepted that it was simply outside of my control. I decided to give in, release my frustrations and simply trust that everything would be all right. I cannot say that it was easy to completely let go of my worry and concern, but I did do my best. Occasionally, I would find my mind drifting back to consider the worst-case scenario of not getting my work done, but I would remind myself that the best place I could ever be is fully present in the moment. I made a choice to enjoy being in the company of people I care about and trusted that everything would work out for the best.

My friend's son is the sort of child that tempts others to go ahead and start a family. Simon's son was incredibly cute, with blond, curly hair, a permanent smile and delightfully blue eyes. If he had started the 'terrible two' stage of tantrums, he managed to contain them all the time during his stay. He had been brought up in a way that encouraged him to be curious, confident and independent. He was either talking or moving or doing, and frequently he managed to do all three of these things together. In the majority of the photographs I took of him, he appears simply as a blur because it was almost impossible to get a photo of him being still. Some photos just reveal a body part of him as he disappeared from camera view. I think that either he moved quicker than the speed of the camera shutter or that I should have selected 'action mode'! He was full of love, fun, adventure, enthusiasm and joy. During the time that he stayed, until he left, he became my teacher and showed me how to reconnect with things that are important, some of which I had almost lost touch with. His name is Elliot.

When the pupil is ready, the teacher will appear

I may not be able to explain all the things that Elliot taught me. Some of them are too difficult to articulate, and I suspect that many of them were experienced at an unconscious level. However, on reflection, I am now aware of how much I learnt, and I treasure every moment that we shared together. I have chosen a name that I think aptly describes seeing the world through the eyes of this two-year-old. It is simply Elliotology.

There is no doubt that Elliot was a happy little boy, and I think that most small children at his age are like this. I intentionally say small children because I am aware that nowadays children seem to grow up more quickly and have worries and responsibilities much earlier in life. At Elliot's age, though, he lived on a moment-to-moment basis and everything was so simple. I doubt that he ever gave much thought to yesterday or tomorrow and just lived in the present moment. He took everything at face value, dealt with it there and then and did not pay attention to things like the weather. If it was sunny, he was happy and playful; if it was raining, he was happy and playful.

He never appeared to suffer from self-doubt. If he wanted to do something, like climb a rope in the playground, he attempted it. If

Warai Festival, Japan

On 8 October, an unusual festival takes place in Japan. It is called Warai Matsuri and it involves a lot of laughter. The story goes that the villagers looked after a goddess at the Nyu Jinja Shrine after she had overslept and missed an important meeting with other deities. She was very upset, but the locals cheered her up by laughing and encouraging her to laugh, too.

A leader dressed like a clown heads a parade through the town to the shrine, instructing everyone to laugh in time to the small bells that he rings. Twelve men called masumochi, *all dressed in formal Samurai costume, accompany him, carrying a chest containing fruits, vegetables and rice ears to symbolize the year's harvest. The laughing procession eventually ends at the Nyu Jinja Shrine.*

he failed, he was not disappointed in himself, but simply tried a few times before giving up without comparing himself to the children who had succeeded. He seemed to accept that doing your best was all you could do. Elliot expressed his emotions immediately and spontaneously. He may have been disappointed that he could not have an ice cream before lunch, but he did not bear grudges and did not hold resentment. Elliot did not carry 'baggage' around with him.

Elliot could not have told you the time and yet his timing was always perfect. He always knew when he was hungry, thirsty or tired; he woke up when he had had enough sleep and went to sleep whenever he needed a nap. He ran around expending energy, and then would suddenly stop and decide to look at a book or play quietly with one of his many cars. Elliot was completely in tune with his body; he heard its messages and responded to them.

How's your day been?

On the first morning of Elliot's stay, he was enjoying a good spoonful of porridge for breakfast when I came into the kitchen. Through his creamy lips he asked me, 'How's your day been, Lesley?' I replied, 'Well, so far, Elliot, very good, but *it is* only 7.30 in the morning!' I laughed and he laughed, too. I had laughed because he had amused me. He laughed because he liked to laugh, and here was an opportunity to share laughter with someone else. His comment made me reflect, though, and I took a moment to become aware of my environment and my circumstances and to appreciate everything around me at that present time. As I looked through the window, the early-morning sun was shining with the promise of a lovely summer's day. The birds were singing, and suddenly everything looked so green and fresh. Here I was, healthy and happy and surrounded by friends and family and the whole day was ahead of us. In that moment I felt blissfully happy. How much better could it be?

Later, as we had lunch, Elliot asked me again, 'How's your day been, Lesley?' I now understood that this was a standard dining-table question that I would hear at every mealtime and sometimes in between. However, every time Elliot posed his question, regardless of what I was doing, I would find myself drawn back to the present moment and into the conscious awareness of what was happening now and how I felt. This regular appraisal and the realization that I was indeed happy and content made me realize that normally I would be more likely to recognize and notice the negative, while taking the positive for granted.

The world through different eyes

Elliot saw the world in a different way to me, yet his was the more accurate and appreciative. He marvelled at the things I took for granted and saw things that I was unable to see. When he came running in from the garden to tell me about the waterfall, I could not imagine what he was talking about. Later, after we had spent three or four minutes watching the water flow from the overflow pipe into the drain outside, I knew what he meant, and he was right, it was worth watching. He spent a long time laughing with his new friend, an ant, picked up in the garden. He laughed as it crawled over his hand and up his arm in wonder that something so small could exist. When it eventually disappeared up the sleeve of his T-shirt and could not be found, he replaced it with a new friend. The garden was apparently full of 'friends'.

The optimist

Elliot's optimism was boundless. We went for a walk, and Elliot spent a huge amount of time and energy trying to catch one of the many birds that were pecking among the heather. His quest to capture another potential friend was, of course, fruitless. As soon as he got close, the birds would take off and land a few yards further on, but Elliot never lost his sense of optimism, enthusiasm and fun and showed no signs of frustration or exasperation. He modelled the behaviour of the cattle grazing on the Forest by having a good long drink from one of the dirtiest puddles I had ever seen and managed to get wet and muddy with seemingly little effort.

Elliot was so full of life, enthusiastic and appreciative of everything that was, and is. He was the epitome of a free spirit and a reminder of how easily we can become disconnected from ourselves and from the reality of life. As I observed him busily moving around here and there, humming a little song, I wondered what happens to us in the process of growing up to cause us to lose this sense of spirit? What would our lives be like if we could retain it or, failing that, recapture it once again? I struggled to identify what Elliot had in abundance and we as adults seem to have lost. Innocence, childhood and total lack of responsibility would be unattainable now, but I had the strongest feeling that if I could put a name to the 'magic' ingredient that Elliot possessed, it might just be possible to recreate it in our lives somehow. But no name was forthcoming and I just could not pin it down.

Simon decided that he would make the long drive home in the early evening so that Elliot could sleep for most of the journey. After he had packed up their belongings and scoured the garden for the assorted toy cars that had been 'parked' in the bushes, we waved goodbye to them. It was sad to see them go. We had so enjoyed their company, and I realized that I would never see this exact version of this little boy again, as two-year-olds grow and develop at such a quick rate. On one hand, I was sorry that they left; on the other hand, a part of me was relieved that at last I could settle down to write my book proposal.

I do not recall exactly what I wrote that evening, but I was not happy with the words that appeared on the page. Eventually, I gave up and decided that it would be best to wait until the following morning and try again after a good night's sleep.

The unconscious mind at work

The thing that has driven my studies and training over the past years has been my fascination with the unconscious mind. This is the part of us outside our conscious awareness, yet is responsible for over 90 per cent of all our decisions and behaviours. Even when we sleep, our brain continues to process information, and if we have an unanswered question, it keeps searching for the solution, just like a computer doing an Internet search.

The thing I love the most, though, is that consequently we often wake up with an answer in our mind that seems to have appeared there as if by magic. It might be the answer to a crossword question from days before, the name of an actor in a film that we have been struggling to remember or the answer to something we have been searching for without success.

This is exactly what happened to me. The following morning, I woke up and my first conscious thought was 'JOY'. Nothing else, and it was not until I had woken up a bit more that I realized the significance of this word. Joy. That was the answer that pinpointed what Elliot was experiencing in almost everything he did! It was joy that made him laugh, joy that made him sing, joy that made him run, play, smile and marvel at the world. He appreciated everything and he experienced everything as fresh, exciting, wonderful and new. I felt the certain truth of this as something that I had already known and had just remembered. I laughed at how simple and obvious it was now. Suddenly, even the concept of having an 'Aha' moment changed. Was it a coincidence that we describe the sudden realization of something as 'Aha'? Had I just had an 'Aha, ha, ha, ha!' moment?

I passionately believe that the answers to the knowledge we seek lie within us, an idea that is repeated in countless different religions and philosophies around the world. I wondered, do we feel joy whenever we connect with our inner truth? Do we feel joy when we reconnect with the essence of who we really are and express that by showing love and consideration? Do we feel joy when we remember to recognize the beauty of the world we live in? Is joy a feeling that says, yes, you are connected, and is laughter a way to express this joy? Do we begin our lives constantly connected to our joy like Elliot and then gradually, as we grown up, do we become more detached from the essence of our true authentic selves?

Joy is felt internally as a powerful emotion and often expressed externally as a beaming smile, an appreciative laugh, a sigh of appreciation and an expression of gratitude. Think of the joy of receiving a gift, being reunited with a loved one, watching a sunset, winning a race or smelling a rose, for instance. Sometimes, though, joy can be expressed through tears, although these are different to tears of sadness. A beautiful melody, a newborn baby, a wedding –

Girl's laughter names

The closest laughter name I can think of in English is 'Joy' – not such a popular choice these days, but why not? Here are some other lovely girl's names inspired by laughter from around the world.

Amura *(Polynesian)* – big smile
Ashi *(Tamil)* – smile
Hasana *(Arabic)* – who brings laughter
Hasita *(Gujarati)* – happy, full of laughter
Harshika *(Indian)* – laugh
Risa *(Hindi, Latin)* – laughter
Tabassum *(Arabic)* – smile, laughter
Teshi *(African)* – cheerful, full of laughter
Whawee *(Sioux)* – laughing maiden

these often bring tears to our eyes. Whenever we connect with joy, we experience the accompanying physical and emotional responses, and this, I believe, makes us feel alive and present in the world.

I found the implication of this idea very exciting because joy is something that we understand and can all connect with. I thought it would be interesting to experiment and to spend time like Elliot, to see whether adopting his behaviour could have the same effect on adults. I also realized that I had a perfect opportunity to try this out – our next laughter session.

Acting like a two-year-old

Before our next laughter session I made a note of the positive behaviours that Elliot had demonstrated. I wrote: *Elliot lives entirely in the present moment and every day is simply 'today', a new day, a fresh start and a new opportunity. He sees things as they truly are, in all their detail with interest in the familiar. He expresses his emotions without inhibition, immediately and honestly. He is in physiological balance (homeostasis) and responds to his physical needs immediately by telling others when he is hungry, thirsty, tired, hot, cold, and so on. He is trusting, accepting and non-judgemental, and he sees the best in everything and everyone. He is full of curiosity and interest in all that he sees, hears, smells, tastes, touches and feels, and he explores each with an open mind. He is a representation of his true authentic self without pretences or critical self-judgement. He is kind, loving, straightforward and uncomplicated. Elliot is an example of what we all looked like before we learnt to see and react differently to our world.*

At our laughter session, I told the group about my new theory of Elliotology, and one of the members, Bridget, shared her personal experience of meeting Elliot. One afternoon when Simon, Elliot and I went for a walk, we decided to call in on Bridget and 'borrow' her dog, Cheeka, a beautiful German Pointer, who despite being a little grey around the muzzle still enjoys her walks in the woods. Cheeka enjoyed her outing with us, and afterwards we took her back home and stayed with Bridget for a while, chatting in the garden.

During our conversation, Elliot pottered around the garden, finding everything fascinating and interesting as usual, and discovered a bucket full of rainwater by the back door. I presume that Bridget used this to water the plants, but, to Elliot, this was another opportunity to have a drink. He held the bucket on both sides, bending over to partially submerge his face and took several large slurps. I think it may have been the noisiness of his drinking that drew our attention to him, and, of course, as soon as Simon noticed, he told Elliot to stop, but by then he had already drunk as much as he could manage.

It was a comical sight seeing him standing licking his lips, with dripping wet hair, a soaked T-shirt and a radiant smile of satisfaction. What really made us all laugh, though, was the disclosure from Bridget that her neighbour had already prevented his Labrador from drinking from this source of water earlier the same morning, because he did not consider the water clean enough for the dog! The group agreed that although this story was charming and amusing, we would have had a different reaction if one of our adult relatives had acted in the same way. The image of our partner or parent having a quick drink from Bridget's water bucket in the same circumstances provoked gasps of horror at the embarrassment that it would have caused, followed by laughter as we imagined what we would have said and done. There was a limit to how much of Elliot's behaviour we would imitate, but we all decided it was worth investigating.

Through Elliot's eyes

We did an exercise we called 'Through Elliot's eyes'. We curled each of our hands into a circle to create a pair of magic binoculars that would enable us to see the world in the same way as Elliot. At first, we could not stop laughing because we all looked ridiculous, but within minutes the laughter changed into exclamations of 'Wow!'. Our laughter session that morning took place in the beautiful gardens that belong to The Rose & Crown pub in Brockenhurst, and a wonderful thing happened as we looked at the world from this new perspective. A cobweb that would have been unnoticed before became the first thing we focused our attention on. Without using any form of communication other than laughter and 'Wow', we marvelled at how delicate and intricate it was and how something as small as a spider could spin a single thread and weave it into such a perfect pattern. I have never failed to appreciate a spider's web since.

Suddenly, we were aware of the microscopic elements of things around us that had previously been outside our conscious awareness. We looked at the tiny weeds in between the paving stones, a raindrop sitting on a petal, a bird's feather, and now the only ridiculous thing seemed to be that we could lose touch with the beauty of the things around us and that these things would be invisible to eyes that only saw what they expected to see. A pair of sparkly shoe laces worn by one of us got another 'Wow!' and so did the jet that passed overhead, appearing to be small enough to fit in one's hand. It was a truly inspiring and moving experience.

We continued the Elliot theme by playing games, building imaginary sandcastles, splashing in imaginary puddles and dodging an imaginary tide as the waves crashed in and nearly soaked us. Someone suggested trying the games we used to play as children, and we 'jumped rope' together, impressing each other with how accomplished we were at skipping without the inconvenience and encumbrance of having to jump over a real rope. There was some very fancy footwork, and a surprising number of people remembered the words and tunes that accompanied this activity, 'salt, pepper, vinegar, mustard' being one that I recall. Imaginary hula hoops were spun at incredible speed without ever losing their momentum, and as we laughed and played like children, we discovered that deep inside us all is a childlike part that finds this sort of activity exhilarating.

Joy and happiness

The difference between joy and happiness is subtle, and we may often experience them both at the same time. Positive Psychology has shown that what we think makes us happy often turns out to be wrong, but joy does not seem to cause the same confusion and there is less of a tendency to become attached to it. Joy can pop up and surprise us at any time, but people do not struggle to hang on to it in the same way that they try to hang on to happiness. Joy is uncomplicated, simple and is always felt in the present moment.

Happiness has these qualities, too, but there seems to be a common belief that happiness can become permanent in one's life after certain things have been obtained, achieved or bought. People are prepared to sacrifice their personal happiness today in order to invest in potential happiness in the future, and if their plans fail, they can feel as though they have somehow been cheated out of the happiness they deserve. I suspect that many people feel so insecure about happiness that they cannot even fully enjoy it when they feel it, fearful that it may not last and that it may fade and never return.

The biggest difference between happiness and joy is our attitude to it. I believe that if you take time every day to look for the joy in your life, you will never need to worry about feeling happy again.

Chapter 6

Laughter Games and Activities

Laughter is an instant vacation.

Milton Berle

Adults can have a real problem with failure of any sort. Even in the midst of some of the silly games we play at our laughter sessions, there will be people who will struggle to do it the 'right way' even though there is no right or wrong way! For them, success becomes more important than fun, and I believe that this can be a barrier to joy.

One of the most valuable lessons I learnt was when I joined Toastmasters to learn the art of public speaking. One of the more experienced members told me to review my own performance by appreciating what I did well and recognizing what I would like to do differently the next time. This stopped me thinking in terms of what I did right and what I did wrong. He illustrated this point by telling me about Thomas Edison, creator of the electric light bulb, who, when asked about his failures, replied, 'I have not failed. I've just found 10,000 ways that won't work.' Getting it 'wrong' is the way that we learn, just like Elliot in the previous chapter instinctively knew. This is another example of an attitude that we develop in adulthood. We may think it serves a positive purpose, but, in fact, it often holds us back. If we fear failure, then we will be reluctant to try new things, and instead of growing and expanding, our world can start to shrink. In this chapter, I explore the importance of games and activities that take us out of our comfort zone and into new experiences – a vital element in uncovering joy and laughter. I also look at some of the other benefits of the activities that we do that are not always obvious.

Anyone who attends our laughter sessions will recognize that I introduce activities and games that offer challenges that few can manage at first, along with games that have absolutely no rules. When you realize this and surrender to the fact that you cannot be right and you cannot win, and you cannot be wrong and lose either, it is possible to just enjoy doing something for its own sake. In my opinion, the worst thing that can happen is that you do nothing, not that you do something wrong.

I sometimes introduce my Clinical Hypnosis patients to the concept of 'Paradoxical Advertising'. This is when instead of fearing that something might happen and people might notice, you tell them in advance. So this might mean informing people that you will probably blush, possibly forget your lines, may stutter, and so on. I have heard that stage actors sometimes deliberately make a mistake to 'get it out of the way', so they can stop worrying about it. Once we relinquish the thought of what might go wrong, or what people may think, we can prevent anxiety building up and often the fear or phobia subsides or even disappears. The fear of fear is frequently more powerful than almost anything that may actually happen.

While studying for my Masters in Applied Positive Psychology degree, there have been many times when I have read research showing that certain activities have been found to have positive benefits, and I have recognized that often they are things that are included in Laughter Yoga groups and in our laughter sessions. It is not necessary to know the science, but I think it is nice to know that while you are enjoying something for its own sake, you are also gaining benefits. In addition, you can pursue some of these activities individually, something you may consider especially if you are not able to access a Laughter Yoga club.

Singing

I imagine the idea of singing at a laughter session would be a horrifying prospect for a lot of people, but this is childlike singing usually done in a group and the songs are no more complicated that 'Row, row, row your boat' or 'Frère Jacques'. Sometimes we will replace the words with Gibberish or laughter sounds, and often we will insist that *everyone* sings out of key. You would expect that this would be easier for some than others, but you may be surprised that the people who sometimes struggle most are those who are used to having the most melodic voices. Singing out of key can be fantastically funny, and it also feels strangely liberating, especially if you have never been a good singer. I remember a particular occasion while we were singing outside in the pub garden at The Rose & Crown: someone came out to see this terrible choir and politely told us that we were 'a bit off key'! Needless to say, this caused a lot of hilarity.

Research shows that there are great benefits from singing in a group. The benefits are similar to laughing and include improved breathing, exercise of the diaphragm and an improved immune response. There is a sense of connection through a shared experience, and I am sure that people who sing in gospel or church choirs also benefit from expressing the positive words that are often about appreciation, love and gratitude. There are studies that show that singing is an effective way to relieve stress and anxiety and increase the relaxation response.

Dancing

This is probably another activity that many people, particularly men (in my experience), tend to shy away from; however, it has been incredibly popular in my group and is often requested – by men!

The difference, of course, is that our dancing is designed to be fun and never serious. Sometimes we play a medley of different types of music such as pop, ballet, waltz, rock, country, folk, and so on, and allow people to do whatever they want. Each piece of music only lasts for a minute or sometimes less, but there are ten pieces of music, so if you have the stamina to get to the end, you will have had a good aerobic workout. Usually everyone joins in and brings as much expression to their interpretation of the dance as they can. Often they will exaggerate their movements and add some silliness, but the body responds to movement to music, and regardless of how we dance, dancing makes us feel good. After a few minutes it is common to feel 'in flow' where conscious thoughts are suspended, and we feel very much in the moment. Not everyone is able to stand and move around, but 'chair dancing' works well, too, and from a seated position it is possible to make expressive arm movements.

Sometimes one of our members will introduce a simple children's dance from circle dancing and teach it to the group. Generally, it consists of simple steps to a piece of music that gets gradually faster and faster and ends when no one can keep up. We have discovered that it is much easier to do these dances when we stop thinking about what we are doing. While we keep our heads down, looking at our feet and concentrating, we make mistakes. The secret is to just enjoy it and realize that it does not matter if we go wrong. When we raise our heads, look at each other and smile, not only do we enjoy ourselves, but we find that we become part of the circle and the group moves together in synchrony. Dance is a good aerobic activity that encourages creativity and expressiveness.

Chanting and NLP techniques

There are two chants that we use frequently: the 'HO-HO, HA-HA-HA' that is accompanied by clapping and indicates that a laughter exercise has finished, and the ever popular 'Very good, very good, YEAH!'.

This last chant is invigorating and connects us with our childlike selves. The more you repeat it, the more it becomes a conditioned response. I am not alone in my experience that whenever I hear the words 'very good', I automatically add on the 'very good, YEAH!' ending. I may not do this aloud, but I always hear it in my head. Most importantly, I get an instant feeling of joy. In Neuro-Linguistic Programming (NLP), this automatic physiological response is referred to as an 'anchor'.

The term 'anchor' refers to what happens when you have a change of mood in response to a trigger or stimulus. These anchors can be positive or negative, and we all have them, although we may not be aware of this. They are learnt responses based on previous experiences, which cause us to react instantly whenever we come across particular triggers. The Russian physiologist and psychologist Ivan Pavlov first theorized about this after he observed that he could condition his dogs to associate food with the sound of a bell. After repeating this exercise for a while, the dogs would salivate at the sound of the bell even when food was not present because of their conditioned response.

We can take advantage of this response by associating a particular state to a unique physical trigger, and each time we repeat this, the association will become stronger. For example, there will be times during our laughter sessions when we feel particularly happy or relaxed. When we are aware of this, we can make a physical action such as pressing the middle finger hard against the thumb or making a tight fist. Any action will do, but it needs to be something that you will not do by accident, as you will want to use this exclusively for anchoring this specific feeling. By repeating this physical action every time you are in this particular positive state, you build up a conditioned response so that, eventually, you will be able to trigger it by simply making this physical movement. This great technique can be used to help build a number of resources that can be triggered when they are needed in special circumstances – for instance, when you want to feel confident, assertive or relaxed.

Clapping

In Laughter Yoga, we do several chants that also involve hand clapping. To the rhythm 1–2, 1–2–3, we clap hands and chant 'HO-HO, HA-HA-HA'. We use this intermittently during the session and also to signify when a laughter exercise is completed.

I have recently included some of the hand-clapping exercises that I recall from my childhood into our sessions that are usually done in pairs. It is interesting that these bring back nostalgic memories for lots of the women and can provide a first experience for some of the

Norman Cousins

In 1964, Norman Cousins was diagnosed with ankylosing spondylitis (AS), a painful inflammatory disease. Finding that his medication was providing little relief, he decided to try treating himself by taking vitamin C supplements and ensuring that he experienced positive emotions, both of which he understood to be beneficial. He began to watch comedy films and read books that made him laugh. He reported that he would watch Candid Camera *and Marx Brothers films until his body had produced enough endorphins to relief his pain and allow him a few hours' sleep. If he woke up in pain later, he would simply repeat the process. Over time he found that his symptoms reduced, and eventually he felt that he had made a full recovery despite the prognosis that his disease was untreatable. He pointed out that if negative emotions could contribute to ill health, then it was obvious that positive ones could aid wellness and recovery. He believed that laughter provided the most effective treatment of his illness. He wrote about his discoveries in his book* Anatomy of an Illness.

men who did not play as children because it was a 'sissy' girl's game. Again, some struggle to get it right and fiercely concentrate on their hands, getting frustrated when they make a mistake. A surprisingly effective way to deal with this is to ask them to smile and to look at their partner, rather than at their hands, or even close their eyes. This places the emphasis more on how the clapping rhythm *feels* rather than trying to work it out with logic. It is surprising how quickly people become dexterous and increase their speed and accuracy, and it also seems to prompt memories of other games played in childhood.

Clapping hands is used to express happiness and to show appreciation in almost every culture. We clap continuously to show our approval at public occasions for sport, music and entertainment, and all nationalities seem to play different variations of clapping games. The rhythm of particular rhymes and songs can sometimes be quite complex and requires a lot of concentration.

Clapping your hands can also have significant health benefits such as improving the immune system. It is said that it stimulates the acupuncture points, and in a study scientists found that small children who clapped each day had improved cognitive abilities, social integration and were more hard working.

Stretching

Stretching accompanies many of our breathing and warm-up exercises, but apart from being good for the body, stretching makes us feel good. When we stretch, we use muscles that are unused to being exercised, and this causes our brain to release endorphins to prevent us from feeling pain. A study at the University of Illinois found that elderly people who followed a stretching programme experienced an increase in self-esteem that was thought to be a result of increased dopamine production, one of the 'happy chemicals'.

When we are inactive, blood pools in our muscles and makes us feel tired and sluggish, but stretching gets our blood flowing more efficiently again.

Chi Kung

We are most fortunate that one of our laughter club members is a renowned Chi Kung practitioner and trainer who has introduced us to the concept of this mind-and-body movement and taught us some simple exercises. Chi Kung originated in China many hundreds of years ago and is known to help combat stress, anxiety and depression. By promoting the healthy flow of life-force energy (chi) around the body, a natural state of harmony and balance is encouraged and enhanced.

Chi Kung includes movements for flexibility, balance, gracefulness, coordination and posture. We use Chi Kung warm-up exercises of shaking (a description of this is included in the 'laughing alone' exercises in Chapter 4) and incorporate Chi Kung movements into laughter exercises, particularly those that require balance.

As people age, their sense of balance decreases, and this puts them at a higher risk of falls, with disastrous consequences. But with practice, we can improve balance. One simple exercise we do is to imagine that we are walking on a tightrope. With our arms out to the side, we carefully place one foot in front of the other and walk for about ten paces before turning round and returning. We imagine that we are high in the air and there is a lot of laughter as we wobble and nearly or completely fall off our rope. Incidentally, another reason older people lose their balance is because of the side effects of medication. Keeping fit, healthy and happy through Laughter Yoga may mean that there is less likelihood of having to take medication in the first place. Many of the benefits are not realized because of their preventative nature.

Cartharsis and resilience

The dictionary defines catharsis as 'the process of releasing, and thereby providing relief from, strong or repressed emotions'. Laughter is a good way to release pent-up emotions, especially those associated with stress. I think a prolonged session of laughter can provide the same sort of relief as smashing up china or screaming into the wind at the top of your voice – and it's fun!

Emotions are supposed to be expressed, after all they are called e-*motions*, but people are often embarrassed about showing their emotions in front of others or think that being emotional is a sign of weakness. Laughter can be cathartic in several ways. If we learn to laugh at our problems, it can help shift our attitudes and, at the same time, help us relieve the stress and anxiety associated with them. Many people feel 'lighter' after sustained laughter, and it may be that through this physical process pent-up emotions are released.

Mindfulness

Mindfulness is a way of paying attention to the present moment and can be achieved with techniques like meditation, breathing techniques and yoga. Practising mindfulness can lead to better insight and awareness of thoughts and feelings without being overwhelmed by them. It has been shown to help with stress, depression and addictive behaviours. I believe that laughter is an excellent way to achieve a state of mindfulness. When we laugh, we are no longer aware of the past or the future, and it keeps us firmly in the moment. When we are fully in the present moment, we can temporarily forget our physical or emotional pain, our list of things to do, our regrets about the past or concerns about the future. When we are mindfully in the present, we usually discover that 'now' is just perfect.

Meditation

I introduce at least two meditations into each laughter session, one of which is a one-minute meditation based on a technique by Martin Boroson, creator of 'One-Moment Meditation'. It's a very effective way to relax that literally only takes one minute of your time. If you want to try it yourself then you'll need some sort of timer that can be set for one minute, it could be a kitchen timer, or a function on your watch or phone. I have downloaded a lovely free meditation APP to my phone that uses the sound of a Tibetan singing bowl to indicate when the time set has elapsed.

First make yourself comfortable, I say something similar to these following words to help people settle but you can just read them slowly to yourself. When you feel that you are ready, set the timer for one minute and then spend the next 60 seconds doing nothing. Although it sounds easy, some people find that they have racing thoughts and get distracted. This is normal. If/when it happens just notice it has happened and direct your attention to your breath. Just notice your breath going in and out. The more you do this meditation, the easier you will find it to do. I practice this once a day, every day without fail. I highly recommend it as a way to ensure that you feel calm and relaxed, especially if you lead a busy and stressful life. This one minute can make such a positive difference to every other minute of your day.

So, now I invite you to take a moment or two to sit and do … nothing. Make yourself comfortable, place your feet on the ground, rest your hands gently on your lap and close your eyes. The next few moments are just for you, for you to do nothing but sit and relax. There is nothing to do, nothing to think about, just enjoy being in peaceful relaxation.

Take a long, slow, deep breath all the way in and then when you are ready, exhale that breath fully on your out breath. With every breath you feel more relaxed, just sitting quietly and still. Feeling your body relax, grateful for the space, for quietness and peace. Listening to the sounds around you, of a busy world, while you just stop and be in the moment, for a moment. Becoming aware of your body, relaxed, comfortable, everything slowing down, and now take one minute to just enjoy the feeling of doing nothing. Start timer.

Afterwards, open your eyes, wriggle your toes and then stretch. You may be surprised at how relaxed you now feel. It is common for people to feel that the minute was only a few seconds. Eventually, with practice the minute can become more expansive. The important thing to note is that there is no 'wrong way' to do this meditation.

Do not expect to be able to spend a full minute without thoughts and distractions. It is a good way of discovering how busy our minds are and if you only spend a couple of seconds in mindful relaxation that's enough to benefit. You may find that 'one-minute meditation' becomes a favourite part of your day, whether you are at home, at work, in a waiting room or travelling on public transport. You can do it as often as you like but never for more than one minute.

Many people have never tried meditation before, and some may believe it is difficult. Everyone, even the busiest person, can find one minute in the day, and this encourages people to practice at home. I like people to discover just how effective a one-minute meditation can be and to experience the deep sense of calm and relaxation from such a small investment of their time.

Research by the Positive Psychologist Barbara Fredrickson has shown that regular practice of loving-kindness meditation, *metta*, can increase positive emotions. As positive emotions are linked to increased well-being (happiness), I often include a loving-kindness meditation, too. Although this meditation's origins are from the Buddhist religion, we use it simply as a way to connect with feelings of love and kindness for ourselves, our loved ones and everyone else in the world. It is a lovely way to end a laughter session, and people often remark afterwards that they feel grateful and more connected to people.

Hypnosis

Although I am a Clinical Hypnotherapist, I do not use hypnosis in my laughter sessions. It would be unethical to use hypnosis without informed consent, and there are a lot of misconceptions about Clinical

Hypnosis as it is often confused with stage hypnosis. However, I have used hypnosis in my practice to assist people connect with their inner laughter, and I have developed a self-hypnosis induction for my clients to use. It has been very successful and has helped a number of people to bring more laughter into their life. You will find more details on my website.

Random acts of kindness

From the outset, I have been determined to try to ensure that each and every one of our laughter sessions is freely available to anyone, without charge. This is part of Dr K's vision for Laughter Yoga around the world, and I am lucky that I was able to facilitate this in my local community. In other parts of the world, laughter clubs are run outside and do not incur any overheads, but this is not practical in the UK. Therefore, most laughter clubs in the UK have to charge a nominal fee to cover the cost of hiring a venue.

At the beginning of our second year, I asked members if they would consider carrying out a 'random act of kindness' (RAK) sometime during the week after our session. I explained this did not have to be anything heroic or difficult but something as simple as allowing someone to go before you in a queue, making a phone call to someone who would appreciate it or posting a letter for someone. I explained that it could be really simple and easy, but there was some personal cost to them, no matter how small.

I provided a list of over 500 suggestions and asked people to write down on a slip of paper what they had done and post it into a large, pink, plastic, see-through piggybank that I had bought for the occasion. I had no idea what we would do with these pieces of paper eventually, but had a feeling that we would be able to do something creative. In the meantime, it was great to see some physical evidence of how many random acts of kindness had been carried out.

At our next session I was really pleased that everyone without exception had done at least one RAK during the week because the thing about doing a RAK is that although you help someone else, the real beneficiary is *you*.

When we show kindness, we get a boost to our positive emotions, and knowing that we have actively chosen to do something for someone else results in us having a higher level of self-esteem and a greater sense of self-worth. The point is not to be recognized and praised for kind acts, but to do them with a sense of altruism.

Some of the laughter group said that they enjoyed doing RAKs and had been trying to remember to do it everyday. This was great news because this behaviour can quickly become a good habit and then you do not have to remember to do it, because your unconscious brain remembers for you. Kind people are the sort you would choose to have as a friend, and if you are kind, or becoming kinder, it can improve your social life and help connect you to other people.

Just like laughter, smiling and happiness, kindness has been shown to have a positive impact on our health, improving our immune system and even helping relieve signs of reactive depression. Doing a RAK can improve the levels of optimism for yourself and others, too. So often we hear about the negative things in our society and how no one cares for each other any more. So, when we display kindness, it can help change our perceptions again. There is a video on my website that I really enjoyed that shows the good things that have been caught on CCTV cameras. It really is heartening and restores your faith in human nature.

I am a great fan of 'pay it forward' – the concept that you receive a gift of kindness and you pay it forward to someone else. When you combine a RAK and 'pay it forward' together, the results are even more rewarding. There have been good examples, reported in the press, when people have elected to pay not only for their own goods or services but for those of the person behind them, paying the toll fares on bridges and roads, paying for some stranger's cup of coffee and even leaving money to pay for someone's meal. People who regularly participate and contribute in this way report that life becomes less stressful and more pleasant. This is probably because, when their focus of attention is placed on looking for opportunities to help others, they are more likely to be connected to the positive energy of loving kindness.

Laughter Buddies

When you follow your natural curiosity and allow yourself to open up to new ideas and possibilities, you will notice that life is full of 'coincidences' and synchronicity. This has certainly been my experience, and although I believe in taking full responsibility for everything that happens in my life, there are many times when things just seem to happen on their own. The creation of Laughter Buddies is a perfect of example of this.

In October 2012, I thought it might be fun to create a kazoo orchestra (another story!), and I ordered some kazoos on the

Internet. As I browsed through the website and looked at the other goods available, I noticed they sold small, yellow plastic figures with wonderful smiley faces. I was immediately attracted to them because they represented fun, laughter and joy, and they were so appealing. On impulse I bought three.

At the end of the month, I travelled out to Hong Kong for work and arranged to meet up with my friend Nat. Nat and I first met on our Laughter Yoga Teacher/Trainer course in Bangalore with Dr K, and, like most of us from the course, we have stayed in touch. I am lucky that my job as part-time cabin crew means that I can get to see her occasionally.

When Nat and I met up for lunch, I took my new toy with me, now named Laughter Buddy (LB). When Nat saw it, she wanted one, too, and so I offered her mine. Nat was insistent that she pay me, but I did not want to take her money. Eventually we agreed that she would pay for it, and I would 'pay it forward' on her behalf and give another Laughter Buddy to somebody else.

By the time I got back to the UK, Nat had taken lots of photos of her Laughter Buddy (now named 'Milkshake') in various locations around Hong Kong and posted them on Facebook. They were really endearing, and I took photos of my Laughter Buddy in the UK and posted them, too. I gave away the other Laughter Buddy and ordered some more as by now I was getting lots of requests for them. Before we knew it, we had started a Laughter Buddies 'pay it forward' community and created a Laughter Buddies Facebook page: www.facebook.com/laughterbuddies

It was astonishing how the concept grew, and within a few weeks

Laughter Buddies had travelled to Australia, Hong Kong, UK, USA, Canada, Bahrain, Egypt, South Africa, Sweden, Chile, Serbia, Italy and Dubai. Something extraordinary started to happen as strangers across the world began to connect with each other by posting photos of their Laughter Buddies on Facebook. Even though, essentially, these figures are just a yellow piece of plastic, people see them as a symbol of happy, innocent, positive, optimistic laughter, fun and love and relate to them.

Perhaps it is because Laughter Buddies appeal to people regardless of age, gender, nationality, religious or political beliefs. They seem to capture people's imagination and creativity. When I gave a Positive Psychology presentation on the subject of positive emotions, it was easy to represent them all by using Laughter Buddy photos.

There are some ambitious plans for Laughter Buddies in the future in which a group of us hopes to raise money for charity projects around the world, and Laughter Buddies feature in a film that is currently being edited.

The positive emotion of receiving a Laughter Buddy as a gift is wonderful, but the positive emotion of 'paying it forward' and facilitating the same experience for someone else is possibly even more pleasurable.

Chapter 7

The Power of the Smile

A smile is a curve that sets everything straight.

Phyllis Diller

I am thankful to Lyn, a regular attendee at our community laughter sessions, for pointing out that 'no one can laugh without smiling first'. This might sound obvious, but she is absolutely right. If you would like to have more laughter in your life, perhaps a first step should be to check how frequently you are smiling. You might like to consider smiling as an important step to master first, rather like crawling before you walk.

After laughing, people tend to keep a smile on their face, and this may be a visual clue to its lasting positive effect on mood. Smiles seem to stay on the faces of people after they have heard a joke, if they are watching something funny on TV or when they are doing something that they find fun. It seems that a smile is the perfect primer for laughter, and I suspect that those people who are already smiling find it much easier to laugh.

Origin of the smile

When you look closely at any human behaviour it can suddenly seem rather strange and odd, like smiling for instance. In order to smile, you have to make a facial expression that involves flexing muscles around the mouth that may also cause muscles around the eyes to contract. Smiling is an expression used to display pleasure, happiness and amusement, but we can also smile when we are anxious, which may turn a smile into a grimace. It is something that we can consciously control and yet sometimes we smile without realizing it.

When we smile, we show others that we are friendly and approachable. By smiling, our ancestors could visibly demonstrate that they posed no threat to strangers, and this could prevent them from being attacked. I imagine many of us today will also search out the friendliest face when we need to ask for assistance in public places or restaurants and shops.

Born with a smile on your face?

There is a lot of disagreement about whether we learn to smile or whether we are born with this ability. The traditional view was that babies learnt to smile at about five to seven weeks of age, and any smiles before this were regarded as 'wind'. However, with the development of modern technology, 4D scanners have been used to capture images of babies smiling in the womb at 28 weeks. The debate goes on whether these smiles are connected to feelings of pleasure or simply natural reflexes. Although there is strong argument that suggests that babies learn to smile by imitating the behaviour of the people around them, it does not quite explain how blind babies learn to smile.

We value babies' smiles highly, and like many other people, I invest a lot of time cooing at babies and making silly noises to get a smile – and if they do, I feel flattered. Several years ago, I was on a trip to Calcutta and visited Mother Teresa's orphanage, where I spent the day working as a volunteer. I soon realized that one of the most important jobs was just spending time with the children who seemed desperate for physical contact. The nuns did a great job of looking after their elementary needs, but with so many children, there seemed to be no time available to just cuddle them. Nowhere was this more apparent than in the nursery where there were rows and rows of cots for the babies who were under a year old. I discovered that as soon as you looked into a cot, a baby would immediately respond with a wonderful smile, and the older ones would also hold up their arms, wanting to be picked up.

I believe that these babies had learnt that smiling made them more appealing so that they were more likely to be lifted up and held. It was also a reflection of the pleasure they got from direct physical contact. Their basic physical needs were met, but emotionally they were deprived of the love and attention that all babies and children deserve. I have never forgotten the lesson I learnt that day. Our age, gender, nationality, religion, politics, health, or anything else you can think of, are irrelevant – we all want to be loved and accepted unconditionally, and we all want to be happy. It is a shame that we spend such a lot of time focusing on the differences that separate us, when we could instead look at the similarities that unite us.

Smiling as a habit

Smiling is a habit. I know this because smiling is an important part of good customer service, a statement that was drilled into me over 30 years ago when I joined Laker Airways. I have been smiling ever since, not just at work, but when I am out and about, too. There are lots of different types of smiling that you can do and they all have a positive effect.

Something as simple as choosing to adopt a slight smile can have an incredibly positive effect on your whole life, changing the way you feel and the way others perceive you and interact with you.

The camera never lies

For an interesting experiment, take a couple of photos with your phone or camera. In one, maintain a neutral expression and, in the other, move the corner of your lips ever so slightly upward. You may not be able to tell the difference between the photos yourself, so make a note that you know which one is which. Then ask someone which one they prefer. Do not be surprised if they say they are both the same, but that they still prefer the one where you are smiling slightly.

A smile is a smile, or is it?

According to the American psychologist Paul Ekman, an expert in the study of emotions and their relation to facial expressions, there are many different kinds of smile. These can be divided into two categories: social or 'polite' smiles and genuine, happy smiles. Real smiles include the muscles around the mouth *and* the eyes and are controlled by a different area of the brain than the part that controls fake smiles. We can perform fake smiles at will because our conscious brain controls them; however, real smiles are spontaneous and generated from the brain automatically, outside of our conscious awareness.

Scientists often refer to smiles as Duchenne (genuine) and non-Duchenne smiles (fake). It was in 1862 that the French neurologist

Guillaume Duchenne studied the physiology of smiling and noted which muscles were used in both types of smiling. The Duchenne smile, the genuine one, involves the muscles around the eyes, the ones that cause laughter lines. The physiology of this smile is that there is a contraction of the zygotic major muscles, which raises the corners of the mouth, *and* the orbicularis oculi muscles, which raise the cheeks.

As a child, I remember that my grandmother would be suspicious of people if, as she said, 'their smile never reached the eyes', which suggests that she instinctively knew what a genuine smile looked like. I expect you have seen someone displaying a false smile on occasions, and maybe, like me, you would rather have no smile than one that is so obviously insincere. Although we can spot these overtly artificial smiles, it is said that, in general, we find it difficult to tell the difference. I found this surprising because I always thought I could tell, but perhaps some of the ones I had counted as genuine were, in fact, fake. If you want to test your ability to spot the difference, there is an online test at the BBC Science website: http://www.bbc.co.uk/science/humanbody/mind/surveys/smiles

My results showed that I am *quite* good at differentiating between the two, but not as good as I thought I was!

You may not fool others, but you can fool yourself

Although fake smiles may not fool other people, science has shown that adopting the facial expression of smiling can cause you to feel happier. A study by social psychologist Robert Zajonc showed that making different vowel sounds could influence people's moods. When participants made a long 'e' sound, their mouth formed a position similar to smiling and their mood improved. However, when they were asked to make a long 'u' sound, the mouth had to adopt a 'pouty' expression that had the opposite effect on how they felt.

However you achieve it, adopting a smile has been shown to make people feel better. When you make the facial changes associated with smiling, this stimulates the brain activities that are associated with happiness. We smile when we are happy, and we are happy when we smile. Putting a smile on your face and keeping it there can make you feel better. However, it stands to reason that the opposite is true as well. We scowl when we are in a bad mood, and we are in a bad mood when we scowl. The next time you are feeling a bit low, try looking back in the mirror and see what mood is reflected back at you, because the evidence suggests that adopting a smile will result in you feeling better almost immediately.

You smile, I smile

The act of smiling is simple and reaps significant rewards in return for little effort. There has been some interesting research that has shown that when you adopt the body language or facial expression of any emotion, your body responds and reacts to match. If 'practice makes perfect', we need to be careful *what* we practise!

If someone smiles at you, the chances are that you will smile back. This is the effect of mirror neurons in our brain that cause us to mimic the emotions that we see in others. A study conducted in Sweden tested this theory by showing people images of smiling faces and measuring their facial response with an electromyograph. Even though the participants in the study were frequently unaware

Mood lifter

You can improve your mood by holding a pencil horizontally between your teeth. This will force you to put your mouth in a smile position; if you make sure that your lips do not touch the pencil, just your teeth, you can make your 'smile' even wider. If you hold it by its end and place your lips around it, you will put your mouth into the 'pouty' pose which will negatively affect your mood.

of having any change to their facial expression, they responded by using the muscles associated with smiling. Even if we choose not to smile, we cannot stop this unconscious response.

In another study, participants were instructed to frown while looking at someone who was smiling, but despite their attempts, it was the muscles associated with smiling that were stimulated. This evidence suggests that if we smile at someone, they will respond *whether they know it or not*, and, furthermore, you may not recognize their response either. So, if you want to make the world a happier place, then *smile* because regardless of whether people choose to smile back, they will have a physiological response and you will feel better, too.

You can experiment by smiling at people and seeing the effect it has. During my flying career, I must have said hello and goodbye to over a million people, and I have always done my best to ensure that my smiles were sincere and genuine. I have always believed that a smile that appears after you have made eye contact with someone will be judged as having more value than a smile that is already present. To make sure that I get good eye contact, I look to see people's eye colour, and the moment I see it, I smile and say hello or goodbye. This prevents me sounding robotic and looking insincere.

For years, this was a successful strategy, but nowadays many people tend to be checking their phones for texts and emails as they board and leave the plane, and many people barely glance at anything or anyone other than their text messages. This phenomenon is not just confined to the aircraft environment either, as I see this trend increasingly in theatres, restaurants and railway stations. Walking down a busy street, it can be hard to find someone to smile at, as people's heads are bowed down over their phones, and their ears are often deaf to any pleasantries because they have earphones on and are plugged into music. Nowadays, the age of people using personal technology stretches from primary school children to those long beyond retirement age, and I wonder how this affects our social relationships. Even if we manage to get the family around the table, how many will be there in physical form only, with their attention focused on social networking and email checking?

Although some people may consider the idea of saying hello and goodbye to lots of people tedious, I consider it to be therapeutic! Whenever you give or receive a smile, you get a physiological and psychological benefit, so if your job involves meeting and greeting, you can be grateful that it is good for your health.

Knowing the theory of this is one thing, putting it into practice another. However, in March 2013, I witnessed someone on the New York subway at Grand Central Station giving out free newspapers with such a sunny disposition that I was intrigued to find out what made him so happy. For hours on end, he never seemed to tire of welcoming people and giving them a wonderful smile and greeting. Eventually, I decided to ask him how he could be so happy all of the time. His reply really shocked me, as he revealed that, in fact, he lived in very difficult circumstances and found life very challenging. His method of coping was to make other people happy, share his smile and be friendly. I am pleased to say that I caught our conversation on video, and it is posted on my website. His name is Prophet, and he is an inspiration to anyone who wants to know the positive effect of smiling.

I am glad that research has not recommended shaking hands with people because I have had a bad experience with that! A few years ago, aviation law changed to make it mandatory to physically check everyone's boarding card. On the first day of the new regulation, I was standing at the door of the aircraft when the first passenger boarded. I smiled, said hello and put my hand out to receive the boarding card so I could inspect it. The gesture was misinterpreted, and the gentleman shook my hand enthusiastically. The person behind him must have thought that this was the normal protocol, and they shook my hand, too. Before I knew it, there was a chain reaction that resulted in me shaking hands with over 100 people that morning, much to the amusement of my colleagues. I was powerless to stop it happening, and some people had handgrips that could

Smiling and hypnosis

Hypnosis might seem an extreme way to get the smiling habit, but it is effective. I introduce almost all my clients to a smiling hypnosis induction regardless of the condition I am treating them for. Most people I see suffer from a degree of stress or anxiety and have some sort of a problem (that is why they seek out a Clinical Hypnotherapist), and smiling is a sure-fire way of helping them relax. When they are in a deeply relaxed, hypnotic state, I help them remember which muscles they use in order to smile and encourage them to smile whenever they see a visual reminder (for example, this could be whenever they look at their watch or see the colour blue). The unconscious mind is very good at remembering to react to these prompts in the periods after our session. Even though the client may not remember the suggestion, they frequently find themselves smiling 'for no reason'. Regardless of the reason for their treatment, they experience feeling more relaxed, happy and contented. Even if you do not learn this technique in hypnosis, you can try using it when you are in a deeply relaxed state. Imagine yourself smiling by either remembering a time when you were happy and smiling or think of a situation that would make you smile. Concentrate on how that smile feels and do not be surprised if you find yourself smiling for real.

crush walnuts, while others seemed determined to shake my arm out of my shoulder socket. I never thought I would say the words 'I know how the Queen must feel', but that day I felt I did and she has my sincerest sympathy.

Why are you smiling?

It seems that it is accepted as perfectly natural for me to smile at anyone when I am in uniform, but it has sometimes led to confusion when I am not. Some people are obviously not used to getting smiles from strangers, and I have been asked, 'Do I know you?' Sometimes

Jaw-relaxing exercise

It is thought that jaw tension may be responsible for up to 92 per cent of recurring headaches, so releasing it might increase your sense of well-being. As you read this, let your jaw relax in your mouth so your teeth are apart, lips together. Then, with your middle fingers, massage in a circular direction around your jaw joint in front of your ears, about ten rotations in each direction. You can open and close your mouth to find the precise area where this joint is. After you have finished, take a deep breath in, then sigh out and notice how it feels now.

people even look behind them to see whom I am smiling at because they presume that it could not possibly be them. So, if you start to smile more, especially in situations like travelling on public transport, in the supermarket or walking through the city, be prepared for people looking at you in a puzzled way. However, console yourself with the thought that you are spreading positivity even though others do not realize it. If enough of us start actively smiling, one day people may ask others, 'Why *aren't* you smiling?' rather than questioning why we are.

There are several campaigns to encourage more smiling. If you want to join a smile movement, you will find some links in the Resources on page 235, or, of course, you could always start your own.

Half smile

Depending on your source of information, 'half smiling' may be described as a therapy, a technique or a meditative practice, but the method is the same and the results are equally effective. It is said that half smiling will help you tolerate stressful situations, lift your spirits and improve your health.

To generate a half smile, you first need to relax the jaw and facial muscles and then form a slight smile. If you are not sure what a half smile looks like, think of the Mona Lisa (I bet you did it automatically!). Adopting a half smile when you are in emotionally challenging situations is said to help you remain positive and not feel overwhelmed.

People who suffer from stress and anxiety tend to hold tension in the muscles around this area, and this can affect the muscles in the neck and shoulders and create pain in other parts of the body. If you suffer from neck or shoulder pain, you may not have considered that the source of discomfort may originate in your jaw and you are likely to benefit from specific releasing exercises.

The sound of smiling

A good friend of mine who trains people in call centres always suggests smiling when talking on the phone. He explains that when you smile, it affects your vocal cords and improves the tone of your voice, so you sound friendlier and more relaxed. He told me that this does not just help in professional situations either. For instance, he always telephones his elderly mother once a week and always at exactly the same time because she enjoys the regularity of his calls. Sometimes, he finds that this fixed time is inconvenient, but

Secret smiling

Smiling has the advantage of being a silent activity, so we can do it without drawing attention to ourselves, and we can do it even when there is no one else present. If you want to practise smiling, but feel self-conscious in public, pretend that you are reading a humorous book, looking at some photos on your phone or listening to something funny on your iPod.

rather than let her down, he rings anyway. 'Smiling,' he says, 'means that she only hears a message of love, concern and understanding in my voice and doesn't associate my occasional frustration and stress as being connected with her. I never want her to feel that she is a nuisance because she never is; it's the pressures of everyday life that are. I smile and she hears that I'm happy to talk to her even when I'm really busy and anxious.'

A study carried out at Portsmouth University showed that participants were able to identify different types of smile in speech and could differentiate between genuine, non-genuine, suppressed and non-smiles just by the sound of the speaker's voice. When I make telephone calls to companies, I am aware that some people sound much more friendly than others, even though they are giving the same message. Now I wonder whether this is because I can detect the ones with a smile on their face?

If you have concerns about the quality of your smile because of concerns about the state of your teeth, you may not smile as much or you may cover your smile with your hand. Restraining the urge to smile or preventing people from seeing it could be preventing you from achieving your happiness potential. If this describes you, then I would urge you to visit the dentist. Modern dental technology means that it is much easier to remedy conditions like discoloured, missing or crooked teeth than it used to be. You may not enjoy dental visits, but would you sacrifice your happiness in order to avoid them?

Research carried out by the British Dental Health Foundation showed that smiling stimulates the reward mechanism in the brain. They found out that one smile can generate the same brain stimulation as 2,000 bars of chocolate and be equal to receiving up to £16,000 in cash! I always keep in mind that this sort of research is often conducted in a laboratory and that the findings are hypothetical and based on statistics. I do not suppose that anyone was actually given £16,000 or asked to eat that many bars of chocolate, but, nevertheless, it does indicate that smiling has a really powerful effect on the brain.

Smile to live longer, look better and be healthier

The research on smiling is persuasive. Smiley people tend to live longer, have happier marriages, more friends and enjoy better physical and emotional health. People who smile are perceived as being attractive, sociable and confident, and these are the qualities of people who tend to pass job interviews and get promoted. A study showed that waitresses who smiled more got bigger tips than those who did not, and the waitresses that drew a smiley face on the bill got a bigger tip, too. So smiling and even a symbol of smiling is recognized and rewarded by others.

Women were judged as far more attractive when they smiled in comparison to when they were wearing makeup, and a study carried out in a bar showed that women were more likely to be approached by men if they smiled. Once a woman had made eye contact with a man, she was approached 20 per cent of the time, but if she smiled, she was approached 60 per cent of the time.

People who smile are perceived as being trustworthy and generous, and we are more likely to trust someone who is smiling.

Apparently, if we do something wrong, but then smile, we will be treated less harshly as people are more likely to forgive smiling people. It seems that most of us seem programmed to smile any time we do something wrong or silly, and we may give a little laugh, too. Next time you accidentally stand on someone's foot, make sure you smile and get forgiven.

Smile to do a better job

Smiling relaxes us, and this improves our ability to concentrate, so when we smile, we do a better job than when we do not. Smiling has been found to reduce the stress hormones of cortisol and epinephrine (adrenaline) and increase the mood enhancing endorphins. Smiling induces relaxation and reduced blood pressure, improves our overall health and strengthens our immune system.

Inner smile

There is another sort of smiling that has been passed down through Taoist traditions for over 5,000 years: the 'inner smile meditation'. This is a simple yet profound meditation centred on generating the compassionate qualities of smiling and directing them into oneself to each of the major organs of the body.

Facial posture

There are many muscles involved in the process of smiling and laughing. It has been estimated that we use around 50 facial muscles to make up to 50 different facial expressions. My colleague Nat Lui in Hong Kong explained that she comes across people who have difficulty in making and maintaining a 'happy face' because they have lost the use of many of these muscles through lack of practice. By laughing and smiling in Laughter Yoga, these muscles get a good workout, and with repetition, they get stronger, just like the other muscles in our body. Regular exercise of the facial muscles leads to us looking younger because we are more likely to smile, and there is also the effect of improved blood circulation in the face that makes us look more youthful. Nat believes that new muscle memory will develop if we exercise unused facial muscles by laughing for extended periods. This means that the body will connect positive emotions with the use of these muscles: consequently, smiling and laughing will become more spontaneous.

By a curious act of synchronicity, shortly after writing this, I came across someone who had exactly the condition that Nat described. I was delivering a presentation about positive emotions and laughter for an organization and had arrived early, mingling with people as they arrived. I got into a conversation with a young man who, unaware that I was the guest speaker, told me that he was being treated for anxiety and depression and that he was interested in positive emotions because he had difficulty in expressing them. As we talked, I noticed that his face seemed quite expressionless, and then he told me that he found it very hard to smile despite doing daily facial exercises. I asked him to demonstrate for me, and with great effort he forced a smile, but it barely changed his expression, and it most certainly did not reach his eyes. By this time, I had told him who I was, and I suggested that he try some of the exercises that I have described in this chapter.

Inner smile meditation

From a comfortable position, take a couple of deep refreshing breaths and close your eyes. Bring to mind a person or situation that makes you smile and revel in this memory, receiving the energy of the smile inside your mind. When you breathe in next, imagine this smiling sense travelling with your breath into your lungs and then around your whole body, for at least three breaths. Slowly open your eyes, with a smile on your face!

At the end of the evening, I ran a laughter session for those who wanted to be involved. As usual, there was a little hesitation and reservation from some, but within a few minutes we were all laughing and enjoying the proceedings. I participated in hand-shaking laughter exercises when, suddenly, the young man I had spoken to earlier was in front of me. The transformation was outstanding! He had a really big smile on his face, and his eyes were creased from smiling and laughter. He was a completely different person, far more relaxed and less intense, and I was thrilled to see how happy he appeared.

We spoke afterwards, and I realized that he had not been aware of how dramatic the change had been. I believe that the positive difference was caused because of spontaneous smiling and the effect of mirror neurons as he made eye-to-eye contact with numerous different people. He did not have to think about how to smile: his brain produced a smile as an automatic response. It was a joy to see, and I was so pleased that he had found a way to connect with that part of himself that he had been out of touch with for so long. I really hope he finds a laughter group where he lives because he is someone who I believe will reap enormous physical and psychological benefits from participating in laughter sessions.

Final thoughts on bringing more smiles into your life

To get into the habit of smiling takes practice and constant repetition. To remind yourself to smile, you can place some visual clues in places where you will be sure to see them. There are various ways you can achieve this, and it does not matter which you choose as long as it works. You may decide to leave notes around that say 'smile', draw a smiley face or use stick-on stars. Place them on the bathroom mirror, by the tea caddy, on your car keys, on your wallet, your mobile phone, near the TV, on the fridge door, your toothbrush, on your computer screen, your desk at work, everywhere! Then, every time you see a star, use it as a cue check to see that you are smiling. If you are not, hitch up the corners of your mouth once again. People who have done this find that after a few days they feel noticeably happier, but it will take between four to six weeks to develop this into a new habit. I know one family who decided to do this together; they noticed that they had far fewer disagreements and the atmosphere at home was considerably better. It is much nicer to interact with people who are smiling at you.

Notice the things that make you smile at home, in the car and at work. It might be a certain photograph, a cuddly toy, a piece of music, the view from a window or an emoticon on your email. Then, if you can, make sure that you get to notice this as often as possible. When you know what pleases you and makes you smile, you can ensure that you get as many opportunities as possible to bring it into your environment.

Make it a habit to smile just before you go to sleep. Make the biggest smile you can and hold it for 5 breaths. Smiling helps us feel relaxed and may aid the onset of sleep. Celebrate that no matter how busy your day has been, you can now allow yourself to do nothing but relax into a deep sleep. When you wake up in the morning, even before you open your eyes, you can once again choose to adopt a huge smile, take 5 deep relaxing breaths and begin your day with a positive intention.

Chapter 8

Stress-busting

The greatest weapon against stress is our ability to choose one thought over another.

William James

So far, this book has been about the benefits of laughter and happiness, and you might judge from the title of this chapter that it is now going to focus on a negative subject, stress. Stress does not have a positive image, and it is common to hear people complain about being stressed. Laughter can play a vital role in helping us manage stress, but we can also do other things to reduce our reaction to stress that will make it easier to utilize the great gift of laughter.

I am going to begin by pointing out that stress is not all bad. Stress is a physiological response, with the positive and useful purpose of helping us survive when we are in physical danger. So we need not regard stress as the enemy, and I believe it is helpful to appreciate the benefits that we get from it, such as improved performance when playing sports, when meeting a challenge or doing something exhilarating. I help people overcome their fear of public speaking by first pointing out the difference between how they interpret their physiological response in comparison to a confident speaker. They both experience the same feelings in their tummy, increased heart and breathing rate, but the anxious speaker will call it 'nerves', whereas the confident speaker will call it 'excitement'. Sportsmen, actors, adventurers or anyone depending on performing excellently would not be able to reach their potential without the *advantage* of experiencing the physiological effects of stress. A lot of how we cope with stress depends on our thoughts, perceptions and our habits; what makes one person stressed may have no such effect on another.

Stress is not always associated with negative events either. We tend to be creatures of habit that get stressed whenever there is change, even when these are changes we welcome. For instance, the impact of getting married, changing job, moving house or having a baby may be welcome, but they will also involve high levels of stress.

Eustress is a term that is often used to describe 'good' stress. This is the sort of stress that motivates us to enjoy actions or behaviours that require increased effort, but bring about feelings of satisfaction. Examples of this would be taking part in physical activities or performing tasks that require a great deal of concentration, such as driving a racing car, or other activities that require a high state of arousal. Our bodies are naturally programmed to maintain a state of balance within our biological systems, which is called homeostasis. Stress, followed by periods of relaxation when the body can recover and maintain this state of homeostasis, does us no harm and can actually be good for us.

'Bad' stress

However, stress can become a problem when it is continuous and when we do not feel able to get on top of the demands placed on us. When stress becomes chronic, we become increasingly exhausted, and burnout becomes a real risk. When we experience chronic stress, we stop functioning effectively and find it increasingly difficult to perform. We are far less likely to laugh and see the light side of life, and consequently miss out on the stress-relieving benefits of laughter. This is when regular attendance at a laughter club is so beneficial as it provides the opportunity to laugh unconditionally despite life circumstances. We can use these techniques outside of the laughter club environment, too, but only once we understand and appreciate how and why it works.

Ironically, it seems that the people who would get the most benefit from laughter are the ones less likely to do it. As we know, it really does not matter if the laughter is real or not because our body does not know the difference. If you have noticed that some people never seem to get stressed and always appear to be laughing and happy, you may have concluded that it is because their life is easier than yours, but this may be more about their attitude and behaviour rather than the difference in life circumstances. They may be laughing *in spite of* their circumstances, having instinctively learnt that this provides the stress relief that helps them cope better. Or maybe they are regular attendees at a laughter club!

The good news is that there are strategies you can adopt to help you manage stress better. If you combine these with the commitment to laugh whenever you can (with or without a reason), you will find that things feel less stressful. You may not be able to change circumstances, but you can change your reaction to them. So, just as we can let laughter reduce our stress, we can also reduce our stress so that we are more able to access and enjoy laughter. The more you practise new ways of dealing with stress, the less stressed you will become. You will be one of those people who always seem to be laughing and happy and people will wonder how *you* do it.

Interestingly, although we often feel stressed when we feel overwhelmed and unable to cope with the demands made upon us, we can also feel stress when we are underutilized and feel bored. Research carried out at York University in Toronto indicates that boredom causes people to feel stressed and has a negative effect on their happiness and health.

Release through laughter

If you worked with Keith, you probably would not recognize him at a laughter session. Few of the members know what he does for a living, but it is a job that carries a lot of responsibility and requires great concentration. He is very well respected at work and in his community, but he says that it is the laughter sessions that have allowed him to be his true authentic self and express himself fully. He is one of the most energetic members and really enjoys the physical aspect of our sessions, like games, singing and dancing. Our sessions provide him with a cathartic experience, allowing him to release the emotions that are frequently suppressed at work.

The mind-and-body connection

Although many people tend to think of the body and mind as separate entities, there is a lot of evidence to support the fact that physical and psychological health are interconnected and influence each other. Research has shown that happy people are more likely to live longer, be healthier and are less likely to experience anxiety, stress and depression. However, this information is useful only if we know how to handle the pressures and stressors we face in our everyday lives so that we can be the happy, healthy people we want to be.

The problem for many of us today is that our 'stress response' is frequently triggered by our thoughts and reactions to situations where, although we are not in any physical danger, our body responds as though we were. When our ancestors got 'stressed', it was in situations when they needed to fight or to run away and they utilized the extra energy that the stress response gave. They either fought the sabre-toothed tiger or they ran away from it, and once the danger had passed, they returned to a more relaxed state.

Today, people feel stressed about things like driving in traffic, exams, redundancy, meeting deadlines and situations where they feel overwhelmed and unable to cope. These are situations when fighting or running away is not a suitable solution, and the stress response can actually make things worse. We do not even need to be in an uncomfortable situation because modern man has the ability to use imagination, unlike our ancestors. We can be in a safe place such as lying in bed at night, but by ruminating on the past or imagining possible situations in the future, we can trigger our stress response.

It is estimated that a staggering 90 per cent of visits to GPs are for stress-related conditions. Nearly everyone I see in my hypnotherapy practice suffers from symptoms of stress and anxiety in some form, even if the problem they present is about something else. Stress has been called the curse of modern life; it is so common that I think people have come to accept it as something unavoidable.

We may not be able to avoid all stressful situations, but by acquiring a better understanding of our biological and psychological reactions, we can learn how to cope better and plan our recovery time. We can protect ourselves against the negative consequences of accumulative stress, but first we need to have the right information, and it is helpful to have a basic understanding of how our autonomic nervous system (ANS) works.

Understanding the stress response

Until I started my Clinical Hypnosis course at university, I am not sure I had even heard of the autonomic nervous system (ANS), and I certainly did not know that it played a vital role in maintaining our physical and psychological health. The ANS is part of the central nervous system, a network of nerves that sends information from the brain to the body's organs. It is responsible for maintaining the body's unconscious functions such as heart rate, digestion, respiration, salivation and perspiration. This system is divided into two parts: the sympathetic nervous system and the parasympathetic nervous system. These systems are autonomous, so you are always either in one or the other, and it is normal to switch from one state to the other, depending on your level of activity.

The sympathetic nervous system is dominant when we are active and using energy, and it is from here that our 'stress response' is activated to enable us to 'fight or take flight' in an emergency situation. This results in the release of specific hormones such as cortisol and adrenaline (epinephrine) and causes an increase in heart rate and blood pressure, allowing more oxygen and blood sugar to be sent to the specific muscles involved in fighting or running away. This is referred to as 'acute stress', a short-lived, temporary physical state, followed by a relaxation response that allows the parasympathetic nervous system to take over. The relaxation response occurs as soon

Laughter epidemic

In 1962, there was an outbreak of contagious laughter in Tanzania (formerly known as Tanganyika). It began with a group of schoolgirls aged between 12 and 18 who started to laugh and apparently 'infected' those who came into contact with them. The laughter epidemic was so severe that schools were closed. Up to 1,000 people were reported as being affected. Outbreaks of hysterical laughter continued to affect people for a period of more than two years.

as there is no longer any perceived danger and the ANS returns to normal.

The parasympathetic nervous system becomes dominant when we do not need to be active and provides the environment where our body can recover and 'rest and digest'. These systems work together to keep our body in a state of balance called homeostasis. Problems occur, though, when the body is continually in an aroused state from perceived threats, and the frequent triggering of the stress response means that the relaxation response does not get activated. Consequently, the overproduction of cortisol in our bloodstream has a negative impact on our immune system; it can become suppressed so that we are less able to fight off infections and we can become more susceptible to illness. Cortisol has also been linked to weight gain, particularly in the abdominal region, sleep problems and blood sugar abnormalities. There can also be a detrimental effect on the digestive system and skin. Many people suffering from conditions such as irritable bowel syndrome (IBS), weight gain, sleep problems and constant coughs and colds may all be suffering the symptoms that are a result of chronic stress. Long-term chronic stress can lead to cardiovascular disease, hypertension (high blood pressure) and pain such as fibromyalgia, diabetes and infertility.

The role of exercise

Being fit does not necessarily mean you are completely healthy: regular exercise and eating well increases your resistance to stressors, but it is not enough just to have cardiovascular fitness. I mention this because I have met people who regularly work out in the gym and control their calorie intake, but do so in a way that is excessive and detrimental to their overall health. When you focus your motivation for fitness on the amount of muscle that can be maintained, the speed or number of miles that can be run and how the body looks, it is easy to neglect the other needs of the body and inadvertently put the body into a state of stress. To put it simply, unless you spend sufficient time in both the sympathetic and parasympathetic nervous states, you will eventually experience some sort of side effect. Although it is possible to spend too long in a state of parasympathetic dominance, the tendency is that most people spend too much time in a state of sympathetic nervous system dominance.

The right way to relax

It may be better if we redefine relaxation as being in the parasympathetic nervous state. Unfortunately, what many people consider to be relaxation may actually have the opposite effect on the body. I always ask my clients what they do to relax: some will describe having a cigarette, a cup of coffee and reading the newspaper as their method for having a break. Many people use alcohol or sugary foods to relax, and although they may feel that this relaxes them, it does not have a beneficial effect on their body; far from promoting the switch into the parasympathetic system, it causes further stress to the body. It is likely the other aspects linked with these behaviours are the ones that cause the feelings of relaxation: for example, being with friends, having a change of environment or taking time to be alone. Going outside into the fresh air to have a cigarette could be a beneficial activity if the cigarette stayed unlit! Many people who find it difficult to relax will eventually suffer from exhaustion, which may be a contributory cause of anxiety and depression.

Stress, anxiety and depression

Anxiety and depression are the most common health problem in the UK and the USA, and in the majority of cases the cause is found to be a reaction to stress. If you feel depressed, sad, without hope or if you lose interest in things you used to enjoy and these symptoms persist for more than a week or two, you should see your doctor immediately. These may be signs you are suffering from chronic depression and will require specialist treatment from a qualified healthcare professional. The treatment for chronic depression is usually very effective and your doctor may recommend one of the talking therapies such as Cognitive Behaviour Therapy (CBT), antidepressants or a combination of both.

It concerns me that it is so easy for people to buy antidepressant drugs on the Internet without a prescription or a formal diagnosis, and there is evidence that many people are using them as a form of self-medication to alleviate symptoms that are likely to have been caused by stress. Antidepressants for those with chronic depression can be effective and helpful when prescribed by a health care

The gift of breath

When you have a moment, perhaps when commuting to work, waiting at the bank or doing a household job or, best of all now *as you read these words, take your attention to your breath, notice air coming in and out of your nostrils. Notice, without trying to change it. Enjoy the gift of the breath. Let yourself relax as you breathe out. Repeat these words to yourself, 'In, I am calm, out, I am relaxed.' After a few moments you* will *feel more calm and relaxed. This is a wonderful technique that you can do almost anywhere in any circumstances. Repeat it during the day and your anxiety level will not rise with accumulated stress.*

professional. I would, however, caution anyone against buying a prescription drug on the Internet and self-administering without medical supervision. There are many fake drugs sold by unscrupulous companies who care more about their profit than about your health.

Managing stress

In 2013, I looked around to see what resources were available to help people manage their stress, and an Internet search took me to the website of the Stress Management Society. This is a non-profit organization dedicated to providing practical help and advice about stress. I liked their statement that said they aimed to turn 'distress to de-stress'. I decided to participate in one of their courses, and I was so impressed with the simple practical information that was delivered that I joined the organization myself and became one of their trainers. I now include some stress management techniques and education in all my workshops because I believe prevention is always better than cure.

You cannot be stressed, anxious and relaxed at the same time, so a key to avoiding or relieving stress is to simply relax. There are countless ways of accessing this state, and working with breath is one of the most effective.

Breathing

We can go without food for long periods of time, only a few days without water, but we need to constantly breathe to stay alive: if we ever stop for more than a few minutes, we will die. Our breathing is controlled by the autonomic nervous system (ANS), so we do not have to remember to do it – most of the time it is outside of our conscious awareness. However, we can consciously control our breath if we wish; this is an excellent way to induce the relaxation response and something that we can do almost anywhere, at any time. People who suffer from panic attacks or anxiety can lessen the likelihood of having a panic attack if they learn to work with their breathing so they prevent hyperventilation (overbreathing). One of

Making your bedroom a sanctuary

Make your bedroom a place of sanctuary to increase your changes of enjoying a good night's sleep. Use it as a room for sleeping, not eating, watching TV, playing computer games, emailing, making telephone calls and working. The only exceptions to this should be when you make love with your partner and when you want to read (uplifting) books and articles before you turn out the light. If you can, try to make sure that your bedroom environment is quiet, cool, comfortable and dark. On occasions when you cannot sleep, remember that you can still rest and relax and allow your body to be in the parasympathetic nervous system. You can use this time to meditate or use relaxation techniques that may help you fall asleep.

Shoulder rolls

People who are stressed often hold a lot of tension in their shoulders. If you work at a desk or computer screen for long periods, it can cause stiffness in your neck and back, too. Shoulder rolls are simple and effective, especially if you do them regularly.

Sit on the edge of the chair with your back straight, feet flat, hip-width apart on the floor. Imagine a thread from the top of your head is pulling you gently upward so that your head is over the centre of your shoulders, not extending forward. While maintaining your posture, lift your right shoulder slowly back, up toward your ear and then forward and down. Next, roll your left shoulder backward, up, forward and down. Repeat this three times and then roll your shoulders in the opposite directions three times each. Finally, finish by shrugging your shoulders straight up toward your ears and then press them down. Repeat this five times.

This is a useful exercise for anyone who works at a desk or finds that they are often in a fixed posture for periods of time.

the most effective ways to do this: is to breathe through the nose. By breathing more slowly and calmly, the brain perceives there is no danger, or the danger has passed, and so the stress response is less likely to be evoked or sustained.

As babies, we breathe naturally by taking slow, deep breaths into the abdomen. If you watch a baby or child sleeping, you will notice their tummy moves more than the chest, indicating the engagement of the diaphragm, allowing access to the richer blood supply available in the lower lobes of the lungs. As we get older, our breathing tends to change, and we breathe less efficiently, which is often a sign that there is tension in the diaphragm that constricts its movement.

Consequently, some people find it difficult to breathe naturally using their abdomen, which, in itself, can cause feelings of anxiety and stress that are associated with the increased breathing rate. Generally, the slower the breath, the more relaxed you will feel.

Laughter Yoga is particularly beneficial as it exercises the diaphragm, encourages us to breathe deeply and clears stale residual air from our lungs. One of the reasons people feel invigorated after Laughter Yoga is because of an increase in oxygen that goes straight to their brain, making them feel energetic and revitalized.

Sleep

Sleep is essential for our well-being, but busy, stressed people tend to get less sleep than they need. On average we need between six and eight hours sleep a night, but there is no hard and fast rule. If you feel tired and lethargic during the day, it may be a sign that you are not getting the amount of sleep you need.

The period during sleep is when your body recuperates and recovers from the physical and psychological stresses and strains of the day. If you do not get enough sleep, you will not have the resources and resilience to cope with the stresses of the day.

Nutrition

Often when we feel stressed, we turn to food for comfort. These foods are usually high in sugar and fat, can lead to weight gain and put extra stress on our bodies. However, we can make wise food choices to help boost our 'happy chemicals' like serotonin. Salmon has been found to improve depression symptoms and increase a positive outlook; flaxseed is rich in magnesium and B-vitamins that help combat the effects of stress.

A lot of pharmaceutical antidepressants work by increasing the body's ability to access serotonin. Tryptophan, an amino acid, is the building block our bodies use to make serotonin. Nuts are particularly rich in tryptophan. A study at the University of Barcelona found that people who ate one ounce of a mixture of walnuts, almonds and Brazil nuts had higher levels of serotonin metabolites. Although nuts are high in calories, a daily portion of 30 grams (a handful) is enough to provide a boost of this 'happy chemical'.

Dark chocolate contains the antioxidant resveratrol, which boosts the brain levels of endorphins and serotonin that both enhance mood. The full benefits are realized after consuming 25 grams, although you may wish to eat more!

Black tea may help you recover from stress more quickly. In a study, tea drinkers felt calmer and had lower levels of the stress hormone cortisol after stressful situations. Caffeine found in coffee can boost stress hormones and raise blood pressure.

Hypnosis

If you have never visited a hypnotherapist, you may hold some misconceptions about what hypnosis is and how it works. This is often because we have seen stage hypnotists on TV or in theatres who appear to be able to hypnotize people by a click of their fingers and then manipulate them to do all manner of embarrassing acts they cannot remember later. Clinical Hypnosis is an altered state of consciousness involving deep relaxation, but although the body becomes completely relaxed, this is not sleep. The unconscious part of the brain becomes more active, and the body automatically switches into the parasympathetic nervous system, the part of our nervous system that is responsible for recuperation. This is one of the reasons that Clinical Hypnosis is so useful because just being in hypnosis has a therapeutic effect. One of the first signs I notice when a client is going into the hypnotic state is the gurgling noise of their tummy, a sure sign that the 'rest and digest' process of the parasympathetic nervous system has begun.

For people suffering from chronic conditions such as anxiety, stress, panic or pain, this can provide immediate relief and allow them to look at their problems from a more conducive physiological and psychological perspective. It enables them to use their own internal resources and reference previous experiences so that they can find their own positive solutions. Hypnosis, then, is a positive, therapeutic, learning experience with many benefits. By learning the skill of self-hypnosis, it is possible to quickly enter into a state of deep relaxation at will, to activate the parasympathetic nervous state and maintain healthy homeostasis.

Hypnosis is a naturally occurring state that we enter frequently during the day when we experience a narrow focus of attention: for instance, becoming engrossed in watching TV, reading a book or daydreaming. As we do this, time often seems to become distorted, and although we feel as though only five minutes have passed, it can turn out to be much longer, or, perhaps, half an hour seems like just ten minutes. This common phenomenon of hypnosis can be exploited so that you can experience the relaxation of a half-hour nap in a five-minute session of self-hypnosis. There are many techniques that you can use to access a self-hypnotic state, and the quickest and most effective way to learn is when you are already in hypnosis. I always teach my clients to do this, as it means that they can practise the work we do together at home and reduce the number of visits they have with me, while learning a useful skill that they can continue to use after treatment. Regular self-hypnosis is relaxing and pleasurable, and it will keep you fit and healthy. It is the perfect antidote to a stressful life.

After a period spent in hypnosis, the body recovers, stress hormones are reduced, and we feel calmer. Consequently, this means that our reaction to stressful situations decreases, leading to an accumulative effect that retrains our physiological response to stress. If we are in a highly agitated or anxious state, we are less able to cope with stress, but when we are able to face the same situation in a relaxed state, we become more resourceful and can manage situations better. An intervention that allows for relaxation and recovery can interrupt the pattern of stress and help us reverse the negative effect. Sometimes this may be as simple as a good night's sleep, a holiday, some extra support or a healthier lifestyle. Many people, myself included, find that regular practice of self-hypnosis keeps them calm and centred. You may want to visit a Clinical Hypnotherapist to learn self-hypnosis techniques; there also are a number of online resources, and I have included a book recommendation in the Resources section.

Our thoughts

It is not just the events of our everyday experience that affect our stress levels but also our negative thoughts. In hypnosis, the part of the brain that regulates our emotions is engaged, and this means that it is possible to create positive emotions by focusing on pleasant thoughts and images. We know from Positive Psychology research that once our ratio of positive emotions to negative emotions gets to 3:1 and above, it increases our sense of well-being (happiness), another reason to practise the skill of self-hypnosis. When we imagine pleasant experiences that involve emotions such as joy, appreciation and gratitude, there is a physical response and our brain produces the biochemicals that match these imagined feelings. Our unconscious brain does not recognize the difference between imagined and real experiences, so what we imagine or focus our thoughts on becomes our experience. Knowing this, we should be careful what we think because when we imagine situations in which we feel sad, depressed, angry or stressful, we also create a biochemical match.

Research by Professor Adrian Owen, a neuroscientist, has shown that when we imagine doing an activity, our brain responds in the same way as if we are actually doing the activity. Using MRI scanning, he was able to show that thinking about playing tennis activated exactly the same area of the brain that is activated when we actually play tennis. This is convincing evidence that our unconscious brain does not know the difference between what is real, imagined, pretended and acted.

We can utilize the power of our imagination and self-hypnosis to create positive emotional responses and feelings of well-being. This is just like regular daydreaming, but with a planned intention and motive. A good way to start is to imagine a special place where you feel safe, secure and comfortable. It might be a place you have visited before, a place you have always wanted to visit or a place completely created in your own imagination. Some people like to revisit the same place in hypnosis and use this as a place of 'safety', somewhere they know they can escape from any worries or problems and always feel relaxed and happy.

Another benefit of self-hypnosis is the opportunity to visualize yourself behaving in new ways that are more appropriate and beneficial for you: for instance, imagining yourself feeling calm and relaxed in a situation where you might normally feel stressed. Every time you 'practise' behaving differently, your brain perceives this as a real experience and learns to respond differently. When you encounter the situation for real, you feel calmer and more in control than you would have done before.

Exercise

Exercise can sometimes provide an opportunity to utilize stress response chemicals that have been released owing to stressful circumstances. Even though it may not be possible to do it at the time, it may still provide relief later. After gentle exercise, the body is more likely to trigger the relaxation response. Walking and swimming are particularly suitable as they are low-impact, aerobic activities. Many people use alcohol to achieve a rapid result, and although this will induce relaxation, excess alcohol consumption will make further demands on the body, interfere with the sleep cycle, cause dehydration and have a subsequent detrimental effect. Sometimes it may feel more appropriate to choose a relaxation activity such as reading, a hot bath or doing a crossword puzzle. Instinctively, you will know what suits you best at the time, but the key is to *actively* choose something helpful in preference to passive distraction activities such as watching TV or using the Internet.

Managing stress over the long term

In an ideal world, once you identified your source of stress, you would simply remove it. However, if your source of stress is your boss, your teenage children or the next-door neighbours, then it is not quite that easy. However, there may be things that you can do to help yourself. If you feel overwhelmed with tasks, there may be some that you can delegate to others or you can ask for help. Tell people how you feel; otherwise, they may assume that you are willing and able to cope with your workload. Try saying *no* when you are asked to take on extra responsibilities and explain that you are unable to help at the present time. Avoid any people who cause you to feel stressed and choose the company of people who you enjoy being with whenever possible. Listening to the news on the TV and in newspapers can have a negative impact on your psyche without you realizing it, so try to avoid it for a while and see if it helps. Many people (myself included) are surprised to find how calm and relaxed they feel when they have a complete break from the news media. If you can manage to abstain from watching TV and using any personal technology, too, the effect is likely to be more dramatic

Psychosomatic Illness

The majority of hypnotherapy clients I see generally suffer from psychosomatic illness. These are real and not imagined illnesses caused by the body being out of balance (homeostasis) and include physical conditions like irritable bowel syndrome (IBS), headaches or disorders such as anxiety disorder and panic attacks. The main cause of psychosomatic illness is long-term or chronic stress. My clients will come to see me about an unwanted habit like smoking, drinking, overeating or nail biting (onychophagia), but it often turns out that these are behaviours that they have adopted in order to cope with their stress levels. Hypnosis is particularly effective at treating psychosomatic illness as being in the state of hypnosis helps rebalance the body by taking it out of the sympathetic nervous state, which is responsible for the stress response (fight/flight response) and into the parasympathetic nervous system where the body is able to rest and recover. I teach people how to utilize self-hypnosis so that they can continue this state of relaxation on their own, but stress is a major problem in our modern society.

The sound of laughter

Some people live in such a permanent state of stress and anxiety that they cannot recognize it as being anything other than normal. Living in such a stressful state frequently leads to terrible health consequences. Those in this condition often find it too difficult to relax and enjoy any form of laughter exercise. In fact, many of them are so 'wired' they would not even be able to sit down for five minutes without feeling anxious. This led me to consider whether laughter could be used therapeutically during hypnosis.

I have noticed that even when people are unable to join in with laughter exercises, they seem to benefit from listening to the sound of laughter. As I explained earlier, this is due to a reaction in our brain that takes place outside of our conscious awareness. With this in mind, I have been experimenting with playing recordings of different sorts of laughter to some of my clients while they have been in hypnosis, and I have had some interesting and promising results. I am currently working on producing a number of MP3 recordings to help people access smiling and laughter through hypnosis as well as facilitating other positive emotions.

Psychosomatic illnesses are caused by mental and emotional stresses that manifest as physical diseases without biological causes. This includes irritable bowel syndrome, upset stomach, muscle aches, tension headaches, chronic fatigue syndrome, hyperventilation or panic attacks, colitis and ulcers, and even infertility. The skill with which a person handles stress affects the potential appearance and severity of psychosomatic symptoms.

Before these conditions can be properly diagnosed, tests must be administered to rule out possible physical reasons for the illness. This step is often frustrating for patient and doctor alike, as test after test comes back negative. This has led some physicians to tell their patients that psychosomatic illnesses are 'all in their head'. Today, most doctors know better. The root may be mental or emotional, but the disease and symptoms are very real.

Psychosomatic illnesses are not faked illnesses: they are real, but, often, psychological intervention is the most effective way to get rid of the physiological symptoms. Unfortunately, many people resist this idea because they think doing so is a denial of their physical symptoms. Although these illnesses respond to drugs, painkillers and other medical help, symptoms are likely to return unless the underlying cause is addressed.

Balance plays a critical role in our mental and physical well-being. Often, when I have given talks about the beneficial effects of laughter to Positive Living groups and other organizations, I notice that although there are vast differences in the personalities and the emotional energy of people when they first participate in a laughter session, these are less noticeable at the end. Laughter seems to have a way of balancing us both physically and emotionally. Those who start out excitable and extrovert appear calmer at the end of the session, whereas those who appeared shy and reticent to begin with show more vitality and enthusiasm at the end. This is why it is impossible to predict how people will react during a laughter session.

Sometimes our bodies and minds produce symptoms that are unpleasant and unwelcome, but once you appreciate that these are messages with the positive intention of keeping you safe and well, you can take appropriate action to relieve them. When we tune into what our body and mind communicate and respond respectfully, we can begin to live a balanced happy and healthy life.

Chapter 9

How to be Happy

If you want others to be happy, practise compassion.
If you want to be happy, practise compassion.
The Dalai Lama

In the final chapter of this book, I want to look in depth at the question of happiness, what it is and how we might find it. I am aware that with the book title *Laugh Your Way to Happiness*, it might sound as though happiness is a destination, somewhere to head toward and somewhere where you can eventually arrive. However, I hope throughout the book that I have shown that the laughter we experience in the here and now is as important as any 'final destination'. And I want to stress that, in the same way, happiness is something that you feel, or do not feel, *now*. You may have been happy in the past, you may be happy in the future, but you can only actually experience feeling happy in the present moment.

To understand what happiness is, we can do no better than to look for the answers in Positive Psychology, which developed as a way of examining the 'science of happiness'. Psychologists have studied what makes us unhappy and what unhappiness looks like since psychology began. Positive Psychology does not disagree with these findings, but attempts to address an imbalance by also looking at what makes us happy and what happiness looks like. The emphasis of Positive Psychology is that rather than focusing on the negative effects of unhappiness, we should shift our attention to the positive effects of happiness.

What do you call it?

You will not find many Positive Psychologists using the term 'happiness', just as you will not find many renowned writers using the adjective 'nice'. The reason is that neither of these words tells us much as they are vague, subjective and too broad. Positive

Psychologists want to measure happiness in terms of your 'subjective well-being' and find out whether you are 'flourishing' as a human being. They also differentiate the kinds of experiences that make you happy by dividing them into the categories of 'hedonic' (pleasure seeking) and 'eudaimonic' (meaningful).

Hedonic and eudaimonic happiness

Surely, happiness is just happiness, easy and simple? Actually, once you start to look at happiness and try to define it, the subject becomes difficult and complex to explain.

Hedonic happiness is linked to the things that give us sensory pleasure and an immediate reward: for example, pursuing pleasure, enjoyment and comfort. However, the effect is short-lived so that what gave you pleasure initially has to be repeated and/or intensified in order to be sustained. This is why one scoop of ice cream may not feel enough and leave you wanting more and feeling dissatisfied. A phenomenon called hedonic adaptation means that we soon get used to the things that initially made us feel happy: although you were really excited when you first got a new car, you soon got used to owning it and the pleasure faded. The constant pursuit of hedonic pleasure can result in addictive behaviours, obesity, relationship and financial problems and, in the long run, can be the cause of much unhappiness.

The pleasure and reward we get from doing things that are worthwhile and give meaning and purpose to our lives is described as eudaimonic happiness. The pleasure associated with this sort of happiness is not usually felt immediately, but the effects are long lasting and can be experienced even after doing an unpleasant task. People who experience eudaimonic happiness are likely to feel that life has a purpose and meaning and enjoy positive relationships.

I do not believe that anyone can prescribe the ingredients of a happy life for you, but it is likely to be your own unique blend of both sorts of happiness. A life without pleasure would be unbearable for most, but a life based purely on transient, minute-to-minute pleasure is unlikely to lead to lasting happiness either. Positive Psychologist Martin Seligman suggests that a life with a balance of hedonic and eudaimonic happiness is the ideal, but if you were only to experience one sort, then eudaimonic would be the most fulfilling and rewarding.

He describes his theory of 'well-being' in his book *Flourish* and uses a model called 'PERMA', an acronym for positive emotion, engagement, relationships, meaning and accomplishment. I believe that laughter as an exercise works because it is the increase of positive emotions, facilitated through laughter, that result in us feeling healthy and happier. There are other simple and effective things you can do to increase your positivity ratio, and I recommend that you read more about Positive Psychology. There are a number of interesting and easy-to-read books listed in the Resources section.

Although I agree that the word happiness does not really describe what happiness is, I have chosen to use it in this book. I believe that you will have your own subjective definition of what happiness means to you, and therefore you do not need to clarify it. As long as you know what happiness *feels* like, then – for the purposes of this book – that is all that matters.

Throughout your life, you will have had certain 'happy' experiences and built up an association with that word, and I don't think there is any benefit in asking you to rename it. If I ask you to look back to when you were happy, I expect that you can do that in an instant and connect with the positive emotions you experienced. You will have lots of memories stored away as 'happy' ones, but few, if any, as moments of 'well-being' or 'flourishing'. So, with my apologies, and while acknowledging my deepest respect to the science of Positive Psychology, let us talk about what makes you happy.

Happiness now

Happiness is something that you can only experience in the present moment; yet so many people anticipate having happiness in the future or spend time reminiscing about happiness in the past. If you are someone who thinks about being happy later – for instance, when you retire, have a romantic relationship, get divorced, have a baby, leave school, win the lottery, and so on – then you may be cheating yourself from getting your full happiness quota today.

Happiness is not something to look or search for or something that you may accidentally stumble across. Try to think of happiness as an experience that is caused by your choices and actions rather than some treasure waiting to be discovered. If you want to be happier, it makes sense to look at what is happening in your life today and then do whatever you can to improve your level of happiness. It may take effort at first, but once you realize what *really* makes you happy, you can ensure that you incorporate these activities and thoughts into your life until they become part of your normal routine.

The key to happiness is to enjoy what you have in your life right now. International business coach and consultant Andrew Machon reminds us that there is no 'on' switch, only an 'off' switch. You can choose to reconnect with laughter, happiness or whatever it is that you have become disconnected from at any time.

First of all, be as happy as you can be *today*! We can all become happier: in fact, Positive Psychology research suggests that it is possible to boost our individual happiness by up to 40 per cent, and the good news is that, as research studies have shown, becoming happier is simple and achievable.

First, you need some information about how and what makes you happy; then you need to have the willingness and determination to make some changes. Most importantly, you need to take responsibility for your happiness and understand that, ultimately, being happy is much more about the choices you make than the circumstances in which you live. Although it may seem unlikely, your life circumstances only account for 10 per cent of the effect on your level of happiness. This explains why some people are able to be happy despite hardship and ill health. So what's stopping you being happier?!

What really makes you happy?

If I asked you what makes, or would make, you happy, I expect you would have no trouble coming up with a list. However, it is a fact that what we think makes us happy is not always true. I wonder how many of you think that wealth, beauty and success would make you really happy? We are bombarded with the 'evidence' that this must be true whenever we look at advertisements, articles in magazines

World record laughing

Belachew Girma holds a Guinness World Record for laughing nonstop for 3 hours and 6 minutes. He explains that after his wife died of HIV-AIDS and he lost his business, he began to read books on psychology and laughter. A born-again Christian, he is now a laughter therapist, activist and motivational speaker.

and people in the TV and film industry. We need look no further than Hollywood to see many examples of people who turn to drugs, drink, addictions and even suicide because they feel they are lacking something in their lives, despite the outwardly appearance of 'having it all'. There are exceptions, of course, but I suspect that the people who are really happy and enjoy their looks, money and their status do not regard them as being the source of their happiness and that they also have meaning and purpose in their life.

No one can say exactly what activities will bring you happiness, but simple acts like being grateful, helping others, connecting with friends and family and pursuing meaningful activities have been shown to be common to people who describe themselves as happy. These are things that are almost always available to us, regardless of our life circumstances. Once we know what will truly make us happy, we can take action to ensure we facilitate it in our lives.

During my Master of Applied Positive Psychology degree course, students were expected to experiment and apply the theories and strategies of Positive Psychology into their daily lives. I discovered that sometimes even the tiniest of changes to one of my behaviours, attitudes or habits would produce profoundly positive outcomes. Small changes in your life can lead to big shifts in how you feel and lead you into an upward spiral of positive emotion, the opposite of the downward spiral of depression that people may be more used to hearing about. I use the metaphor of a central heating system where even small changes to any one part can cause a profound effect overall: for instance, by altering the thermostat, turning off a radiator or changing the timer, you can make noticeable changes in every room. Likewise, changing one attitude or belief can cause a massive change in our life.

Just as I have asked you to consider and accept some facts about laughter, I would like you to consider and accept some facts about happiness because the key to becoming happier is to know what works. The adage 'If you do what you've always done, you're going to get what you've always got' could not be more true. Wishing you could be happier will not change anything and could possibly lead to you feeling worse. I would like you to consider the following five points to see whether you agree or disagree with them.

1. Happiness is an active choice, not something that happens to you.
2. Happiness can only be experienced in the present moment.
3. No one can 'make' you happy, and you cannot 'make' anyone else happy either.

4. If you wait for happiness to happen, you may miss out on being happy now.
5. The key to being happy is to accept and enjoy what is already positively present in your life.

You may resist or disbelieve some of these ideas, but I urge you to accept, or at least open yourself up, to the possibility that they are all true. Ask yourself: would you rather be right or be happy? Even if you just act 'as if' these things are true, even if you have some doubts, I believe you can increase your level of happiness.

These are the five major points that I cover in my 'happiness coach' course with my clients. Many of them are surprised to discover that the 'coach' is not me but a metaphor for their own journey to happiness. They are the driver of their own coach, they decide on the route, whom they invite to share their journey and how much baggage they bring. First of all, though, they have to get on board, sit in the driving seat and take control. There is no point in them just sitting there and wishing that they were somewhere else. They have to take action and accept total responsibility for their own journey. Making mistakes, going in the wrong direction or stalling is not a problem; anyone can get back on track. Perhaps I am like the sat nav, suggesting directions if they are lost and reminding them that there are lots of other routes than just one. After a while, a sat nav is no longer necessary because the driver is able to use his or her own instinct and sense of direction to know which way is best. As the Buddha says: *There is no path to happiness: happiness is the path*.

Happiness is a choice, but in order to make the right choice, you need to have the right information, intention, motivation and commitment. If you have been chasing happiness in the wrong places, or waiting for it come to you, then the good news is that happiness is already present if you look in the right places. Once you discover what makes you happy, and what does not, you can make some simple changes and adopt new behaviours that soon become a new habit.

If the bad news is that many of us having been chasing the wrong things to obtain happiness, then the good news is that happiness is much easier to achieve than we may have thought.

Reasons to be cheerful

There are so many benefits to feeling happy that I could not begin to list them all. I believe that being happy is what every human on earth wants above everything else. It is our motivation to do anything in life, and even if our life's passion is to help others, it is because it makes us happy. You may have lots of desires in your life, but would you want any of them if they did not make you happy? The benefits of happiness and laughter are linked together. We laugh when we are happy; we are happy when we laugh. I believe it is impossible to completely separate them and see where one begins and the other ends.

It came as no surprise to find that the positive health benefits of happiness are virtually the same as those of laughter. People who are happy

- have stronger immune systems;
- get ill less often and recover quicker;
- are more likely to enjoy their work;
- are less likely to suffer from depression;
- are more likely to be creative;
- are less likely to suffer from stress;
- are more likely to enjoy better relationships;
- are less likely to divorce;
- are more likely to live longer;
- are less likely to get heart vascular disease;
- can endure pain for longer;
- are less at likely to have a stroke.

You probably know that laughter is contagious, but you may be surprised to learn that so is happiness. Research using data from a long-term study that measured levels of happiness over a ten-year period shows that happiness can spread just like a virus from one person to another. Although we may expect our level of happiness to have a direct influence on our friends, family and colleagues, the study showed that it could spread by 'three degrees of separation'. This means that your increase in happiness can have a direct effect not just on your friend but your friend's friend's friends. I think this information is exciting and may help us look at happiness in a different way.

Rather than just considering happiness as being something that is personal and subjective, perhaps we should also consider happiness as a collective experience. For instance, if you become happier and that happiness spreads by three degrees of separation, what effect could this have in your life, with your family, friends, colleagues and community? If you have struggled to help someone you love become happier and felt some responsibility for his or her happiness, maybe you could try a new approach. It is difficult and almost impossible to directly create a change in someone else, regardless of how well intentioned the motive may be. Rather like the aircraft scenario of putting on your own oxygen mask before helping anyone else, maybe the best way to help other people be happy is to first be happy yourself.

There are people who think that concentrating on personal happiness is selfish and self-centred, but you could argue that we have a duty to be happy, *especially* if we care about the happiness of others. Perhaps, if enough people get 'infected' with happiness, it will lead to a worldwide pandemic. What a lovely thought!

You may worry that the opposite effect may be true and that sadness and depression can spread in the same way. Well, it appears that unhappiness can also have an influence, but it does not spread in the same way that happiness does. The happiness virus is one that I would suggest you expose yourself to as often as possible. We tend to be attracted to happy, positive people anyway, but now there is a really compelling reason to do so. I have yet to meet someone who complains about being *too* happy.

People who are positive and happy are more likely to attract others to spend time in their company; after all, given a choice, few of us would choose to spend time with someone who is miserable or complaining. Happy people tend to benefit from having better relationships with friends, family and colleagues, and these relationships also provide them with a good support system when they need it.

Feeling happy means you are less likely to become depressed and you are more likely to see the world in a different way. How you feel and behave affects not just you but everyone around you. As Dr K puts it: 'When you laugh, you change, and when you change, the world changes, too.' It is so true, and I have seen many examples of this in my Clinical Hypnotherapy practice and when I have mentored for the Prince's Trust. We tend to notice the things that match our mood. When we feel negative, we are more likely to notice the negative, and visa versa: when we feel positive, we notice the positive.

Unconsciously, we validate our feelings and justify them with the evidence that we see around us. Sometimes we can feel that life is unfair, unjust and 'out to get us'. When things improve, it can appear that the world and the people in it have become a little nicer when, in reality, it is *you* and your perception of the world that has changed. When I work with people who say they are down or depressed (but not suffering from Clinical Depression), I often know when they start to feel better because they start to mention that other people have changed and become more reasonable and positive. It is far more likely that the change is in them, not everyone else, but we are much better at judging other people's behaviour than being fully conscious of our own.

The world is a mirror to your mood and attitude. When you think the world is full of impatient, stressed people who have not got time to be pleasant, you may be getting back some of what you are putting out. It may not be what you intend to communicate, but it is what the world will notice.

I once worked on a flight to Los Angeles and went shopping shortly after arriving at the hotel. This is never a good idea because the time change means that you are essentially shopping in the middle of the night and your body and brain do not function properly. Whatever you buy, you are likely to question it later.

However, on this occasion, I went to a store to buy a dress and felt irritated that there was no sales assistant available to direct me to the fitting room. I headed off in the direction where I thought it would be and was really shocked to see a woman heading towards me who clearly had no intention of moving out of my way. I was even more shocked when I realized that this person was actually *me*! I had seen my own reflection in a mirror, but had been so tired that I had not realized until I almost ran into her (me). It was interesting that I regarded this other women as having a bad attitude, but there could be no doubt about who was the grumpy, stressed and tired person!

How to get more laughter, health and happiness in your life

So how do you get more laughter, health and happiness in your life *now*?!

If you wanted to build a fire to keep you warm and cosy on a cold night, you would know better than to hold a match to a log and expect to set it alight. You would know that in order to build a successful fire, you need to start by lighting some paper or kindling and then add twigs or small pieces of wood until the base of the fire is established. After this, you can add more kindling until the fire reaches such intensity that you can throw on a log or two and know that it will continue to burn. By following this procedure, you would end up with a roaring fire, and then you could sit back and enjoy its warmth and comfort. Once your fire is going well, you would only have to attend to it now and again, giving it the odd poke and throw on another log every so often. If you had insisted on trying to light the log with a match because you were too impatient to bother with the other stages, well, you would still be trying to get it started and would probably be on your third or fourth box of matches!

It is easier to make changes if you build upon small successes and progress gently. There may be setbacks and life will bring you ups and downs, but once you understand what works for *you*, you can choose to do the things that you know will bring you the results you are looking for. Even if something terrible happens and your fire goes out, you will know what to do to build it again. I believe that laughter provides a quick, easy and fun route to health and happiness; it is the firelighter in the metaphor of fire building.

To get your fire blazing, here are a few tips designed to point you in the right direction before you start.

If you want something you have never had, you have got to do something you have never done!

You are probably an expert in what makes you unhappy, fed up and annoyed, but rather than focusing on preventing the things that make you feel this way, you are more likely to succeed when you start to examine the things that make you feel happy, satisfied and even-tempered. In other words, you need to take action. Wishing that things were different has not been shown to be an effective method of change and may actually make you feel worse.

It is not difficult or complicated!

Improving your levels of health, joy and happiness in your life is really simple and requires little effort once you know what works for you. Science has shown that the things that make us feel better are often simple and easily attainable, but until we know what they are, we cannot help ourselves. Remember the saying 'Doing the same thing over and over and expecting different results is the definition of insanity'? No one can say for sure what will be the right way for you, but it is useful to start with things that have been shown to be effective for most people.

Choose ideas that appeal to you ...

Make things even easier for yourself. You are far more likely to stick with a new behaviour if you enjoy it. It is a simple matter of finding what works for you. Professor Sonja Lyubomirsky, author of *The How of Happiness*, calls this 'finding a fit'. By adopting a sense of curiosity and interest in the results you experience, you may learn a lot about what really affects your day-to-day happiness and enjoy the process of experimenting. Laughter and happiness are more likely to occur when you are feeling relaxed, healthy and happy, and the simple steps of redirecting your focus of attention and noticing what is good about where you are today can be enough to help you towards an 'upward spiral' of positivity.

... and those that don't!

Although choosing ideas that appeal is a good idea, sometimes you can gain a lot from doing things that have no appeal at all. You may be surprised to find that you actually enjoy them more than you expect or learn something about yourself that you did not know before. Start with what seems enjoyable at first, though, and save the more challenging things for 'advanced' self-exploration.

Keep an open mind.

You will only know what works for you by actually doing it. During my training on the Master of Applied Positive Psychology course, all the students were required to learn 'experientially' – that is, we did not just learn the theory, we put it into practice and tried it out for ourselves. We used ourselves as human guinea pigs to see what worked and what did not. Students would often do the same exercises or follow the same strategy, but our outcomes would be completely different. What worked for one would not work for another, and what one of us found easy, another would find a struggle. We tried to keep an open mind; nonetheless, we often had preconceptions of how an exercise would affect us, but were frequently surprised at how wrong our initial judgement had been.

You already hold the key.

None of the things suggested requires that you learn something completely new. In fact, it is more likely to be a matter of paying attention to the things that you do not normally notice or you frequently ignore. The key to happiness is appreciating what you have *now*, at this moment, but many people are far more in tune with what they do *not* have.

Only try one or two thing at a time.

I suggest that you only experiment with one or two things at a time. In this way, you will find that it takes less effort to stick to a new habit or regime; most importantly, if something is really effective, you will know exactly what it is. If you try to change too much, too quickly, you will find it difficult and maybe not bother. Be easy on yourself and remember that often it is the tiny changes that are hardly noticeable that create the most dramatic difference to how you feel. In this situation, less really can be more.

There is no deadline.

Although you might like to have rapid results, remember that there is no deadline and life is not a race. If you are someone who likes instant results or immediate gratification and are always thinking of what comes next, then you may practise being in the present moment. You can do this through mindfulness meditation or the practice of 'savouring', giving your full attention to things you like and enjoy. If you always focus on the future, you are likely to miss out on the pleasurable moments taking place in your everyday life.

Happiness is something that you feel now.

Happiness is something to be experienced and appreciated in the present moment. The most important thing is how you feel *now*. All moments pass, whether they are good or bad. Bearing this in mind can change your perception, allowing you to be less anxious when things are not going well and more appreciative when they are going great.

Frequency, not intensity

Positive Psychologist Ed Diener suggests that it is the frequency, not the intensity, of positive versus negative effect that is important. This is good news because it is much easier to facilitate small moments of pleasure in your life than ones when you feel 'over the moon' with joy. Unfortunately, negative emotions appear to be stronger than positive ones: we notice them more and feel their effects for longer. In order to compensate for this, Positive Psychologist Barbara Fredrickson suggests that we need to have a ratio of 3:1 positive to negative emotions to flourish and enjoy improved feelings of well-being. It is important to realize that we are not trying to remove negative emotions as they are often appropriate and will always be part of our lives. Instead, we focus our attention on positive emotions and do what we can to increase the number of these.

Beliefs can hold us back ...

We all hold our own set of beliefs, and these, like our habits, can exist outside of our conscious awareness. Our beliefs and values guide and influence our behaviour and our choices throughout our lives, but some of our deep-rooted beliefs may not be appropriate or serve a positive purpose in our lives today.

When we are young, we believe what we are told by our parents, teachers, friends and family without question. As we grow up, some of these beliefs may need to be updated or replaced or they may hold us back. Many people grow up believing negative things that they were told in childhood: for instance, you are no good at … (fill in the blank) or you will never be able to … (fill in the blank). Perhaps this was true then, but is no longer true now, or maybe it was not even true at the time, but you believed it, and still do! If you find yourself doubting your ability in any way, spend some time examining where your belief comes from, then test to see if it is true. You may find that the belief is better suited to the person who presented it as 'the truth' and you can simply choose not to believe it any more. After all, I don't suppose you still believe in the tooth fairy and Father Christmas, do you?!

Unfortunately, some people may unconsciously believe that they do not deserve to be happy and that life is meant to be difficult and not much fun. It can be hard to resist ideas and beliefs, but once they are in our conscious awareness, we can choose to challenge them.

… and spur us on.

Beliefs can hold us back, but they can also spur us on. Believing that something is possible is an essential component of success. Who would ever achieve their goals if they truly believed they could not? Athletes, sportsmen, inventors, artists, explorers and people who achieve their goals passionately believe it is possible, and they focus on and visualize the positive outcome. When they have setbacks, they believe that these are temporary and learn from the experience. If you want to have more laughter, health and happiness in your life, ask yourself this question: What would I have to believe in order for this to become true? Then ask yourself if you are in alignment with those beliefs. If not, you may like to try this next technique.

Act as if ...

Rather like the principle of 'fake it till you make it' in Laughter Yoga, the similar effect of acting 'as if' can be applied in the same way. When we act 'as if' something is true, regardless of whether we believe it or not, it can have a positive influence on our experience. If you act as if you know that you will achieve the outcome you desire, you will be more likely to succeed.

Have you ever wondered how TV and radio presenters manage to be happy, chatty and energetic every day on air and never have an off day? They must have days when they do not feel bright and bubbly because of illness, fatigue, problems at home, and so on. They are experts in the 'fake it till you make it' and 'as if' principles. Once you have acted 'as if' you are in a good mood for a short period of time, you will find your mood will change to match your behaviour. If you want to feel happy, adopt the mannerisms of a happy person.

... add the word 'yet' ...

Just adding the simple word 'yet' can make such a difference. Consider the difference between saying 'I can't walk three miles' and 'I can't walk three miles yet'.

... and delete the word 'try'.

As soon as we use the word 'try' before something, we are unconsciously predicting that we may fail. If you say, 'I'm going to 'try' and keep a journal', you are far less likely to succeed than if you said, 'I'm going to keep a journal'. It does not mean that you will definitely succeed, but the change in language will affect your attitude and your level of optimism. I do not suppose you would say, 'I'm going to try and drive to work/cook dinner/clean my teeth'!

Track your progress

When you track your progress and see improvements, it will encourage you to continue. You may like to use the 'SMART' approach. This is the acronym for:

S = Specific, **M** = Measurable, **A** = Achievable,
R = Relevant, **T** = Time-bound

It will help you check that you are setting yourself a realistic and achievable goal and do not set yourself up for failure.

Wall calendars are a good way to have a visible record of your success, where you can tick each day of success. A journal is also helpful for keeping track of your emotions and expressing how you feel. There are a number of free APPs for computers and mobile phones. Some of these will log your progress and send you reminders.

Constant repetition is the biggest factor to developing a new habit. If you make a small change in behaviour and repeat every day for 30–45 days, you will most likely break the old habit and develop the new one. There are also websites that allow you to record your progress in a range of different activities and store your information for you (*see* Resources, page 235).

Many Positive Psychology exercises encourage you to scan for positive events in your everyday life. By doing this mindfully at first, you can soon train your brain to notice the positive reasons for feeling happy rather than the negative reasons that support your more negative mood.

Choose your company wisely: you are more likely to laugh and be happy when you are in the company of people who are happy and laugh.

Research

In the Resources section, I have put together a list of books and websites that I think you will find useful. In addition, you will find further information on my website: www.laughyourwaytohappiness.com.

And finally …

It is difficult to separate laughter from health, health from happiness and happiness from laughter. I hope that you will discover that they all interconnect and that you find you possess them all in abundance. Remember: happy people are healthier, healthier people are happier, and laughter is frequently present in the company of healthy, happy people. Trust your instincts and try what appeals most, to begin with. When it comes to experience and understanding, you are your very own best expert.

I can think of no better way to end this book than with a reminder of the wise words I learnt from Dr K all those years ago: '*Keep laughing!*'

Resources

BOOKS

Laughter

Kataria, Dr Madan, *Laugh for No Reason* (revised edition), Denzil, Mumbai, 2011

Hypnosis

Calvert, Tig, *Hypnotherapy For a Better Life*, Hodder Education, London, 2011

Positive Psychology

The following books provide a good basic introduction to Positive Psychology:

Akhtar, Miriam, *Positive Psychology for Overcoming Depression*, Watkins Publishing, London, 2012

Fredrickson, Barbara, *Positivity: Groundbreaking Research to Release Your Inner Optimist and Thrive*, Crown Publishing Group, New York, 2009

Grenville-Cleave, Bridget, *Positive Psychology (Introducing a Practical Guide)*, Icon Books Ltd, London, 2012

Lyubomirsky, Sonja, *The How of Happiness: A Practical Guide to Getting the Life You Want* (paperback edition), Piatkus, London, 2010

Seligman, Martin E P, *Flourish: A New Understanding of Happiness and Well-Being – and How to Achieve Them,* Free Press, New York, 2011

NLP

Miller, Philip, *The Really Good Fun Cartoon Book of NPL: A Simple and Graphic(al) Explanation of the Life Toolbox That Is NLP*, Crown House Publishing, Carmathen, 2008

WEBSITES

www.laughterbusiness.com

www.laughyourwaytohappiness.com

www.laughteryoga.org

www.laughteryogaamerica.com

www.therapythroughhypnosis.co.uk

www.authentichappiness.sas.upenn.edu/Default.aspx

www.ippanetwork.org

www.positivityratio.com

www.thehowofhappiness.com

www.randomactsofkindness.org

Free telephone laughter

Worldwide: www.skypelaughterclub.org

USA: www.laughteryogausa.com

SOCIAL CHANGE IN IRAN

An Eyewitness Account of Dissent, Defiance, and New Movements for Rights

BEHZAD YAGHMAIAN

STATE UNIVERSITY OF NEW YORK PRESS

Published by
STATE UNIVERSITY OF NEW YORK PRESS
ALBANY

Printed in the United States of America

For information, address
State University of New York Press,
90 State Street, Suite 700, Albany, NY 12207

Production, Kelli Williams
Marketing, Michael Campochiaro

Library of Congress Cataloging-in-Publication Data

Yaghmaian, Behzad, 1953–
Social change in Iran : an eyewitness account of dissent, defiance, and new movements for rights / Behzad Yaghmaian.
p. cm.
Includes bibliographical references and index.
ISBN 0-7914-5211-5 (alk. paper) — ISBN 0-7914-5212-3 (pbk. : alk. paper)
1. Social change—Iran. 2. Iran—Politics and government—1997– 3. Civil society—Iran. 4. Student movements—Iran. 5. Iran—Social conditions—1997– 6. Iran—Economic conditions—1997– I. Title.

HN670.2.A8 Y34 2002
303.4′0955—dc21

2001049287

10 9 8 7 6 5 4 3 2 1

Contents

Acknowledgments vii

Preface ix

Introduction
Iran: An Eyewitness Account and Study of Social Change 1

Chapter One
Emerging Social Movements, Victories, and Setbacks in the Battle for Rights 7

Chapter Two
State and the Socialization of Violence: A Narrative of Everyday Life 27

Chapter Three
Children of the Islamic Republic—Part I
The Rise of a New Social Movement for Joy: A Narrative 47

Chapter Four
Children of the Islamic Republic—Part II
Student Movement: Transcendence from a Movement against Rights to a Movement for Rights 73

Chapter Five

CHILDREN OF THE ISLAMIC REPUBLIC—PART III
THE POLITICIZATION OF THE MOVEMENT FOR JOY:
A NARRATIVE OF A NEW STUDENT MOVEMENT IN THE MAKING 91

Chapter Six

A MOVEMENT FOR A FREE PRESS—THE VANGUARD
OF THE BATTLE FOR RIGHTS AND CIVIL SOCIETY 117

Chapter Seven

STATE, ECONOMY, AND CIVIL SOCIETY—PART I
WAGE EARNERS' RESPONSE TO ECONOMIC CATASTROPHE 143

Chapter Eight

STATE, ECONOMY, AND CIVIL SOCIETY—PART II
ECONOMIC DECLINE, DIVIDED STATE, AND POLICY RETREAT:
THE TRIUMPH OF NEOLIBERALISM 181

Chapter Nine

OIL, INTERNATIONAL DIVISION OF LABOR, AND THE CRISIS
OF THE IRANIAN ECONOMY: A POLITICAL ECONOMY ANALYSIS 193

Chapter Ten

THE GREAT DEBATE: A REPUBLIC OR *VELAYAT-E FAGHIH?* 205

Conclusions 225

Postscript 229

Notes 233

Bibliography 263

Index 267

Acknowledgments

The idea of writing this book was conceived after my1995 visit to Iran. I returned to the United States haunted by images of the pain, anxiety, and frustration of men and women who confronted and battled the state's cultural and political violence, rising prices, decline in the value of the national currency, and deteriorating standard of living. I had a story to tell—the story of wage earners working multiple jobs to survive, men and women selling their body organs to feed their children, and youths facing beating and imprisonment by the state's moral police and the security force.

My book is dedicated to the ordinary people, the heroes of everyday life. It is they who inspired me and gave me the zeal and energy to be the narrator of their stories of sorrow and happiness, tears and laughter, and their hopes for a better tomorrow. They taught me perseverance and patience in combating the pains of everyday life, compassion amidst poverty, and living with hope for a brighter tomorrow. They made this book possible.

I benefited from the help and friendship of many individuals in Iran. To protect them from possible actions by the Islamic Republic, I decline to name those who gave me valuable moral support, taught me with their insight and their sober approach to social and political change in Iran, helped me find needed information for my book, and remained my loyal friends. I am indebted to those who lived with me through moments of fear and anxiety, and shared with me the joy of seeing change in the making. I thank them for their contribution to this project.

A variety of people in the United Sates contributed to my thoughts about different issues raised in the book. Many friends among the Iranian expatriate community helped the articulation of my ideas through their critique and discussions of the issues. I am indebted to them for their support. Special thanks are due to Diana Alspach of the Schools of Social Science and Human Services of Ramapo College of New Jersey for her friendship, support, and her fantastic sense of humor. Her steady flow of e-mails helped me retain my contact with the world outside the madness of everyday life in Iran. Her words of encouragement helped me pursue my project, and her brilliant stories made me laugh when laughter was all but forgotten. I owe a great deal to Christopher Madden, a highly promising young journalist and a committed advocate of people's rights, for his meticulous reading of the entire manuscript and his insightful substantive comments and editorial assistance. Christopher's comments and our ongoing dialogue about Iran and other world issues helped the articulation and presentation of the ideas in the book. I am also indebted to Peter Scheckner for his very constructive suggestions and guidance for revising the original manuscript. Many thanks to Jennifer Holland, Charlie Part, and Mark Mikhael for reading the work in progress and for their enthusiastic support.

Finally I would like to thank the editors, reviewers, and staff of the SUNY Press for making this project possible.

Preface

July 20, 1999—The "Web Station," Paphos, Cyprus. Cafes, bars, the Mediterranean breeze, and a fine cup of French coffee: I am free.

Staring at the computer screen, I am sunk in haunting images of fear, despair, and lost hope: bearded men in slippers swinging their clubs on young dreamers; soldiers shooting at the chanting crowd; buses set afire; buildings burnt to the ground; bearded men in slippers roaming in the town. This was the time of revenge, payback time, paying back for two years of dreaming of a better world.

July 19, 1999—The day of fear, the fear that kills, penetrates the deepest part of one's soul. I left the city of fear. Frightened, alienated, I waited for my departure in Tehran International Airport. Will the plane take off? Will I ever be free? Hours of deadly fear, I imagined bearded men in slippers, prison bars, angry laughter of the victors. Will I ever be free?

I left in fear. Alone, I carried with me memories of one year of living in fear, anxiety, and joy. I loved. I feared. I hoped. I dreamed. I laughed. I lived. I took all of my memories with me. The plane took off. I breathed deeply.

Now miles away from the land of bearded men in slippers, a fine cup of French coffee, British tourist playing computer games: I am in the "Web Station." The mesmerizing blue sky and the Mediterranean Sea, I remember the week of death, the week that will be remembered, the week that will not die.

I remember the faces of anxiety, the seventeen-year-old who was hit in the head by the bearded man's club. She died not being embraced by her loving mother, but alone in the hospital watched by bearded men in slippers. She did not feel the soothing hands of her father. She died in fear. The bearded men in slippers laughed in joy.

I remember. I have a story to tell.

Behzad Yaghmaian
July 20, 1999

One day
I shall come
And I shall bring
a message
. . .
I shall come giving
lilacs to beggars.
. . .
On the bridge there is a little girl
without legs
I shall hang Big Dipper around her neck.
. . .
I shall tie a knot—our eyes with the sun,
hearts with love, shadows
with water, branches with wind.
. . .
I shall launch kites into the air.
I shall water the flowerpots.
. . .
I shall come:
on the top of every wall
I shall plant a carnation;
at the foot of every window
I shall recite a poem;
. . .
I shall reconcile;
. . .
I shall walk;
I shall drink light;
I shall love.

—Sohrab Spehri

INTRODUCTION

Iran:
An Eyewitness Account
and Study of Social Change

There are times in a people's history when everyday interactions leave a profound mark on society, events unfold with remarkable intensity and speed, all that is sacred melts in the air and becomes transparent; old taboos disappear, questioning becomes a social norm, ordinary people become active agents of social change. There are times when social pains reach an unbearable scope, individual sorrows become collective tragedy, personal narratives weave closely into a ballad of social drama, and the lives of dissimilar citizens tell common tales of struggle, fear, and pain. There are times when old foundations break down, and the battle cry for the new awakens the earth, volcanoes erupt, heavy rain falls, the earth breathes, and new life germinates.

After four short visits since 1995, I traveled to Iran in Spring 1998 for a visit that would last more than one year. It was the time of change, the time of new movements: clapping hands, smiling faces, women moving back their scarves in public and loudly proclaiming their presence, demanding the right to live, to be happy, to breathe freely. It was the year of dancing in the streets before the eyes of astonished men with guns, the year of students marching for rights, the year of dissent, challenging, thinking, and living differently. It was the year people read newspapers with joy.

It was a year of angry sermons, violence, and terror against intellectuals, of a cable tightened around the neck of a good writer and poet. It was a year of writers dying for freedom. "The writer must carry the burden of two great responsibilities. . . . Serving the truth. And serving freedom," said Mohammad Ja'far Pouyandeh in his last published interview before being savagely killed by saviors of the old and enemies of freedom.

It was the year when a young candidate for Tehran's City Council wrote the words of Sohrab Sepehri on his poster.

> Eyes must be washed
> A different way we must see
> Umbrellas must be closed
> Under the rain we must go
> Under the rain we must take our thoughts, and memory
>
> One day
> I shall come
> And I shall bring
> a message
> I shall come giving
>   lilacs to beggars.
> I shall come.
> I shall give a lilac to the beggar.
> . . .
> I shall love.

Social Change in Iran is primarily based on a narrative of everyday life—stories of everyday people in their battle for survival, tales of young men and women fighting for happiness, and the words of those most deeply carrying the burden of twenty years of an untold tragedy. It is a study of the lives of everyday people, their battles for survival, their pains and hopes—the story of wage earners, students, and young people, and the momentum for change they are creating, the new images they are building. It focuses on the analysis of the citizens of Iran and their collective behavior. It is a narrative of diverse sites of resistance and collective action for change, methods of coping with crisis, and survival mechanisms used in everyday life, focusing on the emergence of new social movements and the players who are implementing social change in Iran. Movements are conceptualized and explained by the telling stories of real people weaving a complex net of interrelated economic, political, and social processes in the everyday. It is an attempt to inquire into the dynamics of social change through the mediation of real-life processes and interactions.

Social Change in Iran is also an analysis of the struggles for power, and the competing factions of the state and their battles for domination, new debates, the surfacing of hidden and latent tensions, emerging conflicts and warfare. It is a social inquiry into the root causes of recent developments in Iran. Though it does not attempt to project the future, the social analysis and pathology of recent developments will lay a foundation for a better understanding of the possibilities and potential of the current sociopolitical intercourse. This is a study and an eyewitness account of social change in Iran.

Chapter 1 is an introduction to the political crisis of the Islamic state, emerging social movements, and victories and setbacks in the battle for democracy and rights in Iran. The chapter is an overview of a new Iran in the making, its actors and players, and its potential.

Chapter 2 is a narrative of state violence against the citizens. It is a story of ordinary people assaulted by multiple forms of violence, a ballad of people living in constant fear, anxiety, and despair. Chapter 2 is a tale of people's vulnerability and the trauma of living under the perpetual fear of being violated by the state and its agents of terror. It is an inquiry into the everyday face of violence in the Islamic Republic—life under the penetrating eyes of the bearded men in slippers, citizens questioning their own innocence, taking shelter in the loneliness of an alienating life under terror.

Chapters 3, 4, and 5 are studies and eyewitness accounts of the youth movement, the defiance of the state by the children of the Islamic Republic, the emergence of a powerful movement for rights, and the revolt of youth against the violence of the state. Having experienced twenty years of social, cultural, and political violence, the children of the Islamic Republic are creating a growing movement for tolerance, pluralism, and the right to live a free life. They are defeating the basic tenets of the Islamic state.

Chapter 3 provides a narrative of the development of an emerging new social movement against the state and its violence. The chapter demonstrates how twenty years of multilayered violence has led to the development of a movement whose central tenet is the right to joy, the right to live with happiness. Through a narrative of everyday life, the chapter demonstrates the development of a grassroots and unorganized movement of ordinary people in defiance of the state's violation of joy and its twenty years of concerted effort to institutionalize "anti-happiness."

A movement for the right to live with joy is emerging as a powerful engine of change in Iran. Using happiness as a weapon, a new politics of deviance is threatening the Islamic Republic.

Chapters 4 and 5 are the narratives of the student movement and the emergence of a new independent movement against the state. Chapter 4 studies the development and evolution of the state-sponsored student movement in the past twenty years. It is a narrative of the ideological and political evolution of official student organizations, their relationship with the state, and their class composition. The chapter begins with a discussion of the composition and dynamics of the student movement in the last years of the Shah's reign and during the 1979 revolution. It focuses on the transformation and development of the *Daftar-e Tahkim-e Vahdat* (Unity Consolidation Office) and The Union of the Islamic Associations of Students and Alumni, and their passage from supporters of state dictatorship to advocates of civil society.

Chapter 5 is a study of what I have called the "new student movement," the movement that created the student uprising of July 1999. Here, too, the dynamics of the movement is explored through a narrative, the narrative of young men and women on a journey of defiance, a journey for change, rights, and joy.

Chapter 5 is an inquiry into the process that led to the events of July 8–14, 1999, and the creation of the new student movement, a movement of young men and women with no political history, ideology, or affiliation.

Soldiers of the new student movement—the children of the Islamic Republic—are a force whose mere existence proclaims loudly the defeat of the Islamic Republic. Dressed in modern Western outfits, reading Pablo Neruda and Milan Kundera, drinking homemade alcohol, escaping the pressures of the state with the music of Pink Floyd and Guns and Roses—they are the children of MTV, satellite dishes, Hollywood movies, the Internet, and e-mail. They are the fearless children of the Islamic Republic. Having no fear of beatings or lashes, no fear of the Security Force, no fear of confinement, they are the children of twenty years of ideological violence and terror.

Chapter 6 is a study of the movement for a critical and independent press, and the importance of the press in the development of civil society in Iran. In the absence of political parties and other institutions of civil society, a critical press articulates the silenced voices of other social agents and those who seek to create the institutions of their collective voice. The critical press is the voice of the civil society in the making.

Chapter 6 studies the role and importance of free press in the battle for civil society since the election of Mohammad Khatami.

Chapter 7 focuses on the tenuous state-wage earner relationship and the forms and depth of citizens' private and collective actions in response to economic catastrophe. Through a narrative of everyday life, the chapter inquires into wage earners' internalization of economic violence in the absence of civil society. Studying ordinary people in their everyday battles, the chapter describes wage earners' various forms of private and collective action, their struggle for survival, and the potential effects of collective dissent and confrontation with the state. Chapter 7 is a study of the potential for the emergence of an independent labor movement—a movement based on economic and political demands. It weaves through different sites of private and collective action by wage earners and inquires into the possibility of transforming the movement for civil society into a wage earners' social movement for justice and equity.

Following the narrative of wage earners' response to the economic consequences of neoliberalism, chapter 8 focuses on the evolution of economic policy and the transformation of the Islamic Republic's earlier populism to its embracing of the basic premises of the neoliberal paradigm. The chapter studies the impact of the state's political divisions on economic policy formation and the potential for the formulation of a coherent policy to resolve the crisis of the Iranian economy.

Chapter 9 is a study and analysis of the current crisis of the Iranian economy. It identifies Iran's position in the international division of labor and the long-term structural causes of its current economic crisis. Studying the historical process of the globalization of economic activity, the role of oil in Iran's economic structure, and factional competition for economic policy formation, the chapter presents a political economy analysis and projection of future developments in the Iranian economy. It provides a theoretical framework for the eyewitness accounts and narratives of wage earners' battles for survival, and examines the potential for their collective confrontation with the state.

Chapter 10 is a journey into "the great debate" in Iran. It is an inquiry into the constitutional debate about the "republic" and *velayat-e faghih,* and a study of the emergence of new "religious intelligentsia" and the movement for religious pluralism and reform from within the ranks of the original architects of the Islamic Republic. The chapter is based on a textual reading and analysis of the constitutional debates around the *faghih,* and the writings of religious reformers, the philosopher Abdolkarim Soroush, the clergymen Mohsen Kadivar, Mohammad Mojtahed Shabestari, and others within the ranks of the established clergy. Chapter 10 lays out the foundation for understanding the widening of the state's political divide and the emergence of the movement for religious reform. It is a study of the ideological crisis of the Islamic state, its loss of legitimacy within its own ranks, and its inability to enforce the ideological premises upon which it was built two decades earlier. The book's concluding remarks follow chapter 10.

CHAPTER ONE

Emerging Social Movements, Victories, and Setbacks in the Battle for Rights

---

Iran is experiencing one of the most dynamic periods of its recent history. Change is occurring in all spheres of life. A powerful movement for reform has emerged. Tired of the old order, seeking a free life, energized by the new discourse of change, ordinary people have broken their silence, joined together by the millions, and created a formidable challenge to the Islamic state. Defying the suffocating behavioral demands of political Islam, they seek the privatization of religion through their bold everyday actions. They demand freedom from religious codes of conduct, repression of thoughts, and limitation of individual rights.

Alongside the grassroots movement for reform, a group within the state has questioned the Islamic Republic's past, its place in the world, and its road ahead. An official movement for reform has emerged within the Islamic state. Finding the earlier project of the Islamic Republic incompatible with the dominant global politico-economic and cultural/technological imperative, a group from within the state has called for abandoning the old order, and embracing a new Islamic state imbedded in the rational synthesis of modernity and tradition. Facing a population hostile to strict Islamic cultural values and a world increasingly shaped by the new technological and information revolution, they seek the modernization of Iran's economic and political structures and the adaptation of the Islamic Republic to the new order. They call for the restructuring of the relationship between religion and the state, and the rationalization of the role of Islam in society.[1]

The official movement for reform is struggling to create a new Islamic Republic—a democratic Islamic state. They seek the building of an Islamic state with a human face—a new Islamic Republic accepted by youth, disempowered women, and citizens tired of two decades of religious monitoring of the most private aspects of their lives. The movement for reform is penetrating the inner soul of Iranian society, becoming institutionalized, changing the dominant political culture, and making a lasting imprint. Perceptions are changing. A sense of empowerment is emerging. Restricted by the entrenched power of the supporters of the old order, attacked and slowed down by the limitations of the official movement, reform is nevertheless taking place. Young people, the urban poor, struggling wage earners, men and women are pushing the limits of the official movement for reform, testing the commitment of the old architects of the Islamic state to the project of reform.

The project of creating a society based on Islamic values and codes of conduct is being challenged by the children of the Islamic Republic, youths with no memory of the old cultural paradigm, the generation born and raised under the Islamic state. Two decades of violent enforcement of Islamic values have led to the emergence of a powerful grassroots movement for the right to live a free life. All attempts to isolate Iranian youth from the increasing flow of global information have failed. A generation of young Iranians is emerging under the influence of the globally dominant youth culture. The Islamic state is most seriously challenged by its own creation—the children of the Islamic Republic. Cultural "deviance" is becoming a norm. All that was condemned, scorned, and banned is becoming dominant. The cultural project of the Islamic state is defeated. It is becoming history.

Politically, the theocracy is being weakened from within. Its own architects are questioning its viability in a modern world. It is a system, in the view of some within the state, unfit to fulfill the requirements of a state in a modern society. The system is archaic. It leads to stagnation and demise. It has to be reformed. The early antagonism to the West and the East must be replaced with the "dialogue of civilizations." Isolationism is being abandoned for coexistence, pluralism in international relations. Angry faces and words are being replaced with smiling faces and a plea for dialogue. Burning the U.S. flag is scorned and repudiated by those who occupied the U.S. embassy in 1980.

THE 1997 PRESIDENTIAL ELECTION— A NEW CHAPTER IN THE LIFE OF THE ISLAMIC REPUBLIC

On May 23, 1997, more than twenty million Iranians poured into the voting stations and defeated Mohammad Nategh-Nouri, the presidential candidate of Iran's "supreme leader," Ayatollah Khamenei, and the dominant political circles within the state. The unprecedented victory of Mohammad Khatami in the 1997 presidential election was the result of a spontaneous and grassroots effort by ordinary people who defied all expected behavior, organizing a most energetic and vibrant campaign after eighteen years of apathy and hopelessness. The election created a new sense of activism, hope, and trust in the power of ordinary people to change the existing order. It replaced the fear and hopelessness of the past with courage and enthusiasm about the future.

Mohammad Khatami's electoral victory was the result of an informal coalition that included millions of women, youths, intellectuals, journalists, writers, artists, clergy, technocrats, and members of the propertied classes, as well as a broad spectrum of individuals advocating some notion of democracy and justice. Despite their different political, economic, and ideological perspectives, diverse and antagonistic social forces and classes united around Khatami's platform. They voted for the creation of a civil society and a government of law, freedom of association and political parties, citizens' right to the privacy of their own space, protection against widespread lawlessness and the violence of the police and armed gangs.

The presidential election was a revolt from below and an open outcry against the institutionalization of people's disempowerment. The defeat of Mohammad Nategh-Nouri was a profound challenge to the political structure set up by the Islamic Republic. It reflected ordinary people's defiance and rejection of the *faghih*—the supreme leader—a quiet revolt against an institution that, situated above all branches of the state, had the power to issue enforceable decrees, nullify legislated law, and act as the commander in chief. The vote against Mohammad Nategh-Nouri proved the people's open opposition to this most sacred institution of the Islamic Republic. May 23, 1997, was a vote for the "republic" and against the *velayat-e faghih* (Supreme Islamic Jurisconsult), a public protest against all that was sacred in the Islamic Republic.

The election was a peaceful referendum against the political, social, and cultural system set up by the Islamic Republic. It was a vote of no confidence for the system's central tenet through the rejection of Mohammad Nategh-Nouri, his candidate of choice. The vote for Khatami was, indeed, a vote against Mohammad Nategh-Nouri, and a vote against the supreme leader.

The presidential election on May 23, 1997, was a quiet revolution for rights on the part of the ordinary people. It was a revolt against eighteen years of violence, of random attacks on youths and women by bands of bearded men armed with clubs and knives, of teenage boys and girls randomly rounded up and detained without reason, and of frightened mothers in search of their missing children.

The presidential election of May 23, 1997, was the beginning of a popular call for rights and the rule of law. The youths' and citizens' latent protest against the *faghih* and the Islamic Republic became a classic street riot later in July 1999. Protest through voting escalated into an open war between young people, on the one hand, and the *faghih* and his loyalists, on the other hand. The events of July 1999 were a warning to the Islamic state that, for the children of the Islamic Republic, voting stations were only the first step on the road to achieving their demands. The children of the Islamic Republic, who had no memory of the 1979 revolution, were prepared to reproduce that experience, this time against the Islamic Republic.

While capturing the imagination of youth and energizing a large section of the population, the 1997 election was also a sign of spreading fractures within the Islamic Republic and the political divide among social forces and groups that shared power for nearly two decades. The victory of Mohammad Khatami and the emergence of a movement for reform from within the state brought into the open the Islamic Republic's political divide. Factional battles were waged using legal and extralegal methods, force and brutality. A crisis emerged. A seemingly united state was splintered into fighting factions, each accusing the others of "betraying Islam," and "weakening the revolution." Twenty years after its victory, the Islamic Republic was shaken by a battle from within. Established practices and policies were questioned. A new future was mapped out. The old and new stood in a haunting competition for control of the Islamic Republic. The competition for hegemony reached a scope and dimension observed only in the formative years of the Islamic Republic.

The election was a struggle fought over different interpretations of the constitution, the institution of the *faghih,* and the republic. While Mohammad Nategh-Nouri and others called for the creation of a Society of Islamic Justice, ruled entirely by the *faghih* and the clergy, others rallied behind Khatami's campaign for a civil society and the strengthening of the republic. Mohammad Khatami's campaign was a call for a rationalized bourgeois civil society within the premises of the Islamic Republic. The support for Mohammad Khatami and his platform by politically powerful and influential groups and individuals reflected a questioning of existing political and social structures and practices from above. It reflected the resurfacing of the power divide relating to the nature of the Islamic Republic, its position within the world community, its future, and its methods of survival. The election was an open manifestation of different paths perceived by the architects of the Islamic Republic about its future—the end of oneness and a crisis from above.

The 1997 election heightened the questioning of the past by those loyal to the Islamic Republic. Tensions rose higher in the following months. Defiant public statements appeared, and old loyalists questioned the Islamic Republic, demanding reform—a demand for change by the architects of the Islamic Republic. "We cannot proceed in the new world by having two or three people making decisions for the country. 'Republic' means the government of the people. . . . We have the *'velayat-e faghih'* mentioned in our constitution. But this does not mean that he runs everything," said Ayatollah Montazeri, who had been instrumental in installing the concept of the *faghih* in the constitution, a powerful clergyman once appointed by the late Ayatollah Khomeini as his heir.

Ayatollah Montazeri's anti-*faghih* sermon was a lecture delivered to a group of seminary students in the city of Qom. The complete tape of the lecture was leaked out and its contents appeared in the press. Violence erupted in Qom. Montazeri's residence was ransacked on November 19, 1997, and his house was seized by a mob of hundreds as the "seizure of the second spy net in the hands of the *Hezbollah*."[2] For days following the attack in Qom, the nation witnessed the outpouring of statements, public proclamations, interviews, and press articles by leading figures of the Islamic Republic about the role and importance of *velayat*-e *faghih*. But the outpouring of supportive statements and harsh words against the opponents of *velayat*-e *faghih* itself was a reflection of a need to defend publicly an institution that was once beyond questioning and did not require a defense in the public arena. It reflected the emergence of a new reality and the need to rally forces to save and fortify a pillar of the Islamic Republic. In the eyes of the public, this was a sign of the weakening of the system. Thus, the challenge would continue throughout the months to come.[3] The state's political divide widened. Challenges to the *faghih* led eventually to the public rejection of the official narrative of the revolution by the loyalists and pillars of the Islamic Republic.

"With the victory of the revolution, four currents wished to gain hegemony in the process of building a new system: the traditionalist clergy, modernist-Islamic left, liberals, and the Marxists. Among them, the clergy and their traditionalist allies gained control. . . . They created a totalitarian system through a comprehensive control . . . of all political, ethical, social, and economic matters. The sphere of private life too, to a large extent, became under the supervision of state agents. . . . Freedom of thoughts was officially banned. . . . The state control of peoples' thoughts and lives expanded even to their homes."[4] This was a narrative of the revolution by Habibollah Payman, general secretary of the Movement of Militant Moslems, member of the Council of Revolution after the victory of the Islamic Republic, and a trusted loyalist of the new system. This was a narrative on the twentieth anniversary of the Islamic Republic!

The challenge to the existing order continued in the days of the state's celebration of its twentieth anniversary. "We have been successful in eliminating the surface of monarchy. But . . . we recreated old relations in new forms. . . . We now have an Islamic monarchy," said Mohsen Kadivar, a theological researcher and devotee of the Islamic Revolution, who was tried and jailed for his unofficial reading of the past twenty years, charged with "propaganda against the system," and "weakening the Islamic Republic."[5]

In the days of the celebration of its birth, the devotees of the Islamic Republic charged the state with preserving the old relations in new forms and creating an Islamic monarchy. Judging freedom by "the degree to which those who oppose the state . . . can participate in society and speak their mind," Kadivar rejected the official claims about the freedom of citizens in Iran. "Without these two years [of Khatami's presidency], it can be said that we have not had a passing grade on freedom in the past two decades," declared Kadivar.[6]

MOHAMMAD KHATAMI AND THE MOVEMENT FOR RIGHTS AND CIVIL SOCIETY—TENSIONS AND CONTRADICTIONS

The 1997 presidential election was a turning point in the battle for rights. Despite the victory of Khatami, a severe struggle remained between the coalition for rights and those defeated in the election. A period of intense confrontation was underway.

The coalition for reform faced formidable political challenges from within the state. The presidential victory of Mohammad Khatami proved to be only the beginning of a long and bumpy road to reform. The *faghih* and his supporters had fortified their position of power in various institutions of the state, further reducing the power of the elected president and weakening the republic. The regular armed forces, the Islamic Revolutionary Guards *(Pasdaran)*, and the security force remained under the control of the *faghih*. The judiciary was left under control of the *faghih* and his loyal forces. Mohammad Nategh-Nouri remained Speaker of Parliament (the *Majlis*) while the antireform members of Parliament maintained a majority position. This did not change until February 2000.

The political division of the state and the entrenched opposition to reform by those in control of most organs of power led to open confrontations. Unable to regain their earlier social legitimacy and defeat the project of reform, the conservatives concentrated on creating social and political crises, and undermining the achievements of the young reform movement. Assassinating writers and intellectuals, jailing prominent journalists and shutting down the pro-reform press, and threatening the president with a coup d' êtat, the opponents of change attempted to create an atmosphere of terror, fear, and hopelessness among everyday people and within the reform movement.

The president's pro-reform interior minister, Abdollah Nouri, was impeached in the first year of Khatami's presidency. The reformist minister of Culture and the Islamic Guidance was condemned in Parliament for his lax attitude toward the press although an attempt by the conservative members of Parliament to impeach him failed. On numerous occasions, freedom of the press became subject to ideological and political assault. Journalists were persecuted and jailed. Abdollah Nouri was finally charged with anti-Islamic activities and convicted in a court system controlled by the conservatives. Nouri's pro-reform daily, *Khorad,* was shut down and he was sentenced to five years in jail.

The assault on the press became a centerpiece of the conservatives' challenge to the project of reform. Defeated and humiliated in the February 2000 parliamentary election, the conservatives waged a new, and seemingly final, campaign against the free press. Sanctioned and guided by the supreme leader, the Justice Department ordered the closing of all pro-reform dailies and journals in April and May of 2000. Prominent journalists and writers and advocates of reform and rights were jailed without trial. The assault on the press was regarded as the least costly and most efficient strategy to defeat the reform movement.

The April attack on the press was preceded by a series of maneuvers designed to create social chaos and pave the way for a coup d' êtat and intervention by the armed forces. "The children of *Ashoura* [the day Imam Hossein, the Shiites' third Imam, and seventy-one comrades were killed in a war in the desert of Karbala] are awaiting a grand and victorious Karbala. . . . The day of action might be near. We must await the final victory," wrote *Alsarat al Hossein,* the organ of *Ansar-e Hezbollah*. And Massoud Dehnamaki, the managing editor of the biweekly Shalamcheh said, "Iran will never become like Turkey. We will not allow our future to become like that of Pakistan and Turkey. Iran will become Lebanon and not Turkey if the situation worsens. We are talking here in codes. Today is no longer a day of silence for the *Hezbollah*. This is the *Hezbollah's* day of uprising. [Our] forces are ready to act behind barricades. Do not think the revolution is over."[7] Iran's elite Revolutionary Guards issued a warning to reformers and the reformist press a week before the last assault on the press. Attacking "those who defend American-style reforms in Iran," the *Pasdaran* threatened that "when the time comes, these people will feel a blow to the head delivered by the revolution."

Responding to the mounting assault against the press and the process of reform, Mohammad Khatami declared to the nation in a press conference in August 2000, "The president is responsible for implementing the constitution, but sometimes he does not possess the levers required to carry out his obligations."[8]

In addition to weathering the political assault by the conservatives, the future of reform also depended on the ability of the new government to deal successfully with Iran's endemic economic problems. Mohammad Khatami's coalition included both the well-to-do and millions of poor and economically disenfranchised Iranians, and his campaign revolved primarily around the issues of rights and building a civil society. Despite their persistence and significance in the lives of the majority of voters, inflation, unemployment, deterioration in the standard of living, and other economic problems were only marginally addressed by Khatami. The burning issue of privatization, the state's role in the economy, trade policy, and commitment to social justice were, by and large, excluded from the presidential campaign.

Regardless, the economy continued to suffer from many deep-rooted ills. The average residential rent in Tehran remained nearly twice the monthly salary of college graduates and the educated work force. Most wage and salary earners received incomes below the state-defined poverty line and were forced to hold two or three jobs to sustain the bare necessities of life. The gap between the poor and the rich continued to widen. Political and social repression, coupled with economic disenfranchisement, created an explosive situation in most corners of Iran.

A commentator wrote, nearly two years after the election: "How long can the desire and enthusiasm for a free and lawful society be a substitute for bread and jobs?"[9] This was, indeed, a fundamental question for Khatami and his coalition for building a civil society.

Mohammad Khatami's coalition in 1997 was supported by social groups with competing economic perspectives: advocates of free markets and laissez-faire, and those promoting the state regulation, planning, and control of the market. This, too, was to become an obstacle in formulating a cohesive and workable economic platform.

Khatami was supported by *Kargozaran-e Sazandegy* (Executives of Construction), led by Hashemi Rafsanjani, Iran's previous president. A loose collective of technocrats and clergy, *Kargozaran* had been, since 1989, responsible for the implementation of the structural adjustment policy in Iran. The group was an open advocate of privatization, a balanced budget, the dismantling of state subsidies, and the reduction of the state's role in the economy. By most accounts, the implementation of *Kargozaran*'s neoliberal policies was responsible for a massive shift of income and resources from the most vulnerable sections of society to the propertied classes and speculators.

Mohammad Khatami's coalition benefited from the selfless participation of millions of unorganized wage earners that, despite their deteriorating and insecure economic status, energetically supported his presidency on the basis of his political and social platform. They were, for the most part, victims of the neoliberal policies of Hashemi Rafsanjani and the *Kargozaran*.

In addition to the advocates of neoliberalism, Mohammad Khatami's coalition included the clergy, Islamic organizations, and individuals with views diametrically opposed to those of the *Kargozaran*. The coalition included Behzad Nabavi (the left-wing minister of industry during the war with Iraq) and many other influential members of the Organization of Mojahedeen of the Islamic Revolution. It enjoyed the support of Mir Hossein Moosavi (prime minister and architect of a quasi welfare state before the presidency of Hashemi Rafsanjani), and the participation of the Collective of Militant Clergy, and as well as opponents of the neoliberal policies of the Rafsanjani administration. Unlike the *Kargozaran,* these groups supported and advocated state regulation of the foreign exchange market and international trade, commitment to "social justice," and the creation of a blend of a Keynesian/welfare state in Iran. Mohammad Khatami thus inherited both an ailing economy and a divided coalition, and it was this coalition that Khatami put in charge of managing and resolving the economy's endemic crisis.

But the mounting political and economic problems did not halt the process of change that had begun in 1997. The demand for reform continued despite difficulties and setbacks. The crack in the Islamic Republic could not be closed. Twenty years after its birth, the Islamic state was experiencing its slow demise.

NEW MOVEMENTS FOR SOCIAL CHANGE—ORDINARY PEOPLE DEFYING THE ISLAMIC STATE

Social Movements in the Making

The May 23, 1997, presidential election resulted in the surprising defeat of Mohammad Nategh-Nouri, the candidate supported by the Ayatollah Khamenei—the *faghih* (supreme leader)—and the dominant political circles around him. What caught many observers' attention in those early days after the election was a deep and genuine feeling of victory and joy, the joy of having achieved the seemingly unachievable: a new nation in the making, a new people, a nation of those believing in their own power. This was a nation of citizens on the path of defiance. May 23, 1997, was the first moment of universal defiance in nearly two decades, defiance that took on new forms and magnitude in the days to come, each time creating a more remarkable manifestation of resilience, creativity, and readiness to fight for change.

Such was the case on May 23, 1998. The anniversary of the presidential election became the day of an unprecedented event, the day of the emergence of a new image and a new face in the Islamic Republic of Iran—the face of young men and women joyfully defying the codes of conduct of the Islamic Republic. May 23, 1998, was the day thousands of young men and women demanded the right to live a free life, to be happy, and to be beautiful. This was the day thousands of well-dressed, clean, happy, vibrant, and indeed beautiful young men and women assembled at Tehran University to celebrate the first anniversary of the Khatami presidency. May 23, 1998, was the magnificent assembly of the face of joy, life, and defiance—faces of those who dared to clap their hands together, scream aloud in happiness, whistle instead of crying *Allah-o Akbar* (God is great), and laugh instead of angrily chanting "Death to America." This was May 23, 1998.

The youths that had made possible the defeat of Mohammad Nategh-Nouri a year earlier now created a new volcano—the volcano of young men and women clapping their hands, smiling, and enjoying their defiant existence. This was the rupture of joy and defiance, a revolt for happiness by the children of the Islamic Republic—men and women who clapped to defy. Happiness—this was a new weapon used by the children of the Islamic Republic: beautiful and creative, defying the bearded men in slippers, creating a theater of joy. May 23, 1998, was the official inauguration of a new social movement—the social movement for joy!

A new reality was emerging—a reality created by women, the immediate targets of control and subjugation in the Islamic Republic. Brave, creative, and persistent, women played an instrumental role in the creation of the movement for joy, collective action for rights, and the transformation of their reality. Not confined to narrowly defined institutional forms, they created a profound movement for women's rights through their everyday practices. They fought for the right to live freely, equal to men. Challenging the Islamic dress code, they used everyday life as the site for gaining rights and respect from the society and the state. They demanded the right to live as free women. Humiliated, assaulted, and arrested randomly for being women, they gained resilience, lost their fears of confronting the state, and battled the repressive social and cultural Islamic codes of conduct. Using deviance as a weapon, they created a reality unimagined by the architects and masters of the Islamic Republic. Unorganized and not trained in political ideology or theory, but led by an instinct for freedom, young women created a powerful collective resistance through private acts of deviance and defiance, proving to be a force undefeatable by the Islamic State.

They waged legal battles to change the status of women in society, established a press dedicated to women's issues and problems, took part in direct street actions fighting the hooligans and the state police, and used the ballot to defeat the Islamic state. They moved to the forefront of collective action for rights, created a new image of women and a reality most feared by the Islamic republic, and formed a women's movement not confined to traditionally experienced forms and institutions. Not limited to activists and vocal advocates of women's rights, their movement included all women engaged in the battles of everyday life. It embraced schoolgirls challenging and ridiculing their religious teachers, teenagers wearing loud lipstick and makeup under the watchful eyes of the moral police, and older women demanding respect and recognition from men in the streets, shops, and the workplace. It became undefeatable. A return to the past seemed impossible in 1998.

The year 1998 was also the beginning of another movement that grew in power and became a formidable force, a force unprecedented in the recent history of Iran—the movement for a critical press, a movement inaugurated by the birth of *Jame'eh* (Society), "the newspaper of civil society." In a few weeks *Jame'eh,* a paper founded by old devotees of the Islamic Republic, became the symbol of new thinking and the demise of the old from within. It was a sign of the death of the old and the birth of the new—a critical press. This was a movement for political and social reform in the absence of political parties and other institutions of civil society.

The publication of *Jame'eh* was soon followed by *Rah-e No* (New Path), *Azadi* (Freedom), *Tavana* (Powerful), and others who dared to challenge the old and demand a new order. New papers and magazines surfaced everyday, and the existing press became more courageous. Colorful magazines and papers for youths, teenagers, women, and elderly people decorated the public displays of newsstands.

This was the birth of a new movement, leading to a fierce counterattack by the pillars of the old, entrenched institutions of the Islamic Republic. A new space was created: a fragile space whose boundaries were constantly pushed beyond its original limits, opening opportunities for the voices of the "other." The state was challenged. Authorities were publicly questioned. Taboos were broken. The untold stories were told. And the unquestionable was questioned.

A specter was haunting the old structure—the specter of critical press. A war was thus waged against the newly born free press. The press was assaulted, papers were shut down, and journalists and writers were imprisoned. Free press became the leading front in the battle for rights.

The year 1998 was also the year of new discourse, the emergence of new concepts, and the generalization of language that had once belonged to small circles of intellectuals and the educated. This was the year when "pluralism," "diversity," "respect for others," and "tolerance" became a part of the everyday language, and an image of postmodernity penetrated the inner soul of premodern Iranian politics and social debate. Diversity was desired rather than scorned. Difference was colorful and a sign of social health.

A postmodern discourse surfaced in the press, in political and intellectual circles, and in society. Those who had supported the destruction of pluralism during the early years of the revolution now campaigned for tolerance of others. Soldiers of intolerance became crusaders for pluralism and diversity. "Political development" substituted for "economic development," and democracy and freedom of expression, association, and participation became the new buzzwords of the development discourse. The year 1998 saw the familiarization of unfamiliar words, cracks in old structures, unexpected ruptures, and new voices of discontent.

The year 1998 was the year of new movements in the making. It was the year of the erosion of the old, the birth of the new, the citizens' rising courage to defy and question the unquestionable. The year of intensified battles within the state. The year when old alliances were changed, new alliances emerged, and the elected government became the "legal opposition." This was the year of rising tensions and conflicts, the deepening of the fracture within the state, defiance from below, new hopes, old disappointments, retreats, and progress.

The Student Uprising of July 1999—A Voyage from the Voting Stations to Street Action

The selfless participation of youth, women, and many other sections of Iranian society who used ballots and conventional democratic means to voice their opposition to the existing order achieved the presidential victory of Mohammad Khatami. The election proved the political maturity of the people and their readiness to use the limited available democratic institutions in defeating the ruling theocracy and moving toward a free and more democratic society. It echoed the people's hunger for democracy, their flexibility, creativity, discipline, and the magnificent power to organize one of the most energetic and grassroots political campaigns in the recent history of Iran. That was May 1997.

In July 1999, seeking freedom of expression and the press, respect, and the right to live a free life, the students and their supporters poured into the streets, turned their energy into nationwide street actions, and demanded an end to the rule of the *faghih*. They left the voting stations for the streets. Their fists in the air, chanting defiant words, marching for rights, they demanded an end to the old order. They voted with their feet.

Between July 8 and 14, 1999, six months after the official celebration of the twentieth anniversary of the Islamic Republic, tens of thousands of jubilant and defiant youths poured into the streets in more than twenty-one cities and gave birth to a phenomenon that shook the foundations of the Islamic Republic. The state's most sacred institution, the *faghih,* was challenged and discredited as the students shouted, "Death to the dictator." The unquestionable was questioned. All taboos were broken. The Islamic Republic's growing crisis of legitimacy was brought into the open. The system lost all vestiges of its legitimacy through street protests by the youth, the children of the Islamic Republic.

The student protest in July 1999 was the first open explosion of the children of the Islamic Republic against the state and all that it represented. It was a loud cry for change by those who were no longer willing to succumb—a social rupture and a revolt by those who, nearly two years earlier, in a peaceful theater of defiance, had made possible the victory of Mohammad Khatami in his bid for the presidency of Iran. The youths had made history, and achieved the unachievable. Now, in July 1999, they were out on the streets with masks covering their faces, and with fists in the air demanding an end to dictatorship and the removal of the *velayat-e faghih*. They demanded the realization of their hopes and aspirations and the promises of the election held on May 23, 1997.

July 1999 was the time for collection, a declaration of existence—the existence of a growing independent movement, independent from the state and all its factions, an independent movement for rights—the right to live a free life.

The July uprising was put down by the use of unprecedented force and violence. More than two thousand students were jailed. Some received long prison sentences. Three were sentenced to death. But, despite the violent clampdown, a new era began in July 1999. The leader's ouster was demanded in the streets of Tehran.

A Return to the Voting Stations: The Parliamentary Election of February 2000

May 23, 1997, was the inauguration of the new movement for reform in Iran—a revolt at the voting stations. It weakened the Islamic state, fractured its structure, questioned its legitimacy, defied its mandates, and began the process of its demise. The parliamentary election of February 2000 was the second revolt at the voting stations, a damaging blow to the Islamic state, a loud rejection of the old order by the people in the young civil society of Iran. The election shattered the state's already weakened legitimacy and humiliated its leaders. It proclaimed aloud that their time was over, that they were the undesired past. The new Iran had passed them by.

The youths that created the July uprising returned to the voting stations in February 2000. Along with other men and women, old and young, they created an unprecedented political scene, surpassed the magnificence of the May 1997 presidential election, and defeated those who had maintained their power through terror and violence. The voters said no to the old guard and elected new faces to the parliament. The proponents of the new discourse of pluralism and rights chose women and the men in ties and Western suits and captured the parliament with ballots. They rejected the old structure and the images of the past. They shouted with their pens and their ballots. They were deviant.

The February parliamentary victory followed a period of intensive preparation for a determining battle. The violent clampdown on the student movement had created a temporary setback for the movement for rights. The hot summer of 1999 was a time of retreat by the battered student movement, proclamations of victory by the guardians of the old order, increased terror against the youths and ordinary people, and a temporary return of the feeling of despair. The opponents of reform seemed triumphant. They had defeated the street action—the collective voice of the youths outside the voting stations. They had tamed the pro-reform president, threatened him with a coup d' êtat.[10] The old guard was on the offensive.

But September began with unexpected results. The clampdown had not succeeded in silencing the new student movement. Protests against the imprisonment of comrades and further demands for rights emerged on campuses. And the assault continued.

The winter of 1999 was the winter of war between the old guard and the press. The critical press was attacked. The dailies *Neshat* and

Khordad were shut down. Abodollah Nouri, the license holder of *Khordad* was jailed. The press continued to expose the opponents of rights, assumed the leadership in the battle for the domination of Parliament, and prepared the public for the February election. It became the voice of the movement for reform.

January 2000 was the month of the final preparation for the voting stations. Writers, journalists, intellectuals, artists, and the leading reformers announced their candidacies for Parliament. They were all declared disqualified by the Guardian Council.

February 19, 2000, was a day of festivity, feeling empowered, collectivity, and triumph. The legislative branch was conquered through the mass turnout at the voting stations despite the disqualifying of pro-reform candidates, the jailing of popular and vocal reformers, and the shutting down of the pro-reform press. Young and old, men and women created a historic turnout at the voting stations across the nation. They forced out of the parliament prominent and powerful figures that had been entrenched in the state and its power structure. They ousted Javad Larijani, Mohhamad Reza Bahonar, Ali Zadsar, Ahmad Rasouli-Nejad, and other conservative politicians who symbolized the past, the years of pain and terror, the arrogance of the rulers, and the political and social system despised by the citizens.

They said no to those who represented the existing power structure, defeated Ali Akbar Hashemi Rafsanjani, the president of the Islamic Republic for eight years, the chair of the powerful Expediency Council of the Islamic Republic, and the third most powerful political figure in the nation. Supported by the old guard, Hashemi Rafsanjani joined the race hoping to capture the seat of Speaker of Parliament. Exposed by the press for creating a financial empire for himself and his family, distrusted by the voters, rejected for his role in the Islamic state, Hashemi Rafsanjani could barely hold on to thirtieth place in the voting in Tehran for thirty seats in the parliament. The voters said no to the *Sardar-e Sazandegi* (caesar of construction), the man behind the economics and politics of the second decade of the Islamic Republic. The vote of no confidence in Rafsanjani was a vote of no confidence in the Islamic state. It was a loud cry for a new Iran.

In July 1999, the youth demonstrated their alienation from the Islamic state and their desire for the establishment of a new order through defiant street actions. Their fists in the air and their faces disguised, they shouted for freedom, rights, and democracy. They made their mark.

With ballots in their hands and their faces undisguised, they ousted the leaders of the Islamic state in February 2000. They set the stage for the next triumph of rights.

Social Movements—"Old" and "New"

The years after 1997 were the years of a deepening economic crisis, the fall in the price of oil, decline in state revenues, rising prices, a continuous drop in the value of the national currency, and the increased impoverishment of wage earners. The economy was trapped in one of its most severe crises since the 1979 revolution. The dramatic drop in the price of oil had drastically cut Iran's primary source of foreign exchange from $11 billion in 1993 to $172 million at the beginning of 1998. The reserves were predicted to reach zero by the end of the year. The tumbling oil prices had left a suffocating impact on the economy (see chapters 8 and 9).

The year 1998 was the year of unpaid salaries and wages by factories, of bankruptcies, layoffs, frustration, and the loss of hope. This was the time of a near collapse of the economy and the potential for social crisis. It was a year when, according to the deputy finance minister, state employees earned an average monthly income of 48,000 tomans (480,000 rials), while average monthly expenditures of a family of four was estimated to be around 113,000 tomans (1,130,000 rials). And a total of 150,000 people, 400 of whom held bachelor's degrees, responded to an advertisement by the Ministry of Education for the hiring of 500 custodians.

Signs of the people's response to the declining economy were indeed emerging. Though still in formative stages, and not entirely outside the control of the state, collective actions around unpaid wages and labor rights increased in number in 1998 and 1999. Fueled by the deepening economic crisis, the sharp decline in wage earners' standard of living, the spread of poverty, and lack of rights at the point of production, struggles emerged with a focus on employee/employer relations and wage earners' share of output. Wage earners seemed to be on the road to questioning their economic status, challenging the state from the point of view of the economic interest of a singular class—the working class. Though not widespread or autonomous, early signs and nuclei of "old" social movements could be observed after 1997 (see Chapter 7).

But, apart from the issues of distribution and economic relations, youths and ordinary men and women created a formidable movement with demands that transcended the interest of a singular class and challenged the state's cultural mandate and its political power. Transclass movements seeking basic civil liberties and rights of "citizenship," based on non-class cultural identities emerged, and movements not associated with the idea of revolution, but with democracy and rights.[11] Mobilizing around a free press, freedom of expression, and the right to political participation, the citizens created parallel movements against the authoritarianism of the state. They fought for a new political and cultural reality, a new image of the citizens not framed by the Islamic Republic.

They gave rise to "new" social movements.[12] Shaped by the cultural and political deprivations of nearly two decades of life under the Islamic Republic, they created movements of deviance, embracing the scorned, desiring what was not to be desired, longing for the forbidden fruits of the life of "decadence," consumerism, and the Satanic West. They lustfully desired and demanded what the new social movements of Europe despised and organized against. And unlike in Europe "where the grand theory had seen social movements as responses to the secular process implicit in Habermas's account of the colonization of the lifeworld, namely the increasing commodification, bureaucratization, and massification," the deviant youth embraced the "colonization of the lifeworld." They desired and used all symbols of massification and commodification, and constructed powerful movements against the state. The Iranian youth created forms and sites of collective action unforeseen by the theorists of new social movements.

They dressed in the symbols of "Western decadence," clapped their hands, danced in public, looked jubilant and defiantly beautiful, demonstrated, voted in elections, and created colorful "repertoires of collective" action and contention.[13] By challenging the cultural mandates of the Islamic Republic in individual acts of defiance (such as looking non-Islamic), their everyday life became a site of public manifestation of youth's discontent. The battle for a new identity—the non-Islamic identity—was carried out boldly by individuals who defied the state-imposed culture and codes of conduct, and transformed the most mundane acts of everyday life into the building blocks of a new powerful movement. Individually, they transformed everyday life into a movement for rights. Together, they formed a new collective identity and made "sustained challenges to power holders . . . by means of repeated display of" their "worthiness, unity, number, and commitment."[14]

The following chapters are primarily based on an eyewitness account of the emerging "new" and "old" social movements in Iran. Social movements are explained through people's everyday practices and living histories, their thoughts, fears, and their "repertoires" for changing their realities. As accurately articulated by John Foran in his 1994 anthology about social movements in Iran, "We need to know more—much more—about the everyday lives of many classes and groups . . . their daily concerns, ways of thinking and feeling."[15] My book is a contribution to this project.

CHAPTER TWO

State and the Socialization of Violence: A Narrative of Everyday Life

---

SURVEILLANCE: A FIRST ENCOUNTER WITH THE ISLAMIC REPUBLIC

It was May 1995. Returning to Tehran after sixteen years, I anxiously awaited the flight to Iran at Vienna Airport in a corridor filled with well-dressed and Western-looking Iranian nationals.

The air was heavy. No one spoke. Everyone's face mirrored an intense sense of anxiety, confusion, and perhaps fear and distrust of others. Distrust! The first return home for many, the airport was an assembly of fear and alienation, filled by people anxiously anticipating the unknown.

The plane touched the ground. Tehran Airport, 2 A.M., May 9, 1995—a shift in landscape—Western outfits now hidden under the shapelessness of long baggy robes and black *chador,* lipstick and makeup wiped away and replaced with pale faces of fear. I was in a world of scarves, veils, long robes, blank faces, and women covered from head to toe. I did not recognize the woman sitting next to me on the plane. Welcome to the Islamic Republic of Iran!

Wall-long pictures of Ayatollah Khomeini, angry-looking armed guards, bearded men in slippers staring at frightened travelers, I was at Tehran International Airport.

Bearded men in slippers! They watched us with penetrating eyes: eyes of surveillance, sharp as a razor blade, cutting through the inner soul. Bearded men in slippers: the union of religion and state power—the embodiment of fear and social control. They were ready for a crusade.

Waiting nearly an hour on line, I finally reached the first passport control. A man with a short beard and the face of an interrogator, or perhaps an executioner numbed by the reality of his actions, entered my name in a computer. He did not smile. His head down, he handed me the passport. I proceeded with fear to the second passport control.

The second passport control: an angry-looking man searched for my name in an old book with a black cover, interrogating me with eyes that were as cold as ice. Every cell in my body seemed vulnerable to the suspicious eyes of a bearded man in slippers. I felt exposed, riddled with guilt for an uncommitted crime.

Engulfed in fear, I moved forward to the third passport control. Not a single person was smiling. No joy was seen on the faces of frightened travelers. A child cried. The man behind me dropped his handbag. A woman was commanded to pull forward her headscarf. A bearded man in a black shirt and slippers stared at the travelers with a face echoing hatred and suspicion. Fear on a young woman's face, innocent people doubting their innocence, this was Tehran International Airport in May 1995.

The final passport control at last. I declared my dollars, got my passport stamped, and began a journey into the familiar unknown.[1] I was free at last.

MOUNTAINS, FRESH AIR, AND THE PRESENCE OF FEAR

June 1995. I went for a refreshing visit to Darakeh, where century-old trees stood tall above smog and noise and the chaos of everyday life, a peaceful river carved its way through the quiet Mount Alborz, and humble-looking cafes ornamented the river. Bright neon lights breaking up the darkness of the night. Young boys and girls played joyfully and ate their berries and sweets, men and women sat on benches covered by hand-made *klims,* drinking tea and smoking from heavenly water pipes. I felt the sensation of joy and freedom, sipping my tea in Darakeh.

Darakeh! It was a beautiful, mild summer night in Darakeh. An old man stared at the sky, counting the stars with his grandson. The magnificent smell of kebab and barbecued corn in the air, the sound of water played a beautiful music to the ears of tired citizens of despair. The peaceful summer wind danced through the leaves, singing the songs of liberation from everyday life.

And there was a sudden end to tranquillity and peace, brought by the arrival of men with guns—the Security Force in patrol cars. I saw the return of the familiar faces of anxiety and fear.

"Time to leave," shouted an angry-looking man with a gun. Shutters came down. Lights went off. Grills were turned off. Benches were evacuated. The water pipes were put away.

"It's midnight. Time to leave. Hurry," shouted the man holding the automatic rifle in hand with his finger anxiously rubbing the trigger. Eighteen or younger, he demanded with authority, "Time to leave." Half asleep, children ran after their parents. "Time to leave!"

It was time to leave. We slowly drove toward the highway, waiting in a long line before the Chamran Expressway's entrance. Armed men screened every car at a roadblock, children asleep in back seats, a bright light from a flashlight traveled inside every car—a light dancing on hiding faces of fear and anxiety.

We were cleared. Free at last. We drove in fear and tears of anger. I kissed the beautiful face of my six-year-old nephew.

THE SECURITY FORCE

Summer of 1997. I left the security force building in fear. Slowly finding my way out of the room and the courtyard, I escaped the suspicious eyes of men roaming around with their automatic rifles. Not even noticed by the bearded man at the entrance, I was out, free.

Robbed by men on a motorcycle, I had gone for help to a local security force office—a four-story building, dirty, crowded, and noisy. Two bearded men in slippers guarded the door. A narrow hallway opened to the courtyard.

"What do you want?" the man sitting at a desk at the entrance to the courtyard asked angrily. "Write your name and address here," he said with anger and resentment.

I entered my name in an open book and walked to the courtyard. A group of armed men laughing and playing with their automatic rifles in the room to my right, a bearded man in slippers suspiciously watching the passersby, I felt the penetrating eyes of surveillance, eyes of fear.

I looked inside a room from the open window facing the yard. An officer screamed at a handcuffed man. A bearded man looked busy and angry in the next room. A short man entered the room. Two people laughed loudly. An officer screamed at a woman. I entered the building.

Two Afghanis were handcuffed to a bench. A tired and unkind officer left the room. My eyes followed the officer.

"I told you to sit down. I'll see you when I want," an officer shouted at an old woman standing in front of his desk.

"Where should I go? I need help. Someone should take care of this."

"Sit down! I'll have you arrested," shouted the officer.

The old woman moved back a step or two. "Sit down!" the officer shouted again.

I stood by the door, anticipating the need to escape this madhouse of fear and violence. I could not move.

"I have been here the whole day. Look at them. They are so vicious. Animals," a middle-aged woman sitting on the bench whispered to me.

"What are you doing here?" the woman asked. "Two bikers stole my rug. I am here to file a complaint," I replied.

"Tell everyone to move back," the officer ordered a bearded man wearing a black shirt. Noise in the hallway, men entering and leaving the room angrily, I stood by the door in fear.

I was frightened, afraid of being charged with a crime I did not commit. Shaking with fear and trying to maintain an appearance of innocence, I slowly left the room and escaped to freedom. Fearful of being noticed in my escape, I carefully disappeared from the gaze of suspicious eyes. Free at last!

POLLUTION AND SMOG: THE KILLING OF INTELLECTUALS AND WRITERS

November 1998. This was the beginning of the days of death, the assassination of activists and writers.

November 23. Daryoush Forouhar and his wife Parvaneh Eskandari were assassinated in their home in Tehran. Stabbed fifteen and seventeen times each, they were assassinated exactly the same way as other opposition leaders: Shahpour Bakhtiar, stabbed to death in his home in Paris; and Dr. Saami, killed in his office in Tehran. Member of the nationalist *Hezb-e Mellat* (Nation Party), the first minister of labor of the Islamic Republic, and a long-time political activist during the rule of Shah, Daryoush Forouhar was killed on November 23, 1998.

Thousands attended the funeral of Forouhar and Eskandari. Participants chanted slogans against the state. The hooligans of *Ansar-e Hezbollah* attacked them.

December 9, 1998. It was mid afternoon. I read in the paper the news about the disappearance of prominent poet and writer Mohammad Mokhtari. Mokhtari had been missing for six days. In October, Mokhtari had been questioned briefly by authorities along with five other authors, for planning to seek legal permission to re-institute the banned Writers Association of Iran. He disappeared in December 1998.

Six in the evening, I received a devastating call from a close friend. Mokhtari's family had been called by the coroner's office to receive his body. Marks on Mokhtari's head and neck; he was murdered by strangulation.

Mokhtari once wrote, "It seems it will happen again once I cross this tunnel. The house is so far, and the cemeteries repeat so often. The cemeteries repeat so often."

Wednesday, December 9, 1998. The news of the disappearance of Mohammad Ja'afar Pouyandeh, a prominent translator, sociologist, and writer, shook Tehran. This was the disappearance of the second writer from the group of six. Pouyandeh left a friend at two in the afternoon on Wednesday to attend a meeting at "the Union of Publishers and Booksellers." That was the last time he was seen by friends and loved ones.

December 12, 1998. "The dead body of Pouyandeh was found in the outskirts of Tehran," I read in the daily *Iran*. "Pouyandeh was strangled by cable, his gold ring and watch not removed, his identification cards left out of his pockets"—another sign of a deliberate murder in the chain of political assassinations.

Pouyandeh once said in an interview, "A writer must carry the burden of two great responsibilities: Serving truth and serving freedom." He died for serving the truth and freedom.

December 12. Tehran had been covered by deadly smog for days. The air was dark gray and heavy. People were asked not to leave their homes except in case of emergency or work. The heavy weight of poison in the air had made breathing a dangerous life-supporting activity. Tehran was dark, day and night—a deadly and inescapable darkness, sickness, nausea and vomiting, burning throat and eyes, and fatigue.

The number of the missing and the dead on the rise, six were killed in less than a month, and one missing. Anxiety, anger, and fear abound.

December 14, 1998. Elementary schools were closed for a day to avoid unnecessary exposure of young children to the deadly smog. Fear lingered on.

December 15, 1998. The smog and pollution reached an unprecedented level. All elementary schools, high schools, and pre-university educational institutions were ordered closed. Tehran looked increasingly like the setting of a science fiction movie. Masked men and women moved like ghosts inside the hazy and dark air, coughing and going about their everyday struggles! Twelve were reported dead due to high levels of pollution in Tehran.

December 15, 1998. I left home to take part in Mohktari's funeral. A woman left a taxicab. Covered head to toe in a thick black *chador,* a black scarf covering her forehead and chin underneath the *chador,* she wore a white mask enveloping the part of her face allowed to be exposed according to the Islamic dress code. She was carrying an expensive leather briefcase. Perhaps she was a business-woman. I was frightened.

I arrived at Karegar Avenue, the sight of the historic student uprising nearly half a year later. The crowd formed slowly in front of the mosque. There were fewer than three thousand mourners. Occasional weeping by the immediate family broke the deadly silence every few minutes. New friends and family arrived, embracing, crying silently. Silence among the crowd in front of the mosque, a woman sobbed aloud, a man covered his face to hide his tears. And there was silence again.

A relatively small crowd, mainly writers, journalists, and intellectuals, gathered to mourn the death of the victims of civil society in Iran. Writers and secular intellectuals were the first to die on the road to civil liberties in the Islamic Iran.

It was ten in the morning. Mokhtari's silenced body was carried out of the mosque. The crowd followed the body in silence. We walked without talking. There were speeches and sobbing in the cemetery, and the words of Iran's famous writer and one of the six questioned writers who said, "We received your message. Repression of thoughts! We are ready for you."

The funeral of Mohammad Ja'afar Pouyandeh was held a week after the burial of Mohammad Mokhtari. Back on Karegar Avenue, the crowd gathered outside the mosque. There were flowers, words of defiance, the image of Pouyandeh's calm face on a big banner, tears rolling down the wrinkled and broken face of his father, and placards decorated with words about human rights from his last translation. Nazanin, Pouyandeh's sole daughter, read a poem of courage and hope. I will never forget that day.

KILLING THE BODY, KILLING THE SOUL

I embraced the old man, kissed his kind wrinkled face, and slowly moved away from the car. Feeling the fresh wetness of his tears on my face, I aimlessly walked among the men and women hurrying to end another day in their journey of life.

Old, and full of pain, he was a retired mechanic driving his car as a private taxi. Unshaved face, shabby clothes, he had a gaze that cried out tales of anguish and open wounds.

"How is life?" I asked the old man. He told me of many years of hard and unending labor, holding two jobs, a loving wife, and four sons, the eldest educated with high degrees from universities in faraway lands.

He broke down in tears telling me the saga of his boys. Tears falling on his wrinkled face, his words broken and interrupted by intervals of soundless cries, he painfully told me the tale of his two oldest sons. Tortured for their thoughts, his sons were executed on a lonely night by angry men with guns.

He told stories of the brilliance of his boys, his unending struggle to secure them a future unlike his own, and the horrors of losing loved ones to the firing squad.

Driving in the darkness of a suffocating evening, quietly sobbing while struggling to finish his tale, the man told me the ballad of the third son: bullet in the heart, bullets in the eyes, and a broken old man embracing the bloody body of a ravaged son.

We embraced and I left the car. He drove on in search of yet another customer. Another chance to continue a life of pain and sorrow.

STATE VIOLENCE, EVERYDAY LIFE, AND THE LONGING FOR LIFE

Eyes must be washed
a different way we must see
umbrellas must be closed
under the rain we must go
under the rain we must take our thoughts, and memory

—Sohrab Sepehri

February 25, 1999, was the day before the country's first councils election. My nightmare over, I had my last court hearing in the morning.

We were both cleared. Yes, we are clean and allowed go on breathing the fresh air of the mountains of Tehran. Freedom! I sat in my room, closed my eyes, and broke down in tears. I was free. The beatings, insults, angry guards, and the jail seemed so far away now.

Tehran had become an interesting place in those pre-election days. The city was wallpapered with election posters. The councils election had led to the highest amount of poster production in the history of this land. Yes, a record was broken. There was hardly a wall not covered with posters in Tehran, posters and large billboards.

It was a windy day, the morning of February 21. I saw flyers dancing in the air, men and women pausing and reading the colorful posters. Colors in the Islamic Republic of Iran.

Wind—the most treasured gift of nature in the city of smog, the savior from the smog and pollution, at times more precious than gold and the dollar—I like the dance of the flyers in the wind, the theater of life, the breathing of clean air. That was a clear and windy morning. I was dressed up and excited. Wearing a brown velvet vest ornamented with my grandfather's pocket watch, brown trousers, white shirt, and a long brown winter coat, I was to meet and talk to one of the leading religious intellectuals in the country—a philosopher, outspoken, brave, and controversial.

I left home not knowing what was awaiting me, purchased one of the philosopher's books from a bookstore on 16 Azar Street on my way to the meeting place, and strolled on the streets surrounding Tehran University. Reading the election posters plastered on the walls and fences around Tehran University, I felt the sensation of clean air, wind, and the new message of hope created by the fantastic collage of colors, new names, smiling faces, and words of love on the walls of Tehran.[2]

This was Tehran, February 1999, a land of new faces, images, political ideas, a new election and political space—smiles on the faces of candidates in the councils election. I saw images of deviance—pictures of a beautiful woman staring straight at the passersby, a man in a red jacket, a woman showing a good part of her hair, a young candidate posing like a movie star. I saw images not seen in twenty years—ties and Western outfits in the Islamic Republic, faces of handsome men and beautiful women on election posters—a new political landscape in the making.

There was the near absence of the clergy, the usual faces and images of bearded men in turbans, only a few known faces in turbans and long religious robes, but even they were forced to smile! Smiling was the compelling public image in the Councils election in February

1999. Posters of unknown men and women, educated and determined, self-confident, and brave—these were the faces of tomorrow, men and women making history in the Islamic Republic. A new life and a new message, a new reality was seen on the horizon—men and women shining with their clean outfits, smiling faces, and colorful posters—a change in language, a new discourse.

My eyes were suddenly fixed on the words of Sohrab Sepehri, now the favorite poet of young Iranians—the poet of love, the poet of life—the words of Sohrab as the campaign message of a young candidate for the city council in Tehran. He was a son of Kashan, thirty-seven years of age, an engineer. I read the loving words of Sohrab—a manifesto of compassion. This was the candidate's message for the tired citizens of Tehran.

> Eyes must be washed
> A different way we must see
> Umbrellas must be closed
> Under the rain we must go
> Under the rain we must take our thoughts, and memory
>
> One day
> I shall come
> And I shall bring
> a message
> I shall come giving
> lilacs to beggars.
> I shall come.
> I shall give a lilac to the beggar.
> . . .
> I shall love.

It was nearly eleven in the morning and the stories of the night not yet written. Excited and full of life by the poems of Sohrab and the collage of colorful posters on the city's walls, I was finally at the place where I was to meet the dissident philosopher. I entered the gate. Standing before the security booth, I watched the bearded men walking around with no smile on their faces. I was in a strange world. There were no poems of Sohrab on the wall. I approached the guard and introduced myself. He was polite and friendly.

My counterpart had not shown up at his office for nearly three months, the guard told me. "But I have an appointment with him today," I said. "Is he in Iran?" asked the guard. "He must be. We have an appointment." The man seemed puzzled. "You can wait for him if you want. But we have not seen him lately. We cannot promise anything."

I waited for nearly thirty minutes. The philosopher did not show up. I went inside again. The guard apologized. I smiled and said goodbye.

Disappointed, I left the meeting place and walked aimlessly on Vali-e Asr Avenue—the beautiful and picturesque old Pahlavi Avenue—once the symbol of elegance and wealth, still a landmark in Tehran amidst all the changes that have occurred in the past twenty years. I walked slowly on Vali-e Asr Avenue along *Park-e Daneshjoo* (Student Park), thinking about Sohrab and my memories of the Pahlavi Avenue.

Already forgetting my disappointment, I remembered the posters and the messages of "Green City" and love. And from afar I saw the jubilant and cheerful face of a friend approaching me with love. She was happy to see me. I was delighted by her unexpected presence. We talked, laughed, and decided to take a journey into the land of posters on the walls and melt in the world of new words and images.

Once again Sohrab! We read the poster of another candidate with his words of love as his political manifesto.

I will tie
eyes to the sun
hearts with love
shadows with water
branches with the wind.

I will tie hearts with love! She read to me a poster with the militant words of the poet Hamid Mossadeq. I remembered the day Mossadeq died, three months earlier, a sudden death of the poet whose words inspired passion, militancy and the will to fight.

A candidate stated: "In search of fresh air. For a new breathing." And a young independent candidate promised, "We will never lose our youth." I remembered a piece of graffiti I had read on the rocks going up the Mount Alborz near Darband three years ago. "I lost my youth. Long live life!" I lost my youth. Long live life!

Standing in front of Tehran University, posters plastered on the campus fence, all I could see was posters with promises of a green city, peace, comfort, security, a bright future for youth, sports, cultural development, free press, and respect for youth. Was this a mirage comforting my tired eyes?

Filled with joy, I smiled at my friend. She responded with eyes full of love. She read aloud the posters. I wrote down her words with excitement. We had smiles on our faces.

A candidate promised a clean city, a green earth, blue sky, and "intellectual production." "The best city is a secure and happy city," declared the candidate. "Happiness is not a sin. It is a need of youth," wrote another young candidate. "A free Iran, developed Tehran, with a happy people," promised the "grand coalition of the youth."

Five days before the elections, the city was filled with the message of love, happiness, tolerance, and diversity. Even those fighting happiness for twenty years now had to promise "life, and a green city." A "green city" was promised by those who built prisons, and outlawed all signs of joy and life, banned music and dance, put behind bars and tortured those who dared to laugh and demand happiness. This was a promise of a "green city" by those who shut down the monthly *Adineh* for publishing an article about the absence of smiles on the faces of the youth.

The message was heard. Even the enemies of love had to campaign with the promise of love. This was indeed a victory for the emerging movement for joy. A triumph for life, this was history in the making. A new movement had put its stamp on every wall of the city, forcing its opponents to follow its tracks, resentfully wraping themselves in its image. The poetry of life written on the walls, a new image of politics, an unimagined collage of ideas, this was the politics of postmodernity in the heart of the premodern Islamic Republic of Iran. The twenty-year old "independent" candidate of "workers, students, and artists" declared on his poster:

> faith in social justice
> faith in the abolishing of class differences
> the unknown poet
> a "messenger" of wandering lovers

A messenger of wandering lovers in the Islamic Republic, this was a magnificent eclecticism of ideas and messages: love, arts, and the working class in Tehran in February 1999. "Allow the youth to breathe," demanded a candidate.

Wrapped in the jubilant image of life and happiness, I said farewell to my friend and continued my journey. Late for her theater workshop, she departed with a smile.

The blue sky of Tehran and the clean air created by the heavenly wind had given me a sense of the realization of the "green space and a clean city" promised by the candidates of hope and love. We had the blessing of the wind, the transparent gold for the city of smog. I could clearly see the mountains from afar. I saw white snow shining under the bright sun. Snow on the mountains, fresh air, and wind—I felt alive and filled with joy.

Walking away from Tehran University with no aim, I sat on a park bench at *Park-e Laleh* (Tulip Park). Copies of *Khordad, Neshat,* and *Sobh-e Emrooz* in my hands, I drowned myself in reading the latest news about the elections. It was five days before the elections, four prominent candidates once again disqualified by the supervisory board. Abdollah Nouri, Saeed Hajjarian, and two other close allies of the president were disqualified while their campaign posters were posted throughout the city.

I put the papers away and left the park and heard my named called aloud. This must have been a day of unplanned meetings by friends. The sight of a kind friend delighted me. Unemployed for nearly a year, married and the father of two, he invited me to lunch at his flat. I accepted his invitation.

It was nearly four in the afternoon, a few hours away from the end of joy and the blue sky. I left my friend's flat and walked slowly on Taleghani Street towards Vali-e Asr Avenue after a wonderful day of meeting friends and journeying in the world of green space, joy, peace, and love.

It was a few minutes past six in the evening and I found myself on Vozara Street entering the famous *Park Sa'ee*.

Truly, this must have been the day of accidental meetings between friends. Hearing my name called by a gentle voice, I looked behind me and saw the fine young woman I had met a month or two earlier in the College of Economics of Allameh Tabatabaee University. She too was strolling in the park. Happy to have met, we walked and talked about all that intellectually inspired the two of us. This was a refreshing conversation with a young student eager to inquire and learn. Learning was her hobby she had told me once. She was brilliant indeed. We settled on a bench near the park's playground.

Quiet for a moment or two, a boy in shabby clothes stood before us. Holding a cage with a small bird and poems of Hafez in sealed envelopes, the boy asked me to test my fortune by having the bird pull a poem from the collection. I agreed and gave him two hundred tomans. “This is too much,” said the boy. I smiled. He accepted, and stood by while I opened the envelope.

I asked the boy’s age. “Eleven,” he replied. “Do you attend school?” I asked. He nodded and said no. “My sisters attend school. But, I have to work.” The boy seemed stressed and uncomfortable. “Does your father not work?” I asked. Injured at work, the father had become disabled. The meager disability pay from the government was not enough, and the boy was now the major breadwinner of the family of six. I looked at the young boy without speaking. He broke into tears and told me the sad ballad of his life.

A shoeshine for two years, his belongings were taken away by the security force earlier that day. Not allowed to work in the park, he was told. He sobbed quietly and told me of the fear of being beaten by his father. The birdcage was the property of a friend. The boy hoped to earn some money before the end of the day to avoid the beating by his father at night. I offered the boy one thousand tomans. He refused to accept. “This is a loan. You pay me back later. You will find me here in the park,” I told him. Moments of hesitation, he accepted the money. I asked him to buy new materials and begin the shoeshine business again. He wiped his wet face, and walked to the playground where his friend stood astonished by a man speaking on a cellular phone while tending his young boy. The two friends held hands and began their search for other customers.

Walking along the park, we sat on another bench close to Vali-e Asr Avenue. We talked about poverty and despair in the Islamic Republic. The sun was gone. The night had come. And the story of the boy had darkened my memories of the day. We talked about the tears on the boy’s face and the fear of violence by his defeated and broken father.

And once again I heard someone calling me. But, this time, the voice was angry and violent. I was not addressed by my name. “Hey, get up and come here,” was what broke the quiet of the night and made me aware of unhappy moments to come. I looked behind me and saw two bearded guards in security force uniforms. “Take your bag. You have to go with me,” shouted one bearded guard. I looked at my friend and walked away from the bench. A young man and a woman were also with the guards. “You too, get up and come,” shouted the other officer at my friend. She picked up her bag and we stood before the four strangers in the park.

Ordered violently to follow the guards, I asked for reasons. They demanded identification cards. I surrendered my faculty ID from the United States. That was all I had carried with me. Unable to read the English text, they demanded explanation. I told them of my occupation. "A professor in the United States," the guard repeated. "A university student," my friend said to the guard. The guards looked at us with a sense of pleasure, a pleasure I could not understand at that moment.

"Come with us," shouted the guard. I asked again for explanation. He shouted louder and demanded my silence. It was dark. We followed the uniformed guards and entered a building on the north end of the park. There were two arrested young men in a room, a few uniformed officers, and a middle-aged man in plainclothes behind a desk.

"Against the wall. Stay right there," shouted the arresting guard. I was in a state of disbelief. The day had nearly ended. Gone was the blue sky, the promises of a green city, and security. I looked at my friend. She stood strong and defiant.

The man in plainclothes inquired about my friend and me. The guard showed him our identification cards. "A professor from the United States," said the guard with a sense of pleasure and irony. "Get over here," shouted the man in plainclothes.

I approached his desk and said, "Why am I . . ." A heavy hand crashed on my face. I hit the wall behind me. Unable to hear for a second or two, shocked by the strike, I said "Why . . ." again. A second strike on my face, and I hit the wall. He smiled triumphantly. This was a moment of pleasure for him. The guards seemed victorious. They looked at me with a curious sense of joy. I said joy! I had now understood the pleasure on the face of the arresting guards and the sickening joy in the eyes of the man in plainclothes. Indeed that was the joy of having caught a perfect victim. Joy was what I saw on the angry face of the man in plainclothes, joy amidst anger, the joy of revenge.

There were three arrested young men in the room. They were not hit. They looked frightened. I was insulted again by the man in plainclothes. "I will break you into pieces before I let you go," said the man. "Do you think this is Los Angeles? We will show you where you are. This is Iran not America. We will show you." The man in plainclothes continued his insults. I heard words I will never be able to repeat even in a court of law in my own defense, words of anger, words of hate, words to break me down and defeat my sense of being, words I will never forget.

Shocked by the incident, my friend asked for explanation. Assaulted by the violent language of the man in plainclothes, she stood defiant and firm and heard the violating words of the man in plainclothes. She was visibly defiant, defiant without words.

The guards searched my bag. My heart nearly stopped beating. I trembled. "I am finished," I said to myself. Will they see the copy of the *Communist Manifesto* in my bag? Will they find the five pages of questions from the philosopher about the constitution, the *faghih* and his absolute power, the Islamic *hijab,* and all other symbols of the violation of basic human rights in the Islamic Republic? I trembled in fear, closed my eyes, and anticipated the new wave of verbal and physical attacks. "The counterrevolutionary from the United States, spy," I expected to hear from the officer. I was finished. I was a perfect catch. Engulfed in fear, I watched the copy of the *Manifesto* in the hands of the man in plainclothes. The end of freedom, I thought to myself.

Holding the *Manifesto* and searching the bag, the man in plainclothes shouted. "What is this?" He had found my Swiss Army knife. "Possession of a weapon," he cried. I protested. He insulted me and threatened me with more violence. "Possession of a weapon."

And a state of disbelief! "Take your bag," shouted the man in plainclothes while placing the *Manifesto* in my bag. Was this a mirage? I picked up my bag and stood against the wall. Cold sweat rolling down my face, the *Manifesto* in the bag, I was assaulted by the continued words of insult from the man in plainclothes—words that actually made me lose my fear. I stood against the wall in disbelief. The man in plainclothes had no interest in the contents of my bag. He was in search of other signs of "cultural invasion" in my bag. I was saved. And for a second or two, I remembered the election posters again. I saw joy, life, green space, and the words of Sohrab.

Pushed against the wall by an officer, I watched them joke about my appearance. I was dressed differently. Looking modern and clean, I exemplified all that they resented, and all that they wished to destroy. But, it was now too late. Appearances like mine had covered the walls of the city. They saw the election posters in me. This was their chance to strike back.

They spoke about the United States again. They laughed. I looked at my friend. Firm and defiant, she stood calm and in control.

A charge was filed against us. I was handcuffed. "Why?" I asked gently. They shouted again. Taken out of the park, handcuffed, I followed the two guards on Vozara Street. A guard between my defiant-looking friend and me, we stood before the green metal gates of Vozara Monkerat building—a temporary jailhouse for the moral "deviants."

"Your home for tonight," said one of the guards while entering a room on the first floor. There were three uniformed officers, four accused men, a woman, and my friend and me. Whispers and staring eyes in the room, a woman in black *chador* took my friend away. I was put on a bench facing the wall. Half an hour passed, the interrogation began. I filled out and signed a report prepared by the questioning officer. A case of "illegitimate relationship" said a colonel. I was relieved. This was not a political case. No trace of the *Manifesto* in the report!

I was allowed to make a call to my brother. A soldier arrived. I was taken down to the basement. A metal door opened. I entered. "Take off your belt and shoelaces," said the prison guard. I handed him my keys and other "sharp objects." The metal gate closed behind me. I was jailed!

Seven cells and a dungeon, a long filthy hallway to the bathroom, no windows, forty prisoners, and me, that was to be my home for the night.

They placed me in cell number 6. Packed and smelling bad, ten inmates in the cell, men sitting wall to wall on the floor, I was welcomed by the inmates and offered a place on the floor by a gentle young man. We joked. They were amused by my presence in their cell! "Professor" was what they called me. Young and old, there were ten inmates in cell number 6.

Inmate 1—He was Captain of the jailhouse. Twenty-three years of age, ten days in the jail, he was arrested with a male friend and two girlfriends in his car. They were charged with having an "illegitimate relationship." The women were sent to the Evin Prison the day before my arrival. I spent a few hours puffing cigarettes and talking with the Captain that night. Cigarettes were not allowed in the jail. But I smoked with the Captain and the prison guard.

Inmate 2—He offered me a place on the floor next to him. Anguished and restless, he asked about my life in the States. "What kind of music do you listen to?" whispered Inmate 2. We talked about Pink Floyd. He too loved Roger Waters. He asked me about concerts I had seen. I listed Pink Floyd, Roger Waters, U2, Sting, and others. He seemed amazed! We talked about Pink Floyd again. Pink Floyd in the jails of the Islamic Republic!

Inmate 3—He was older than fifty and a bathroom attendant in a city park. He had been in temporary confinement for nearly a week.

Inmate 4—A young man in his early twenties, he was noisy and mischievous. He enjoyed calling me "Professor." We laughed. He wanted to know about the States. "How can I get a visa to America?" he asked a few times. "Tell me about the 'girls' in the America." America was what almost everyone was interested. I was asked about America, music, and the "girls."

Inmate 5—Maybe in his sixties, he sang the songs of the famous prerevolution female singer Hayedeh at the request of other inmates. The singer of the time of "sin," "cultural invasion," and all that represented the "decedent past," her music was what the young and the old asked for from Inmate 5. They all enjoyed his singing. I do not know why he was jailed.

Inmate 6—In his late twenties, jailed for a week, he was caught with a girlfriend like most others. We managed to speak later in the morning. Inmate 6 gave me some useful information about the court system. We spoke after his early-morning prayer.

Court10503 was the fear of all inmates. The judge had never released anyone without severe punishment and long days of indeterminate imprisonment. Inmates 1, 3, 4, 5, and 6 were all tried in Court10503.

An hour gone, I had a visitor. I left my cell for the small "office" of the guard by the metal door of the jail and saw my brother on the other side of the gate with food and cigarettes. I had to spend the night in jail. The guard allowed me to smoke in his office. The Captain arrived. The three of us stayed in the office, smoked, joked, and talked about the "girls." I too had now become a privileged inmate. I smoked cigarettes with the guard and the Captain. I was above the other prisoners. They did not have the right to smoke.

It was 1:30 in the morning. The guard read to the Captain and me the love poems he wrote to his wife when she was his "girlfriend." A poetic guard in his late twenties, a decent man with a great memory in poetry, he was married to the "girl friend." They had a one-year-old daughter, the guard said proudly. His salary was fifty thousand tomans a month. He paid forty-five thousand tomans for rent. He did accept "gifts" from prisoners. I asked him to write some of the poems he read that night. The guard wrote:

> I like to be calmed in this house of sadness,
> I traveled anonymously and like to die anonymously
> There is no one to free the bird of my heart,

Wings closed, and the heart broken, I will die in this cage.
I aged in sorrow and pain.
I became old, though my face is young.

He wrote words of pain, words of love—words of a prison guard in the jails of the Islamic Republic. It was nearly two in the morning, we heard men coming down the steps to the basement. Standing at the door, a man pleaded in a sad and trembling voice: "Excuse me sir. Can you help me please? My brother has disappeared since last Thursday. We have no news from him for five days. Can you please check to see if he is here?" The man gave the guard his brother's name. The guard called the name. No one answered. He returned to the door. The man thanked the guard and walked up the stairs. We smoked more cigarettes.

I heard men coming down the stairs throughout the night. Three very young men, eighteen or younger, a man in his thirties, others who became Inmates 33, 34, and the rest—all arrested for having been seen with women not married or related to them.

I spent some time with the Captain. We befriended and exchanged numbers. We promised to meet and breathe the fresh air once out of jail. I never saw the Captain again.

The wakeup call was at seven in the morning, half an hour for washing and the rest. We were all lined up on the hallway to the bathrooms, not allowed in the cells or the main hallway. We sat on the cold floor. Some stood on their feet until nine.

They began calling names. My name was among those to be taken to court that morning. We were handcuffed in pairs. I had a funny young partner. We laughed amidst anxiety, sat handcuffed for nearly an hour and half in the cold, and were separated later and sent to different courts. I heard Court 10508 after my name. I was relieved.

I was released the next day. Returning two days later for some legal procedures, I met Inmate 7, handcuffed and on his way to the court. He was taken to Court 10503 and still in jail. Surprised to see him, I asked about the Captain. The Captain had gone nearly mad the night before, shouting and banging on the walls the entire night. He was close to a nervous breakdown, said Inmate 7. That is the last I heard about the Captain.

I am a free man now. My friend and I are free. Barred from meeting each other. That was the court's verdict. We did not discuss our experiences in the jail. She said "a madhouse" a few times.

That was while we waited outside the courtroom. I may never know what she saw that night. A "madhouse" is all I know.

Forced to leave abruptly after the July student uprising, I left Iran without seeing the Captain or my friend who spend a horrifying night in the "madhouse." I wish the Captain and all the inmates a life free of fear, anxiety, random arrest, and imprisonment. May they breathe the fresh air of Mount of Alborz and gaze at the eyes of their loved ones in a world free of the eyes of surveillance of the bearded men in slippers!

CHAPTER THREE

Children of the Islamic Republic—Part I

The Rise of a New Social Movement for Joy: A Narrative

Beyond the seas there is a town
wherein windows open to epiphany.
Upon roofs dwell doves who watch the spout of human intelligence.
The arm of every town kid is a bough of insight.
The townsfolk behold a clay wall
as if a flame, a tender dream.
The earth hears the music of your feeling,
and the fluttering sound of mythical birds come on the wind.
Beyond the seas there is a town
wherein the sun spans the eyes of early risers,
and poets inherit water and wisdom and light.
Beyond the seas is a town!
A boat must be built.

—Sohrab Sepehri

The right to joy is a fundamental right in a civil society.

—Mohammad Nikfar

The cultural transformation of society by the creation of hegemonic Islamic social and cultural norms was, from its inception, one of the pillars of the Islamic Republic. Central to this new cultural design was opposition to Western social values. Opposing Western "cultural invasion," the state sought to eliminate all forms of cultural plurality and "non-Islamic" social behavior. Through a process of social engineering, the Islamic Republic hoped to culturally mould a postrevolution generation of young Iranians as the backbone of an Islamic state in the future. The Islamic cultural project was designed and enforced through multiple processes of coercion and the application of laws and means of state repression, co-optation, and habituation and socialization.

Forcing the Islamic *hijab* on women, separating male and female students in universities, and banning all contact between them, the state sought to create a society of virtuous Moslem men and women—a society of repressed worldly desires. The Islamic Republic opposed and banned music, arts, and all cultural symbols of modern life. Through diverse means and methods, the state sought to construct a culture in which secular happiness was a sin, human love an unforgivable crime. Bright colors of joy were replaced with dark colors of anger and fear. Happiness was a worldly sin, laughter a crime.

The construction of the Islamic culture was further assisted by the eight-year war between Iran and Iraq. The war created a marriage between patriotism and devotion to Islam. Now happiness was a sign of unpatriotic feelings, a crime against both Islam and the nation. What was now celebrated was mourning and self-beating, and death. The desire for martyrdom and death replaced the celebration of worldly love, passion for life, and the joy of being. Death was the final word in the new culture.

Now, two decades after the victory of the Islamic Republic, a growing movement for joy, a movement against the state's cultural project is emerging. Defining and creating a personal and collective identity outside the premises of the state's accepted behavior and codes of conduct, an unorganized grassroots social movement has taken shape. A movement embedded in the experiences of everyday life and shaped by ordinary people's deviance and their embracing of the scorned and the unacceptable has surfaced—a movement shaped by the desire to "sin."

Against the celebration of death, a movement for life, the right to be, and the right to live a free life is emerging—a movement for the celebration of life. Defying the eyes of surveillance of the Islamic state, openly confronting the state with the symbols of "cultural invasion," a movement is loudly announcing the defeat of the Islamic Republic of Iran.

What follows is a narrative of the defeat of the Islamic Republic's cultural project—the making of a movement for joy by ordinary people in the process of everyday life.

CHILDREN OF THE ISLAMIC REPUBLIC—DEFEAT OF A CULTURAL PROJECT

> Is Happiness Lost in our City? Is Laughter a Sin?
>
> It was a few years ago. I went to a restaurant with my parents, husband, and my child. We ordered our food and waited. Thinking that we were ordinary people, like other ordinary people in other parts of the world, we talked and laughed quietly. A few minutes gone, a boy approached us. Thirteen or fourteen years of age, armed, angry, he was as rude as one could be. Looking at my mother he shouted: "Are you not ashamed of yourself for laughing in public?" . . .
>
> It was last year. My son and daughter had gone hiking to the mountains. Talking and laughing, and innocently enjoying these moments away from the city, they were confronted by a band of armed youngsters. Treating them with most indecent words they shouted. "Are you not ashamed of yourself for laughing in public?" . . .
>
> My son went to the mountains alone one night after that incident. He was assaulted by a band of armed boys. As a result, my son and his sister kissed goodbye going to the mountains forever.". . .
>
> And now, all of our youth somehow consider laughing a sin. Our youth are depressed and frightened. They have forgotten being young. . . .
>
> Tell us once, why laughter is a sin.
>
> —A mother in the Islamic Republic

Football is Happiness; Football is Defiance

June 13, 1998. Half an hour before Iran's first encounter in the 1998 World Cup, the country was anxiously waiting for the match between the "boys" and the world-class Yugoslav national team. I decided not to watch the game and wander on the streets of Tehran instead.

The game had just begun. Tehran, a hyper, overcrowded city of thirteen million had turned into a ghost town. A few cars on the streets, passersby running to get home for the game, piece and tranquility in Tehran, this was an amazingly unusual scene for this city of old cars, smog, and frantic citizens!

Nearly dark by now, I found myself walking aimlessly. A narrow alley to my left, I heard the loud cry of a sports reporter—excitement, a moment of silence, and loud cry again—radio waves competing in the smoggy air of Tehran. There were whistles, jeers, and more whistles. I felt the sensation of joy and pride, and the magnificent music of the poetry of oneness—the poetry of love.

Tired of walking, I took a cab—private car and a bearded driver in a black shirt—the familiar face of a man of religion I thought to myself. A passenger in the backseat, in her fifties I thought.

"Would you mind if I drop her off first?" asked the driver. "That will be fine. I am in no rush. Everyone is watching the game. I don't mind getting there when the game is over," I replied calmly.

A sudden rush of words of astonishment broke through the air in the car. Shocked by what I had said, the passenger in the backseat erupted. "Are you not a patriot?" said the woman in a voice filled with disbelief.

"I do not care for football very much," I replied.

"You must still be happy for the success of your country," interrupted the driver. "How could you not care?" interjected the woman again. I looked at her and smiled.

We drove without anyone speaking, the announcer's excited voice in the air, and the driver spoke again. "What matters is that people are happy for a short while. That is the point for me. Everyone is happy today. This is a temporary relief from a life of pain and hard work. We deserve these moments of joy," said the driver in a gentle and kind voice. "I drive this car from seven in the morning until ten at night every day. Life is not easy here. Always running." He spoke with a warm smile on his face. His kindness and love for happiness defied his black shirt and neatly trimmed beard—the profile of a Moslem fundamentalist that he was not. I was ashamed of my blind judgement of his appearance.

I had reached my destination. The driver stopped the car. I asked for the fare and paid the driver. I was overcharged!

I had arrived nearly twenty minutes before the end of the game. I too watched the remainder of this historic competition between the "boys" and the powerful Yugoslav team. We were all proud of the "boys." They lost with dignity.

The nation was anticipating the historic game between the American and the Iranian teams on June 21, 1998. The countdown had begun, only a week before the game of the century for this nation of tired citizens.

June 21, 1998, was an important day. Abdollah Nouri, the secretary of the interior, was impeached by a marginal vote in the *Majlis*. To many, this was the first step in what appeared to be a political coup against the government of President Khatami. The daily Hamshahri called the impeachment "revenge" against the president by those defeated in the last election.

The news of Nouri's impeachment was made public by late afternoon while the country was preparing itself for the historic football match between Iran and the United States. The impeachment news was received by most observers and ordinary people as a setback in their civic struggle for social and political reform. A cloud of despair and sadness engulfed the soldiers of everyday life. The battle between the forces of reform and the fundamentalists had entered a new stage. Despite the sugar coating of the event by various political figures, what was clear to most ordinary people was that June 21 opened a new chapter in the battle for reform in Iran.

But amidst the feeling of temporary defeat the nation slowly withdrew from the streets, deserted all public spaces, and sat in front of their television receivers for the second event of the day, the football match between the United States and Iran. Life goes on!

By 11:00 P.M. nobody was to be seen on the streets. Cars speeded to reach home on time. Men and women ran home after their daily battles of survival. Children said goodbye to friends to join their loved ones in the anticipation of the game of their life—this was the evening of July 21, 1998.

At twenty minutes past eleven, Tehran was a ghost town never seen before. No noise to be heard except for the loud air waves rushing out of open windows to announce the coming of the "event."

Minutes before 11:30, all eyes fixed to television screens, I took a glance at the dead-end alley and closed the window. The game started.

At half-past one in the morning, June 22, 1998, this was a historic time in the memory of the citizens of the empire of fear. The game was over. The "boys" had won the game. Sixty million people screamed in joy.

Words will not be able to capture the feelings and sentiments, the sense of celebration, and the collective spirit that engulfed the streets and alleys of Tehran in the early hours of June 22, 1998. Doors opened. Waves of men, women, and children poured into the streets. Iran erupted in an orgy of festivity never seen before.

At two in the morning, traffic jams created by cars and trucks overloaded with cheering men and women. I watched the dance of moving windshield wipers decorated with white napkins and cloth—symbols of peace. Armies of dancing bodies chanted words of joy and love. Light, noise, and traffic jam—this was a spontaneous outburst of ordinary people in a revolt for joy and pride.

In the early hours of June 22 the nation observed a spontaneous coalition of ordinary people from diverse social groups, classes, ages, and genders. All boundaries were torn down and a powerful united front was formed on the streets of Tehran and other cities of Iran—a united front for joy. Football and the victory in the match with the United States were catalysts that brought into the open people's passion for happiness, pride, and an ordinary life outside the cultural and social boundaries of the Islamic Republic. The street celebrations in those early morning hours were the manifestation of people's defiance of the fundamentalists and their organs of repression.

What we saw was a powerful theater of defiance and poetry of love. Even the security force and the *Basij* (The Volunteer Corp) could not stop this frenzy of festivity and joy. They were booed and forced to retreat after attempting to stop people's celebration. In Karaj, *Basiji* intruders were confronted with the loud cry of "*Basiji* must dance." No power was able to stop ordinary people's fury of love and defiance.

Dance! "*Basiji* must dance!" A new weapon was discovered by ordinary people, a weapon more powerful than the violence of the *Basiji,* a weapon later used by the student movement in the battle with the hooligans of the *Ansar*. Satire, ridicule, joy, and laughter—these were the new ways found by ordinary people in their struggle against the agents of violence and hate. "Dance!"—Horror for *the Basij,* deadlier than death, worse than burning in the volcanic fires of Hell. "*Basiji* must dance," they cried aloud. This was the time of defiance, a public show of collective deviance: "sin" on the streets of the Islamic Republic of Iran. Happiness was the weapon with which ordinary people tore down all walls of fundamentalist repression and transformed June 22 to an unforgettable event that transcended football and all nationalistic feelings of the victory in the match. Through their spontaneous impulses and hunger for joy, they created new forms of collective action against violence and terror.

The early hours of June 22, 1998, manifested ordinary people's joy in being able to present themselves as civilized, competent, and honorable people to other citizens of the world. The waving of the

Iranian flag was a demonstration of the pride in being a people equal to those from whom they had been kept away for twenty years. June 22 was a loud pronouncement by a nation to the rest of the world of their readiness to be a part of the modern world community. It was a celebration of coming out of isolation and the archaic social and cultural norms of fundamentalism.

People's enthusiasm about football, wrote a commentator, "is nothing but the result of isolationist policies pursued by anti-democratic forces in recent years."[1] In an article entitled "Life, Football, and Nothing But," in the weekly *Iran Javan* (Young Iran), a commentator wrote. "Life is a ball. The earth is green. Life is a picture of Ronaldo [the Brazilian player] on the wall. . . . Life is football."[2]

> The presence of hundreds of thousands of people and the eruption of joy and happiness on the streets of Tehran was an unexpected and unusual event. To many young people freedom does not mean the freedom of speech, the right to public gathering, the freedom of association, or the liberal or religious interpretation of freedom. To many youth freedom means happiness. . . . Happiness is a need for humanity. Happiness is a need in our society today.[3]

Football is happiness. Football is defiance.

Nearly half a year later, having defeated its rivals, Iran's national football team became the number one team in Asia. Once again, joy and pride engulfed the Iranian youth and people poured out into the streets to celebrate this victory. This time, at least in one city, as reported by the press, clashes occurred between the celebrating youth and the fundamentalists. Gangs of *Hezbollah* hooligans in Isfahan attacked the joyous young men and women. The youths broke store windows and smashed cars. The details of this incident were not clear. But, as alluded to in a Friday prayer later in the month, the youths chanted militant slogans that defied the repressive organs of the state.

On December 24, during the Friday prayer in Zahedan, the Friday Imam criticized the people "who poured into the streets, broke windows, and chanted "Cannons, Tanks, and *Basiji* Have No More Effect."[4] This was a replay of events twenty years earlier when tens of thousands of young people defiantly stood before the guns and tanks of the Shah and chanted with their fists in the air "Cannons, Tanks, and Machine Guns Have No More Effect." Twenty years later, a generation that was not even born on the eve of the revolution now repeated the same slogan, this time against the Islamic Republic.

"Cannons, Tanks, and *Basiji* Have No More Effect" was to become a unifying cry of the young students battling the *Ansar* and the Security Force on the streets of Tehran nearly half a year later in July 1999.

"God is Dead, Zappa is God"

July1998. It was an early evening after a hot summer day in Tehran. I was told of the arrival of Sebastia Salgado's latest book of photos. An unexpected and pleasant surprise for the fans of Salgado's penetrating gaze into the lives of the deprived and underprivileged, this was a real thrill for me and the friend who invited me to the viewing of the book, *People Without Home*. The book had journeyed from house to house overnight. It was now waiting for our arrival at Soheil's upbeat apartment in a wealthy neighborhood of Tehran.

Son of a very prominent contemporary Iranian intellectual and writer, charming, handsome with an air of carelessness and authority, a good deal of wealth, and a "fuck the rest of the world" attitude, Soheil was a photographer living in an apartment owned by his writer father. No furniture, a naked hardwood floor, a small metal statue of a bending man in the middle of the floor, large pictures on the walls; we sat on the floor feeling cool and upbeat. There were five young men and a sharp-looking young woman on the balcony, smoke in the air, "good wine," and a couple of hours of the music of Frank Zappa. Zappa in the Islamic Republic of Iran!

Never expecting to meet a Frank Zappa fan in the Islamic Republic of Iran, I was filled with amazement and a sense of mischievous joy. They knew the meaning of "cool." "Zappa is cool," I was told. Cool is talking philosophy, listening to Zappa, classical music, and of course a good dose of famous classic rock, and Pink Floyd. Children of the Islamic Republic, not older than twenty-five, they were the "intellectual underground."

"Zappa is the last word in music," declared the young photographer. A photographer himself, the Zappa fan seemed to be not much interested in Salgado. Zappa had it all. He admired Hume and even Marx, I was told later.

The lights were off, a couple of candles on the floor, nonstop smoking, and Frank Zappa's loud melodies in our ears. "Zappa is all." God is dead. Zappa is God.

I challenged Soheil with my own pretentious talk about Roger Waters of Pink Floyd. "Roger is God," I told Soheil. He disagreed.

"Roger has nothing to teach Zappa. But, Zappa has a lot to teach Roger," said the Zappa fan with authority. "Zappa is God!" We shook hands, wished each other good days ahead, and said farewell.

"God is Dead, Nietzsche is God"

Late summer, 1998. "I'm into Hume," said Leyla. I was surprised. "Nietzsche," said Shahla. "Only Nietzsche, he is my philosopher."

I had heard of "Nietzsche fundamentalists" among the "baby intellectuals" of Iran. This was what a photographer friend called the young admirers of Nietzsche. He told me of wars and even fistfights between the fans of Hume, Nietzsche, and other Western gurus at some parties!

"God is Dead, Nietzsche is God!"

I do not recall now, but I made a passing reference to dialectics, something about the unity of opposites! It was a joke I was making about something we saw on our way up in one of the usual Darakeh hikes with friends. "Dialectics," cried Leyla with sparkles of life, excitement, and surprise in her eyes. "Dialectic! Why dialectics?" she asked.

I was obliged to explain my mischievous reasons for using this almost mysterious philosophical terminology. Yes, I had to explain my understanding of dialectics and talk about Marx and his dialectical materialism. She had understood dialectics differently. Asking if she was referring to Hegel, Marx, or anybody else, I did not get an answer.

"Are you a student of philosophy? Do you read much philosophy?" I asked with excitement, excited to meet a young enthusiast and someone who talked about dialectics! Indeed, I got the response that came to me over and over in the following weeks from the fans of philosophy. She had only read Hume. She was a Hume fan. I never understood why! Why Hume?

Three weeks later, bearing Hume, Nietzsche and other grand names in mind, I went with friends to the bon voyage party of a young male painter. Talented, funny, sociable, a fine fellow he was. I was in an apartment in a wealthy neighborhood. Reminded of the stories about the underground culture in eastern Europe before the fall of official communism, I was intrigued by the assembly of cool, hip, intellectualism, carefree attitude, and wealth. This was in Tehran, the Islamic Republic of Iran. Smoke in the air, a crowd of youngsters sitting on the floor, a couple of "sixties-looking" young men with non-Islamic beards and an air of ease and peacefulness conversing on a big couch; I too sat on the floor and began the journey into the world of hip in Iran. Modern, hip, and non-Islamic, they were the children of the Islamic Republic. Watching a number of hip-looking young men and women dressed cool and sharp, I felt back in New York City, away from bearded men in slippers and all the usual madness of life in the Islamic Republic.

I was introduced to a graduate of the Pratt Institute in NYC—an architect fascinated with intellectualism and thrilled at meeting a man from his own planet. I was delighted to meet him too. He had done some writing and was aspiring to make a film about the "sociology of the city," he told me later. I told him of my interests and projects. He told me I reminded him of the "sixties intellectuals." I was thrilled! That was a compliment.

Massoud was quietly listening to our conversation. A young sculptor, Massoud was a dropout from the college of sociology at Tehran University. Sitting on the floor with a sense of confidence belonging to the men of thought and ideas, distinguished with his full dark beard, he came closer to the architect and me. I introduced myself. A minute or two later, we were talking about intellectuals and the "intellectual project" in Iran. Massoud's hand movements and facial expressions were perfect. In less than half an hour we talked about the Iranian Bolsheviks, the identity crisis of the old Left, and the "road ahead." The road ahead! For some curious reason, I recall nothing of the content of our plan for the future! I was not buzzed or drunk. There was no alcohol or drugs at the party—very unusual for parties of that type. There was no Hume or Nietzsche in our conversation, no Zappa either! But I recall nothing!

High-Tech Dating in the Land of Islam

The crowd in front of Alborz Restaurant defied all of my earlier expectations of the youth in the Islamic Republic. A friend had invited me there on a Friday afternoon to show me a taste of the good life and pleasure in this land of Islam and fundamentalism. Curious to see the other side of this mysterious planet, I accepted his invitation.

We arrived at half past one in the afternoon. "No, we are too early," my friend complained with a sad voice. He was disappointed, apparently his favorite scene and the mix of young men and women had not formed yet. "Too early," he said again and again. But, we had no choice. We stood in line with a dozen or so parents, grandparents, and children. This was not the crowd he had expected. The line went all the way from the second floor of the building to the street. Half an hour gone, we were directed to a table in the middle of a cheaply decorated and not-so-charming restaurant. And we ordered. Soon came huge kebabs and gigantic portions of rice. Eating a meal big enough for four in less than thirty minutes, we paid the bill and proceeded to the door. We were rushed in and rushed out. Stuffed and paid up, we had to leave. We were not allowed to wait for my friend's expected scene.

"Too early. They will just be coming now. Too early" my friend repeated with even more sorrow now. Frankly, I was tired of hearing his regrets and yet eager to see his crowd.

We sat foot on the stairs leading to the ground floor. And there they were! Citizens from another planet, they were. An amazing spectacular—teenage men and girls beautifully dressed and made up, cellular phones in their hands, chatting and laughing and creating a sight far removed from the Islamic Iran. "This is it. I knew it. We were too early," cried my friend with sorrow and regret. More than a dozen youngsters were conversing on their cellular phones. They had discovered a brilliant way of overcoming the Islamic obstacles to finding quick pleasure and love. My friend explained how the youth exchanged phone numbers while waiting on line for the second floor, setting up their dates through undetectable electronic waves while having their lovely kebab and rice. This was indeed high-tech dating in the premodern Iran, every Friday from 2:30 to 4:00 in the afternoon—a paradise for wealthy kids with their high-tech toys and top-of-the-line European outfits, expensive perfumes, and all the scorned instruments of joy.

I said farewell to my saddened friend and entered the known side of the Islamic Republic. Taking a cab to Azadi Avenue, I talked about the heat and rising prices with the driver.

Passion for the Scorned—Passion for Music

Winter 1998. To my surprise, a weekly newspaper in Tehran carried a full-length two-page article about the legendary rock band, Pink Floyd. The article was both accurate and intelligent, presenting a well-informed appraisal of the important contributions of the band to music.

A translation of Pink Floyd lyrics was on the market now, one of the highlights of this year's International Book Fair—*The Division*

Bell. Facing an insatiable appetite among the youth, the publisher had brought out a fourth edition of the volume. This was while a separate volume of Pink Floyd poems also became a hit. Two separate translations of all the Floyd poems in one year, four editions of one translation—passion for rock & roll in the Islamic Republic of Iran!

The year 1998 was the year of partial retreat by the state on the cultural front. Prerevolutionary Iranian music, once scorned as representative of all that was decadent and immoral, was slowly and quietly returning to postrevolutionary Iran through the sound waves of the state-controlled television and radio. Produced and promoted by the state, we could now hear reproduced the voices and music of prerevolutionary artists—the scorned, the unwanted, the "other." A new industry, cloning the voices of "sin," emerged in the Islamic Republic!

After twenty years of banning happiness and the right to enjoy life, the Islamic Republic organized its first festival of "pop music" in 1999. Pop was now a reality no longer ignored. Music, Western music, "decadent" music—music was slowly becoming a weapon in the hands of youth, forcing the state to retreat.

Valentine's Day in Islamic Iran!

Love—the expression of earthly affection between humans—a forbidden subject and a taboo in the Islamic Republic—love has been slowly emerging as a powerful magnet among the children of the revolution. It was nearly a decade ago when Mohsen Makhbalbaf's movie *The Turn of Love* became a subject of debate in the parliament and was finally banned by the state. Now, helped by the change in the leadership of the Ministry of Culture and Islamic Guidance, love was returning to the print press, movies, and music. Farsi translations of love poems by Pablo Neruda and other poets of love became the most popular gifts among the youth.[5] Magazines and journals specializing in youth wrote openly about love—love not for God, but for other humans—earthly love. Milan Kundera's books decorated the windows of bookstores on Enghelab Avenue. I asked a very dear friend what I could send him from New York. "Kundera," he responded. "Whatever that is new from Kundera," he wanted from me.

February 14, 1999, was the celebration of Valentine's Day in the Islamic Republic, postmodernity in action, the celebration of love with red roses and chocolate in the state that had celebrated death for twenty years! This was 1999, the Islamic Republic of Iran.

For two or three weeks beforehand, bookstores and shops catering to the young were carrying signs of the day of love, Valentine's Day in Iran! I asked a younger friend about the signs. "Oh, yes, this is a big thing here, but unfortunately not as big as in the States. There, they have the real thing. We have a long way to go."

I saw Navid the night before Valentine's Day. Seventeen years of age, he had spent a big chunk of money on gifts for a "girl" he wished to date. And Ali, a wonderful and bright young man, a friend close to my heart, a bundle of joy, he bought candles a couple of weeks earlier. And of course, he bought candles for more than one girlfriend! He had many.

I went for a lovely walk with Mojgam two days before the "day." She made sure to remind me of the significance of February 14 while having lunch. "Do not forget Valentine's Day," said Mojgam with smile on her face.

February 14 finally arrived. I spent some good hours writing at home. Ali visited and used my phone to wish happy Valentine's Day to quite a few girlfriends. We saw Mehrjooi's *The Pear Tree* in the evening. That was a fine movie about love.

Late in the evening, February 14, we decided to go for coffee. This had now become a ritual for us—late evening coffee at Hotel Homa, the old Sheraton—the only twenty-four-hour restaurant in Tehran, spacious and decorated like a fancy diner, and relatively empty late at night.

We arrived at the restaurant at Hotel Homa near Vanak Square in Tehran on the day of love. A line of young men and women had formed at the entrance of the restaurant. The place was full of the children of Islamic Republic celebrating the day of love only two days after the grand celebration of the twentieth anniversary of the "Islamic Revolution" by the state.

Having given up the hope of getting a table at Homa Hotel on the day of love we proceeded to the "Strawberry"—another cafe/restaurant and a magnet for young West-loving Iranians. Finely decorated, designed like a Parisian bar, serving no alcohol of course, I felt I was no longer in Iran. Actually, liking the place, I visited there often.

A walking distance from Hotel Homa, we arrived at "Strawberries" in a few minutes. The place was open and full, but we managed to get a table on the evening of love. It was nearly midnight now. The bar was full of young women and men, out to celebrate love and life, defying all tenets of the Islamic Republic, all looking good, pleasantly dressed, and happy to be out celebrating the day of love. We joked, laughed, paid the bill, and took a taxicab home.

"Five hundred tomans to Sa'adat Abad," I said. The driver agreed. We entered the car. I sat in the front still thinking about the day of love. The car took off. The driver passed two red lights. Suddenly, seeing a gigantic truck facing the taxicab, I screamed. The driver steered the car away. A near miss, it was. He speeded again. I looked at the driver. He said calmly: "I did not see it."

Speeding on the highway, a sharp turn, the driver did not reduce his speed. I objected. "You must be suicidal," I said with a voice filled with fear. "I have been this way for a while," responded the driver.

I took a good look at the driver. He was young. With anger on his face, he turned toward me and asked, "What is there to live for?" He sped, passing two cars on the freeway, nearly smashing one. We were near home now. I was frightened. And my friends were laughing in the back seat.

"Why are they so happy?" asked the driver. He had not smiled. I asked him to stop the car. He said something jokingly. I do not recall his joke, but he did not smile while joking with me. We left the car. My friends continued to laugh. I told them of my fear of dying while in the car. They laughed! We said goodbye.

Hunger for Joy in the Islamic Republic

January 4, 1999. The last day of the Fajr International Theater Festival, a theater carnival to celebrate the festival's finale was to kick off at 4:00 from Enghelab Square. This was the site of angry cries of "Death to the opponents of *velayat-e faghih,*" and "Death to America"—a busy place for hustlers, and drug dealers. The square was now host to a street carnival twenty years after the birth of the Islamic Republic.

The first in twenty years, the first organized show of happiness, a carnival of joy, dancing puppets, clowns, music, and traditional dancers—this was the day of dancing on Enghelab Avenue twenty years after the birth of the Islamic Republic. A theater of friendship in the empire of anger and hate—trucks loaded with dancing men, and young women freely talking to the amazed spectators. "Hello my baby," said a young puppet artist to the children and women following her truck. "How are you, my friend?" said a clown.

A joyous crowd of working people, poor laborers, soldiers beginning their weekend away from their barracks, men and women, old and young—they were out to watch the spectacle of joy on Enghelab Avenue. Loud laughter, unending smiles, and the liberty of happiness in public—this was a celebration of the inner soul of the citizens of despair.

Hearing the music from his region of the country on Enghelab Avenue, frantic and broken into endless laughter, a young soldier revealed the last few teeth in his mouth. I saw the face of life. How badly the soldier wished to dance with that music. He did not dance. He followed the carnival.

A laborer ran after the truck of puppets. He had never seen a monkey so tall, a monkey who shook his hand! The laborer smiled and disappeared with the truck from my sight. "A man inside the monkey," he will tell his friends in the village.

"The hunger for happiness by the poor, the hunger for joy on Enghelab Avenue," I wrote to a friend.

Hossein Party: Turning the Sacred into an Instrument of Joy

It was the month of *Moharram* again, around the *Norouz* (New Year), I recall. It was in *Moharram* that, nearly fourteen centuries ago, Imam Hossein, the third Shiite Imam and a grandson of Mohammad the prophet, was martyred with seventy-one comrades in a battle with a large army of enemy soldiers in the desert of Karbala.

I remembered *Moharram* from my childhood days in Tehran—a month of mourning, self-beating, religious parades at nights, and free food on the day Imam Hossein was martyred. I always liked going to the parades with my friends. We could stay out until really late at night. We also beat our chests imitating the adults, men in black shirts, and the kids who seemed much more devoted than us. They cried for Imam Hossein, beat their chests nearly to death, passed out, and were carried away by the men in black. Brave, heroic, and devoted, they were envied by other kids. Oh, how much I would have loved to be able to cry like them, and get carried away by the men in black. But I could not. I was not really hurt, no matter how much I tried to convince myself of the psychological pains of the loss of Imam Hossein thirteen hundred years back. I guess I was not a good Shiite.

That was then. Now I was back in Tehran during the month of *Moharram* many years later. This was *Moharram* in the Islamic Republic, the state that celebrated martyrdom and dying for God and Islam, and made a virtue of mourning, self-beating, sorrow, and worldly pain. This was *Moharram* during the twentieth anniversary of the Islamic Republic: no music on radio or television for a month, unshaved men in black shirts, Quran readings, black flags, and magnificent religious parades.

The last Wednesday of the year, a couple of days before the New Year, I took a cab to meet some loving family friends for dinner at a flat near Karegar Avenue. The driver was unshaved, wearing a black shirt, listening to Quran recitation on the radio. He was speeding on Chamran Expressway. Off the expressway, we waited for nearly ten minutes at the intersection of Karegar Avenue and Second Street for a parade to pass. The radio was now turned off. The driver was cursing and rambling without pausing. Cars were lining up behind us.

I watched with amazement the long parade of chanting men and women, and very young children, some younger than four years of age, I thought. The parade was going south on Karegar Avenue toward Enghelab Square. Long and loud was the parade. Searching with my curious eyes for unshaved men in black shirts, I saw young men and teenage boys dressed in jeans, T-shirts, with nice hairdos, and body gestures that betrayed their joy of the outing, not the sadness of mourning the death of Imam Hossein. The parade passed the intersection, we proceeded, and the driver turned on the radio. I was in front of my friend's flat. I later told my friends about the parade. They nodded!

A few days later, having spent long hours writing, tired of staring at my computer screen, I heard the phone ring. "You are invited to a party tonight, a Hossein Party," said the happy young relative, wishing to show me "the other side of the Islamic Republic." I laughed, thinking that this was a bad joke by my bored relative. A joke this was not! I was told of Hossein Parties across the city that night. Curious and tired of writing, I accepted the invitation.

A mild night in early spring, I waited for my sixteen-year old relative in front of her parents' flat, waiting for the "girls" to get ready. And the girls appeared before my eyes in a column of seven. They came dressed up, made up, wearing loud lipstick and shoes with high soles—the fashion in the Islamic Republic. They came with nicely brushed hair, scarves pushed back to reveal their young hair, and the scent of all types of expensive and cheap perfumes filling the fresh air of this early spring night.

On our way to the party, we were joined by other teams of young teenage girls and boys, all dressed in their best, wearing strong perfumes and colognes, joyfully marching toward the big party of the night. Youthful laughter, occasional ringing of cellular phones in the hands of the voyagers of joy, and secrets whispered into the ears of friends—this was the night I went to a Hossein Party in Tehran, twenty years after the victory of the Islamic Republic.

Finally at the Hossein Party, I stood in the middle of a street in a state of disbelief. A bright street, busy, noisy, and active—this was the site of the Hossein Party I attended during the twentieth anniversary of the Islamic Republic. I stood facing the local high school, with its walls covered with black and green flags, loud Quran recitation from the loudspeakers inside, and young men going in and out of the school, looking busy and important. Young men brought out banners from the school, lining them up in the middle of the street, preparing for the parade. Organizing parades and the customary rituals of mourning and self-beating, feeding the numberless mourners, comforting them after the fatigue of their sorrowful parades—a *hay'at* the school had become for three days.

Hundreds of teenage boys and girls, festive looking and beautiful, they created a spectacle of deviance in the Islamic Republic of Iran. Boys on one side of the street, girls on the other side, boys driving around in fancy cars, girls going up and down eyeing the boys—they were the boys and the girls of the Islamic Republic on the night before the martyrdom of Imam Hossein. They stayed out late, marched in the parade, returned to the school, and stuffed their sensual selves with the free food—rice and curry, courtesy of the Hossein Party!

Boys in blue jeans, hip hairdos, and cool shirts. They stroked their chests in mourning, blinking at the girls marching behind them. Girls in expensive shoes—their best shoes indeed—paraded, chanting words of "sorrow" after their heroic boys. Eyes meeting eyes, hearts opening to hearts, the sensation of desire and lust in the air, they exchanged phone numbers during opportune moments, secretly arranged dates, found new mates, and made a theater of deviance under the watchful eyes of the bearded men of the Islamic Republic. They sinned, broke rules, transformed mourning into joy, and self-beating into sensual body movements of young men and women in search of love. They were the children of the Islamic Republic.

The next morning I was on my way to the Caspian Sea with friends for a short vacation away from the chaos of Tehran—a ritual for all those fortunate citizens with a car, a villa by the sea, or money to pay exorbitant rental prices during national holidays. Excited about the night before, I told a friend about the Hossein Party and all that I had seen with my astonished eyes. It was only then that I realized I had not been to the best of the parties, that my friend had spent the night at the Grand Hossein Party on Pasdaran Avenue, "chasing girls" and finally succeeding in giving his phone number to someone at 4:30 in the morning. He was indeed happy that morning.

I had a memorable time by the beautiful Caspian Sea.

APPENDIX

CHILDREN OF THE ISLAMIC REPUBLIC—A DOCUMENTARY OF THE DEFEAT OF THE ISLAMIC CULTURAL PROJECT

To document and prove the impact of "cultural invasion" on the youth, the state-run television network launched a special project that was to be aired as a part of a series about Iranian youth. A group of researchers conducted interviews with young people (mainly teens) on the streets, in parks, and in schools. They asked them for their views about life, culture, and music. To further support their case, the researchers interviewed youth in the prisons of the Islamic Republic. They spoke with young men and women convicted for social and cultural wrongdoing.

Though prepared as a political project to benefit the state, the documentary forced the producers into retreat. The state decided against the airing of the series. Instead of exposing the "cultural invasion," the filmed interviews revealed the severity of the defeat of the Islamic Republic's cultural project. The edited film was thus archived.

But like many other forbidden films, videos, and cultural products, this documentary was leaked out. Copies were made and widely distributed. A friend gave me a copy of this forbidden documentary. What is presented here is a transcribed excerpt from the documentary entitled *Mirage*.

Interviews in Different City Parks

Interviewer: How should one dress in your opinion?

Interviewee—boy: However one likes. We dress however we are comfortable—"Heavy," "Rap," or whatever else we like.

Interviewer: You said you go to parties. Tell us about these parties.

Interviewee—boy: We go late at night, without the family. We go with friends. We are happy. We dance, have a good time, and return home. The result is happiness and joy.

Interviewer: What is fashion?

Interviewee: What everyone wears.

Interviewer: Do you think the type of clothes one wears can lead to deviance?

Interviewee—boy: Not at all. I wear what I like. Whatever the fashion is.

Interviewer: Why do you prefer the park?

Interviewee—girl: Because it is quiet. It has green space.

Interviewer: What is fashion?

Interviewee—girl: Whatever looks good on you.

Interviewee—another girl: What is wrong with my pants in your opinion? Why do they [the security force] come and take us in their minibuses?

Interviewee—the first girl: One must be open-minded. Wearing certain clothes does not at all lead to deviance.

Interviewee—boy: Wearing a type of clothes does not lead to deviance at all. It is not possible.

Interviews in Different Schools

Interviewer: Do you encounter any restrictions in school?

Interviewee—girl: We have many restrictions, restrictions that have a negative impact on the kids, for example cutting the kids' nails by the principal.

Interviewer: Are you happy with the school uniform?

Interviewee: Yes. I think that is what is necessary.

Interviewer: How many groups are there in the school?

Interviewee—girl: There are a few groups: The carefree group, the religious group, and those exactly against the second group and the school officials.

Interviewer: What is the name of the third group?

Interviewee—girl: “Rap,” “Heavy” [short name for heavy metal], and “Metallica” . . .

Interviewer: Are these groups very different from each other?

Interviewee: Yes! They even compete for followers.

Interviewer: Which group has more followers?

Interviewee: I think the Heavy. I am a Heavy myself. You would not believe if I told you I was *Hezbollahi*. My appearance in school is entirely different from what I am outside the school. I believe everything has its own place, God in his place, and what I do has its place. It is my own business if I commit a sin. Look, they don’t put me in the same grave with a *Hezbollahi* person! I have a religious family. They pray. They are not my role model.

Interviewer: What is “Rap”?

Interviewee—boy: Wearing European and fashionable clothes.

Interviewer: How do you find the newest fashion?

Interviewee—boy: Video and foreign shows.

Interviewer: How do you like to be?

Interviewee—girl: I like to look good. Wear makeup. But I know my limits.

Interviewer: Have you ever been arrested for wearing a certain type of clothes?

Interviewee—girl: Yes, many times. Now you tell me, why do they import or make these clothes if there is something wrong with them? Why do they sell them at all? There are many things I like to wear. But, there is no use! They don’t let you wear them. *[A girlfriend arrives.]* See sir, right now, here, people have gathered to watch us because of our clothes. The culture must be raised! *Roosari* is *Toosari* [Headscarf is a smack on the head].

Interviewer: What is “Rap”?

Interviewee—boy: A type of music. But the government views it as a type of cultural invasion.

Interviewer: How much pocket money do you have?

Interviewee—girl: Seven to eight hundred tomans a day. We go to cafes everyday. My friends pay if I don't have enough.

Interviewee—girl: I want to leave Iran. I don't like Iran at all. I feel I am in a prison here even when I am sitting in the park. So far, they have arrested and jailed me thirteen to fourteen times. I have spent three to seven months in jail. This is all because I was caught with boys, or I didn't have the proper *hijab,* or they wanted to know why I don't live with my family. Why? Because they are prejudice! They want me to wear the *chador,* or not wear colorful clothes . . . I don't think I have chosen the wrong way. I like to speak with boys, to go out, to live alone, go anywhere I want, with anybody I want. But the law does not allow this. What can I do?

Interviewee—girl: I like to be free. They complain about everything, our clothes, and our hair. Of course, the way we make ourselves is not really right! But we have to. Because we are full of complexes . . . I am in the third grade in high school. The way I dress outside is totally different from the way I am in school. I try not to be seen by the school officials when I am out. I am afraid of them. My parents don't say anything about my clothes. This is because they are high cultured.

Interviewee—boy: I am in the second grade in high school. I have many problems. For example, today is Thursday, the beginning of the weekend. The *Basiji* ripped off my shirt. It was worth seven or eight thousand tomans. Of course the price is not really the question. They hit me. Cut my hair. Slapped me and kicked me. They wanted to know why I had the American flag on my shirt.

Interviewee—girl: Someone who told me he was a *Basij* hit me because I had not worn socks. I didn't asked for his identification card because I was scared. He pressed on my ankle with his boots like smashing cigarettes. [She cries.] I was in bed because of the pain for two or three days. Tell them to give us young people some freedom for God's sake. What have we done to deserve this?

Interviewee—a group of boys: Their restrictions have led to a lot of problems for young people. Many kids in *baalay-e shahr* [wealthy part of Tehran] have become addicted. This is all because of taking our freedom away from us. Let's go to Golestan [name of an upbeat shopping mall in a rich neighborhood of

Tehran]. I bet they will arrest us. I will show that to you. I don't think our problem is one of identity crisis. Look, if the system wants us not to wear certain clothes or do certain things, they should give us an alternative.

Interviews in the Shopping Mall

Interviewer: Why did you choose these clothes?

Interviewee—boy: I liked them. I bought them and wore them. Whether an outfit is good or bad is a matter of personal taste. I wear what I like. I don't allow my family to interfere in this matter.

[The film shows that the same young people express regret after being arrested by authorities or the Basij.]

Interviewer: Do you know "Rap"?

Interviewee—girl: Yes. It came from the West. Doctor Alban is its founder. I know him from his tapes and from the satellite dish and video. I spend my free time hanging out with friends. I go to classes, and to parties. We have a good time. We smoke cigarettes. But, I am not a Rap. Not everybody can be a Rap.

Interviews in Prison

Girl: I have been arrested many times, for different crimes, mostly stealing, of course, insulting the regime and fighting with law enforcement officers have also been a part of my convictions. I know I have committed many crimes. Only I know these crimes, even execution would not be enough for me if I wrote down all that I have done. *[She cries.]*

I always liked to attract people's attention. That is why I became a Heavy. I imitated TV shows . . . The leader always had the final word in our group [Heavy]. We used special slang like "shit" and "fuck you" *[both said in English]*. We all looked alike: tight pants . . . We would cut deep in our hands with broken glass and tattoo the word Heavy. We wore long boots with a lock on one side and a key on the other side.

The Heavy boys plucked the middle of their eyebrows. The girls' gangs were not allowed to be in contact with the boys. Those who had contact with boys were expelled from the gang . . . In parties, only the Heavy kids were invited. There were both alcohol and hashish. We would start with the bottle game. Sometimes we would become completely naked . . .

I do not believe in religion. I mean, I don't believe in anything. You are born one day. You die another day. Everything is empty and meaningless in my opinion. My only wish is for the regime to change. I have promised to stay Heavy for the rest of my life. I will never break my promise."

Girl: I never thought I would be in prison some day. I only thought of having a good time. I said fuck to everything . . . My family is not responsible for this. Of course, my father complained a lot. He complained even when I went out with my girlfriends and paid no attention to the boys. But I had my freedom. Sometimes my mother gave me advice . . . I finally met a boy. I thought he loved me. He called me all the time. I was young and immature. I finally did what I should not have done. Of course I did not want to . . .

I believe clothing has a lot to do with being drawn into this. We spent all of our time taking care of our appearance, buying and wearing expensive name brands. Approximately, three hundred thousand tomans was spent on each *teep* [total appearance, hairdo, clothing, and the subculture coming with that]. We bought our clothes from the Sorkheh Bazaar Mall. Some of the things we bought were smuggled . . .

I'd let my runaway friends in my house. Otherwise they had to spend every night at some boy's place. My father did not like this and became angry.

I now regret my past. I will not do this if I return. I am very tired. I also promised not to speak to anyone. I won't do anything without the permission of my mother. I won't go anywhere. Of course, I preferred outside to home before. This was because of my father's bad temper. But, I know now that I made a mistake.

Girl: The fact that I am in jail now is fifty percent my family's fault and thirty percent the society's fault. I only see myself twenty percent at fault. The bad attitude of my family, my husband . . . I was deceived very easily. Bad friends gave me the smoking habit. I finally ran away from home. I escaped from the town with a friend. I like to escape when I'm home. I like to go home when I'm here . . .

I slept at Mehrabad Airport at times, sometimes in parks, of course in the park toilet. I don't know why I did this, why I ran away. I think I have no way out. Life is meaningless for me. I am indifferent to everything. I tried to kill myself once, but it didn't work. I mean, I ate broken glass, but that was not enough. I didn't die. I have no hope. My family does not want me any more. I am eighteen now. I think perhaps being in jail is more comfortable for me.

Girl: Our house was near the army barracks. It all started with going to parties. It was too late that night and I stayed at a friend's house. I stayed the next day and did not go home for three days. I was then arrested and returned home. My father treated me well. They actually treated me better than before. I ran away again . . . I was a part of the Heavy gang in school. Once you choose a gang, you must have all the characteristics of the group . . .

I am very tired now. I won't do anything if I return, because I am tired. Of course I would have continued this if I were not tired, but not now, not any more.

Girl: They took me to the room by force. I didn't want to go. I told on everyone to the authorities . . .

First I ran away for three months. I was Rap. We drank whiskey in the school bathroom, smoked cigarettes with friends. We saw porno movies. It was the school principal's fault . . . She was a dictator. We did not ever dare to speak to her. We hung out on the streets the whole day. Our worry was the nights. Where could we sleep? . . .

I hate myself. It is six years now that I have not seen my father and brothers. When told about me by my mother, my brother said, "Let her die." They don't want me anymore. I am lonely. I have no one other than my sister. Mother says that I shamed her. My wish is to return home. I will marry the person my mother chooses for me. I will have a family.

Boy: We bought expensive clothes in order to be a part of the gang. Of course we didn't have the money. I got money from friends. Their shoes were sixty thousand tomans. They made fun of my shoes. Sometimes they exchanged shoes. Sometimes they stole them. My friends stole many things from my house. They took cassettes . . .

I myself liked Rap. I thought having the right *teep* and wearing the right clothes was very important. I am an addict now. It has been a month. My family realized this early on. They brought me here . . . It was for this *teep* that I met certain people and went certain places. The kids use cocaine, LSD . . . Of course it is possible to be a Rap without doing all of this. But ninety percent of the kids used drugs.

Boy: I went to parties two or three times. There was both alcohol and cigarettes. I was a Heavy. Of course I myself liked Rap. I liked how they dressed. But, you couldn't be a Rap in my neighborhood. Of course my father did not like my way of dressing. So, I became a Heavy, with all its ways. I started with hashish. There is a girl who is pregnant by me. They love our *teep* and our clothes!

Girl: You know what? I am confused. My wish is either to be hanged or be with Vahid [her boyfriend]. I damaged myself a lot with the things I did. I didn't know what it meant to smoke hashish . . . I am nineteen now, with two kids. I have no life. I have no respect for myself. All I like is to fight with someone. I hit myself until I see blood when nobody else is around. I calm down after that.

CHAPTER FOUR

Children of the Islamic Republic—Part II

Student Movement: Transcendence from a Movement against Rights to a Movement for Rights

---

STUDENT MOVEMENT AS A PILLAR OF STATE VIOLENCE: THE RISE OF UNITY CONSOLIDATION OFFICE (THE UCO)

I left Iran in February 1976. Though a nonpolitical student, I had become acquainted with the student movement and its demands in my high school years and later in the four years of college. I witnessed the quiet disappearance of classmates and the taming of vocal students by the late Shah's government, saw the armed guards occupying Tehran University and the area around the campus, and heard stories about brave actions by students organized in radical political groups. I heard tales of heroism and courage of students at the most prestigious universities, and crackdowns by the Shah and his police. Like many other citizens, I had sympathy for those who sacrificed their bright future trying to make a change for others, shared their demands for greater freedom and democracy and independence.[1] We sympathized with young idealists—the children of semi-modern middle classes with very bright futures in society—who fought for a more egalitarian society and improvements in the living conditions of the urban poor and the peasantry. Their movement was a crusade by the children of the middle class for the economic liberation of the poor—a social project to bring the political and economic promises of modernity (or the Shah's modernization) to all citizens.

Marxist or Islamic, the pre-1979 student movement was principally a movement with secular demands. It was a movement based on political thoughts that had emerged from the West and Western ideals of democracy and social justice. It sought freedom of expression, democracy (though not clearly defined and understood), and an economically independent Iran.

The student movement was a movement independent of the state. It was autonomous, both organizationally and ideologically. The movement defined itself by its opposition to the state. It was respected and admired by all citizens resentful of the Shah and his government. A symbol of heroism, selflessness, and intelligence, the movement was the gate to a better world for all—a world of freedom and rights. That was my image of the student movement when I left Iran in 1976.

All these features were later transformed with the formation of the Islamic Republic. No longer a symbol of the battle for rights and freedom, the postrevolutionary student movement became the embodiment of fear, terror, and all that was resented by millions who had enthusiastically supported the fall of the Shah. The student movement was now a movement against rights. It defined itself in opposition to the modern and democratic sentiments of the citizens, and represented the new state against its citizens. It was feared and resented. Gradually, after an intense process of elimination and recruitment of new forces, what became the Islamic student movement was a state-sponsored antimodern force composed primarily of children of more traditional and economically disenfranchised sections of the population. The postrevolutionary Islamic student movement became characterized by adherence to "revolutionary" violence and semi-militarism, hostility to modernity and all modern values and culture, and intolerance of others.

I visited Iran in July 1979. Still in its formative days, the Islamic Republic had not yet established its cultural and political hegemony in the country. Universities had not yet been taken over by the new emerging official "Islamic student movement." But a new reality was already emerging. Universities were to be tamed and put under the control of the new state. This occurred nearly a year after my last visit to Iran in Spring 1980 through the implementation of the so-called cultural revolution. The visit in July 1979 was to become my last visit to Iran for sixteen years. I witnessed from afar the implementation of the cultural revolution in the universities—the demise of hope and the dominance of archaic and repressive norms in Iranian universities, the alienation of Iranian youth, their hopelessness, and their fears.

The cultural revolution ended the modernist tenets of the student movement. Culturally and politically, the new student body organized in official student associations was premodern in its essence. It promoted and helped enforce premodern (Islamic) cultural norms regarding relationships between men and women, hostility to modern music and arts, and all that was outside the confines of the premodern Islamic values. Their suspiciousness of the relationship between men and women went so far that it led to the installation of curtains in the middle of classrooms to separate male and female students, in some universities.

Socially and politically, the student movement became the agent of absolutism, the monopolization of power by a single group, and hostility to diversity. The movement manifested the Islamic Republic's animosity to happiness. It helped instill in universities an atmosphere of fatigue, gloom, terror, and alienation—the pillars of domination by the Islamic Republic in universities and in society at large. Separate seating for men and women, a ban on the use of music, prohibition of all contacts between male and female students, and surveillance by angry young bearded men led to the emergence of a suffocating atmosphere of terror and unhappiness in universities across the country. Far from a site of free intellectual and social nourishment of the young generation, the universities of the nation became semi-militarized zones ruled by order, obedience, and terror. They became lagoons of apathy and alienation.

The cultural revolution transformed the universities and the student movement in Iran. It led to the elimination of all existing political groupings among the students and the domination of universities by *Ettehadieh-e Anjomanhaye Eslami-e Daneshjooyan-e Daneshgahhaye Sarasar-e Keshvar, Daftar-e Tahkim-e Vahdat* (Unity Consolidation Office, the UCO). Organizing a large number of Moslem students around unconditional and total support for Ayatollah Khomeini and his ideas, the UCO became the embodiment of the Islamic Republic in universities. It represented all facets of the state's political and cultural projects in universities.[2] The UCO was gradually elevated to the position of gatekeeper of the student movement, an organization funded, morally supported, tolerated, and used by the state. It became the embodiment of the state in universities, an instrument used to cleanse universities of all opposition to the state.

THE TRANSFORMATION OF THE OFFICIAL STUDENT MOVEMENT: A METAMORPHOSIS TO A MOVEMENT FOR RIGHTS

Unity Consolidation Office (the UCO)

After sixteen years of absence, I returned to Iran through a UN sponsored program for lecturing at Allameh Tabatabee University. This was May 15, 1995. I arrived in fear. Engulfed in the heavy image of a decade and half of unprecedented repression, I lectured for students and faculty about international political economy and the implications of World Bank/IMF neoliberal policies in the Third World. The visit in 1995 was the first of a number of visits in following years. I returned to Iran every year, lectured, got acquainted with Moslem and secular students, and witnessed the slow transformation of universities and the student movement. I witnessed the emergence of a powerful secular student movement and the transformation of the official movement from a state-supported institution against rights to a movement for rights.

Already, in May 1995, the old Islamic student movement had acquired a transformed face. I was pleasantly surprised by the open criticism of Hashemi Rafsanjani—Iran's president at the time—and his economic program by Moslem students. Students had waged a successful crusade against Rafsanjani's neoliberal economic policy and its impact on the livelihood of the working poor and most wage earners in the country. As a political economist and a critic of the World Bank–sponsored policies of economic liberalization, I was pleased by the critical articles published in *Payam-e Daneshjoo,* a weekly published by the group led by Heshmatolla Tabarzadi, the controversial student leader, unknown to me and many others at that time. All this was new to me. I bought copies of *Payam-e Daneshjoo* from polite and clean-looking young men at crowded city intersections. They even smiled and engaged me in conversation. This was my first exposure to the Islamic student movement on the road to a major transformation to advocates of reform, plurality, and tolerance. I witnessed the gradual transformation of campuses, the change in the language and the dominant discourse in universities, and the emergence of loud voices of dissent from the ranks of those who had once institutionalized the state and its violence in universities. A sea change was occurring before my eyes.

Two years later, in the summer of 1997, I met Abbas Abdi, an editor of the daily *Salam,* which was shut down in July 1998. We met in Abdi's office at the paper's headquarters in Tehran. A veteran of the U.S. embassy takeover, a prominent figure in the postrevolutionary official student movement *Daftar-e Tahkim-e Vahdat* (Unity Consolidation Office, the UCO), Abdi looked calm and gentle. He was distrustful of me. Once a radical Moslem, anti-Western, and a faithful devotee of the original model and project of the Islamic Republic, Abdi was now an editor of a pro-reform daily. I explained the reason for my visit. I was there to inquire about the social responses of wage earners to economic policies of the Rafsanjani administration. Abdi remained quiet. A gentle and distrustful look on his face, he politely allowed me to finish my tale. Cautiously exchanging a few words, he finally referred me to an economist at Allameh Tabatabaee University. The message was clear. Though a proponent of change and reform, he did not wish to be affiliated, in any form, with a stranger from the United States.

This was the summer of 1997, weeks after the unprecedented victory of the pro-reform Mohammad Khatami in the May 23 election. By now the old Islamic student movement had become an integral part of the movement for reform and civil society. A new discourse had emerged. The old language of hate and violence was replaced by words of tolerance and coexistence. Alongside the jubilant and Western-looking non-Islamic students, I saw smiling Moslem students—neatly dressed, articulate, and kind looking. This was the new image I faced in rallies and forums organized by the UCO. The political landscape of Iran's universities had changed. A new reality had emerged.

I met, befriended, and held classes with eager and enthusiastic Moslem students. I saw a new surge of passion for change—Moslem students genuinely seeking to learn the teachings of Marx and other Western philosophers, lamenting the lack of pluralism and diversity in Iran. I partook in rallies and meetings organized by the UCO, heard speeches against absolutism and for civil society, and saw well-dressed and articulate Moslem students joining force with secular students in a joint battle for rights. I witnessed Moslems clapping in public.

A new Iran was in the making. The war with Iraq was over. Ayatollah Khomeini, the leader of the Islamic Republic, was dead. The 1980s were long gone. A time for reawakening and questioning had begun.

The 1990s were the years of changes in the demographics of the student body in Iran's universities. The old guard, the generation of the embassy takeover and the cultural revolution had already graduated, become absorbed in the job market (mainly in state institutions, becoming relatively influential individuals), or withdrawn from politics. A new generation of students was being admitted to universities—a generation resentful of the repressive social and cultural atmosphere created by their elders—a generation of youth in the world of MTV and satellite dishes, a world increasingly intolerant of despotism and archaic social norms.

Not veterans of the war with Iraq, or early warriors of the Islamic Republic, even the new Moslem students aspired for a different world free of the negative social heritage left by the older generation. Not hostile to beauty and cleanliness, the new generation of students had a transformed appearance. Gone was the predominance of angry young bearded men, women covered from head to toe, and the violating anger on the faces of young men and women looking at the "other" with eyes of surveillance. Even the Moslem students now sought a normal social life. The revolution was long gone for the new generation of students. Now was the time to live. A time to enjoy the fruits of life, a time of social stability and normalcy.

Fatigue after a decade of revolution and war, state of emergency, isolation from the world beyond the ideological and cultural confines of the Islamic Republic, and the predominance of a general sense of social exhaustion had made the continuation of the old approaches to politics untenable. Not attracted to the discourse of the old guard, the new student body, Moslem and secular, reflected a passion for immediate "worldly" gratification and access to the fruits of life available in the world of the non-Islamic "other." Resentful of the images of the past, they were embracing a new image of life—a life of beauty, happiness, and nonideological existence.

No longer dominated by angry and bearded young men and Islamic women, the universities were now home to a diverse student body, a collage combining the dying images of the past and the emerging images of tomorrow. Smiling men and women in Western outfits, men and women who desired all that was scorned, broke all social taboos, and represented defiance of the past through their mere being—this was the new generation of students the UCO was facing in the second decade of the Islamic Republic. The old ideological approach was no longer tenable. The UCO had to respond to this sea change.

The 1990s were also years of profound political and philosophical change among a number of the architects and devotees of the

Islamic Republic. While in the United States, I had become aware of the emergence of a new movement for religious reform based around the teachings of Abdolkarim Soroush, a philosopher and an architect of the cultural revolution. Soroush's courses in the philosophy of religion, logic, and other related fields became an intellectual Mecca for many young Moslems energized by his ideas of religious and political reform. Privatization of religion, political and social pluralism, and other modernist ideas galvanized a new movement of "religious intelligentsia"—a movement of people loyal and committed to the state, but disillusioned by its institutionalized repression of thought and expression—a movement of Moslems seeking to modernize the archaic Islamic Republic.

While in Iran, I witnessed the effects of these ideas in the UCO and Moslem students. The clash between the "modern" and the "traditional" and the optimal mix between the two social projects had become a subject of widespread debate and interest among the supporters of the state. What was now resented by many, was the Islamic State's innate hostility to modernity. Achieving modernity (or aspects of modernity) became a desirable social objective among many Moslems in universities and the society at large. Ideas of pluralism, civil society, and respect for citizens' rights became critical to many Moslem students, including members the UCO.[3]

The termination of the war with Iraq and the death of Ayatollah Khomeini, the charismatic leader and primary architect of the Islamic Republic, were fundamental factors leading to the metamorphosis of the UCO and other supporters of the state. Here too, similar to many historical experiences in other revolutions in the world, the loss of the leader and the charismatic figure directing the energy of many devotees of the new order created a leadership and spiritual vacuum, leading to disillusionment and the questioning of the Islamic Republic. The disillusionment was compounded by the state's retreat from many of its earlier economic and social policies. The death of the Ayatollah removed the Islamic Republic's veil and exposed to the eyes of the state's loyalists what had been shielded by the presence of the unifying leader. Ayatollah Khomeini's death was, in many ways, the beginning of the end of the Islamic Republic—the surfacing of hidden and latent conflicts, tensions, and political division—the surfacing of the crisis of the Islamic state.

The years following the death of Ayatollah Khomeini and the termination of the Iran-Iraq War were years of political evolution, and a change in outlook for many organizations and individuals affiliated with the state. The postwar years saw the expulsion of the Islamic Left from the state, the replacement of the Islamic Republic's earlier populist economic policies with policies of market liberalization and privatization, and the slow erosion of the economic role of the state in the economy (see chapter 7). An era had come to an end.

The purging of the Islamic Left from the government eliminated the power base of the UCO within the existing political structure. After almost a decade of being the mirror image of the state in universities, the UCO now found itself in a precarious new situation. Although it was still a devotee of the Islamic state and committed to its preservation, the new administration and the parliament no longer shared many of the ideological standpoints of the "movement."

The UCO, like other elements of the Islamic Left, embraced both a populist critique of capitalism and vague notions of social justice and equality. It regarded state ownership of the means of production and economic enterprises as "noncapitalist," and opposed privatization and other aspects of the neoliberal policies of Rafsanjani. To the UCO and other leading organizations of the Left within the state, the policy metamorphosis from welfare state to neoliberalism reflected a movement away from the economic ideals of the revolution and the Islamic state, leading to the "rule of capital" and its subsequent injustices.

A distinguishing tenet of the UCO was always, explained Farahani, "its emphasis on economic policies that reduce class differences. This was the common feature of all groups within the left tendency. . . . Justice and freedom were always on the agenda of Islamic Associations. . . . The associations focused on the questions of poverty, wealth, and the structural adjustment policy when it felt that the implementation of the program would primarily lead to the creation of class differences."[4] The new economic policies of the state thus gave rise to a new zeal in the UCO to defeat the "rule of capital" in defense of the original (populist) ideals of the Islamic revolution and the "Imam's Line."

Thus, in the postwar years, the UCO was slowly transformed into a loyal opposition—a force within the system but critical of those "deviating from the ideals of the revolution." Once a pillar of the sectarianism of the state and its negation of citizen's rights, the UCO was on the way to becoming an advocate of civil society, pluralism, and rights. Once a pillar of state repression in universities, the

UCO was now seeking a new Islamic Republic—a more tolerant Islamic Republic—an Islamic Republic based on social stability.

The UCO's direct political activities peaked after the 1997 presidential election and the victory of Mohammad Khatami and his platform of reform. With the election of Khatami, the UCO became a vocal force opposing the policies of the conservatives and state institutions under their control. The new political tension between the conservatives and the official movement for civil society made an imprint on the UCO's activities. Moving away from its earlier focus on economics, the UCO concentrated on advocacy of the political platform of President Mohammad Khatami. It played an important role in Khatami's coalition for civil society and rights and became one of the primary legal/official groups organizing mass rallies in protest against the conservatives who were cracking down on free press and rights. Though still loyal to the Islamic Republic, the *faghih,* and many Islamic tenets of the state, the UCO became a paramount force exposing the judiciary, the security force, and other state institutions controlled by the conservatives.

Given the general lack of secular student associations and other alternative student groups, the secular students and young people seeking to express their resentment of the Islamic Republic and all that it represented joined the UCO-sponsored activities against the conservatives and the state institutions under conservative control. UCO activities thus became events that brought together secular and Moslem students, both men and women defying Islam and all Islamic values and those still loyal to the principle of the Islamic Republic.

The activities organized by the UCO energized and activated the youths alienated by Islam and the state. It brought out those who resented all Islamic values shared and promoted by the UCO, and those who would later defy the UCO's leadership in the events of July 8–14, 1999. The UCO planted the seeds of its own demise as "the student movement" and the leader of opposition to the conservatives. Raised seemingly to the status of the leader of the opposition student movement between May 1997 and July 1999, the UCO was reduced to a force desperately seeking to lead and control the student movement during the events of July 1999. The student protests in July 1999 revealed that the UCO had been merely a front used by secular students and the new student movement as a venue to express their anger in the months preceding the student uprising. There was no need for a front in July 1999. The new student movement declared its independence from the UCO and the state.

Though still addressed as "the student movement" by state officials and the press, the UCO proved to be a loyal opposition without the ability to influence a grassroots independent movement that was forming throughout the nation. It had become a force opposed by Right-leaning forces within the state, and discredited and isolated in the universities among youths with no historical ties to the state and its different factions. The new student movement was not to be led by those affiliated in any form with the state, and still advocated an Islamic Student movement. The July student protests marked, in a large sense, the end of the UCO as "the student movement."

The Union of the Islamic Associations of Students and Alumni: A Journey from Religious Fundamentalism to the Rejection of velayat-e faghih

Perhaps more than any development, I was intrigued by the ideological and political changes within the small radical student Moslem group known as the *Seday-e Daneshjoo* (Voice of the Students) or *Ettahadieh-e Anjomanha-e Eslami-e Daneshjooyan va Daneshamookhtegan* (The Union of the Islamic Associations of Students and Alumni). A group small in size, The Union of the Islamic Associations of Students and Alumni was transformed from a staunch supporter of the supreme leader, to the first organized group openly calling for constitutional reform to reduce the power of the *faghih*. Once supported and financed by the state, the union and its members became scorned by all factions within the state, attacked by state-sponsored gangs, beaten, arrested and imprisoned, and banned from existence. A month before the student uprising in July 1999, Hesmatollah Tabarzadi, the secretary of the union, was arrested and jailed along with other leaders of the organization. His recently published biweekly, *Hoviat-e Khish,* was banned. The union was silenced. No one condemned the state for silencing Tabarzadi and shutting down of *Hoviat-e Khish!*[5]

I attended a number of rallies organized by the union. Between 1995 and 1999, the union evolved into the most radical opposition student group in the country. It trespassed on all sacred grounds. It openly challenged the supreme leader two years before the July 1999 student uprising when "Death to the dictator" was heard on the streets of Tehran and other cities. I faithfully followed the communiqués issued by the union, read its publications, and followed its development. I met many students with nationalist tendencies at rallies organized by the union. What was least apparent in all those activities was any adherence to the state's version of an Islamic society, or even Islam. The activities organized by the union had a different tone and feeling from those organized by the UCO. They were more radical, more critical of the state, and more secular. This was appealing to me.

I was intrigued by the political evolution of the union. A splinter of the UCO, the union was founded under the name "Moslem Associations of Students and Alumni of Universities and Institutions of Higher Education" in 1983. It was founded as a student group with right-wing political and social views, a counter to the (Islamic) Left-leaning policies of the UCO.[6] In 1988, the union published the first issue of its publication *Payam-e Daneshjoo-e Basij* (Voice of *Basiji* Student), under the leadership of the controversial figure, Heshmatollah Tabarzadi. In later years, after changing its political position, *Payam-e Daneshjoo* was closed down by the state and its office ransacked by members of *Ansar-e Hezbollah* a number of times.

In an unprecedented and remarkably honest self-assessment, Tabarzadi explained the history of the organization before his arrest and imprisonment in the summer of 1999:

> In those days [the forming years of the Islamic Republic] . . . we were a minority faction [in the UCO]. . . . We were [a] radical religious [faction]. . . . Between 1979 and 1983 we worked as a part of Islamic Associations. I can say that in this period we were among staunch supporters of the *Khat-e Imam* (Imam's Line). . . . We have revised and changed our activities since 1983. There were positive and negative aspects to this revision. The positive point was that we protested the domination of universities by the Left faction [the UCO]. . . . Meanwhile, we fell into a type of political backwardness. That is, while we protested the status quo, we were not able to go beyond the context and framework of existing factions and present slogans and programs that would activate the student movement. . . . There were many students who were interested in being active on this level and did not trust us. [They trusted] neither the Left faction that had a monopoly control [in universities], nor us. Although posing reformist slogans in confrontation with the Left, we supported the state in a different way. And this ambiguity and static nature of our positions held us back. These were our two distinctive features until 1991.[7]

This type of self-criticism was indeed unique in Iran's political circles. The UCO never criticized and questioned its past. Tabarzadi's self-criticism was a sign of the group's readiness for a more complete transformation to an advocate of a broader concept of pluralism in Iran. This became further apparent in the group's writings and activities.

The death of Ayatollah Khomeini was a fundamental factor leading to the metamorphosis of the union, said Tabarzadi and his comrades. A decade after his death, the union reflected on the death of the Ayatollah, bravely challenging the new leadership.

> It became clear after 1989 that, *velayat-e motlagh-e fardi,* resulted in financial and administrative corruption, injustice, discrimination, and deep class divide under the eight-year rule of Hashemi Rafsanjani and his family.[8]

Most important in this political metamorphosis was the change in the union's position on *velayat-e faghih,* the sacred institution of the Islamic Republic. "We believe in *imamat* [the leadership of a spiritual leader], the same *imamat* established by Imam Ali [the first Imam of the Shiites]. *Vali-e faghih* can also have the same rights," said Tabarzadi in 1996.[9] But later, Tabarzadi rejected his earlier position about the *faghih,* publicly challenging the unlimited power of the *faghih* and calling for his direct election by the people and a limited term for his service.[10] Comparing the *faghih* to a monarch, on June 6, 1999, a statement by the Union declared:

> Three types or models of state have existed in the past hundred years in Iran: The absolute monarchy model that was supported by foreigners. The people-centered system proposed by the Constitutional Movement and later by religious-nationalist figures. And the system based on *velayat-e faghih* (governance of the Islamic Jurisconsult). This was later changed into *velayat-e motlagheh-e faghih* (absolute and unconditional governance of the Islamic Jurisconsult), or *velayat-e motlagheh-e fardi* (absolute governance of an individual).

Criticizing *velayat-e motlagheh-e faghih* as the dictatorship of an individual *(fard)* and declaring the political system under the Islamic Republic as a continuation of the old system of monarchy in different forms, the statement openly declared the kidnapping of the revolution by the leaders of the Islamic Republic and the turning of the revolution into the means for the dictatorship of an individual.

> *Velayat-e motlagheh-e fardi* has survived twenty years and is before us now. It is meanwhile necessary to consider people's wishes in the past and at present to find out the extent to which *velayat-e motlagheh-e fardi* is compatible with their demands. . . . The leaders of the revolution have substituted their theories for people's wishes. . . . Independence from foreigners, freedom from the dictatorship of monarchy, justice, equality, ethics and spirituality were among the demands of . . . the people . . . in February 1979. . . . By no means, what they [people] demanded of the Islamic Republic was the absolute rule of *velayat-e faghih*. . . . There would have been no need for a revolution . . . if the *faghih* were to replace the Shah . . .

Challenging the *faghih* and his constitutional power became the cornerstone of a comprehensive political and programmatic transformation of the union and Tabarzadi. Having argued once that "people's wants and power must be judged based on religious criteria,"[11] the union declared two years later that "even Imam Ali ruled on the basis of people's wants and satisfaction."[12] *Payam-e Daneshjoo* became the most vocal student organization advocating for people's participation in the government of the country.

"Participation" became a key concept in the union's political work after Mohammad Khatami's election to the presidency of Iran. The union criticized the project of "[economic] development" for its lack of clarity about "people's participation in politics."[13] It advocated the use of a free press as a tool for people's participation—an activity that goes beyond organizing rallies and demonstration, to include formulating and expressing opinions about the current policies of the state.[14] The union demanded people's right "to freely and clearly express their opinions about different policies [of the state]."[15]

After three years of being banned, on May 1, 1999, *Payam-e Daneshjoo*, an organ of the union started publication under the name *Hoviat-e Khish* (One's Identity), with Heshmatollah Tabarzadi as editor-in-chief, and with all members of the council of writers of *Payam-e Daneshjoo*. Licensed to Hossein Kashani, the new paper used *Payam-e Daneshjoo*'s old staff to re-launch their banned paper.[16] Soon, *Hoviat-e Khish* became a magnet to all those closely watching the student movement and its developments. It was there that Tabarzadi and the union spelled out their most critical assessment of the state and their own past, presented an inclusive and pluralist political framework for the future, and discussed the psychology of the metamorphosis both of the organization and of many Moslems outside the union.

In its very short life, *Hoviat-e Khish* focused on the "identity crisis" among the disillusioned old devotees of the Islamic state, while trying to articulate a new identity. In an article entitled "In Search of Identity" Fatollah Moradi argued that "defending the ideology of a part of society and the distribution of wealth and power based on ideology has led to a deep identity crisis and division among the people."[17] Hossein Kashani, the license holder and managing director of the paper wrote:

> The identity that was found in "Fakkeh" and "Dokoohe," matured in "Macoot," reached its climax in "Shalamcheh,"[18] and perfected under the leadership of Imam [Khomeini] . . . reached a crisis [in later years]. And most fair-minded, selfless, and thoughtful forces coming from the people and the revolution faced an "identity crisis."[19]

And Tabarzadi explained the "identity crisis" and the political evolution of the group and many other Moslems:

> Like Marxism that has a utopia . . . a utopia was shaped in the minds of Moslem and revolutionary forces. Our utopia was to establish a world Islamic government. In that Islamic government we were to have justice, equality, ethics and spirituality, and the victory and rule of the oppressed in the world. . . . In this environment, civil society was meaningless. . . . The Islamic movement could itself present a new model. For example, in our model the leader had a special and superior position. He was viewed and propagated as a charismatic and sacred person. Revolutionary forces . . . were judged by the degree of their closeness to the ideas of the leader. . . . This is contrary to civil society. . . . Power is distributed based on people's vote in a civil society. . . . The system of *velayat-e faghih* showed its limitations in the political, economic and administrative system especially after [signing] the resolution [ending the war between Iran and Iraq]. It became clear that [despite] many of the slogans . . . like justice, and the defense of toilers and the deprived . . . the

> country was pushed back instead of approaching its utopia and achieving more justice and equality. Injustice led to deep class differences. It was there that the first sparkle of self-questioning and criticism were surfaced, and intellectual debates found their space in the society.[20]

Tabarzadi defined the identity of the citizens of Iran as a mixture of Iranian, Moslem, and what he called "our culture and civilization." Clearly, a shift had occurred in the political orientation of the organization. After two decades, a type of nationalism was slowly emerging as a powerful sentiment in the union and the larger student movement. Even radical Moslem student organizations were no longer immune from this shift in tendency. A new brand of nationalism was being endorsed as a response to religious despotism. A new identity! The end of the "identity crisis"!

The departure from Islamic fundamentalism meant a more eclectic and open approach to politics, embracing ideas of inclusion and citizenship based on a person's place of birth rather than ideology. The union moved closer to Iran's nationalist organizations, the remnants of Mohammad Mossadegh's *Jebh-e Melli* (The National Front), and *Hezb-e Mellat* (Nation's Party),[21] forming alliances with and helping create a number of parallel secular student and political organizations.[22]

Once again, twenty years after the death of the independent student movement in Iran, Tabarzadi and the union proclaimed the need for the autonomy of the movement from the state and all its tendencies. Unlike the UCO, with its close ties with the Left faction within the state, the union now advocated a complete break from the state. This was a significant departure from the past—the sign of emergence of the nuclei of the student movement as a genuine social moment. Once a fundamentalist student organization, the union now defined itself in independence from the Islamic state and all its fractions. Tabarzadi explained the independence of the union in an interview with the weekly *Aban:*

> We find ourselves in one front with Khatami's programs. Of course he is a part of the regime. We are an independent group. Independent groups must not put themselves behind the regime or any part of that.[23]

After the election of Mohammad Khatami and with the help of an associate, Manoocher Mohammadi, Tabarzadi formed a number of parallel organizations with nationalist and religious tendencies. They included *Sazman-e Melli-e Daneshjooyan va Daneshamookhtegan-e Iran* (The National Organization of Iranian Students and Alumni), *Jebhe Motahede Daneshjooi* (Student United Front), and *Daneshjooyan-e roshanfekr-e Iran* (Iran's Intellectual Students).

The Student United Front organized a series of student activities criticizing the conservatives and their institutions of power, during the period between 1997 and July 1999. Eclectic in their political ideology, the Student United Front and affiliated parallel organizations embraced a combination of nationalism and Islam, promoting the secularization of the state, the creation of a civil society, the defense of citizens' rights, and other policies deemed dangerous by the state. Manoocher Mohammadi was later arrested as the main instigator and leader of the July student uprising. He was charged with inciting the unrest that shook Iran in July after traveling to the United States and Turkey for meetings with "counter-revolutionaries and so-called Western human rights groups." Mohammadi was accused of trying "to ride the wave of student protest . . . and to promote the line of violence and clashes." A scapegoat was found for the events of July 1999.

At the time I write these lines, Mohammadi and all leaders and important activists of the National Organization of Iranian Students and Alumni, and the Student United Front remain in the custody of the Islamic Republic, their status and fate unknown.

And five weeks after the appearance of its first issue, *Hoviat-e Khish* was shut down by a decree from the Revolutionary Court.[24] Copies of the last issue of the paper were collected and removed from all newsstands across the country. Tabarzadi, Kashani, and other associates were arrested and imprisoned. A new voice was silenced. A new beginning was aborted.

> [We propose]: The country's political structure must be a free republic in which all parties and tendencies, including the nationalists, Islamic, and socialists, can present their platform to the people. Ultimately, the majority vote must determine [who governs]. According to this perspective that is based on a parliamentary republic, it is the people's vote that determines what tendency and for what length of time it will rule.[25]

This was the last public declaration of the union before the closure of *Hoviat-e Khish* and Tabarzadi's imprisonment in June 1999.

Twenty years after its transformation of universities into sites of surveillance and control, the state lost the unconditional support the official student movement. Its pillars in the universities challenged the tenets of the system they once helped fortify. The Islamic state was questioned. It lost its social legitimacy. And the students revolted. That was July 8–14, 1999.

CHAPTER FIVE

Children of the Islamic Republic—Part III

The Politicization of the Movement for Joy: A Narrative of a New Student Movement in the Making

---

There are times in a people's life when events unfold with remarkable intensity and speed, all that is sacred crumbles before the irresistible power of questioning minds, the hidden becomes transparent, old taboos disappear, questioning becomes a social norm, and ordinary people become active agents of social change. Such were the days of July 8–14, 1999, the week when taboos were broken, the unquestionable was questioned, the fearful were fearless, estranged warriors held hands and created moments of collectivity and love. This was the time of love, the reunion of the estranged, the birth of new citizens—the youths who cried "Down with the dictator," and young men and women who dared to demand the ouster of the sacred *faghih*—the leader of leaders, and the "discovered saint."

In July 1999 a vibrant and energetic movement captured the attention of the world through the student protests in Tehran and more than twenty other cities in Iran. A new force with the potential to transform the Islamic Republic was born. No longer a tool of repression in the hands of the state, an independent movement announced its existence, a movement independent of all factions of the state. Defying the control and leadership of the official student movement, and announcing the irrelevance of the old, a new student movement proclaimed its existence in July 1999, a movement that betrayed and defied all expectations and created a nonrepairable crack in the foundations of the Islamic Republic. This was a movement of the children of the Islamic Republic against the state!

Twenty years of fear and submission, tight control of the student movement, and lifeless existence for those outside the cultural and political norms of the state were brought to an end. A new reality was created in the week of July 8–14, 1999. All that had been forbidden and scorned was flaunted by defiant youth. Looking beautiful and full of life, marching shoulder to shoulder, young men and women announced the death of the old order with their smiling faces and words of defiance. They defied the old, the state, and the old student movement. They were the warriors of freedom, the children of the Islamic Republic!

The following chapter is a narrative of the processes that led to the events of July 8–14, 1999, and the creation of a new student movement—the movement of young men and women with no political history, ideology, or affiliation. Born and having come to adulthood during the past twenty years, they were objects of the state's ideological and political propaganda and its hope for creating a new generation of citizens unaffected by the ideas of the West and modernity. They were to build the future of the Islamic Republic—a distinct Islamic state.

Soldiers of the new student movement, the children of the Islamic Republic—they dressed in modern Western outfits, reading Pablo Neruda and Milan Kundera, drinking homemade alcohol, escaping the pressures of the state with the music of Pink Floyd, Metallica, and Guns and Roses. Children of MTV, satellite dishes, Hollywood movies, the Internet and e-mail, and all that the Islamic Republic had fought to destroy for twenty years—they are the children of the Islamic Republic, eight years of war, twenty years of violence, random arrests, and imprisonment. Beaten by bearded men in slippers, flogged for having been seen and caught with the opposite sex, forced to spend nights in the temporary confinement of the state—they are the fearless children of the Islamic Republic. No fear of the beatings and flogging, no fear of the security force, no fear of confinement—they are the children of twenty years of violence and terror.

THE NEW POLITICS OF DEVIANCE—CLAPPING FOR RIGHTS

A New Beginning, a New Voice—Clapping on May 23, 1998:

May 23, 1998, was the day of an unprecedented event, the emergence of new images and new faces in the Islamic Republic of Iran—faces of joyous young men and women, faces of those who dared to clap their hands together, whistle, and scream aloud in happiness. They whistled instead of crying, "*Allah-o Akbar*" (God is great), clapped and laughed instead of angrily chanting, "Death to America," and created thunders of joy and excitement. This was May 23, 1998.

A new image was born when thousands of energized young men and women gathered on the campus of Tehran University on May 23,1998, to hear Mohammad Khatami speak on the first anniversary of his victory. They created a sight never seen in the history of the Islamic Republic—an orgy of joy and happiness, festivity, and defiance. They created a new politics of deviance. Clapping and whistling, they defied the dominant images of anger and violence. Laughing and screaming aloud, they defied the behavioral norms of their society. And standing closely together, men and women, rubbing shoulders and feeling each other's warmth, they defied a fundamental mandate of the system—the separation of genders. They transformed universities and the face of student politics. They defied twenty years of angry faces of young men in Islamic beards, surveillance on campuses, the separation of men and women, alienation, fear and terror, the death of joy on campuses, attacks on all semblance of independent existence, the death of thinking, the death of life. They created a new reality.

The students arrived with smiles and proclaimed their existence, the existence of a generation defiant of the cultural and social norms of the Islamic Republic, a generation determined to live and defy. They were the generation of deviants! Alien from the system, the proclamation of their existence was a powerful sign of the defeat of a project, the project to mold a new society, a new generation of the youth of the Islamic Republic. They were the youth of the Islamic Republic, a force the state could no longer control, a force energized by the will to live with joy and proclaim aloud its existence.

They dressed beautifully, defying the unattractive and violent appearance mandated by the state. They came wearing makeup, defiling the face of the "virtuous" Islamic woman. They came in tight blue jeans, T-shirts and deviant sunglasses, defiling the face of the "zealous" Islamic man. They had attractive hairdos, moved elegantly, and not for a moment did they abandon their beautiful smiles. They sounded the death knell of the cultural project of the Islamic Republic.

May 23, 1998, was the official inauguration of the politicization of the social movement for happiness, the birth of a new student movement! It was the birth of a new enemy. They had to be stopped.

"They whistle instead of saying the *Salavat* [praising Prophet Mohammad and his family] . . . I hope this mistake will immediately be corrected. I request our President to unequivocally declare this a mistake," said Ayatollah Khaz'ali at Tehran University on May 13, 1998.[1] "*Alloh-o-Akbar* [God is Great] is gone with people clapping and whistling in the month of *Moharram,*" lamented Ayatollah Khaz'ali on May 29, 1998. And Ha'ji Bakhshi, a known leader of *Ansar-e Hezbollah,* responded to the students, threatened to "stand up" to those who clap and whistle instead of crying *Allah-o Akbar*. We "will not allow them to clap and ridicule us," said Ha'ji Bakhshi.[2] The conservative weekly *Shoma* made a comparison between the anniversary rally and those organized by the supporters of Banisadr (the Islamic Republic's first president), reminding its readers that Banisadr distanced himself from God "with each clap and whistle." This was a warning to Khatami! And warning Mohammad Khatami in a Friday prayer in Tabriz, Abolfazl Moosavi Tabrizi declared, "I warn you Mr. Khatami not to allow the 20 million votes on May 23 [the 1997 Presidential election] to become a tool to destroy *Hezbollah* forces. . . . I swear to God Mr. Khatami that the [Tehran University] rally served the United States and had its roots outside of Iran." Nearly 40,000 seminary students and mullahs marched in the city of Qom, canceling religious classes in protest against the clapping and whistling by the youths.[3]

But despite these warnings, the clapping and whistling survived. They became a symbol of deviance and the new student movement, engulfing all political rallies and meetings in the months to come. And such was the tribute to Abdollah Nouri on June 30th, 1998.

A New Weapon Discovered—Deviance:

Abdollah Nouri, the first secretary of interior under President Khatami was impeached by a marginal vote in the *Majlis* on June 21, 1998. The impeachment of Nouri led to a widespread response by his supporters and the coalition of civil society in Iran. The student movement also responded. A tribute to Nouri was organized by the UCO at Tehran University on June 30, 1998.

June 30, 1998, 3:00 P.M. The auditorium of the Technical College of Tehran University was packed with enthusiastic students and supporters. Young men and women had gathered to voice their opposition to the assault on the process of reform. Fanning themselves with newspapers and pamphlets to escape the suffocating midafternoon heat in this overcrowded auditorium, they were patiently awaiting the start of the meeting.

3:30 in the afternoon. The usual separation of men and women into different rows was totally ignored. The room was transformed into a gender-mixed meeting place, increasingly resembling the public gatherings and rallies of the days before the 1979 revolution. A short, bearded man behind the podium recited verses from the Quran for fifteen minutes. Loud noise could be heard outside the auditorium. Hundreds of young students desperately tried to find their way into the room.

The Quran recitation ended. A thunderous burst of excitement followed. The entire crowd on their feet, clapping, whistling, and cheering endlessly. The festive sound of colliding hands echoed in the auditorium. Standing side by side, they erupted in a frenzy of clapping and cheering, exhibiting an unprecedented level of excitement and deviance. The youth created an unprecedented event, clapped after the Quran recitation, whistled and screamed in joy. New grounds were broken.

For most participants, the tribute to Nouri was indeed a celebration of the right to defy. Though organized by the UCO, the crowd's main manifestation was secular. Seldom heard were the usual religious chants. They transformed the image of political gatherings organized by the UCO—a front for youth energized and excited by a new opening in society.

The loud cheering and clapping were the background to a diverse set of chants and slogans that manifested the emerging level of political consciousness among young people and their courage to stand up to forces of repression. The cries of "Students are awakened, they despise absolutism," and "Death to absolutism" reflected a new level of courage and an emerging student movement. These were the slogans that were heard on the streets of the capital nearly a year later during the July1999 uprising.

Though gathered in support of Khatami and his cabinet, the crowd also articulated a demand for firmness and a more resilient approach by Khatami to the opponents of reform. "Khatami, Khatami, resilience, resilience," was their demand for a more radical approach to the political and social crisis of the country by Mohammad Khatami, reflecting the restlessness of the youths ready to push to its logical limits the president's platform for reform and civil society. They demanded true "political development" and freedom—freedom to be, to live, and to think. "Freedom of thoughts, always, always," cried out loud the students present in the auditorium.

By now the emergence of nuclei of a new student movement was apparent, a movement impatiently striving to materialize the platform of civil society. And once again, a concerted assault on students was begun by the frightened centers of power. This time, even those supporting Mohammad Khatami and his platform added their voice to the barrage of condemnation of the students. A new activism and a new sense of power had become evident among the young. It was the young people that brought about the victory of Mohammad Khatami in the presidential election of May 23, 1997. It was the young people that threatened the integrity of the Islamic Republic. Young people had to be demobilized.[4]

And the battle continued.

The country prepared itself for the election of the Assembly of Experts, a body empowered to supervise, appoint, or remove the *faghih*. Like all elections, this too was controlled by the Guardian Council and the discriminatory rule of "approbatory supervision" *(nezarat-e estesvabi)*, a principle allowing the conservative Guardian Council (dominated by the traditional right tendency) to supervise the selection of candidates and unilaterally reject the credentials of undesired candidates. All expected the rejection of pro-Khatami candidates by the Guardian Council. And the student movement reacted.

October 18, 1998. Five days before the election of the Assembly of Experts, a rally was called by the Union of the Islamic Associations of Students and Alumni in *Park-e Laleh* (Tulip Park) to present the views of the union concerning the election and fight for the "rights of citizens." The union had obtained a permit from the Interior Ministry for a two-hour rally with four speakers, including a one-hour speech by its chairman, Heshmatollah Tabarzadi. The permit was later changed to allow a one-hour rally with two speakers by the ministry a day before the rally. Tabarzadi was allowed to speak for fifteen minutes.

1:00 in the afternoon. The park was filled with riot control police and members of the security force. A collage of the supporters of the union, independent students and other young enthusiasts, and *Ansar-e Hezbollah* awaited the speech by Tabarzadi. Bearded men in slippers suspiciously roamed among the crowd. The air was filled with tension. Bearded men in slippers patiently filmed everyone in the crowd. Cameras slowly moving in different directions, they captured the faces of those wishing to escape the eyes of surveillance. These were cameras in the hands of bearded men in slippers.

And finally, Heshmatollah Tabarzadi was on the stage. The crowd moved forward. Fifteen minutes to hear the views of the union by its chairman—beaten, brutalized, and hospitalized for expressing his views about the *faghih* at a rally a year earlier. The direct pronouncement of the same views had the potential for leading to more violence and persecution and imprisonment. Brilliantly using his short time, Tabarzadi made references to the rally a year earlier and its consequences for him and the weekly *Payam-e Daneshjoo*.

It was a year ago, he told the crowd, that he was badly injured and later tried by the Revolutionary Court after having pronounced the union's proposal for the direct election of the *faghih* by the citizens, and the need for a term limit for the elected *faghih*. Thus, once again, this time indirectly, the union called for a constitutional revision and a fundamental change in the institution of the supreme leader. He called for direct election and a term limit, and treatment of the *faghih* like all other elected officials.

Fifteen minutes gone, a member of the union announced the termination of the rally. A bearded man in slippers held high a poster of the supreme leader. The *Ansar* slowly moved close to the stage and behind the bearded man in slippers. The cluster of hate among the dreamers of a better tomorrow was formed. The directive was given. The time for a showdown had arrived for the *Ansar*. Pictures of the *faghih* were held high in the air. A loud cry of "Death to the opponents of the *velayat-e faghih*" erupted. Angry faces, violent words, a call to kill, this was the message of the *Ansar* in white shirts, camouflage pants, carrying chains and knives.

And a sudden spontaneous response by the students in the park confronted the message of hate with the music of clapping hands. Clapping rhythmically to the call to kill, the youth transformed the slogan of death into a deviant music for dance and joy. A continuing duel between the two forces erupted. The agents of violence angrily raised their fists shouting words of hate. The children of the Islamic Republic whistled and clapped in rhythm, minimizing the power of their opponents by ridiculing their actions.

Disarmed and ridiculed by the music of the clapping hands, dizzied with defeat and helplessness, the *Ansar* continued to shout in disbelief. But the clapping continued. The laughter became contagious. And the call for death became louder.

This was the new student movement confronting the *Ansar*. Brilliant, brave, joyous, and defiant, they used new methods of collective voice, new tools to combat hate—the weapon of happiness, smiling faces, dancing hands, all that is scorned by the Islamic Republic.

May 1999—The Prelude to the July Student Uprising:

May 16, 1999, was the beginning of the weeks of tension and bloody clashes, the politicization of the new student movement, the first open confrontation between students and the state.

Waging a sitdown strike to demand the ouster of the president of the Islamic Azad University in Qom, students were confronted by members of the intelligence office of the university on May 17, 1999. Marches and rallies were also reported by students of Islamic Azad University in Varamin, protesting the change in the management of the university. A management shakeup designed to instill a more capable team to control the rising tide of student protest and their demands was on the way.

The country was awaiting the arrival of May 23, the second anniversary of Khatami's victory in the presidential election. All anticipated a new showdown, a new celebration of rights, a new confrontation.

Abdollah Jasbi, chancellor of Islamic Azad University, spoke before the main sermon in the Friday prayer at Tehran University on the occasion of the seventeenth anniversary of the founding of the university. An unusual and suspicious event, a non-clergy civilian was invited to address the Friday prayer at Tehran University. Verbally assaulting the students of Islamic Azad University, Jasbi threatened the students, charging his student critics with being "agents of some of the newly-emerged print media," vowing severe punishments for the politically active students. An official warning had been issued—a warning from the stage of the Friday prayer at Tehran University. A new showdown was in the making.

And May 23 finally arrived. This was one year after the official inauguration of the movement for joy and the loud declaration of the defeat of the cultural and social project of the state by the youth of the Islamic Republic.

May 23, 1999. They held red and white carnations in defiance of the violence of the state. They laughed and screamed in happiness, said no to the angry faces of bearded men in slippers. They had come in the thousands to *Park-e Laleh* to commemorate May 23. There were young men who wore T-shirts with pictures of Bon Jovi and Axl Rose, shaved their faces and combed their hair in style, and women who showed their beautiful hair, announcing their womanhood, rejecting the image forced on them by the state and the student movement of the past. Their jubilant energy led to a thunderous declaration of their existence. They existed. They were out and could not be silenced. They were the new student movement.

Powerful and determined, beautiful and joyous, loud and defiant, they returned to reclaim their rights. They returned to reclaim their movement. They were in the thousands, young women and men with no fear—the children of the Islamic Republic. Colorful lipsticks on the lips of beautiful young women, proud of their being, they loudly rejoiced in their existence as women in a collective voyage for rights. And the young men with their defiant T-shirts and Western outfits, they came with carnations. They came with smiles. They were assaulted. They refused to submit. They were beaten. They held high their carnations. They sang songs and clapped their powerful hands together—the dancing hands of men and women of tomorrow, moving together in the air, joining and departing, and playing the melody of life. A fantastic theater of defiance!

They came with pictures of Mossadegh and Khatami. Holding high Mossadegh's posters in defiance of the barrage of his denunciation by high-ranking members of the state, loudly chanting "Salute to Mossadegh." Mossadegh was now a hero for thousands of young students, born many years after his removal from power, born in the Islamic Republic of Iran, students who had not even studied the legacy of Mossadegh. Aware of the hatred of the conservatives for Mossadegh, they held high his posters and saluted him in public gatherings. A hero was reborn, a man scorned by the conservatives in the state—thus, a man worthy of support.[5]

They denounced the judiciary and called for the resignation of Ayatollah Yazdi, the judiciary chief. They cried loud "Freedom of thoughts for ever," and "Death to despotism." For nearly three hours, they stayed together and continued their demand for rights and freedom of expression amidst the assault by the hooligans in black uniforms supported by the security force and the anti-riot police.

They waved their hands, held high their posters and carnations, and smiled. They chanted with smiles and confronted the soldiers of fear and despair with a weapon the soldiers could not match—laughter, the joy of being. They were resilient and unbeaten by faces of anger and violence. They were defiant, deviant.

And they defied the supreme leader's warning against the criticism of the Guardian Council and the approbatory supervision. They chanted slogans against the council.

Three days after the attack on students by Jasbi at the Friday prayer in Tehran University, hundreds of energized and defiant Islamic Azad University students came to *Park-e Laleh,* demanding aloud the resignation of Jasbi. "Jasbi, Jasbi, resignation, resignation," chanted the students surrounded by the security force and the *Ansar* hooligans.

Defiant, jubilant, beautiful, and modern, these were the children of MTV and satellite dishes, computer games, rock & roll, techno music, and all that was forbidden. Once again they declared their existence on May 23rd, 1999. And they were noticed. Soldiers of life and joy were noticed by the state.

And it was the existence of this army of joy and defiance that the supreme leader had to deny. "Those around the country who exhibit wrong behaviors, words, and mindset under the influence of the enemy's propaganda," said the leader the day after May 23, "are not representatives of our young generation." Our youth, continued the leader, "are the same generation who will, once again, show their deep belief in Islam if there is a reason to fight for God today."[6]

And Nategh Nouri, Speaker of *Majlis* declared, "Using the pretext of freedom, they miss-educate [our youth] with books and novels. They sometimes promote prostitution and sin. . . . The youth that get instigated this way will no longer be a man of war and martyrdom." He had clearly heard the message of May 23, 1999. Will the children of the Islamic Republic fight a war for God? Will they be a "man of war and martyrdom"? The answer frightened the leaders of the Islamic Republic.

Children of the Islamic Republic, they were the warriors of a different war—the war for rights, the right to be. These were the warriors of joy and life and not the project of the Islamic Republic. "Freedom must be confronted if it plots against the system and fights against Islam. . . . The enemy wants to take away, especially from the youth, religious beliefs, purity, and sacrifices for the [war] front. . . . This is dangerous," lamented Nategh Nouri.[7]

They were preparing the ground for their assault. The new student movement had to be stopped.

A meeting of high-ranking Justice Department staff headed by Ayatollah Yazdi was organized to deal with the student crisis. "Unfortunately, in these days, while celebrating May 23rd . . . some individuals and groups . . . are attacking the Islamic principles and values and the authorities of the system . . . in the name of freedom and . . . through illegal gatherings and published articles." An order to crack down on the new student movement was issued by the judiciary. "Judges in different Justice Department branches across the nation, following their religious and legal duties, will deal according to law with all agents of conspiracy and all tension-provoking activities . . ."[8]

A war was in the making!

The students in Tehran and other cities continued their protests and demands for rights, confronting the violence of the *Ansar* and the members of the Security Force and the anti-riot police.[9]

May 25, 1999. This was the day of an event unprecedented in the twenty years of the Islamic Republic. The third grade students in Tehran waged a street protest demanding the repeat of a physics exam that they conceived of as unreasonably difficult. The Ministry of Education conceded. A date was set for the new physics exam. A victory was won by the youths in their first public protest.

Wednesday, May 26. A prelude to the July student protests, a rally was organized by students of Islamic Azad University to protest Jasbi's Friday prayer remarks. Beginning in front of Islamic Azad University's main gate on Palestine Street, the protest continued as a sitdown strike at the university parking lot after the physical attack by the Security Force.

A student explained the reason for the protest. "We began our protest by complaining about the [low quality of] food services and conditions of the dormitory. . . . In addition to educated professors and suitable classrooms, we demand the right to political activity."

The riot police responded. The Islamic Azad University students were violently attacked by the police. Many were injured, hospitalized at Imam Khomeini Hospital or moved to the dormitory for treatment. A number of students were arrested, taken away by the anti-riot police.

The pretense of neutrality of the security force and the state was now removed. Students were directly assaulted by the state and not by the *Ansar*. This was a new precedent after the cultural revolution, a new imprint on the memory of the children of the Islamic

Republic—those with no memory of the violence of state forces in the early years of the Islamic Republic. May 26, 1999, was a turning point in the new student movement and relations between the state and the students.[10] The war had begun.

JULY 1999 STUDENT UPRISING: THE NEW STUDENT MOVEMENT BATTLING THE STATE

The following is a narrative of events in the week of July 8–14, 1999, the week that shook the Islamic Republic, transformed Iran's universities, brought to an end the domination of universities by the official student movement, and politicized and transformed the children of the Islamic Republic. The children of MTV were attacked by the security force, chained and cut by bearded men in slippers, gassed, arrested, and declared the enemy of the state. A new chapter was opened in the history of the Islamic state in the week of July 8–14, 1999.

Thursday, the morning of July 8, 1999. The parliament passed the "basic framework" of the repressive and limiting press law. One of the most significant achievements and pillars of the reform movement was seriously threatened.

Thursday, the morning of July 8, 1999. The daily *Salam,* the most important organ of the supporters of Khatami, and a paper closely affiliated with the Collective of Militant Clergy, was shut down by an order of the Revolutionary Court.[11]

Thursday, the morning of July 8, 1999. A small contingent of students, two hundred in total, left the housing compound of Tehran University on Karegar (Worker) Avenue. Marching northbound, they protested the passing of the press law and the closure of *Salam*.

Midnight. The protesting students returned to the housing compound calm and quiet. Time of rest!

July 9, 1999, nearly 2:30 in the morning. The housing compound of Tehran University was ambushed by the *Ansar,* the security force, and anti-riot police. This was an unexpected night attack in an undeclared war. There was fire, chaos, burning rooms, clubs on the faces of sleeping students, chains breaking the bones of fleeing young men, blood, and death. The police and the hooligans occupied the compound. This was in the early hours of Friday July 9, 1999.

Friday, July 9, 1999. A war was waged in the housing compound. Hooligans and the security force on the rampage, injured students wandering in parks and streets nearby, and crying neighbors.

Friday afternoon. Students from across Tehran joined their embattled brothers and sisters. Ordinary citizens joined the protest. The student protest moved to the streets. There were burning tires, unarmed students facing the men with guns, barricades on Karegar Avenue.

The crisis in the housing compound was now transformed into a full-blown street riot. Citizens on the scene, the crowd was on the rise, the guards and the hooligans were ousted from the compound. Students were in control, masking their faces, young men guarded the barricades. Barricades on the streets, this was twenty years after the birth of the Islamic Republic.

Friday night, July 9, 1999. Hundreds of students of Shaheed Beheshti University assembled on the street in front of the university entrance, protesting the attack on Tehran University students. They were assaulted by the security force, arrested, and imprisoned.

Saturday morning, July 10, 1999. Attempts by the government's top officials to gain the release of injured students and their transfer to city hospitals had failed. Many injured students were in critical conditions under the custody of the security force. The number of the dead was reported on the rise.

The ministers of interior, higher education, and health threatened to resign. The Ministry of Interior called the attack "unauthorized and without coordination with the Interior Ministery." Mustafa Tajzadeh, the deputy interior minister, called for either giving total control of the security force to the Interior Ministry or releasing the ministry from all responsibilities related to the force. He too threatened to resign if those behind the attack were not brought to the law. The political divide within the state was deepened. The Ministry of Education declared the attack on students a "premeditated plan to create chaos" in the country, a plan to defeat President Khatami's project for reforming the Islamic Republic. A crawling coup d' êtat from above, declared others.

Saturday, July 10, eleven in the morning. Thousands of students and youth gathered at the entrance of Tehran University, protesting the violence in the housing complex and the brutal attack on students by the police and the *Ansar*. Enghelab Avenue in front of the historic entrance of Tehran University was the site of scenes reminiscent of the days of the 1979 revolution. Bookstores along the southern side of the avenue were shut down in fear of violence, shutters were going down, and people were strolling with faces of defiance. Fearless, students were mourning the death of the lost ones. They declared July 9 a new National Student Day, the "December 7" of the new student movement.[12]

Young and defiant, they came with masks, covering their faces to protect themselves from the eyes of surveillance. They mourned. They defied. They made a theatrical recreation of the days that had led to the downfall of the Shah some twenty years earlier.

Fists in the air, men and women stood in a united front for rights. Smoke in the air from a burning motorcycle, this was the near-occupation of Enghelab Avenue, across from the university entrance, by students. They were there by the thousands, there to declare their existence, demand respect from the state, and challenge twenty years of Islamic codes of conduct. They were there to defy all codes of conduct.

A new tidal wave of unorganized grassroots student movement shook Tehran and twenty other cities during the week of July 8–14, 1999. Free from all control by the state and the official student movement, operating outside the ideological and political domains of the Unity Consolidation Office (UCO), they defied the state and all attempts by the UCO to put an Islamic stamp on the new student movement. They were not to be led by the official Moslem Student Association, those who had ruled the universities for all the years of repression and censorship, the soldiers of the cultural revolution, the reformed old guard—the old repressors now seeking reform and freedom. They were not to be led!

Nearly eighteen years after the cultural revolution, the UCO was now a part of the protest in front of Tehran University, the university they once helped close. They were now assembled to protest the conservative faction of the state and the killing of students in the housing compound. They protested the entry into the housing compound by the police. They chanted against "disrespecting the sacred university." They cried, "*Allah-o Akbar,*" and read verses from the Quran.

And in front of the main entrance, thousands of students assembled along with the members of the UCO, thousands who reluctantly cried, "*Allah-o Akbar,*" and chanted after the loudspeaker in the hands of members of UCO. Thousands were there to protest the state and all that was old and entrenched in the power structure. They were there to demand a new life and a new structure. They were independent of the UCO and its attempts to lead the student protest. Demanding freedom from all forms of control, they walked on all sacred grounds, and openly chanted for the ouster of the supreme leader. They cried loud, "Khamenei, shame on you; leadership is not for you," and "The Commander in Chief! resignation, resignation." The sacred supreme leader was now the subject of the protest by the students, students who cried: "Sayyed Ali Pinochet, Iran will not be another Chile."

Saturday, July 10, 1999. For nearly three hours Enghelab Avenue in front of the university entrance was the scene of a war of words and chants between the students and the UCO. For nearly three hours the UCO tried with no success to contain the crowd's anger and construct a disciplined Islamic student movement. And the students defied all that was not to be defied, moved outside the domains of the old, responded to the UCO's Islamic chants with brilliantly constructed secular slogans.

"Mourning, mourning today, Islamic students are mourning today" was heard from loudspeakers controlled by the UCO. And the crowd repeated, "Mourning, mourning today, the militant students are mourning today." The duel continued throughout the day. The UCO tried, helplessly, to take the crowd inside the campus and into the University Mosque. The students rejected the plea, crying "No, right here," refusing to be taken to the mosque. They were not to build a new Islamic student movement. They refused to recreate the old, and manifested the existence of a brilliant, vibrant, and militant non-Islamic student movement. And they clapped when directed to cry *"Allah-o Akbar."* They mourned while clapping. They mourned differently.

They did not trust their "leaders" even when they were kindly requested to "trust the pioneers of fighting against repression." They did not trust, stayed outside the campus, and did not enter the mosque. They were out to create history—a powerful secular and independent student movement.

And students in other cities including Rasht, Shiraz, and Tabriz entered the protest movement in sympathy with the students in Tehran. A number of merchants in Tehran's Bazaar shut down their stores in sympathy with students. The crisis was reaching uncontrollable levels. The division within the state escalated.

July 10, 1999. The minister of higher education announced his resignation. Moosavi Lari, the interior minister, resigned from his post in the security force and handed the force entirely to the supreme leader. The president of Tehran University and all the presidents of its colleges resigned in protest against the attack on students. The deepening crisis of legitimacy and the split within the state was now more apparent than at any other time in recent years.

The UCO's failure to lead the masses of participants in the daily rallies was now a reality. Students openly defied the UCO, accusing its leaders of compromise with the state. And the UCO called "infiltrators" the students who manifested their uncontrolled outrage by their secular and anti-*faghih* slogans.

Sunday, July 11, 1999. UCO called for a rally at the housing compound, now in the hands of the students and the UCO. A few thousand students responded. Repeated attempts by the UCO to gain the leadership and control of the students inside and around the compound failed. A young woman, younger than twenty-two, dared to take the stage in the compound and declare the following: "I am not an infiltrator. I am a student. I do not belong to any group or party. But, I do want explanation about the attack on students. . . . Is not the leader in charge of the security force. He must explain about these killing. Or else, he should step down." This was the general mood on July 11, the mood of fearless defiance and questioning. Questioning the powers that be!

Cabdrivers, street vendors, bystanders, shopkeepers, all and all manifested a level of openness in their protest that could not have been dreamed of a few days earlier. Strangers spoke with each other about the attack on students. The young man selling newspapers on the street corner shouted, "Students are killed." He knew well that this would bring him more customers. The news about the attack on students was a new way to hustle a few more tomans for the warriors of everyday. This too reflected a new level of courage.

And on Sunday, July 11, away from the compound, in front of Tehran University, hundreds of defiant students gathered in an unauthorized rally against the attack on students. By noon, their numbers had reached nearly a thousand. And they marched on Enghelab Avenue toward Karegar Avenue and the compound, recruiting new members, chanting, and calling for support of their cause by the people. Proceeding on Karegar Avenue, the crowd grew in size. Bystanders joined in. Neighbors helped, giving water and fruit to the marching students. Others brought sandwiches and bread. And the students marched defiantly. "We shall kill that who killed our brother," chanted the marchers. And they cried loud:

"Death to dictatorship."
"Liberated student, unite, unite."
"Cannon, tank, machine gun, have no impact any more."
"Cannon, tank, *Basiji,* have no impact any more."

They held high copies of daily *Khordad* and its pictures of the attack on students as a proof of their grievance. Marching on the

streets, they were greeted by welcoming gestures of citizens Tehran. "Student, student, we support you," chanted a busload o fans going to a football match in Azadi Stadium.

July 11, 1999. By early evening on July 11 the official posture and language had changed. In the earlier days of the crisis, the focus of all official statements was condemnation of the attack on the students. But a new focus had emerged now—on the "infiltrators," "instigators," and "those benefiting from chaos and violence."

The interior minister issued a statement condemning "suspicious elements." He condemned slogans that "did not belong to our students," and "behaviors that did not belong to our students." The national television and radio repeatedly aired the minister's statement and other official warnings against the "infiltrators." After four days of near-silence, the official broadcasting services aired warnings against "those trying to take advantage of the crisis" throughout the night into the morning of July 12.

July 11. The National Security Council banned all unauthorized gatherings. "All unauthorized gatherings are considered illegal. The violators will be dealt with according to the law," declared the council in a public statement. The stage was set for an attack on the "infiltrators."

But Tehran was not the only scene of student activities on July 11. Students of Tabriz University organized a mass protest in support of their counterparts in Tehran. The security force and the *Ansar* attacked them. The bloody encounter at the university was later moved off campus. Street battles between students and the hooligans supported by the Security Force continued into the evening. Cars were set afire, banks and travel agencies were attacked and damaged. Other protests were held in different cities across the nation. Citywide protests erupted by students in Mashed, Isfahan, Oroomieh, Ardabil, Semnan, and other places. In Tehran, the students of the University of Arts began a strike and vowed not to take their final exams. In Zanjan, the students of Zanjan University held a mourning ceremony in commemoration of those killed in the Tehran University dormitory complex. In Khomeini-shahr, the students of Islamic Azad University issued a statement condemning the recent tragic incident. In the provinces of Bushehr, Hormuzgan, Sistan-Baluchestan, Ardabil, Mazandaran, Gilan, and Lorestan and in the cities of Birjan and Kashan, university students staged demonstrations and rallies. The student protest had gained a national dimension. The time for clampdown had arrived. A communiqué by Tehran's governor's office on Monday, July 12, declared:

> e of some unfavorable elements who want to dis- quility of the residents of Tehran and foment turmoil, nforcement and security force have been notified to effec- prevent any and all of those who try to stage a demonstra- on or a sit-in. All those who disrupt the peace and create turmoil will be arrested and handed over to the appropriate judicial authorities. No form of gathering is allowed. No permission is granted to hold any sort of rallies on Tuesday.

Monday, July 12. The first public address by the supreme leader since the attack on the housing compound was aired across the nation. The leader spoke before a large group of devotees and loyalists, outlining the course of official action against the protesting students, in a superbly prepared theatrical performance. Amidst the hysterical weeping of men and women faithfully listening to the leader's sermon-like address, Ayatollah Khamenei changed the official language used in addressing the protesting students. For the first time since the beginning of the protests, some among the students were referred to as the "enemy," financed by the United States to infiltrate the Islamic Republic and damage the country's national security.

The message was clear. The enemy was to be defeated by any means necessary. The national security had been threatened. The protests had to be put down. No tolerance or moderation was allowed.

The initiative was now out of the hands of Khatami and his administration to defuse the crisis by meeting student demands. Four days into the uprising, Mohammad Khatami failed to visit the students in the compound. His condemnation of the assault on students could not contain the rising anger of the embattled youth. The new student movement demanded immediate action. That was not delivered. And the leader had spoken.

The *Hezbollah* was called on to act indiscriminately and without any "unnecessary patience" to clamp down the protests. An army of "the faithful unknown soldiers of the Islamic Republic of Iran" was called to the streets to put down the protests. The leader said:

> What I tell the students is to watch and identify the enemy. . . . Strangers disguised as friends come among you. Identify them. You should look out for hidden hands. . . . The enemy has targeted the students in the past few years. . . . When some infiltrators take advantage of an opportunity to fish in the troubled waters and enter student circles, making some slogans and change some words, they should not think that we make mistake. No we will not make a mis-

> take. We know our audience and our enemy. . . . This is the enemy that wants to infiltrate the ranks of students . . . the students themselves should . . . be vigilant. . . . Be careful. . . . The enemy is making attempts to infiltrate the country. . . . The enemy has now targeted our national security. . . . Everything is destroyed in the absence of security. The enemy has targeted this. . . . Our main enemies in spying networks are the designers of these plots. . . . Where is the money allocated by the U.S. Congress to campaign against the Islamic Republic of Iran, spent? No doubt that the budget and a sum several times this budget are spent on such schemes against Iran.[13]

And having lost total control of the events and the initiative to resolve the crisis, President Khatami addressed the nation in a televised press conference, vowing to deal with the "deviation" in the student movement. Careful to avoid addressing students as "enemy" or "spies" of foreign countries, Khatami continued to press for adherence to law and order and maintaining peace. Khatami said, on Tuesday July 13, 1999:

> What I want to say here in a few words is this: A day or two after the events on Thursday night [July 8], a deviation took place. And in my opinion this deviation was not for the good of Iran. The aim was to inflict damage to the foundation of the system and engender violence, tension and disturbance in society. Fortunately, with regard to this event, the student movement [meaning the UCO] has declared its innocence. The behavior [of the rioters] was not based on any principles. The students declared that the event had no connection with the university. They said that some people were taking advantage of the situation. Some of the arrested people were not students.
>
> Undoubtedly, some will take political advantage of the situation. Basically, the violence and disturbance were against the interests of the system. They were against the interest of the nation, and against the policies of the government. . . . These events are neither deeply rooted nor widespread. It is easy to engender violence or disturbance in society. We want, as far as possible, to show society that we should confront violence without violence and it is for this reason that our dear forces responsible for law and order have sustained injuries.
>
> The issues raised, slogans chanted—inflammatory slogans against the values of the system and our nation's beliefs, and also deceitful slogans which for instance support a section of the system or the government—are all meant to create divisions and engender violence in society. Our noble nation will not be deceived by these slogans.[14]

By now, any possibility of tolerance toward the students had disappeared. Mohammad Khatami had lost the opportunity to address students' demands and resolve the crisis in a more peaceful manner.[15] Even in his televised press conference, Khatami failed to directly address and condemn the main perpetrators of violence, the bands of "the faithful unknown soldiers of the Islamic Republic of Iran," and the bearded men in slippers who clubbed students to death on the streets of Tehran. Khatami's call for law and order failed to identify and condemn the main advocates of lawlessness.

By Tuesday, the day of Khatami's press conference, the protests had taken new forms and dimensions. The UCO had ceased the occupation of the housing compound and ended all protest activities on Monday.

The targets of the student protests were using the situation to create justification for a bloody crackdown on the movement. Students were to be charged with lawlessness, threatening the national security, looting, and other intolerable actions.

After three days of retreat, and following the call by the leader, the security force occupied main corners of the city. Armed and supported by the security force, the "the faithful unknown soldiers of the Islamic Republic of Iran" began an indiscriminate attack on students. They looted banks and office buildings, set fire to cars and buses, broke windows, and even attacked a mosque. Students and their supporters were accused of the rising violence and lawlessness. The images of burning buildings and cars were shown on the national television to prepare the public for the assault on the students. The leader's address was repeatedly aired on radio and television.

Meanwhile, the protests spread to other corners of the capital. A war had broken out in Tehran. A call was issued by the Organization of Islamic Propaganda for a nationwide rally against the protesters and in support of the system on Wednesday, July 15. For two days, the call was constantly aired on the national radio and television. All the loyalists and supporters of the state were organized to take part in the rallies in Tehran and other major cities to show support for the leader. A showdown was in the making. Wednesday, July 14, was to be the end of all protests and the beginning of the state of siege.

Thus arrived Wednesday. There were hundreds of thousands on the streets of Tehran, paid devotees of the system, families of veterans of the war with Iraq, the armed forces, bands of hooligans armed with chains, knives, clubs, and other weapons. And a call to kill was issued by the deputy speaker of the Iranian parliament, Hassan

Rowhani, in an address in Tehran University—a new and heightened level of violence was authorized against the young dreamers for a better tomorrow. And a new language emerged in addressing the protesting students, calling them *mofsed-e fel-arz* (corrupt on earth) and *mohareb ba khoda* (warriors against God)—a charge only punishable by death. A call to kill.

> Over the past few days . . . the people have tolerated the events like thorns in their eyes. This revolutionary patience was very interesting. The people maintained calm with vigilance, but were ready to take orders. . . . Had the authorities not instructed our people, our Muslim, zealous and revolutionary youth to show patience, they would have torn these thugs and the mob to pieces. . . . Two nights ago we received decisive instructions to deal with these elements. And at dusk yesterday we received a decisive revolutionary order to crush mercilessly and monumentally any move of these opportunist elements wherever it may occur.

And the crowd chanted, "Death to counterrevolutionaries!"

More than two thousand were arrested on Wednesday and in the days after. The July protests ended.

Thursday, July 15, 1999. An undeclared martial law and a state of siege was imposed in Tehran. Plain-clothed armed men were assigned to the capital's streets, harassing, stopping, and questioning citizens of the embattled capital, *Ansar* and the *Basij* were on a rampage. This was the beginning of all-out revenge, savagery, terror. A semi-coup d' être was waged against the reform movement and its achievements of the past two years. Bearded men in slippers, riding high on their motorcycles, were unleashed to take revenge.

July 16. A day of confusion and fear was passed, a day of suspicion, distrust of others, a day of defeat and questions. Where are we now after six days of protest? Newspapers openly reported the looting, car burning, and violence by the *Ansar* and the men unleashed to attack and kill by the state.

We had been set up, victims of a plan to create violence and disorder and manufacture reasons for the return of the old faces of hate and fear, declared pro-reform papers. Where will we go now? What is the future of the reform movement? Will the press be assaulted next? Who will end up in jail? Who will be eliminated?

July 18. An official narrative of the July events was prepared. Manouchehr Mohammadi, members of the National Union of University Students and Alumni, and those affiliated with the jailed

Heshmatollah Tabarzadi were identified as the main culprits of the uprising, the main instigators of "the plot against the state."

The Ministry of Intelligence declared to the public: "One of the arrested persons was a Manouchehr Mohammadi who in the past few years had organized unlawful groups such as the Organization of Iranian Intellectual Students, Students Defense Committee for Political Prisoners, and National Union of Students and Alumni." Mohammadi and a colleague traveled to Turkey and the United States and met with counterrevolutionary groups in 1998. The counterrevolution had ordered Mohammadi to engage in a series of operations that included "organizing a National Students Union with the idea of leading student sentiments towards certain goals . . . provoking the young generation towards a reconciliation with pro-monarchy feelings, legitimizing violence and violent encounters with the idea of creating a political and social crisis in Iran," declared the ministry report.

A new round of arrests began of people allegedly affiliated with Mohammadi and Tabarzadi. In a televised recantation, Mohammadi "confessed" to having met with "counterrevolutionaries" abroad. A list of names of the "agents of Zionism" was made public.

September 1999. The Revolutionary Court convicted to death four students arrested in connection with the July uprising. The Ministry of Intelligence charged, once again, members of the small secular organizations created by Manouchehr Mohammadi and Tabarzadi in the past two years as the instigators of violence, looting, and other acts of civil destruction.

Mustafa Tajzadeh, the deputy interior minister, called for an open trial of those responsible for the attack on the housing compound.

The opening of Tehran University was postponed twice.

The Youth Movement after the July Uprising:

In July 1999 a new student movement took to the streets and created the first national struggle against the Islamic Republic. A new movement shook the Islamic Republic, a movement created by the spontaneous instincts and sparks of creativity and political consciousness of the youth—untamed, and fearless, without political education or experience, defiant of all attempts to be controlled, defiant of the state and the formal student movement. A movement was born free of control from above, free of leadership.

The July uprising, once and for all, closed the book on the control of the student movement by Moslem students in organizations guided by the ideology of Islam and affiliated with the state. It made history. It transformed universities and the relationship of the state with the student movement. It broke the chains of imprisonment of the energy and creativity of the youth. July was a loud moment in the struggle for rights.

Not led by the UCO or "misguided" by Mohammadi and associates, the July uprising was a revolt against twenty years of humiliation, social and cultural imprisonment, and an entrenched dictatorship felt in every moment of everyday life. It was a rupture created by ordinary people, those not trained in the intellectual discourse of the New Left or the Old Left, those not embedded in postmodern theoretical jargon. This was an outburst created by the children of MTV and satellite dishes—the children of the Islamic Republic. The July uprising was a significant moment in the long battle for rights in Iran. Though crushed by the state, the legacy of July remained. The imprint of state violence upon the minds of the young warriors remained. The battle for rights continued.

Following postponement and delays, the country's universities opened in the fall. Sporadic collective action erupted by the students in support of their arrested sisters and brothers. Not tamed by the July assault, the student militancy and determination to win reform and rights seemed on the rise. They waged demonstrations in support of freedom of thoughts, took to the streets demanding the reopening of the banned reformist press and the release of reformist writers and journalists. Determined to defeat the conservatives and win the legislative branch, they voted en masse in the parliamentary election of February 2000, creating a humiliating setback for the conservatives and their leading candidates.

The defeated conservatives responded. They assaulted the press. Nearly all reformist newspapers and journals were shut down. Respected and popular writers and journalists were arrested and jailed without trial. The attempt in the parliament to reform the repressive press law was aborted by the supreme leader. Using his constitutional prerogative, the leader demanded that the parliament refrain from changing the existing law. The government of Mohammad Khatami and the official reform movement seemed paralyzed and helpless. They responded to the continuous conservative assault with "passive resistance," hoping to defuse the potential for open physical confrontation and the escalation of the crisis. The conservatives proceeded. They attacked a UCO meeting in Khoramabad in late August. Citizens and the supporters of the students responded.

A street war emerged. A police officer was killed. Armed men occupied the city. Fifteen hundred people were arrested.

Rank and file students and the more radical student groups challenged the strategy of "passive resistance." Action was demanded. Expressing its disappointment with the official reform movement, the Union of the Islamic Associations of Students and Alumni accused the supporters of the president of pursuing a strategy of "growing silence." Upon his release from prison, Heshmatollah Tabarzadi, the chairman of the union, vowed to continue to fight for reform. "Reforms within the establishment have reached a deadlock. We need to launch an active but peaceful movement for freedom to achieve our democratic objectives," declared Tabarzadi.[16]

The rank and file members of the UCO voiced their impatience and dissatisfaction. They too demanded a change in strategy. The leadership defended the existing approach, called for calm and wisdom in preempting the attempts by the conservatives to provoke violence. The debate continued. The conservatives were winning new ground. The official reform movement was in crisis. It feared the disillusionment of youth and the students, or their further radicalization and escape from their control. The leaders of the May 23rd movement accused the conservatives of trying to radicalize the students and youth through their assaults on the hard-won gains of the reform movement. In a press conference in New York during the United Nations Millenium Summit in early September, Mohammad Khatami demarcated himself from the "extremists" on both the conservative and reformist camps. "Extremism in any form, in any direction, is unwanted, whether it's in the name of freedom or of suppressing the rights of the people, so we must create a balance," said Khatami to reporters. He too called for patience and calm, not demanding change that would go beyond the system's current capacity for reform.

Khatami's presence at the United Nations was an important international victory for the president and his allies. Capitalizing on Khatami's international popularity and success, the UCO and other youth groups within the May 23rd movement called for a welcoming ceremony at Tehran Airport, inviting the youth to greet the president with 2,001 carnations. Hoping for a disciplined show of support for the president, they called on young people to assemble at the airport and turn Khatami's arrival into a show of victory for the May 23rd movement. The call for assembly was heard. Nearly 5,000 Western-looking and jubilant youths responded to the call. Dressed in T-shirts and jeans, wearing makeup, and defying the accepted Islamic appearance, they came to greet "the architect of the dialogue of civilization."

But this time too, the crowd was not willing to be contained by the narrow demands and objectives of the organizers. The youths had come to welcome Khatami, but also to demand resilience, determination, and forwardness in the struggle for reform. They demanded action, showed their impatience with the strategy of the official reform movement, and turned the welcoming ceremony into a day of protest against the conservatives and their organs of power. They refused to be controlled by the organizers, challenged the slogans aired from the podium, cried loud for the freedom of the imprisoned writers and journalists. They demanded the reopening of the reformist press. Challenging and defying the order of the supreme leader to the parliament, the youth demanded the reforming of the existing press law. "Free political prisoners," shouted the youth. "Re-institute the freedom of press," "Reform the press law," and "Resilience, resilience, the reformist parliament," demanded the young men and women at Tehran Airport. They saluted the nationalist leader Mossadegh, and vowed to support Khatami and the reformist minister of culture and Islamic guidance, Ata' Mohajerani. This was September 9, 2000, nearly three weeks before the opening of the universities. The student movement was alive and determined.

Anticipating new rounds of collective action on the part of the students, the nation awaited the reopening of universities on September 23, 2000. How would the young people respond to the summer assault on the reform movement and the press? That was the central question for the conservatives and the official reform movement.

CHAPTER SIX

A Movement for a Free Press—the Vanguard of the Battle for Rights and Civil Society

The movement for civil society reached a new stage and gained unprecedented momentum after the election of Mohammad Khatami to Iran's presidency on May 23, 1997. New social movements for rights and freedom of expression emerged. Independent citizens' organizations were formed. Collective action for rights spread. Wage earners' fear of state reprisal slowly declined, job actions and collective action for improvement in their living conditions increased. Students revolted. New independent student organizations emerged. Women's efforts to change the archaic and repressive Islamic laws intensified. Environmentalist groups, independent charity organizations, and associations representing the independent interests of citizen groups forced their way into the new political landscape of Iran.

A civil society was in the making—a new reality expressed in the multitude of emerging independent organizations and movements, a new culture of social activism, and a new understanding of rights by the citizens—the right to collective defiance. And underlying the actualization and sustainability of this new momentum was the dynamic, persistent, and powerful movement for a free press and the realization and institutionalization of freedom of expression and ideas in Iran.

The election of Mr. Khatami gave rise to an explosion of newspapers and other print media in Iran. Once dominated by *Kayhan, Resalat, Jomhouri-e Eslami,* and fewer than a handful of other state-financed or controlled dailies, in less than two years, numerous new publications began their operations, each representing a specific political and social perspective. A large number of newspapers and journals specializing in women, youth, politics, culture, sports, and literature emerged. Flooded with colorful new publications, newsstands became magnets attracting a diverse population of young and old, men and women, teenagers, and all those searching for news and information pertinent to their needs. The press emerged as the frontier of civil society. The assembly of everyday people before the newsstands reflected the power and influence of the movement for a free press.

With the explosion in the number of print media came the transformation of the nature of the press, and the entrenchment of a critical press—the central embodiment of the project of creating a civil society in Iran. Bold and aggressive, the critical press became the echo of people's opposition to religious dictatorship, sectarianism, and political/social norms that had deprived them of their most basic human rights for two decades. The press exposed the serial killings of writers and intellectuals in Winter 1998, made public the involvement of the Intelligence Ministry in the killings, forced the resignation of the minister of intelligence, Dori Najafabadi, and prevented the continuation of the state-sponsored terrorizing of intellectuals. The press openly criticized the language and culture of violence and intolerance practiced by the opponents of change, brought before the eyes of the world the lawlessness of the judiciary and the security force, and exposed the apparent connection between violent gangs attacking citizens and various state institutions. And it was the press that made public the brutalizing by the security force and the bearded men in slippers of the students in Tehran, Tabriz, and other cities in July 1999—an event that would have passed unnoticed prior to the emergence of the movement for a free press.

The press fought the citizen's fear of state repression, the security force, and the bearded men in slippers. It transformed fear into empowerment. It wrote openly about what had been taboo for two decades, exposed the sacred, broke boundaries, spoke of the unspoken, and pushed the limits of the emerging civil society. A new social movement for a free press was born—a gatekeeper of the emerging civil society, a new collective voice—the voice of the "other," the voice of those not represented and those silenced in the past.

In the short years after the election of Mohammad Khatami, the press became the battleground of different factions and political tendencies within and outside the state. In the absence of independent opposition, political parties, and amidst continuing intolerance of non-Islamic political organizations, the free press became the primary venue for secular intellectuals promoting freedom of expression, political participation, democracy, and the secularization of politics. Embattled, assaulted for nearly twenty years, put down and isolated, and lacking financial resources, a small independent press had survived in the years preceding the election of Mohammad Khatami. It exploded after May 23, 1997. The secular print media, magazines and books, were given a boost. New translations of Western critical political theory, philosophy, economics, sociology, literature, and the arts were published, helping spread an intellectual culture that defied the dominant ideology and practices of the recent past.

But the free press also became the primary instrument for change for the now-reformed Moslems—the emerging group of "Moslem intelligentsia," the old architects of the Islamic Republic, and the new warriors fighting to reform what they had once struggled to build. The free press became the most important instrument for fostering religious and political reform by the "Moslem intelligentsia." They challenged state institutions controlled by the opponents of change, published articles and news stories about the antidemocratic laws and the violent language and practices of powerful individuals and organs, and used the widely read newspapers to put forth ideas of religious and political pluralism and tolerance. Publishing articles on political theory, philosophy of religion, economic sociology, and other theoretical issues, they aimed at popularizing ideas and paradigms essential for the transformation of the cultural and political landscape.

The press became the manifestation of the political and cultural divide in the nation. Papers and journals echoed the voices of different tendencies within the state and in society at large. Financed and controlled by the religious Right, the dailies *Kayhan, Resalat,* and *Jomhoori-e Eslami* continued to represent and defend the world view of those in control of the judiciary, the armed forces, the Guardian Council, and the Assembly of the Experts. Others, including *Salam, Asr-e Ma, Mobin,* and *Payam-e Hajar,* echoed the views of a wide spectrum of the religious Left. *Hamshahri* continued to be the main voice of the modern Right, the *Kargozaran*. New dailies *Khordad* and *Sobh-e Emrooz* became the public voice of powerful and important associates of Mohammad Khatami. And a host of independent weekly and monthly publications spoke to their constituencies outside the state. They addressed secular intellectuals, youth, and women.

The free press thus became the "enemy" of the political regime that had survived nearly two decades by blocking all channels of information, censoring all public manifestations of thoughts and ideas, benefiting from a political and social culture rooted in fear, suspicion, distrust of others, and self-censorship. The movement for a free press cracked the walls of this social structure, fractured the foundations of the state, and helped the formation of a culture of courage, defiance, self-respect, and collectivity. Free press was declared an "enemy" of the state. It had to be stopped. Hence, a concerted assault on the free press by the judiciary and powerful institutions controlled by the religious Right.

THE MOVEMENT FOR FREE PRESS AND THE LEGACY OF *JAME'EH:* "THE FIRST PAPER OF THE CIVIL SOCIETY"

The daily *Jame'eh* (society) was the first pro-reform newspaper that began publication after the presidency of Mohammad Khatami. *Jame'eh* gradually became the most consistent supporter of civil liberties, the most vocal critic of the fundamentalists and their attacks on freedom and on the new and weak institutions of civil society. While published only for approximately three months, the daily was faithfully read by intellectuals and students, and ordinary people excited by the prospects of the triumph of personal freedom and a civil society in Iran. *Jame'eh* echoed people's innate desire for change and their resentment of fundamentalism and its legacy of social control and the infringement of rights.

Published by Mashaallah Shamsolvaezin and Hamid-Reza Jalaeipour, and other old devotees of the "Islamic Revolution," *Jame'eh* was the voice of dissent from within, a sign of the erosion of the old structure and the state's loss of support of selfless veterans of the Islamic project. Echoing the voice of the growing "Moslem intelligentsia," *Jame'eh* popularized the call for change from within the ranks of those who had once comprised the pillars of the Islamic state. It was a symbol of the defeat of a grand social and political project, losing the support of its loyalists amidst the rising challenge from "others." *Jame'eh* was the loud echo of the growing loneliness of the Islamic state. It reflected the old guards' psychological pains of isolation, loss of popularity, and its eventual demise.

Jame'eh thus became the "enemy of the state," a threat to those opposing change—a voice to be silenced.

Three months into its life, *Jame'eh* was charged with slander, the falsification of truth, and the publication of materials against Islamic morals by the Islamic Republic's Revolutionary Court. The charge of slander was brought against the daily by Rahim Safavi, the chief commander of the *Pasdaran* (Islamic Revolutionary Guards Corps), and Mohsen Rafighdoost, the (now deposed) chair of the powerful *Mostazafan Foundation,* both from the ranks of the fundamentalists and the conservatives.

One month before its closure, *Jame'eh* had made public a statement by Rahim Safavi about reformers in Iran. In a closed meeting of high-ranking officers of the *Pasdaran,* the commander had declared his readiness to "cut the tongue" and "slit the throat" of the opponents of Islam. And a few days before the court ruling to ban *Jame'eh,* in a talk before a group of *Basiji* students, Safavi stated:

> A third tendency is hiding and attempting to create conflict and war between forces loyal to the revolution. . . . We have identified many members of the third tendency. However, we allow them to form their groups and organizations and establish their journals. But, we will encounter them at the right moment. . . . At this point the fruit is not ripe. When it ripens, we will pick them with the help of the *Basij*.[1]

The preparation for the assault on *Jame'eh* and the free press had begun. To defeat the project of reform and civil society, the critical press had to be demonized and stopped. To protect Islam, the agents of "cultural invasion" had to be stopped. The assault on *Jame'eh* reflected the fundamentalists' regrouping against the movement for religious reform, pluralism, and the call by the "Moslem intelligentsia" for remaking the Islamic Republic on new foundations—an Islamic Republic based on a plurality of religious beliefs, and democracy. The battle had begun.

Mohammad Bagher Ghalibaf, the commander of *Pasdaran's* air force, announced the readiness of the force to intervene in domestic cultural affairs to preserve the revolution.

> In its defense of the revolution and Islam, the *Pasdaran* is organized in a way that it is ready [to intervene] in all spheres, including the military matters, the presence of foreign forces, domestic difficulties, and the cultural invasion.[2]

This was an open declaration of war by the *Pasdaran,* a powerful branch of the armed forces, against its old friends, the earlier architects of the Islamic state, and those who had fought armed battles for its protection. Ironically, Hamid-Reza Jalaeipour had held important positions in *Pasdaran* in the past. He had been among the first group dispatched to Kurdistan to put down the autonomy movement in the spring of 1979. Jalaeipour had been for ten continuous years the commander of *Pasdaran* in Naghadeh and Mahabad, and a head of the security council in the Kurdish areas of the country. He had been the organizer and head of Islamic student associations in seventeen cities in England (during his graduate studies). A decade later, the force he had served in the past was organizing to silence his voice. New lines of demarcation were being drawn.

In his address to the *Basiji* students, Rahim Safavi spoke of the intention to shut down a newspaper on June 11. The events of the second week of June were preceded by a series of attacks on Khatami's government and the reform-minded press by a number of religious leaders and influential members of the Right tendency in Friday prayers and other public gatherings. Ayatollah Mesbah Yazdi, a leading Islamic philosopher, and a leading ideologue of the fundamentalists said: "Having lost hope in plotting against the Islamic revolution, the enemy has now gathered all its forces on the cultural front. After 20 years, no one could have expected a challenge to the most fundamental pillar of the revolution, *velayat-e faghih*. Discussing such issues (questioning the legitimacy of the concept of *faghih*) is nothing but a plot [against the revolution]."[3]

Indeed, the sacred *velayat-e faghih* was now a subject of discussion in the press. The press had crossed sacred frontiers, frontiers painstakingly safeguarded for nearly twenty years. It thus continued to be the focus of attack by the Islamic Right.[4] In the Friday prayer at Tehran University on June 12, Ayatollah Mesbah Yazdi attacked the proponents of freedom and civil society. He declared the following:

> In a famous American university and out in the views of other, a male and female student did something that I am ashamed of naming. . . . Others gathered around them and watched them while applauding. Sometimes they were proud of the longevity of the encounter. . . . What can be said about this by those who speak of freedom and cry about the lack of freedom in Iran? The fact is that they have heard stories about the West, or watched films and videos [about the Western life style] and now wish to have a life like theirs.[5]

Finally on June 11, 1998, *Jame'eh* was convicted and banned by court order. But the daily was allowed to publish until a decision was made by the appeals court.

"I request the press court to continue its work to end the activities of those journals that are run with the pen of paid [foreign] agents, and fight against those who spread western ideas in the society," said Ayatollah Mojtahed in Tabriz following the banning of *Jame'eh*.[6]

In an editorial on June 8, 1998, the conservative daily *Resalat* wrote, "We should not allow those who spoke with people with gun to repeat the same words today through the use of their pen. . . . Why should not the system and people find their track and give them the proper response?" Three days later, the conservative daily *Kayhan* wrote in an editorial: "We can find the track of foreign elements that have a black history of animosity against the people and the revolution by a passing look at the press . . ."[7]

And the press responded to the assault. The independent weekly *Aban* called the banning of *Jame'eh* "a threat to independent press."[8] *Aban* wrote defiantly: "The right tendency attempts to stop the society's [forward] movement. But, the truth is that while they might succeed in slowing this process, they cannot push the society back to the past. The epoch of censorship and the limitation of freedoms is over."[9] The weekly *Mobin* called the recent events a "political night-attack against the May 23 phenomenon."[10]

June 1998 was the time of the conviction of the mayor of Tehran, Gholam Hossein Karbaschi, a supporter of Mohammad Khatami and his project of reform. June was also the month when the nation was engulfed in the frenzy and excitement of the 1998 World Cup, and the historic football match between the United States and Iran. The independent weekly *Tavana* accused the Right of using people's preoccupation with the World Cup to launch its orchestrated attack on the government of Mohammad Khatami.[11]

Various political commentators also condemned the rulings against Karbaschi and *Jame'eh,* while criticizing the judiciary. Emadoldin Baghi accused the judiciary of "acting like a political party."[12] Ezatollah Sahabi, the managing editor of the monthly *Iran Farda,* called the simultaneous closure of *Jame'eh* and the conviction of the mayor "a crawling coup d' êtat."[13] Coup d' êtat was a topic of discussion in the press in the days that followed. The independent and provocative weekly *Rah-e No* (New Way) published two articles about coups d' êtat in its July 25 issue. In a translation of a 1996 article by Ian Campell, conditions very similar to those in Iran were described as a pretext for a coup d' état and the takeover of power by the armed forces.

Thursday, July 23, 1998, was the last publication day of *Jame'eh*. The appeals court revoked the license of *Jame'eh*. *Jame'eh*, "the first paper of Iran's civil society," was no longer to be read by the everyday people energized and emboldened by the critical press. Sorrow and disbelief engulfed those who, for a short period of freedom, had begun their battles of everyday life reading their copies of *Jame'eh*.

But, *Jame'eh* was not to disappear with the court order. Using remarkable creativity and devotion to the ideals of free press, and anticipating the decision of the appeals court, *Jame'eh*'s staff had already made arrangements for the reappearance of the critical daily. *Toos*, a pro-reform weekly published in Mashed, was to replace the banned *Jame'eh*. On Saturday July 25, the daily *Hamshahri* announced the continuation of *Jame'eh* as *Toos*, now published by the staff of *Jame'eh* as a daily in Tehran.

The new week began with the colorful pages of the daily *Toos* in the hands of the loyal readers of *Jame'eh*. *Toos* had replaced *Jame'eh* with the same format, the same staff, and the same politics—the politics of change. There was a feeling of triumph in the streets of Tehran, a victory for the proponents of change, and an unprecedented humiliation for the state. This was a new chapter in the battle for rights in Iran. *Jame'eh* was now *Toos*. The free press remained defiant. The fundamentalists responded. The war continued.

Ayatollah Yazdi, then the head of the judiciary, launched an unprecedentedly harsh verbal attack on *Toos* in his Friday prayer sermon at Tehran University on July 31, 1998. Indirectly addressing and criticizing the minister of culture and Islamic guidance for his liberal attitude toward the press, Yazdi said:

> There are those newspapers that grow like mushrooms without any strong roots, but are using their pen to attack the strong roots of Islam. . . . Let me tell you discreetly. The public officials must remember that this is an Islamic country. Islamic laws rule this country. . . . The country, families of the martyrs, and the youth that support the government will not tolerate any assault on Islam. . . . I expect the minister of Islamic guidance to act in advance so that there would be no reason for action by others.

This was an open call by the nation's judiciary for a mob attack on the free press. "There are hundreds of thousands of families of martyrs in this country. It is impossible for them to sit idle and watch you step on the clean blood of these dear martyrs with ridicule," threatened Ayatollah Yazdi.[14] The continuation of *Jame'eh* as *Toos* was indeed a public humiliation for the judiciary and the opponents of a free press. Angered and frustrated by this development, they continued their attacks on *Toos* and the free press in general.[15]

The call for the mob attack on the press was heard. On Saturday morning, August 1, 1998, a group of twenty-five hooligans gathered in front of *Toos* headquarters and threatened death to Mashaallah Shamsolvaezin, the managing editor of the daily. "When the judiciary protested the publication of *Toos,* the minister of guidance not only failed to order the shutdown of the paper, but also said that the publication of the paper cannot be stopped on legal grounds. Thus, since the law is silent on this matter, we found it our religious responsibility to take action," said an assailant to the daily *Hamshahri.*

Toos was shut down on that Saturday morning. But once again, the disappointed and broken subscribers of *Jame'eh* (now *Toos*) woke up Sunday morning finding yet another new daily sent to them by the *Jame'eh* Corporation. The Ninth issue of *Aftab-e Emrooz* (Today's Sun) was mailed to the subscribers of *Jame'eh* as a replacement for *Toos.* Another existing daily now replaced the assaulted *Toos. Jame'eh* and *Toos* remained.

Once again excitement and joy was felt all over the capital. Friends called friends, family members paid visits to loved ones, shopkeepers congratulated their customers, and everyone made the effort to be the first one to break the news about the survival of *Jame'eh* to their friends. Defiance and power was all that was seen on people's faces. Yes, *Jame'eh* was alive. In less than a few hours *Aftab-e Emrooz* gained fame and popularity unmatched by any other publication, becoming the public voice of the civil society. The free press was not to die.

The citizens of Tehran were solemnly celebrating this grand victory when the evening news on the state-owned national television sent shock waves all over the country by announcing the decision by the Justice Department to allow the resumption of *Toos. Toos* was back in print! Free press marched forward with a great sense of pride and power. Monday morning the city anxiously awaited the first issue of *Toos* after its one-day ban!

And the attack on free press continued to be the subject of sermons in other Friday prayers across the nation. Reacting to the closure of *Jame'eh* and its immediate replacement by *Toos,* the speaker in the Friday prayer in Semnan lamented: "How long should we witness so much lack of discipline in the press? The minute a newspaper is shut down and its activities prevented, another newspaper replaces that."[16]

The Friday prayer sermon by Ayatollah Yazdi caused a severe reaction in the press. The judiciary chief was charged with inciting violence and illegal activities by his supporters, and creating an atmosphere of chaos, fear, and lawlessness. The managing editor of *Toos* filed a lawsuit against Ayatollah Yazdi with the Justice Department—an unprecedented event in Iran.

September 16, 1998. Finally, the short orgy of free press was brought to a halt with the final closure of *Toos*. The daily's editor-in-chief, Mashaallah Shamsolvaezin, manager, Hamid-Reza Jalaeipour, a popular satirist and columnist, Ibrahim Nabavi, and Mohammad Asgar Sazegar, the general manager of Jame'eh-e Rouze Publishing House, the license holder of *Toos,* were arrested and jailed. The daily *Toos* and its arrested staff were charged with endangering the nation's national security, and opposition to the sacred regime of the Islamic Republic. Mohammad Asgar Sazegar and Mashaallah Shamsolvaezin were called *Moharab be Khoda* (enemies of God)—a charge that carries the death penalty.

September 1998 marked a temporary setback in what was the most important social gain of the presidency of Mohammad Khatami. The fall of Mazar Sheriff to Taliban forces and the killing of Iranian diplomats in Afghanistan in September gave new ammunition to the fundamentalists in beating the war drums and repressing their opposition under the pretext of securing Iran's national security and preserving national unity.

The statement by the speaker of the parliament, Mohammad Nategh-Noori, was a telling example of the fundamentalists' use of the Afghan crisis in attacking freedom of the press.

> We cannot deviate from our religious beliefs and the obedience of the *faghih* when the country faces bad economic conditions . . . the betrayal of Pakistan, the presence of Taliban in Afghanistan and drug dealers on the northern borders of the country. Who would sacrifice their lives, if our people lack such beliefs? The enemy has cleverly entered [the battle] and unfortunately, some with clear allegiance [to the enemy] are expressing views that weaken people's beliefs. Would our youth join [the battle] front with one order, if their belief in the *faghih* is weakened?[17]

Faith and religious belief became the main themes used in the battle against a free press. On September 15, in a meeting with the commanders of *Pasdaran,* the leader of the Islamic Republic, Ayatollah Khamenie, criticized some members of the press for their abuse of freedom and their targeting of people's faith.[18] The attack on the free press escalated. Ayatollah Yazdi suggested persecution of the writers of articles that "insult the sacred beliefs," in addition to the editors and those in charge of the press.[19] Soon after, the managers of *Rah-e No, Tavana, Aban,* and *Iran Farda* received threatening phone calls demanding the closure of their journals. Two days later, the manager of *Tavana* announced the closing of his weekly. After nearly a decade of cultural activity, the independent monthly *Jame'eh Salem* (Healthy Society) stopped printing. Independent weeklies *Mobin* and *Navid-e Isfahan* were shut down. The bimonthly *Asr-e Ma* was convicted in court and ordered to close publication. *Asr-e Ma* was allowed to continue its publication pending a decision by the appeals court. The newly formed independent and critical weekly *Rah-e No* was closed by its editor and license holder Akbar Ganji after receiving a call from the court.

September 1998 seemed to many to be the final days of the movement for a free press, and the beginning of a systemic assault on rights. Retreat and caution became the dominant mood among those remaining in print. Self-censorship reappeared. The newsstands were no longer the exciting places they used to be. There were no lines of men and women eagerly searching for their choice of this most colorful critical press. The sorrowful sight of the newsstands reflected the sorrowful demise of the most fundamental pillar of the hope for civil society in Iran. The deadly shadow of self-censorship under the fear of closure and persecution made most remaining journals the living symbols of a society whose life vessels were closed—a society in a coma.[20]

The attack on the free press continued in public speeches and declarations. Rahim Safavi, the commander of *Pasdaran* declared: "The *Pasdaran* will deal with any counter revolution group in any cover . . . if the plots of the agents of the cultural coup d' état reach unbearable levels."[21]

The imprisoned staff of *Toos* was released on bail after nearly a month in solitary confinement. Ibrahim Nabavi, writer and columnist, and the author the most widely read daily column, the satirical "The Fourth Column," said the following after his freedom: "I oppose the principle of solitary confinement. . . . Prison was not an interesting place. Its doors were closed 24 hours a day. . . . From now on, I will write my subjects concisely, well—calculated, and with wisdom and cleverness."[22] This was the painful confession of a man of imagination and creative mind—a man whose humor wounded the body and soul of the opponents of freedom, and brightened the day of those who avenged their years of misery with laughter and joy. Nabavi did not write with wisdom in the months to come. Two years later, he was arrested and jailed without trial along with many other reformist writers and journalists.

Mashaallah Shamalvaezin, the editor-in-chief of *Toos,* was released after twenty-seven days of solitary confinement. Though not directly claiming torture and mistreatment by prison authorities, Shamalvaezin described the verbal abuse and psychological "pressure" that he and others were subjected to during their confinement. "I was told," said Shamalvaezin, "you will rot here, if you do not confess." But despite these pressures Shamalvaezin remained defiant. In numerous interviews after his release he condemned his illegal arrest and the illegal closure of *Toos,* while defending a free press and the need for a press that is financially and institutionally independent of the state and its various organs.[23]

Toos was banned. But "the first paper of the civil society" survived the assault. In a few months *Jame'eh* returned to stands under the name *Neshat* (Joy). "Joy" was the name chosen by the publishers of *Jame'eh* for their new newspaper of the civil society. "Joy"—the ultimate weapon against the violence of the state, the inner foremost passion of all warriors of the everyday—"Joy" was the word in the large print that decorated the colorful front page of the new replacement for *Jame'eh*. "Joy" was the chosen weapon against violence. "Joy" was brilliant, defiant, critical, bold, creative. Joining the other newly formed papers after the temporary moments of retreat, "Joy" became a leading paper in challenging the fundamentalists, exposing the killing of the intellectuals and writers in the deadly winter of 1998, making public the brutal treatment of the students by the Security Force in July 1999. It published articles and letters challenging and opposing the *ghesas* (the law of Islamic retribution), and openly questioning and criticizing the role of the leader in the society. "Joy" was the "enemy" of the state. It had to be stopped. *Jame'eh* was to be no more.

On September 1, 1999, addressing a group of *Basij* forces in the city of Mashed, the supreme leader said the following about the press:

> Nobody can deny that I am a supporter of the freedom of expression and thoughts. . . . The pen holders [writers in the press] who deny the twenty-year struggle of the Iranian people against the repressive and plundering powers use the public funds to justify the

> needs of the enemy. . . . Their actions are no less than the actions of the bandits. They might even be more dangerous. Those who oppose the *ghesas* are *mortad* [apostate]. There is no question about the punishment of a *mortad* in Islam.[24]

The critical press was declared more dangerous than bandits. Two days later, on September 3, the substitute leader of Friday prayer in Tehran University and chairman of National Expediency Council of Iran, Akbar Hashemi Rafsanjani, told thousands of worshipers: "Everyday certain newspapers fuel the fire of tension in the country." And the next day, on September 4, 1998, *Neshat* was shut down by court order. "Joy" was banned.

But the battle continued. The publishers of "Joy" remained defiant. The creativity of *Jame'eh, Toos,* and *Neshat* now reappeared, in less than a week, in a new daily, *Akhbar Eghtesadi* (Economic News). Published by the same staff as "Joy," the "Economic News" was about anything but economic news. Devoting two pages to economics, the daily continued the defiant tradition of *Jame'eh*. *Akhbar Eghtesadi* was the new daily by the publishers of the first paper of the civil society. It gained respect and recognition from inception. On October 7, 1999, nearly a month after the closure of *Neshat,* the publishers of *Jame'eh* engulfed their loyal readers with joy, this time with *Asr-e Azadegan* (the Epoch of the Freed)—a daily with *Jame'eh's* staff and following the format, platform, and the appearance of *Jame'eh*. And on November 2, Mashaallah Shamsolvaezin, editor-in-chief of the pro-reform *Asr-e Azadegan* was called to appear before the court on charges of insulting Islamic values. These were charges related to the publication of the banned *Neshat*. Shamsolvaezin called the court illegal and refused to defend himself before an illegal court. He was later sentenced to three years in jail.

But the daily *Jame'eh* continued its publication under a new name. The first paper of the civil society survived the assault. Its death arrived in the spring of 2000. The supreme leader charged it with being a "spy net" in a declaration against the free press. *Jame'eh* ceased to exist.

FREE PRESS IN THE WINTER OF SMOG AND DEATH

The long and deadly winter of 1998 arrived.

November and December 1998 were the months of sorrow and pain, the disappearance and death of writers, activists, and intellectuals.

And the attack on the press continued amidst political assassinations in the month of December.[25] But now the independent press responded with a new zeal and energy. Forced to retreat earlier, it now emerged out of self-censorship and the mood of defeat. The press, once again, became a vanguard in the movement for civil society. The days of self-censorship were over. The movement for a free press was to lead the national anger and desire to expose and punish those responsible for the murders.

While the dailies *Rasalat, Jomhoori-e Islami, Kayhan,* and other conservative papers joined the voices of their influential political leaders, blaming the murders on "foreign conspirators," the CIA, and world Zionism, the independent press focused on domestic forces, and the violence perpetrated by the fundamentalists. The political assassinations gave rise to open criticism of the faction in control of the judiciary, the parliament, and the security force. Some charged the head of the judiciary and other fundamentalists with advocating violence, and not responding to the recent spate of political killings. Others accused the fundamentalist faction of the state of having organized the killings to defeat Khatami's project of political and social reform. The monthly *Iran Farda* in its December editorial addressed "those within the rulers who promote violence and chaos under the pretext of preserving Islam." The editorial defended the "republic, as the real and final guarantor of Islamic values." It concluded that Khatami was "the last chance for the survival and development of the Islamic revolution."[26]

Addressing the reaction of influential conservative figures and their charging "foreign arrogance" and the "Zionists" for the recent spate of murders, Taghi Rahmani wrote in *Iran Farda,* "Such refusal to accept responsibility from an important part of the rulers is an important warning. Such reactions allow this faction to declare a state of emergency, interfere as the savior [of the nation], and take control of the situation."[27] The press challenged the fundamentalists. The fundamentalists continued their assault on the free press.

In his Friday prayer sermon on the occasion of Christmas at Tehran University, the supreme leader challenged the press. The leader said:

> I criticized some newspapers but they cried out that there was no freedom. I am a strong advocate of freedom myself. But, there are some that take advantage of this freedom and create tension in the society. Some of these newspapers choose their headlines in a way

> to pit people against one another. Our press must work to bring political factions closer to each other. They should not exaggerate existing differences.[28]

On that same day, the Friday Imam of Ganaveh attacked the press and called for cutting the tongues and breaking the hands of the "mercenary press."[29]

Amidst the pressure by state officials, threatening speeches and proclamations by influential clergy, and the orgy of murders of writers and intellectuals, the press exhibited a remarkable degree of bravery, commitment, professionalism, as well as the spirit of freedom. It became the voice of all who were angered by the killings, a free podium for all who wished to challenge the state, and the loud cry of all ordinary people who demanded justice and an end to violence. The press was indeed a new form of a social movement for justice and freedom. And it was the pressure of the free press that finally forced the state to reveal the deadly connection between the Ministry of Intelligence and the killings—a revelation that would not have happened under other circumstances. The press was a symbol of the public discontent. It challenged the state, forced it to abide by the rules of civil society. The critical press said no, it refused to be silenced, and boldly confronted the forces of terror. A new movement was born in the young and fragile civil society of Iran—the movement that forced the state to retreat.

Thus, on January 5, 1999, the Ministry of Intelligence issued an unprecedented statement about the killings of writers and intellectuals. "With much regret, a number of our irresponsible, devious, and willful colleagues in the ministry [of Intelligence] who were undoubtedly used as tools by unknown [foreign] agents in furthering their cause, were among those committing these crimes."[30]

For the first time in Iran's recent history an important state institution assumed responsibility for the terror and murder of its citizens. The press had forced the state to a historic confession. Other writers and activists on the death list were saved. This was a new chapter in the history of the struggle for civil society in Iran.

The state had to be saved. Mohammad Nategh-Noori, the Speaker of Parliament proclaimed: "The Ministry of Intelligence forces did an excellent job in unfolding these plots. Their performance should indeed be praised." The dailies *Resalat, Kayhan,* and *Jomhoori Islami* also carried articles and interviews with *Majlis* MPs and state officials praising the performance of the ministry and still accusing foreigners of being connected to these crimes. But others in the press began a widespread campaign for a further investigation into the murders and the trial of those in the leadership of the killing gang.

In a column for the newly established daily *Sobh-e Emrooz* (Today's Morning), Akbar Ganji, the editor of the banned weekly *Rah-e No,* wrote about the "Directors of Terror." Ganji referred to a claim that three judges from a judiciary unit had convicted the murdered writers and activists to the death penalty in a closed trial. Ganji asked for their arrest, the revelation of their names to society, and an immediate trial of the judges:

> The directors [of these crimes] are not necessarily homed in the Ministry of Intelligence. The devious and politically defeated [forces] can infiltrate [the ministry] and influence obedient individuals and order them to take part in terror. The directors wish for an expedient dealing with the killers so that their role will disappear from the public's memory. Focusing on the Ministry of Intelligence is a visual error. . . . We must identify the directors in any clothes and any position.[31]

Ganji called for the criminalization and prosecution of hate speech and physical assault. He became the most articulate and vocal member of the press exposing the organs of the state and their involvement in the killings of their opponents. His columns about the killings became a nightmare for the fundamentalists in the months that followed. Two years later, Ganji was jailed without trial. He remains in jail at the time of this writing.

Other critics including Mohsen Kadivar called for a fundamental restructuring of the Ministry of Intelligence and an immediate resignation of the minister. Kadivar said: "I suggest to Mr. Dori Najafabadi to immediately hand his resignation to the President. But, if he lacks the power and courage to do so, it is the public's demand that the President fires him." Kadivar criticized the parliament for not calling for the impeachment of the minister. Ezatollah Sahabi, a leading member of the Freedom Movement and the managing director of *Iran Farda,* publicly demanded a search for the instigators of these crimes within the high-ranking members of the state. Sahabi said:

> To find the reasons for these crimes necessitates searching for those who benefit from them. Regarding this matter, it is not believable

> that a cell within the Ministry of Intelligence has acted alone. Indeed, the instigators of these crimes must be sought within the repressive tendencies [of the state].

Challenging the view of many within the state about the nature of these crimes, Sahabi said:

> Before being a national security question, these crimes are political. The faction in control of power is by no means committed [to law]. It uses fear and terror to impose its power. Thus, I believe that even with the freeing of the Ministry of Intelligence of their agents, they will continue their methods through secret and illegal channels.[32]

The grassroots movement against violence and for the arrest of the instigators of crime and violence continued in the press. Newspapers and weeklies including *Salam, Khordad, Sobh-e Emrooz, Hamshahri,* Zan, *Iran, Aban, Neshat,* and others maintained a high profile and filled their pages with critical articles, news stories, interviews, and public opinion polls about the killings. They pressured Khatami and his administration not to stop at the level of arresting and punishing only a few employees of the Ministry of Intelligence. They demanded the restructuring of the state.

It was clear to the public that the killings had been ordered by high-ranking members of the state. What had happened in Iran was state terrorism against its own citizens and nothing seemed to be able to stop the public demand for justice. The press was the main vehicle in the movement for justice. The call for the resignation of the minister of intelligence became a public cry in the days after January 6, 1999. The crisis reached unprecedented dimensions. The state had to be protected.

On Friday January 10, 1999, the supreme leader blamed foreign forces as the instigators of recent killings, while praising the services of the Information Ministry in the past twenty years. The leader's Friday prayer speech was, in a sense, a historical speech that highlighted and clearly presented the political culture and perspective of the dominant faction of the state regarding the recent events. It was an attack on the press. The press was, once again, acting like the "enemy." Ayatollah Khamenie said:

> I do not think the issue is over. This seems to be a long story. I cannot accept that these murders took place without a foreign scenario behind them. This is impossible. . . . I am not surprised at

> the propaganda ballyhoo of the foreign media. But, I am surprised at what some of our own media, including the press, are doing. They are acting exactly like our enemies. They are like a stupid child who would make fun of his father when he is at odds with someone else . . .[33]

The victims of the crimes became the "harmless enemy," and those responsible were asked to "defend the nation" against the enemy. The press had indeed brought fear to the state. And despite the speech by the leader, the press continued to publish reports, statements by student groups and other political organizations, and interviews that openly contradicted the official view, targeting high-level and influential forces within the state for the killings. *Khordad* and other dailies carried the statement by Ayatollah Taheri, a vocal critic of the conservative faction. Taheri called for the identification and arrest of those who ordered the killings, and criticized "those who should have stood firm before these deviations," those who "consciously and intentionally chose silence."[34]

The press continued to publish stories about more incidents of past killings, illegal arrests, and disappearances of citizens. What was once published only in the opposition papers outside Iran, was now openly published inside the country in the legal press. They wrote about murder by the state!

The daily *Khordad* reported of an open letter to the president by Ali Sabati, the managing editor of the monthly *Payam-e Shomal* (Voice of the North). Sobati was harassed and threatened by authorities after publishing two editorials about the killing of intellectuals. Sabati wrote: "My life is endangered by Office of Intelligence and [branch of Ministry of Intelligence] and Ansar-e Hezbollah." The prominent writer Hooshang Golshiri and others published their accounts of the murders by the state.

February 2, 1999. The monthly *Adineh,* a well-respected cultural/literary magazine was banned after a decade of surviving censorship. The managing director of the monthly was charged with "publishing lies" in an article titled "Happiness Has Been Lost in Our City, Laughter Is a Sin." On February 12, 1999, a few days after his resignation as the minister of intelligence, Dorri Najafabadi used the opportunity in the Friday prayer sermon in the city of Ray near Tehran to attack the press. Echoing the central theme of the conservative attack on free press, Dorri Najafabadi said, "Some in the press do not play the role of friends of the revolution, the system, and the martyrs. . . . These are not the friends of the revolution but its enemy. They play the role of the fifth column [of the enemy]."[35] Rahim Safavi, the head of Revolutionary Guards Corps had threatened to use force against the press a week earlier. Safavi said:

> The enemy in foreign press and the domestic press affiliated with outside want to create a division [in the system], and say that there is a power struggle and a political war in Iran. . . . If the leader allows us, the plotters will not [be able] to stand before the *Basij*. Internal and external enemies must know that *Basij* and the *Pasdarans* are the children of Ashoora and their model is Sied-al Shohada [Imam Hossein], and in defense of Islam, they will not compromise with anyone.[36]

And the war continued.

FREE PRESS AFTER THE SEPTEMBER 1998 ASSAULT—REVIVAL AND SETBACKS

Many developments had occurred since the closure of *Toos, Tavana, Jame-e Salem,* and other papers and magazines in September 1998. The publishers of *Toos* obtained a license to publish a new daily. *Toos* was published under the name *Neshat* and two new reform-minded newspapers, *Khordad* and *Sobh-e Emrooz,* began publication directed by high-ranking officials of Khatami's administration. Published by the impeached interior minister, Abdollah Nouri, *Khordad* soon became a well respected and widely read paper among the reform-minded citizens. *Sobh-e Emrooz,* published by Khatami's political advisor Saeed Hajjarian, became a powerful voice of the legal opposition. *Tavana* was once again published under the same name. *Zan,* the first newspaper focusing on the problems of women, started publication under Fa'ezeh Rafsanjani, daughter of the ex-president Hashemi Rafsanjani and an MP from Tehran. Also published were the weekly *Hajar* and a host of other critical papers and magazines.

The temporary retreat of the free press movement was indeed over by the end of 1998. The press continued its march forward with more power and momentum in 1999. The boldness and critical edge of the press increased. There was no possibility of defeat of the free press except by a coup d' état and the escalation of violence against members of the press and the movement for change. Such was the nature of the "Moharram Project" in April 1999, a month of continued attack on the press. The danger of the coup d' êtat and the spread of violence was brilliantly defused by the advanced exposure of Akbar Ganji and others in the press. But the press itself became a target of attack once again.

The daily *Zan* was shut down, charged with having published a letter by Farah Deeba, the late Shah's queen. The representative of the *faghih* in the Pasdaran warned the press and writers against the consequences of their attack on sacred religious beliefs of the people. "Newspapers and writers should remember the country they live in," said the *faghih*'s representative. Addressing a group of clergy in the city of Babol, Mohammad Nategh-Noori, the speaker of the parliament said: "Papers and magazines like *Kian, Aban, Negah-e No,* and *Iran Farda* go beyond the Imam, the Leader and the revolution in their discussions and publish anti-Islam and anti-prophet material."[37] And in its April issue, the conservative bimonthly *Sobh* wrote:

> [T]he newly emerged liberalism from within the system and the counter revolutionaries outside the system . . . are making attempts to form an alliance. . . . [The] liberals, reformists, foreign agents, and those penetrating [the system] . . . are the political and cultural soldiers of world imperialism. . . . They are . . . the main enemy and a serious threat for us. It is main responsibility of . . . the real guardians of the system, Islam, the people, and the country's independence, and those loving the Leader to rush to destroy the infectious centers of liberalism . . .[38]

Unable to stop the boldness of the press despite their physical assaults, the fundamentalists focused on the minister of culture and Islamic guidance, a reformer during whose administration free press was allowed to flourish. In April 1999, thirty-two conservative MPs issued a call for the impeachment of Ata'ollah Mohajerani. Mohajerani's impeachment hearings were held on May 1. And what was ostensibly aimed at the minister proved to be an impeachment of the movement for a free press. It was a trial of the press masked by the impeachment of Mohajerani. Mohajerani was criticized for his lax attitude toward the press and book publishing. The criticism and condemnation of free expression was the major theme of all addresses in support of the impeachment.

Reza Taghavi, MP from Tehran, head of the *Majlis* Commission on Culture and Islamic Guidance said: "The cultural environment of the country is one against the main pillar of the system and its loyal forces. . . . Those pens that are inked by unhealthy ideas, target freedom more than anything else." Ali Akbar Moosavi Hosseini, MP from Tehran, said: "I must admit to this sad reality that what has happened to the press lately does not at all comply with the legal objectives of this Ministry. . . . Do you believe that any writing or book should be free without any criteria and that people themselves must decide what is right and not right?" Morteza Nabavi, MP from Tehran, said: "Do you not hear the footstep of America in some papers?" Mohammad Azimi said: "The despicable attempt by some members of the press cannot be ignored. . . . Some papers print truly shameless and despicable material. . . . Modesty does not allow repeating these materials [here] because doing so can imply promoting prostitution. . . . Poisoned pens try to pave the way for the objectives of their masters and themselves by promoting prostitution."

After a six-hour long deliberation, the motion for the impeachment of the minister was defeated. The failure to impeach Mohajerani was, in some sense, a failure to impeach and stop the movement for a free press. It was an indication that, at least through acceptable parliamentary measures, the momentum of free press could not be stopped and defeated. And the aggression continued.

May 1, 1999. The banned *Payam-e Daneshjoo*, organ of Islamic Association of University Students and Alumni, started publication after a three and a half year absence as the bimonthly *Hoviat-e Khish* (One's Identity). On Saturday, May 1, 1999, *Hoviat-e Khish* appeared in newsstands with Heshmatollah Tabarzadi as its editor-in-chief, and all of the members of the council of writers of *Payam-e Daneshjoo*. Nearly six weeks after its birth, *Hoviat-e Khish* was banned, its copies collected and withdrawn from newsstands across the country by the authorities, and its license holder and editor-in-chief jailed.

May 1999 was a month of renewed widespread attack on the free press. The managing directors of a number of dailies including *Azad, Aria, Iran, Khordad, Neshat,* and *Sobh-e Emrooz* were called to court, charged with variety of violations. The state demanded extraordinarily high bail for the release of the accused journalists. The managing directors of dailies *Aria* and *Iran* were kept in jail for a few hours and released on bail of more than 200,000,000 rials (more than the assets of some papers).

The Ministry of Culture and Islamic Guidance intervened on behalf of the press in an unprecedented move in the history of the nation by paying the bail to secure the release of imprisoned journalists. On May 31, newspapers reported an allocation of 5,000,000,000 rials to be used for the release of other accused journalists in the future by the ministry.

The director of the daily *Azad* was directed to fire the paper's managing editor as a condition for its continued publication. The editor, Ahmad Zeidabadi, resigned from his post to protect the publication of the daily. The weekly *Tavana* announced its decision not to publish for one week in protest against the new wave of attacks. Fereidoun Verdinejad, managing director of the state news agency and director of the English-language *Iran Daily* and Persian-language daily *Iran,* was arrested in connection with a cartoon his newspaper ran showing a television serving as a toilet's cistern in May 1999. Mohammad Reza Zohdi, editor of *Arya,* was arrested on charges of disclosing military information. Others in the print media who were summoned for hearings included Latif Safari of *Neshat* and Said Hajjarian of *Sobh-e Emrooz*. Abdollah Nouri, the publisher of *Khordad,* was summoned by the Special Court for the Clergy. *Neshat* was shut down on September 4, its managing director and editor-in-chief arrested and imprisoned. Latif Safari, the director of *Neshat,* was sentenced to two and a half years in prison and banned for five years from press activity. Abdollah Nouri, the publisher of the vocal and pro-reform daily *Khordad,* was charged with betraying the revolution and insulting the sacred values of Islam and tried in the Special Court for the Clergy. *Khordad* was shut down. A few weeks later, *Fatth* substituted for *Khordad* with the same staff and politics.

ABDOLLAH NOURI'S TRIAL—THE INDICTMENT OF THE FREE PRESS

Following the assault on the critical press by the conservatives within the state, the daily *Khordad* was shut down and its license holder, Abdollah Nouri, was put on trial and charged with weakening the state and Islam. Nouri's trial became a historic event, manifesting many weaknesses and contradictions of the Islamic Republic. Though an attempt by the fundamentalists to bar Nouri from running in the upcoming parliamentary elections and seizing the position of the speaker of the parliament, the trial was also an indictment of the free press as a threat to Islam and the integrity of the Islamic Republic. The charges made against Nouri reflected the conservatives' inner hatred of the critical press, their fear of losing control and the last vestiges of legitimacy through its criticisms of the Islamic

Republic's cultural values and social norms. Earlier, Ayatollah Yazdi had reiterated this fear in a Friday prayer sermon at Tehran University. Ayatollah Yazdi stated:

> There are no disputes among religious leaders about principles like inheritance, martyrdom, and *hijab*. They [the press] play with these principles and then claim that this is not a disruption of Islam. Is not the weakening of *hijab* a disruption of the principles of Islam? Doubting inheritance is a disruption of the principles of Islam. I argue that these issues must be determined by Islamic experts . . . Islamic experts are the teachers in the seminaries.

The critical press questioned the unquestionable, crossed the "red line" and walked on sacred grounds. It instilled fear in the old guard of the Islamic Republic. The critical press was the embodiment of the movement for change, the cornerstone of the movement for civil society in Iran, a voice heard by all, a voice hard to silence. It was the enemy of the state. It was tried on charges of betraying Islam and the state.[39]

The trial of Nouri and Shamsolvaezin, and the shutting down of *Khordad* and *Neshat* before the parliamentary elections of February 2000, revealed the intertwining of the free press and the political crisis of the Islamic Republic. Abdollah Nouri, one of the highest-ranking statesmen of the Islamic Republic was tried and jailed through charges made against him as a result of his press activities. It was Nouri's role in the press that brought against him the charge of "siding with the plot of cultural invasion." He was jailed for having published articles that saw no difference between expressing one's joy and happiness through "clapping, whistling, and jeering" and crying *Allah-o Akbar* (God is Great), and writing, "People express differently their feelings, happiness, and sorrow."

Charged with publishing articles and stories questioning the Islamic Republic and the legitimate institutions of the state, challenging the supreme leader, deviating from the Imam's (Ayatollah Khomeini) views on the United States and Israel, Nouri's trial revealed the vulnerability of the Islamic Republic and its political institutions. It revealed the state's defensiveness in the face of public scrutiny. The charges of "publishing materials against Islamic principles" exposed the fragility of the cultural institutions created during twenty years of fear, intimidation, and terror. The trial of Nouri was a powerful testimony to this fear, a historical document revealing the vulnerability of institutions whose epoch had long passed, and a politico-cultural system on the verge of demise and extinction. It was a historical self-indictment of the Islamic Republic.

The battle against a free press became the cornerstone of the conservatives' battle for survival. Ali Sarzadeh, MP from the city Jeeroft, said. "We shall create a sea of blood" if feeling "endangered by some of the newly established press."[40]

APRIL 2000 AND THE POLITICAL COUP D' ÊTAT AGAINST THE REFORM GOVERNMENT—THE CLAMPDOWN ON THE PRESS

Despite the continuous assault on the press, the critical press continued to grow, gain more popularity among the intellectuals and everyday people, and become a culture—a new way of living, an undefeatable reality. Popular respect for the critical press reached unprecedented levels. As the social legitimacy of the state declined, the popularity of the press increased. Critical press became the guardian of the vulnerable civil society in Iran, the image of a pluralistic society, the embodiment of people's resentment of the state, the true enemy of absolutism and the guardians of the old order.

The critical press housed the legal dissent. It bridged the gap between the intellectuals, Moslem and secular, and the everyday people. Not through theoretical journals and books, the intellectuals chose the popular dailies and magazines to reach out to the citizens. They used the popular press to build a mass movement for rights and civil society. The critical press became the engine of the struggle for rights.

Newsstands became sites of colorful collages of diversely dressed citizens—men, women, young, and old—debating important political and social issues, searching for their press of choice, creating a sense of community. The newsstands became a public space of dissent. Vibrant, colorful, full of life, they became dispersed sites of defiance, magnets for citizens eagerly seeking words that defied the state—the stories not told by the state, the "other" voice.

By February 2000, the time of the crucial parliamentary elections, the press had become more powerful than mass political parties in democracies. It had the power to mobilize, organize, and change the dominant reality. Thus, the attack on the press escalated. The elections arrived. The conservatives received a humiliating defeat. The press went on the offensive. The battle between the old order and the press reached higher levels. The Revolutionary Guards entered the war of words against the press, threatening the president with a coup d' êtat to end the chaos created by "those who defend American-style reforms in Iran." Trying to defuse the anger of the guards and the possibility of a military coup, the supreme leader targeted the critical press, proposing the use of "legal violence" instead of "illegal violence" to stop the "enemy's" infiltration in the country. Calling the critical press the "enemy strongholds" the leader said, "What they are doing is a grave danger to us. If their leaders do not put a stop to it, the enemy will move ahead." He called on the government and the nation's legal institutions to stop the press. A green light for a mass clampdown on the press was issued.

In less than a week, the judiciary acted upon the leader's directives. A witch hunt emerged. Prominent journalists were summoned to court and jailed. Twenty-one critical dailies and popular journals were shut down. *Asr-e Azadegan* (the replacement for Joy), *Akhbar-e Eghtesadi, Fatth* (replacement for *Khordad*), *Sobh-e Emrooz, Azad, Arya, Payam-e Hajar, Iran Farda,* and others were forced out of existence. Akbar Ganji and Shamsolvaezin, Emadoldin Baghi, Ebrahim Nabavi, Masood Behnood, and other leading journalists were put behind bars. Newsstands became graveyards of the popular victims of the battle for reform. Fifteen thousand journalists and press employees became unemployed. The public reacted. A press-support fund was created. Tens of thousands of ordinary people contributed to the fund from their meager earnings. They stood behind the vanguards of the battle for civil society.

CHAPTER SEVEN

State, Economy, and Civil Society—Part I

Wage Earners' Response to Economic Catastrophe

The dominance of capitalist relations of production failed to bring about civil society and its institutions in Iran. The revolutionary period of 1978–1979 that culminated in the overthrow of the Pahlavi regime resulted in the creation of nascent institutions of civil society. But, the triumph of the Islamic Republic in February 1979 led to the further erosion of civil society in Iran. The Islamic Republic, from its inception, created its own institutions of control of economic, political, and cultural spheres, and destroyed all independent forms and institutions of social and cultural life. The spheres of family and private life were invaded by the state, creating a haunting and over-repressive presence in one's most private domains. Through the Islamicization of the society, the state dissolved all venues of independent social, political, and cultural action.

Independent workers councils, women's groups, and other grassroots organizations formed during the temporary political respite of the revolutionary period of 1978–1979 were brutalized, dissolved, and banned. The state invaded universities and institutions of higher education, dissolved student and faculty associations, arrested and executed student leaders, and fired the politically undesirable members of the faculty. Newspaper headquarters and bookstores were assaulted, books set on fire, and a multilayered and comprehensive system of censorship was established. Political parties were banned.

The state-controlled *Shoraha-ye Eslami* (Islamic Councils) and the notorious neighborhood committees or *Comiteh* were instituted in all public enterprises, workplaces, schools, and neighborhoods, replacing the newly formed and fragile institutions of civil society. The process of building a civil society was aborted.

The attack on the young institutions of civil society and the invasion of the spheres of private and public life were carried out through a network of officially established organs of repression and a host of unofficial *gorouh-ha-ye feshar* (pressure groups). Using a populist and pro-poor platform, and riding on people's ideological sympathy to Islam, the state successfully recruited from an inexhaustible pool of the economically disenfranchised and ideologically backward and antimodern sections of the population and organized a powerful network of urban gangs and "pressure groups." The attacks on bookstores, movie theaters, public meetings, and citizens' private assemblies were carried out by the bands of loyalists and state devotees financed and supported by different organs of the Islamic Republic, *Sepah-e Pasdaran* (the Islamic Revolutionary Guards Corps), and other paramilitary groups.

The independent institutions of the wage earners were the subject of a concerted assault from the inception of the new state. In 1979, the Iranian wage-earning class was a relatively young class without significant historical experience in trade unionism or other forms of class organization.[1] But, despite this, the class exhibited a remarkable potential for creating the necessary conditions for its self-rule, presenting a fundamental challenge to the state during the course of the revolution.[2] The potential was manifested in the organizational networks and workers' collective decisions and actions during and immediately after the revolution. The quick politicization of workers' demands on one hand, and their fantastic ability to control and regulate production on the other, were not only instrumental in defeating the Shah, but also indicated an innate threat to the new state, the Islamic Republic of Iran.

Striking workers' demands during the revolution included: pay raises, control over finance and profit sharing, change of management, freedom of political prisoners, a five-day working week, a forty-hour week, freedom of expression, an end to censorship, and the abolition of the Shah's regime. After the overthrow of the Shah, the Iranian wage-earning class created militant *shoraha-ye karegari* (Workers Councils) in factories across different industries. The Workers Councils demanded the payment of delayed wages by the new state, and protection against lockouts and layoffs. Though not theoretically informed, the councils showed an innate tendency toward egalitarianism. In various industrial establishments, they demanded the narrowing of the gap between wages for manual and mental labor, an increase in the income of low-wage members of the Workers Councils, and decreases in salaries of managers and high-paid employees. In some factories, the Workers Councils took on the direct control of production or established some forms of *control-e karegari* (workers' control). Overall, the councils were involved in trade unionism, the struggle against authoritarian relations at the point of production, control over the conditions of employment and financial affairs, and the actual administration of production.

Although the council movement did not follow a theoretically clear platform, it nevertheless imposed a formidable threat to the rule and authority of the new state both economically and politically. But despite its enormous energy and success, the Workers Council movement was finally defeated by the new state. The councils were attacked, and their members (especially the identified leaders) were arrested and imprisoned. Independent Workers Councils were destroyed and replaced with state-controlled *Shoraha-ye Eslami* (Islamic Councils) in factories. The Islamic Councils became powerful tools used to prevent the recreation of the independent council movement and the rise of workers' dissent in factories. They were the signs of the death of new and independent institutions of civil society in Iran.

The years following the assault on workers' independent institutions were the years of retreat, fear, and submission on the part of the wage earners. Surveillance by the watchful eyes of the Islamic Councils, the turning of factories into military camps, imprisonment, and the fear of unemployment silenced the fatigued wage earners. Except in rare and isolated occasions, created a working class tamed by the state and its regime of labor control.

This was the general situation on May 23, 1997, the day of the presidential election that led to the victory of Mohammad Khatami.

WAGE EARNERS AND THE LIMITS OF THE OFFICIAL MOVEMENT FOR CIVIL SOCIETY

Mohammad Khatami won the election with the promise of a new Islamic Republic based on the institutionalization of rights and civil society. With Khatami's election, civil society, participation, and rights became a part of the everyday discourse and vocabulary. The print media became a medium for the public discussion of civil society, its requirements, and its benefits to the citizens. The belief in civil society became the line of demarcation between the reformers and the opponents of reform.[3] But despite its popularization by Khatami's camp and the press, many fundamental aspects of civil society remained unexplored and neglected.

After twenty years of coercion and repressed workers' rights, the wage earners' unconditional right to independent institutions was ignored by the advocates of civil society. *Khaneh-e Karegar* (House of Labor), the only existing workers' organization, remained under the tight control of the Islamic Left faction of the government and its affiliates in the Ministry of Intelligence. While advocating "participation," party building, and the government of law, workers' rights at the point of production, their right to collective and free representation, and the right to challenge their public and private employers were excluded from the discourse of civil society. The official language of rights and participation excluded the wage earners as a specific social group with a defined collective interest and rights. A civil society was to be built without the institutionalization of workers' rights. The narrowness and limits of the official movement for civil society, and the neglect of wage earners and their independent institutions, resulted in the continuation of the old regime of labor control at the point of production, and, ultimately, fear and intimidation in the society at large.

Mohammad Khatami's program of reform and "political development" called for "citizens' participation," "citizens' empowerment," and the "citizens' mastery over their destiny." But "citizens' are a heterogeneous group, with structurally differential social, political, and economic power. The materialization of political development is contingent upon the recognition of the differential power of the social groups (classes) that constitute the "citizens." The differential power of citizens is the reflection of the existence of social segmentation based on race, gender, ethnicity, and class.[4] Civil society is an amalgamation of institutions used by these social groups in their confrontation (dealings) with the state, the market, and one another. The project of "citizens' empowerment" cannot be realized without the recognition of the social power differentials and the rights of different groups in creating their mediums of collective voice. Civil society rests on the institutionalization of such mediums. Wage earners' deprivation of the ownership and control of capital (as a class) leads to a subordinate economic, social, and political power position and structural inability to bargain for the realization of rights, thus a hindrance to their "participation."[5] The creation of independent institutions of wage earners for the articulation of their collective voice partially counteracts the structural determinants of inequality of power and facilitates the move toward "citizens' empowerment."

Independent unions, workers' councils and associations, factory committees, and all other mediums for formulating and enforcing wage earners' collective voice partially reduce the weight of their structurally subordinate social power. The independence of wage earners' institutions allows the articulation of ideas and their realization into collective voice and action without fear of the employers (public or private) and the state. Independent institutions partially change the balance of power at the point of production and the society at large.

In the case of Iran, the realization of civil society rests on the formation of both ideologically and organizationally independent institutions of wage earners. The ideological independence of wage earners' institutions is fundamental to freeing the workers' and employees' associations from the forced adherence to Islam and what the Islamic state sanctions as religiously (thus politically) viable and admissible. The existence of "Islamic Unions" and "Islamic Councils" manifests control, surveillance, and subordination to the state or its factions and affiliated organizations. The official movement for civil society in Iran remains, in this respect, within the parameters and confines of the practices of the past twenty years. The materialization of civil society rests on a departure from this.

Signs of such a departure are emerging. Workers' collective voice, though still embryonic, is being formed.

MOVEMENT FOR CIVIL SOCIETY AND WAGE EARNERS' RESPONSE TO ECONOMIC MALICE

The wage earners' response to economic marginalization is diverse and socially determined. The specificity of the forms and degree of these responses are, among other factors, determined by the extent to which a civil society and the institutions of collective action exist. In countries where civil society is institutionalized and entrenched, reactions to economic disenfranchisement often occur in the form of collective action and public protest sanctioned by the law. Where unions and labor associations, grassroots non-class organizations representing the group interest of the affected population, and in general, social movements (old and new) are institutionalized and collective action (even partially) is a part of the everyday culture, public opposition becomes a dominant form of reaction by citizens. Such reactions, by and large, remain within the confines of legally defined citizens' rights. Resistance and collective action at the point of production, strikes, and class and non-class struggles, collective lobbying for favorable state regulation, etc., are common forms of collective response in such societies.

Contrary to this public manifestation of dissent and discontent, where civil society and institutions of collective action are weak or nonexistent, a process of internalization of economic and social catastrophe occurs, leading to individual (private) reactions on the part of the affected population. Private response takes the place of public reaction and protest. State regulation of the private sphere and its control of the life channels of the society, and the absence of citizens' rights and the freedom of assembly make improbable (impossible in most cases) the formation of a public voice within the confines of legally sanctioned action.

In the absence of the sites of collective action and public voice, a process of retreat to personal struggles for survival occurs, leading to diverse manifestations of individually crafted coping mechanisms. The internalization of discontent produces a complex set of responses and/or mental and physical reactions. Corruption, bribery, manic anxiety, fear and depression, suicide, heart attack, and crime become social epidemics, leading to alienation and social hostility among the victims of economics. The fear of tomorrow and the anxiety about one's ability to survive the battle of everyday life further deepen the retreat to the sphere of private struggle. The generalized internalization of discontent leads to intensified competition for survival, and an acute sense of estrangement.

The internalization of discontent thus shields the state from collective opposition. At the same time, the ban on collectivity and public manifestations of economic discontent leads to sporadic, unorganized, and spontaneous ruptures and collective actions that take place outside the parameters of legally sanctioned public voice. Collective action in such cases takes the form of riots, looting, burning of the property of the "other." It leads to direct confrontation with the state and its organs of repression. Here, economic protest is inherently political. The fusion of the "political" and the "economical" occurs in practice from the inception of public action. The state often responds with the use of force, brutalizing those who dare to step outside the sphere of private and internalized reaction. In such cases, collective opposition to economic policy is, by nature, a challenge to the integrity of the state and its power. It is that fundamental challenge that leads to immediate repression of the public voice.

From its inception in February 1979, the Islamic Republic systematically annihilated all newly born institutions of citizens' power and banned all manifestations of collective voice. Being denied the institutions of civil society, wage earners primarily reacted to economic and social marginalization through private struggles and the internalization of their disempowerment. Unable to react collectively to the pains of economics, they retreated to the sphere of private life and enwrapped themselves in private struggles for survival. Indeed, survival became the dominant motto of life for the embattled citizens living under constant surveillance and fear. Alienated, divided by fear and distrust, and defeated, wage earners sought salvation from the painful realities of everyday life through privately crafted additional sources of income. Denied the right to collectively organize for higher wages, fearful of severe punishment by the state for the open and public expression of their needs and frustrations, demoralized and atomized, they sank into the abyss of internalizing their misfortunes, seeking survival as lone warriors on a painful odyssey.

The following is a tale of survival in the battle of everyday life. Everyday life—the space where the monster of economics feeds its unending hunger for the actors of the theater of despair. Men hustle their way through two or three jobs—humbles men who do not succumb. Everyday life—the site of lies, cheating, and desperately victimizing other victims of despair, where walls of resistance crumble, the unordinary becomes customary, morality succumbs to the pressures of rising prices and a falling standard of living, ordinary people submit to what was revolting and unthinkable yesterday.

PRIVATE RESPONSE TO ECONOMIC MARGINALIZATION: THE INTERNALIZATION OF ECONOMIC CATASTROPHE—A NARRATIVE

Anxiety, Fear, Helplessness: Wage Earners and Currency Devaluation—A Narrative of Everyday Life

This was the summer of 1995, six years after the inauguration of the structural adjustment policy: privatization, exchange rate liberalization, and cuts in state subsidies. Perhaps more than any other aspect of structural adjustment, exchange liberalization had a fundamental impact on wage earners' social psychology and their mechanisms of coping with everyday life. What emerged in the process was the mental enslavement of a population facing an unending decline in the value of its national currency, the violence of exchange rate liberalization. They helplessly witnessed their impoverishment and the decline in their purchasing power (see Appendix A).

Dizzied by the ever-rising value of the dollar and the decline in their standard of living, and unable to rationalize and comprehend the unfolding events, some sought individual salvation by transferring their meager wealth into dollar holdings, while others watched the erosion of their purchasing power with disbelief and despair. The rising dollar brought wage earners, the retired elderly, and even children to their knees, helplessly worshiping the emerging new master. Speculation about the future value of the dollar became the national preoccupation, pulling all layers of the society into the abyss of uncertainty, anxiety, and fear of the future, internalizing the violence of economics.

Six years after the initial attempt to liberalize currency markets, the value of the national currency hit a record low in 1995. The country was overwhelmed by an insatiable thirst for dollars. The first few days of April were days of total confusion.

I read aloud the daily paper's headline about the dollar at a family gathering: "A Week Long Plunge in the Exchange Rate." The currency had dropped in value from 180 to 320 tomans (from 1,800 to 3,200 rials) to a dollar. The room was filled with anxiety about a farther drop of the local currency. There was speculation, conspiracy theories, fear, fear, and fear.

I was repeatedly asked about my prediction of the future. The exchange rate was now at 400 tomans to a dollar.

The exchange rate was a hot topic in family gatherings, bus lines, and work places. Even children discussed the foreign exchange market. What could be the future?

"The dollar will reach one thousand tomans," said an old man waiting on line to buy freshly baked bread.

"Good investment. My neighbor sold his car a week ago and bought dollars with the money. Smart guy," said another man with admiration and jealousy.

"It has to stop somewhere," cried an angry passenger.

"Four Hundred Seventy Tomans for One Dollar," read the headline of a popular daily.

The soaring prices of consumer goods were now the burning topic of discussion at every gathering. A man asked me at the ice cream shop for an explanation of the collapse of the currency. The shop owner had his own theory. A customer disagreed. The owner offered a free ice cream to the customer if he was proven right. They laughed, continuing to argue with energy and an air of authority. Another man dressed in shabby clothes spoke frantically without making sense.

Five hundred twenty-five tomans to each dollar! A friend complained about the doubling of his business expenses in less than three weeks.

A long hot summer day in Tehran, pollution, smog, traffic jams, and the dollar climbed to 590 tomans.

Finally all conversations focused on a new subject—the U.S. trade embargo against Iran. The market reacted immediately, and the local currency plunged even further.

Six hundred ten tomans to a dollar! Prices rose overnight. Rice, eggs, meat, locally manufactured cars, computers, anything and everything had become more expensive. A growing madness was felt everywhere. Some stores only accepted dollars for their products.

"One thousand tomans. I told you guys. One thousand! This is how the Americans will get rid of the mullahs," said a relative. Rumors spread around the city that Bill Clinton had announced his readiness to push the dollar up to one thousand tomans to sabotage the Islamic Republic.

People argued about the price hike at the vegetable shop. The streets of Tehran were filled with anxiety, rage, and anger at shop owners, cab drivers, and other victims of exchange rate liberalization.

"Why should the price of eggplants increase? What does that have to do with the dollar?" asked an angry woman under a thick black veil. "Bandits," said another woman. The shopkeeper screamed back. The women left with hatred and frustration.

It was now the month of *Moharram*. The month of national mourning for the martyrdom of Imam Hossein some thirteen hundred years ago, a time for chanting, self-beatings, and wearing black clothes. And the dollar reached 650 tomans.

"A hundred percent increase in the price of a kilo of cucumbers overnight," a friend reported to me with a sense of helplessness and despair.

"Did the price of the dollar go up because of the assassination of Imam Hossein?" asked my six-year-old nephew. "Did the price of the dollar go up because of the assassination of Imam Hossein?"

Seven hundred ten!

The city was filled with rumors and speculation about the future of the dollar. "An American plot." "Foreign conspiracy." "Seven hundred and ten!" screamed a neighbor.

Madness and open rage! Newspapers were filled with images of people's fear and anxiety—"Higher Than Ever," "Once Again the Toman on Sale," and similar headlines decorated the front pages of newspapers and magazines.

The speedy decline in the value of currency was such that, without thinking about the reasons for this event, everyone was rushing to turn their liquid savings into the dollar, or gold, anything but the toman. A commentator reported:

> In those days, [toman] was like fire, burning everyone's hands, and forcing them to rush frantically to turn their [money] into dollars, gold, refrigerators, televisions, automobiles, or any other commodity. The severity of the situation is revealed in the anxiety and nervousness of people, lost and confused by the steady decline in the value of the national currency and the uncontrolled increase in the prices of basic necessities. In less than four months, people's feelings have traveled the long journey of ambiguity, fear, anxiousness, and finally, the loss of trust in the power on the national money.

Tehran was on the verge of a social explosion.

May 10, 1995. An unexpected intervention by the state shocked the market. A fixed exchange rate of three hundred tomans per dollar was set by the central bank, marking an end to three years of floating exchange rates. The security force occupied the trading district. A few traders were arrested. "Defeat of foreign enemies," declared a daily paper.

A petty investor committed suicide. The price of cucumbers declined. My nephew played with his friends. We enjoyed the temporary respite from the violence of exchange rate liberalization.

For nearly two years, the exchange rate was relatively stabilized while prices continued to soar. The standard of living of most wage earners plummeted, pulling the citizens of despair into the abyss of the battle of everyday life. The bitter memories of the sinking national currency were slowly erased from their minds.

This was May 1997. The election of a new popular president had given rise to the hope for freedom and moments of cultural respite and the birth of new dreams.

Two years after the intervention, the state was gradually easing the exchange control. The old pains were reappearing. The national currency continued to decline in value, now facing a resigned and defeated army of ordinary people—resignation and defeat amidst rising exchange rates. Tired, they toiled to survive, accepted the rising exchange rates, and succumbed.

Summer of 1998. Once again an unbearable orgy of heat, smog, and noise assaulted the citizens of despair dizzied in the struggles of everyday life.

Summer of 1998. Prices of many basic necessities doubled in less than a year. The free market exchange rate rose to 560 tomans to a dollar. The standard of living of wage earners declined farther to exceptionally low levels. Not a single soul discussed the exchange rate. The unacceptable had now become the norm. Individual coping mechanisms overshadowed and tamed all sentiments for a collective response to the crisis.

I visited the ice cream shop I had often visited during the hot and long summer of 1995 hoping to engage the owner in a discussion of the exchange rate again. He did not respond. I mentioned the bet he had made three years earlier. He did not recall. I bought an ice cream and said goodbye.

October 26, 1998. The economic conditions were deteriorating everyday. The dollar had reached, once again, as high as 650 tomans. There was no reaction by ordinary people, no newspaper headlines on the subject, and no public frenzies. The same exchange rate had brought the country to a state of psychological panic and a near-social collapse three years earlier. The demon was now accepted. The pain was too familiar. Life goes on!

November 9, 1998. Continuing its downward slide against the dollar, the national currency reached its lowest level in three years—703 tomans to a dollar by lunchtime. No state intervention, no suicide by investors, no execution of traders—this was an Iran different from the summer of 1995.

November 14, 1998. The market reacted to the statement by the state about its intention to halt the three-year effort to stabilize the value of the local currency. The dollar reached 711 tomans, dropping to 700 tomans the next trading day.[6] Seven hundred eleven tomans, but no reaction by ordinary people. Numbed and defeated, they accepted an unavoidable destiny.

January 23,1999. A relatively cold night in Tehran, I took a private cab to the Ghoroub (Sunset) Restaurant off Vali-e Asr Avenue.

A young man driving his car as a taxicab pulled over. I sat in the front. He was young and happy-looking. We smiled and talked about the dollar.

"The dollar reached seven hundred and forty-five tomans today," said the young driver almost immediately after the takeoff. Excited by the young man's comment about the dollar, I asked: "Where did you read that?" He had purchased dollars for a friend. "Where will all of this end?" I asked, expecting a response from the driver. He threw his hands up in the air and was quiet for a few long minutes. I tried again to continue the conversation about the dollar. He was no longer interested. He spoke of the difficulties of getting married!

"Twenty-eight years old and unmarried," said the driver. He drove his car as a private taxicab from five to eleven, seven days a week.

"Is this all you do?" I asked, knowing the answer. The young man was a full-time employee of a private firm, holding two jobs and unmarried. He talked about the problems of not being married in Iran. We were on Vali-e Asr Avenue across from *Park-e Mellat* (People's Park). I left his car, paid the fare, and said goodbye.

January 20, 1999. Early evening, I left home for a heavenly hike on the barren Mount Alborz at night, seeking freedom from the city smog, moments of joy away from the bearded men in slippers, men with guns, and from the anxiety of everyday life.

I shouted, "Daraḳeh." A car pulled over. "Are you going hiking?" asked the driver. "Yes," I replied. The driver smiled. "How is business," I asked. He smiled. "The dollar reached seven hundred and forty-five yesterday," I said to the driver. He smiled again.

"Do you go hiking very often?" asked the driver. "Sometimes," I replied. "I love to hike too," he said, "but who has the time these days? Have not done this for ten years. Who has the time these days?"

The driver spoke in a calm voice and without anger. He told me of his hiking voyages in the past. Adventurous and brave, he smiled telling me about his "days of living a free life"! I did not talk about the dollar. He was excited to remember his joyous past. I watched him smile. Short moments of freedom from the battle of everyday life, I did not talk about the dollar. We arrived in Darakeh. I shook the driver's hand and paid his fare.

The hike was heavenly. I did not think about the dollar. Staring at the reflection of the moon on the patient earth of Mount Alborz, sitting in peace and quiet, singing songs, laughing, walking fearlessly in the dark of the night, sucking the marrow of the short moments of freedom, I held hands with Maryam under the protection of the stars. We joked, laughed, dreamed.

January 24, 1999. He was young and talkative. An owner of an old domestic car, caught with bottles of smuggled scotch the first time, arrested while strolling with a "girl" a month or two later, he told me of his problems with the authorities in the past. I talked about the dollar.

He had heard the news. "Seven hundred fifty tomans now. It will be twelve hundred tomans by *Norouz* [the New Year]," said the driver. "What could people do in these conditions?" I said with rage.

He lamented about the pains of everyday life and the absence of joy and breathing space. He wished to talk about "girls." A beautiful woman crossed the street. We both smiled. We talked about women and marriage and not the dollar. I paid my fare and said goodbye.

January 22, 1999. We talked about heart attack and suicide. He told me that he would probably die in a few years. I did not talk about the dollar.

January 27, 1999. Driving a relatively new domestic car, he was handsome and well dressed, clean-shaved, proper, and pleasant.

"Have you heard about the new rise in value of the dollar?" I asked after a few ordinary comments about pollution and the not so nice weather in Tehran. "It is incredible. I know it will hit one thousand toman by *Noruoz*. This is what Clinton has said," he replied gently.

Yes, once again the one thousand toman scenario was beginning to surface in Iran. I had heard this earlier during the week. One thousand tomans per dollar, this was the height of all conspiracies! Iranians thrive on conspiracy. That is how they often explain change.

We remained quiet for a minute or two. "What do you think about Reza Shah?" I was abruptly brought back to my real surroundings by this unusual question of the gentle driver. "Reza Shah?" I asked with surprise. "Yes, Reza Shah. Do you agree that he is one of the very few people who did something for Iran?" This too had become an emerging sentiment in Iran in the past few years, a national passion for the benevolent dictator.

"Do you agree with me? What do you think about Rafsanjani? I know he enriched himself in the past twenty years. But, I think he is also one of the great leaders of Iran. Only Reza Shah and Rafsanjani, do you agree with me?" The driver spoke with intensity and excitement. He patiently awaited my response. I could not escape his inquisitive mind, trying once or twice to return to the dollar, he was more interested in my views of Reza Shah and Rafsanjani.

"You know, history made a mistake about Hitler. But, now, everyone in the world has a different view of him. The truth is out. He was a great man. We know it now. The world owes him a lot. Look at the Jews. He left five or six thousands of them and they control the world. He should have ended the job." He spoke about "killing the Jews" in perfect calm and peace. He was not interested in the dollar.

We had arrived at my destination. The cars behind us sounding their horns, the driver pulled over, continuing his stories of Reza Shah and Hitler. I saw my friend waiting for me on the corner, paid the fare, and left the car.

January 31, 1999. The dollar was 850 tomans in midafternoon, 870 tomans by late evening, and finally 900 tomans. I continued my fruitless efforts to gauge the public sentiments about the decline in the value of the national currency. No one had any interest in discussing the subject. The feeling of defeat had long sunk in. There was an epidemic of submission and the internalization of a crisis that seemed without solution. If only they could survive the crisis by harder work, longer hours of toil, another job, or cheating the other victims of the violence of economics.

But the rapid plunge in the value of the currency could not escape the attention of the press. Speculations and rumors about the causes of the plunge abounded, the English language daily *Iran News* wrote, in an editorial on February 2:

> We should not forget that the psychological impact of the increase in the value of hard currency against the rial would worsen the economic situation, because it could lead to a rush by the people to buy dollars. Who is responsible?

And the daily *Sobh-e Emrooz* proposed the possibility of the government's deliberate actions in the market to raise the value of the dollar in order to finance its New Year payments later through the sale of its reserves at a higher price.[7]

February 16, 1999. After a week of sharp decline in the value of national currency, the exchange rate stabilized around 800 tomans to dollar.

May 15, 1999. I sold a few hundred dollars at 819 tomans to dollar. There was still no panic and no discussion about the slide in the value of the national currency.

July 3, 1999. I exchanged dollars for 945 tomans.

July 19, 1999. An unexpected end to my voyage in Iran, I left Iran in fear a week after the student uprising.

A Theater of Survival: Working a Second or a Third Job

Holding multiple jobs or working for twelve or fourteen hour shifts had become a growing epidemic in the1990s in Iran. There are no statistics on the number of citizens working more than one job or shifts longer than ten hours. The growing number of men dividing their days and nights between different income-generating activities (including paid jobs in the formal market) is not known. State statistics are fruitless. They do not reveal the severity of the economic pain and the coping mechanisms of the wage earners. The numbers are misrepresentative.

The rising cost of living, salaries that do not suffice to meet the monthly rent of a humble flat, the fear of tomorrow, and economic insecurity transformed the labor market in the 1990s. All boundaries broke down. Job classifications were practically removed from existence. Doctors engaged in real estate activities, buying and selling homes. College graduates traded in the black foreign exchange market. Those fortunate enough to obtain a car became cab drivers, driving through smog and heat, competing for survival with other desperate warriors of the everyday. They borrowed at notoriously high interest rates to buy a car, to become a cab driver. They sold their meager belonging to be a cab driver. From Tehran to Shiraz and Isfahan, teachers, army officers, civil servants, even doctors became cab drivers. Economic marginalization of the wage earners transformed Iran into a nation of cab drivers.

And a new industry emerged. Private taxi service companies mushroomed. A new method of survival surfaced. Young and the old, employed or without work, educated youth, fathers and grandfathers, all became cab drivers in private taxi service companies. Private taxi service became a booming industry, providing the opportunity for an extra shift of labor for the fortunate citizens owning four wheels under a rusting box of steel. It provided the last chance for survival for Massoud, Rahim, Akbar, and other warriors of everyday life.

Massoud—thirty-five years old, married, a father of two, four years of university education in German language, he worked in a private taxi service agency.

Rahim—twenty-seven years old, married, a father of two, four years of university education in accounting, he worked in a private taxi service agency.

Akbar—seventy-three years old, retired state employee, married and a father of four, charming and pleasant, he worked in a private taxi service agency.

Ahmad—thirty years old, lost his business a year earlier, married, angry, unshaved, he worked in a private taxi service agency.

He did not tell me his name. A colonel of the Security Force, honest, committed, and kind, he drove his car after finishing his daily shift in the Security Force. He too worked in a private taxi service agency.

Hossein—twenty-five years old, thin, well dressed, and handsome, a shoemaker in the grand bazaar, cheated by a lifetime friend, bankrupt, he borrowed money to buy an old Peykan. Driving twelve hours a day, Hossein worked in a private taxi service agency.

And while Ahmad, Hossein, and others worked in private taxi agencies, many more drove around the busy streets of Tehran and other cities, hustling, searching to steal customers from private taxi service agencies, and the real taxis now facing an unbeatable competition from other warriors of the everyday. They drove their old domestic cars many long hours between other jobs. They did not sleep. They did not see their loved ones. They drove to survive. They did not work for private taxi service companies. They told their stories of toil and pain.

The old man chose to survive. Like others I met in the city of cabdrivers he was determined to survive the abyss of economic despair. He drove his old Peykan in the suffocating heat of midafternoon summer days in Tehran. He spoke with a kind, a gentle voice.

"I'm seventy-two years old," said the old man with a mixture of pride and anger. "Thirty-five years of honest work for the government. I retired fifteen years ago. Have been doing this for eight years. Twelve hours a day, everyday. Yes, twelve hours a day!" A long uncomfortable and haunting silence, unspoken words, he spoke again.

"My pension is seventeen thousand tomans a month. And my rent!" A long pause. "Thirty thousand." The old man looked at me and continued. A different tone in his voice, his words were wrapped in rage, and a fatigue that was as old as seventy-two long years of hard work. His wrinkled face covered by the heavy dust of a history of pain and anger, seventy-two years of hard work, a cigarette in his hand, deep sighs, a sense of sadness, and the boredom of mere existence, he hustled on the streets of Tehran at age seventy-two. We said goodbye. He smiled and continued on the road to survival.

It was October 25, 1998. "Sa'adat Abad," I said waiting for a ride to my family's flat. A rundown domestic car, a young and fatigued driver in shabby clothes, I entered the car. "How much?"

asked the driver. "Eight hundred tomans," I answered. He nodded. I shut the door closed. "How is business?" I hoped to start off a conversation.

He told me his painful tale of a hard work and agony. He had left home thirty-six hours earlier. Started work at the water company at six in the morning the day before. A twenty-four-hour shift, a night without sleep, a quick breakfast, he started his next job at 6:30 in the morning. A full day of driving in the nervous streets of Tehran. It was eleven at night and he had not had dinner. Two more hours of work, he would be home at one past midnight. Another morrow, he would leave home for a twenty-four-hour shift at the water company at six in the morning.

He rarely saw his young daughter. He could not forget what she told him one day. "I wish Uncle Ali was my father. I never see you. You never take me anywhere." He could not forget what she said. He did not see her often, leaving home when she was in bed, returning when she was long asleep. "I wish Uncle Ali was my father," he repeated calmly trying to hide the tears rolling down his fatigued face. He had chosen to survive. He drove his beat-up car around the city and cried silently for his young daughter.

Victimizing Other Victims of Economic Despair

Trapped in the endless battle of survival and alienated from the society, some adhered to violence and criminal activities. Though small in scale, such acts of individual violence rose rapidly, especially in the 1990s with the implementation of economic liberalization and structural adjustment. Drugs and bad checks ranked as the highest two reasons for people's incarceration.[8] Corruption and victimizing other victims of economic despair became a social epidemic.

Summer of 1996. It was now two years since the state had drastically cut the funding for health services. Even public hospitals were asked to move toward financial self-sufficiency. A new epidemic in Iran, hospitals and clinics demanded advanced payment before hospitalization and the delivery of services. Helpless men and women waited for a miracle and admission for care. I read in the paper the story of the woman who was turned away by the hospital without receiving care. I told the story to a friend.

The woman cried.

"Please have mercy on me. I have sold all my belongings. This is all I have. Please. I have no other money. Help me. I am dying."

The clerk was moved by the woman's desperate pleadings. But he had to follow orders. Admission to the hospital required a hundred thousand tomans advance payment in her case. She had half.

"Where should I go? For God's sake, help me. I am ill. Help me!" She wept and pleaded. Where can she go?

Her doctor had sent her off to Tehran for the treatment of her illness—hundreds of kilometers away from her family and home. Her loved ones waiting for her safe return, she prayed day and night that she would survive this ailment. Where could she go? They had sold all they could and borrowed money from friends. Fifty thousand was all she had.

"This is the hospital rule. I only follow orders," said the clerk with shame.

"Please help me."

She remembered her loving young boy. She could not die. No. Who would care for him? Who would send him off to school every morning? She could not die. But fifty thousand was all she had. She pleaded to her God and cried.

"Sister, sister, please do not cry."

She opened her reddened eyes to the kind and soothing voice of the stranger. Kind looking. Gentle, and warm. He spoke to her with affection and compassion. Touched by her predicament? He promised to use his contacts at the hospital and arrange her admission with only half of the necessary advance payment.

Hope in the woman's eyes. Oh, was he the messenger of God? Could he persuade them? "You are sent by God to save my life."

He departed. The woman patiently awaited the return of the kind man. Her prayers were finally answered. She imagined returning home to her boy. Life without illness, can that be true?

The kind man returned with a smile and good news. Yes, the hospital officials had finally conceded. She was to be admitted with only fifty thousand tomans.

To start the admission procedure, the kind man asked for the woman's papers and her money.

"God bless you. God bless you."

The cry of joy and happiness, joy in her eyes, she continued to thank the kind man and her God for this miraculous turn of events. The kind man left the room. She waited half-shaken, frightened and filled with joy.

Hours passed. The ill woman continued to wait. The room emptied. The clerk fell asleep behind his desk. The guard smoked a cigarette. The woman continued to wait.

New patients arrived. The kind man did not return. The woman cried. The kind man did not return.

A new guard arrived. A new shift, a new day, the woman continued to wait. The kind man did not return.

"Who is the real criminal? The kind man or the hospital officials?" I asked my friend. "Who is the real criminal?"

July 1998. The boy was crying frantically. No more than ten years of age, dressed in black pants and shirt, an empty tray in his hand, tears rolling down his face, desperately gazing at the cherries now spread on the hot pavement, he was ignored by the passersby. He sobbed endlessly.

"What is the problem son?" I asked with affection. He answered while crying. He had tripped and dropped all his belongings. Black cherries on the pavement, his only capital now decorated the boiling asphalt. He hopelessly watched the shoes of men and women carelessly walking on his only hope for survival in the jungle of despair.

"How much did you pay for all of this?" A pitiful existence, a capital worth less than two dollars, he had lost all he owned. I gave him one thousand tomans. The boy walked away immediately. Feeling satisfied about saving the boy from his misery, I proceeded toward my destination.

August 1998. This was a hot summer afternoon in Tehran. I entered the cab. Twelve hundred tomans from Darakeh to Azadi I offered. He accepted. He was well dressed, gentle, and kind. We talked about football and the desperate economic conditions of the country, long hours of work, inflation and loss of hope, unemployed youth wandering on the streets of capital. Hopeless existence!

A long expressway connecting Tehran from the west to the east, heat waves dancing on the asphalt, I noticed a teenage boy sitting on the curb separating the two sides of the expressway. His head down, he was covering his mourning face with his hands, escaping from the shame of mourning in public—mourning the death of hope, the loss of belongings. Strawberries ornamenting the hot gray asphalt with dark red, another desperate soul was mourning the loss of his capital, watching his morrow crushed under the old tires of smoking cars, I said to myself.

Lamenting about this sorrowful picture, we were now a few kilometers away. I saw tears in the driver's eyes.

Two weeks gone. The expressway connecting the west to the east, mid afternoon, two teenage boys stood by the tall trees surrounding the expressway. Black T-shirt, torn jeans, a tray of strawberries in his hand, one boy approached the highway. Emptying the tray on the asphalt, he moved quickly to the curb separating the two sides of the expressway. Red strawberries ornamenting the hot gray asphalt, the boy sat on the curb, his head down, his hands covering his mourning face.

The other boy, short and chunky, hiding behind the trees—he was anxiously looking out for his friend. A new theater of survival in the jungle of despair, I thought to myself. Children are learning the art of survival!

Violence of Economics: Stolen Childhood

Children—victims of economic violence, engulfed in the anxiety and fears of the world of older men and women. Children—faces of innocence, voices of purity, waiting for a future of pain and fear.

Children, the new victims of the violence of economics—boys and girls strolling on the alienating streets of Tehran, begging, selling chewing gum and candy, desperately staring at the toys and the forbidden food behind the protective glass of shop windows. They are the new victims of the violence of economics.

Summer 1995. A hot summer day in Tehran, waiting for a cab at a busy intersection, trapped between old cars, and the deadly weight of noise, and smog, I watched the heat dance in the air, mingle through the melting steel of old domestic cars. I saw the heat mix with the suffocating fumes released from the tired mufflers, forming a dark gray cloud pressing everyone to the ground.

"Please buy one. Please buy." A young boy grabbed the edge of my T-shirt. Maybe six or seven years old, sweating, he held a few cheap chocolate candies in his small hand. I bought two candies. He smiled and ran off.

"I told you no. Get away from me," a driver screamed at a boy trying to sell him a potato peeler. The boy pleaded. The driver rolled up his window. The traffic light changed and we moved a few inches ahead.

Overwhelmed by the heavy weight of the driver's anger and frustration, the image of the child selling chocolate candy, and the heat—the unbearable heat—I sank into a deep feeling of alienation, gazing at the faces of drivers impatiently waiting for any opening in the traffic. An afternoon of intolerance, I paid the driver and found my way out of this massive cemetery of hopeless men and women buried under melting metals.

Summer 1996. He was younger than eight, sitting on a piece of cardboard near the grand bazaar. An old scale, an opened book, a pen, and an empty cup, his eyes were desperately following the feet of the passersby.

A man on the scale, the happy sound of dropping coin in the cup, the boy smiled.

Pen in his hand, eyes on the shoes of the passersby, no sound of dropping coins, he waited in despair.

A man on the scale, the boy smiled.

July 1997. It was summer, a time for childhood games, playfulness, and easy breathing. I noticed the round-faced boy, Madjid, selling chewing gum at the entrance of the freeway.

Big round eyes, unwashed face, worn-out shoes, sweating, and a few packs of chewing gum in his hand, he was in search of customers under the burning sun of Tehran in a hot summer day in July. I bought a pack of chewing gum. He smiled. I bought another pack.

"What do you like to do for your summer vacation?" I asked Madjid. He smiled again, answering me with most refreshing joy:

I like to have a drawing book and color pencils at home.
I like to watch television after lunch.
I like to stay home and play with my brother and sister.
I like to go to the seaside and play in the water.
    But mother says it is expensive.
I like to go to the zoo and see the animals.
I like to own a toy gun and play police and thief with my friends.
I like to go to the park with my parents.
I like to go to *Shahr-e Ba'zi* [amusement park] with my family.
    But mother says that is expensive.

Madjid chased a potential customer and disappeared from my sight. His voice echoing in my ears—"I like to go to my uncle's village and play with the goats."

Migration: Fleeing the State's Economic and Political Violence

"Forgive me for intruding. I overheard your conversation. I feel the same way as the author of the poem you just read. I too have an urge to fly away. I cannot stay here, but I have nowhere to go. Who is that poet?"

Sipping tea with a friend on the bench next to mine, the young man looked restless and uneasy

"Sohrab Sepehri. He is my favorite poet. Do you know him?" I asked.

"I heard his name in school. I'd like to read his poems. Maybe it will help."

I wrote the titles of Sohrab's poems on a piece of paper. He thanked me, staring at the paper.

"Do you come here often?"

"Sometimes," I replied. "I like Darakeh. It helps me stay away from the chaos of the city."

An unending gaze on his face. "I hope to see you and talk to you again" said the young man.

But I never saw him in Darakeh again. I returned to the same spot, drank tea, and breathed the fresh mountain air. Lost in the crowded collage of the forgotten young men and women of Tehran, the young man was never to be seen.

His face reappears when I voyage through the penetrating words of Sohrab Sepehri.

> I must leave tonight.
> Pack a suitcase the size of my loneliness,
> I must leave tonight.

"I must leave tonight." Stories of men and women on the unending road to their escape.

Summer of 1996. I met Amir one morning. Twenty or younger, using his car as a taxicab after work, a lifeless face, grim and withdrawn, looking absorbed or perhaps lost, his clothes unwashed and old, Amir drove with little attention to the world around him.

"Is this your only job?" I asked Amir.

"I work in an office five days a week," he replied with the same lifeless face. "I do this on the weekends to make some extra money. But I'm still behind. Cannot catch up."

Amir's face revealed anger and hopelessness. "I blew it," he burst out abruptly. "I blew it. I should have stayed longer. Instead, what did I do?"

His face seized with sadness and despair. "I had a golden opportunity. You make mistakes when you are young. I could have built a great future for me. I blew it."

The anger in his voice giving way to a mourning sigh—mourning the death of a great future, the death of hope—his eyes staring at the faraway, I interrupted again.

"What did you do?" I asked Amir.

"I moved to Japan with another friend for work. I got homesick and came back after a year. He stayed on. He is a multimillionaire now. I had this car before I left. That is still all I have to my name."

Amir's voice was filled with resentment, perhaps deep anger. "He sent money home to his family. They bought two vans, a minibus and refrigerators for him. Just kept them somewhere without using them. Everything he bought is worth three times more now. Smart! And me, this old car is all I have to my name."

Amir's tale of disappointment and failure remained with me for a long time. I met many young men with the same broken dreams, longing for the opportunity to defeat and tame the monster of rising prices, or perhaps longing for a chance to survive. I met young men leaving their homes for a chance to labor in Japan, Dubai, Cyprus, and Turkey—new Mecca for the struggling Iranian youth, a golden chance to escape the miseries of unbeatable inflation and economic deprivation, a hope for a better tomorrow. But this was only a foggy dream and a mirage for the young driver who envied the fortunes of his friend, and for Ali.

"I came back from Dubai two days ago. They called from the hospital." Ali looked anxious and withdrawn. He had a private pickup truck.

"She needs an operation, some type of cancer the doctor says. I went to work in Dubai to save money for the operation. But I had to come back. She needs the operation now."

He was called back home for his wife's cancer operation. He was home without the money for her treatment. His face wrinkled by anger, fear, and a sense of failure and defeat. Defeat!

A Voyage of Fear: Young Men in Search of Toil in Faraway Lands

Salute to Life, I Lost my Youth.

—Graffiti on a lonely rock in the mountains surrounding Tehran

It was September 9, 1998, Iran Air flight 747 to Larnaca, Cyprus—a Mecca for the Iranian middle class, a place of temporary respite from a deadly existence riddled with the constant pains of inflation, economic insecurity, and cultural boredom. This was a journey to the Mediterranean Sea—a place for co-ed bathing and swimming, women free of the suffocating head-to-toe Islamic outfit, food, wine, music, and all that is worthy of human desire. The Mediterranean Sea—where it is possible to be human once again, live and love like humans, breathe the fresh air like the humans do. Hours away from the chance to stroll on the beach without the watchful eyes of the Security Force and the Islamic Volunteer Corps, hold hands and watch the beautiful sunset, smile and love without fear, the passengers waited anxiously for flight 747 to Larnaca.

Smiles on their faces, men and women dreamed of good times ahead and a temporary freedom from the pains of everyday life. Still covered by the Islamic dress code, women dreamed of the moment they would take off their long robes and allow their skin to be touched by the heavenly sensation of the Mediterranean sun and the fresh air dancing on their deprived skin. This was the kiss of life.

Filling out customs forms, I was approached by a nervous-looking young man. Pale and worried, he did not know his way around. First time leaving home, riddled by fear and worry, he asked me to help him fill out the forms. Following me around, he requested to stand by me while waiting for the boarding time. Suspicious of the young man, I found an excuse and left the lobby to say farewell to Maryam. We hugged under the suspicious eyes of passersby, stared at each other's eyes, and departed in silence.

Half an hour gone, aboard the Iran Air flight to Larnaca, thinking of Maryam, I heard the young man's voice. "I am glad to find you again. 24C. Yes, my seat is next to yours. I am so happy to be with a friend." The young man sat next to me in row 24, smiled, placed his handbag under the seat, and thanked God for being seated next to me.

He spoke after minutes of uneasy silence. "Have you been to Cyprus before?" asked the young man. He was once again anxious and fearful. Worried eyes, his body destabilized by a fear deadlier than death, I responded affirmatively to his question.

"How much dollars do you take with you?" I did not wish to answer this question. My suspicion of the young man in 24C was intensified.

"Is three hundred dollars enough?" he asked, hoping for my affirmation. Three hundred dollars! This was the amount I heard over and over from other anxious and fearful young men on that short flight to Larnaca. "Is it enough?" I smiled and avoided the question.

"Will you stay in Larnaca?"

"No," I responded without hesitation. I told 24C of my plan to visit a friend in Paphos, a well-respected Cypriot, an educator, and a man of wisdom. I was to visit Andreas Georgiades and his loving wife Stella in Paphos.

"Are you staying in Larnaca?" I asked 24C. He hoped to leave Larnaca. Limasoul was where 24C had planned to go. 24C told me of an Iranian man who would give him work as a construction laborer in Limasoul. He told me of the money he would save and his future plans in Iran. I was not sure that 24C himself believed his dreams.

"Have you spoken to the man?"

He had not. The young man only had a phone number. He was on a journey away from home with three hundred dollars, a small handbag, a phone number, a dream, and a face that betrayed the inner secrets he wished to hide. I remembered Sohrab Sepehri's poem.

> I must leave tonight.
> Pack a suitcase the size of my loneliness.
> I must leave tonight.

I had lost my suspicions of 24C by now. His journey was not for the Mediterranean sun, the fresh air, and as he told me, "not for women." He closed his eyes for a few short minutes waiting for the takeoff. I thought about his tale, turned to my left, and for the first time noticed the man in 24A. He was young, in his early twenties. I smiled. He said hello. We greeted one another with respect.

The plane took off. I read my newspaper. 24A smiled again. 24C broke the silence. "Will you stay with me when we get to the airport in Larnaca? Can you help me not get deported?" Suddenly hijacked from my own reality and taken to the world of fear and anxiety of deportation, I nodded and looked for ways to hide my uneasiness and feeling of awe after this abrupt encounter.

Deportation was to become the common theme of my conversations with 23A, 23B, 17D, 25G, 19D, and many other young Iranian males on the plane—young men in search of the scarce opportunity to toil, and a chance to live. Deportation was the common fear of the young men on the flight to Cyprus—a heaven not too far away, a garden of hope protected by tall walls and immigration officials who could spot foreign men in search of toil. This was Iran Air flight 747 to Larnaca, Cyprus—an uneasy collage of happy travelers in search of joy and those nervously awaiting their first encounter with the guardians of the heaven—the deadly collage of comfort and despair.

The frightened man in 24C told stories of young men, young like him, men in search of toil, men deported and returned to Iran from the airport, never reaching their dreamland, never toiling under the blue sky of the Mediterranean Sea.

"Can you help me not get deported?" 24A listened in silence. He too looked frightened now. "Do you think they would deport me?"

I asked 24C to be calm. How can I promise to save him from deportation?

The plane took off. I turned to 24C. His eyes closed, his face revealed an intense sense of fear. "Be calm," I told 24C holding his hand. A few minutes of silence, a flight attendant covered head to toe in dark blue appeared with a tamed smile and a basket of domestic candies, plates of snacks, bread, packaged sandwiches, and fruit—last wishes of men awaiting their execution. I did not eat my bread. His eyes on my plate, 24A smiled. "Can I have your bread?" he asked. I offered him my plate. He calmly put the bread in his shirt pocket. "I could use it later," said 24A with a strange smile. I offered 24A my fruit. He accepted.

My journeying neighbors had never flown before. Amazed at the wrapped package of food, they asked me to explain every piece. Small packs of salt and pepper—creations beyond the imagination of 24C, curiously staring at the pack for a minute or two—symbols of the world of the "others"—others so near but so far, clustered with them on flight 747 to Larnaca, Cyprus.

"I hope they do not deport me. That would be the end of me," said 24C after the short minutes of peace of mind created by the amazing package of food. The man in 24A put two packs of fruit in his handbag, and a coffee cup too before the flight attendant returned.

Half an hour before landing, surrounded by men of despair, I too felt the suffocating sensation of fear and anxiety now. "Can you stay with me on the line?" pleaded 24C. And once again, I told him to control his fear. "Self-control is your only chance." 24C put his head down, covering his anxious face in his hands that betrayed years of toil, and nothing but toil.

The flight attendant in dark blue handed out arrival passes written in English. Nervous whispers erupted in rows around me. Men moved from one row to another, searching for help to fill out the forms, asking for possible ways to hide their plans for their odyssey. I was approached by frightened young men, looking for a way to disguise the real reason for their journey. No knowledge of English, no money, no hotel reservation, no real occupation at home—private business was what everyone asked me to write on the arrival forms.

One-thirty in the afternoon, landing in Larnaca Airport, I was followed by 24C, 24A, 17 B, and other frightened men on their desperate voyage in hope of a better tomorrow. I consoled 17A. "Will you speak to the officer for us?"

Line 1. The buzzer sounded. A door opened. 17A approached the booth. An unfriendly officer asked questions. 17A stood before him in fear. The officer picked up the phone. I looked at 17A. A plain-clothed security man arrived. Young, no smile, he escorted 17A to a room. A locked room behind the passport booths. He unlocked the door. 17A entered. He locked the door.

The realization of what was feared, 24C turned to me with a deadly fear on his face.

Line 2. The buzzer sounded. The door opened. 24C approached the booth. An unfriendly officer asked questions. 24C stood before him in fear. The officer picked up the phone. I looked at 24C. The plain-clothed security arrived. Escorting 24C to locked room behind the passport booths, he unlocked the door. 24C entered. He locked the door.

Line 5. The buzzer sounded. The door opened and 22A approached the booth. We looked at each other, saying our last farewell with our eyes.

The buzzer sounded again. I said farewell to 18A.

An hour and a half passed. All the frightened young men were behind the locked door. This was the end of their dreams.

The buzzer sounded. The door opened. I approached the booth with my American passport. The unfriendly officer smiled. We shook hands. I was on my way to Paphos.

September 10, 1998, Paphos. I was in the small garden of the Georgiades Marilena's Apartments, enjoying the fresh breeze from the Mediterranean Sea, heavenly grapes, sweat figs, the forbidden red wine, feta cheese, and olives. Drowned in joy of life, I closed my eyes and remembered the haunting image of 17A entering the locked room. I opened my eyes, looked at the kind face of Andreas Georgiades, and took a sip of Othello, vintage 1983.

October 13, 1998. I was back in Tehran shortly before the days of smog and deadly pollution, and the murder of the intellectuals and writers.

Death by Heart Attack—Free from the Battle of the Everyday

Heart attacks rose sharply among the young men trapped in the complex web of economic uncertainty and cultural and political invasion by the state. Others fell into the abyss of depression, anxiety, and the manic fear of tomorrow.

It was late Winter 1998. I do not recall his name. He was young, angry, depressed, and unshaved. I paid him one thousand tomans for a ride to Darakeh. Cheated by a childhood friend, in debt, he had sold all his belongings to pay a part of his debt. A driver for twelve hours a day, seven days a week, he lamented about his pains. We talked about suicide and death by heart attack. He told me of the fatal heart attack of a young friend. He spoke with no emotions on his face. I never saw him again.

Perhaps Pirooz or Ali, he was young and angry. Having lost a business to a brother, a cabdriver for less than half a year, he spoke with rage. I met him in the spring of 1999. "You cannot trust anybody," he repeated the whole way to my destination. He told me of the death of a close friend at age thirty. Recently married, leaving a pregnant wife behind, he too died of a heart attack. He said farewell to the world of anxiety. Died at age thirty.

February 4, 1999. I saw him at a family gathering. He was withdrawn and looking pale. Never smiled, he had lost weight. "What will happen to the economy?" he asked me with a sense of urgency. "What can be done? Is there any solution?" He heard my reply, sat quietly, and said in pain, "So, no solution!"

A mining engineer, married, and a father of two. He had lost his job two and a half years earlier. One year of unemployment, selling family belongings, and coping with the humiliation of unemployment, he found employment at a mine far from home. Eight months of hard work, day in day out, far from home, the killing heat of Chabahar Port, he returned home without any money after eight months. Forced to leave the job, he returned home after eight months. Eight months of work, he was not paid his salary. No one was paid. There was no money he was told. Now unemployed again. Owed eight months of pay. Unable to find a new job, he asked, "Is there anything that can be done?"

Suicide—the Final Act in the Battle of the Everyday

When death by heart attack failed to free the victims of the battle of the everyday, suicide offered the terminal respite from the overwhelming and unbeatable agony of life. In 1998, Iran suffered from a rate of suicide twice as high as the highest rate in the world. In 1990, there were 244 cases of suicide filed with the security force of the Islamic Republic in the areas under its jurisdiction. In 1995, the number of cases filed had increased to 3,472.[9]

Suicide—the final act in the lonely battle of the everyday. Although the decision to terminate one's life is set in motion by a multitude of factors, the sharp increase in suicide after 1989 supports the conclusion that poverty and economic uncertainty aggravated people's living conditions, leading to suicide in many cases. Suicide was on the rise in both densely populated cities and more remote places in the country. Half of all suicides occurred in cities, while the rest took place in smaller towns and villages. According to some reports, between five and seven thousand people committed suicide every year.[10] Despite its condemnation on religious grounds by the state, suicide continued to increase. Desperate and defeated in the battle for survival, and feeling total estrangement from society, some took the lives of their families to free their loved ones from the pains of everyday.

Poverty was reported to be the cause of suicide by fire by four teenage girls, ages twelve, fifteen, seventeen, and nineteen, in the city of Darab.[11] The newspapers reported about a "psychotic," "mentally ill," and "demented" man who set his family on fire. He terminated the lives of nine children, his wife, and himself. Medical and legal experts, the police, and the public condemned the action. A few days before the "psychotic" act, he told a surviving son: "We are inflicted by the black leprosy of poverty." He finally rid his family of the disease. A moment of pain, and a chapter was closed. Eleven people died. Free at last. Poverty remained for others.

And I read the story of Ja'afar Goorani. Thirty-four years old and a father of two, he was fired after thirteen years of labor in the same company. He hanged himself in the bathroom of his apartment.

COLLECTIVE ACTION IN THE MAKING: WORKERS' RESPONSE TO THE CIVIL SOCIETY

The poor and the wage-earning class primarily reacted to their economic disenfranchisement through an alienating process of internalization and the formation of noncollective survival mechanisms. The internalization of social discontent and the predominance of isolated and individual sites of struggle for survival shielded the state from potential collective responses to its policies for nearly twenty years. But, on rare occasions, public discontent produced open social ruptures in which the totality of the state was challenged by disenchanted protesters. On these occasions, a form of spontaneous collectivity was generated, channeled against the state. The severity of political and cultural repression and economic marginalization led, in some case, to the formation of collective action that crossed the usual boundaries of economic protest and challenged the legitimacy of the state.[12] In addition to scattered riots, there were occasional job actions against rising prices and the declining standard of living of the wage earners. In most cases, these manifestations of a collective voice were settled by the use of force and occasional wage concessions on the part of the state.[13]

The press in Iran rarely reports the occurrence of strikes and other job actions and protests by workers. Independent organizations rooted in the working class with the ability to collect and distribute reliable data and information are also lacking. The rare and infrequent reports of strikes and protests in the official media are often distorted and not entirely reliable. As a result, an accurate assessment of the degree of collective action by the wage earners is not possible. But, given all these limitations, the available information indicates an increase in job actions, rallies, and protests by workers since the election of Mohammad Khatami in May 1997.

The presidency of Mohammad Khatami and the promise of reform and freedom of expression on one hand, and the deepening economic crisis, on the other hand, resulted in a relative surge of collective action on the part of the wage earners throughout the country. The severe economic crisis and the new political space created after the election of Mohammad Khatami led to more incidents of collective action on the part of affected workers. Like students and youths, wage earners appear to have been gaining a new consciousness of their collective interest, more frequently responding to their rising economic disenfranchisement through the non-private methods dominant earlier. In the common backdrop of alienation, apathy, and private struggles for survival, new elements of collectivity are emerging.

Despite the continued presence of the official organizations and institutions of state repression, surveillance and control in factories and economic units, and the dominance of the House of Labor and the Islamic Councils as the only officially sanctioned workers organizations, signs of independent action by the workers have emerged.[14] Though still riddled with illusions about Islam and the

Islamic state, workers have been gaining a new sense of courage, collectively reacting to their immediate economic conditions, protesting against the management at their enterprises. For the most part, collective action on the part of the workers has been confined to local (firm-based) economic demands.

The deepened economic crisis and the consequent nonpayment of salaries and wages have been a primary reason for workers action. Collective action to demand the payment of deferred salaries became a common occurrence across the country and in different industries (see Appendix B). Of 181 protests reported by the media from March 1998 to March 1999, a total of one hundred were concerned with unpaid wages.[15] In many cases, these actions were organized against enterprises owned by the state or the very powerful non-state public foundations (the Mostazefan Foundation and others) under the direct control of the *faghih*.

Inspired by the new opening in society, workers have been using different forms of collective action to voice their frustrations. In addition to job actions, in many cases, the workers had brought the grievances away from the point of production, protesting in front of state offices, demanding action and support from the state.[16] Of 181 protests and strikes by workers reported by various press and media from March 1998 to March 1999, there were forty-six strikes and sixty-three demonstrations and protests away from the factory, in front of local state offices.[17] Instead of focusing on the owners of their enterprises, protesting workers have been holding the state responsible for resolving their crisis and ridding them of their dire conditions. The continuation of the economic crisis and the inability of private and state enterprises to meet their current payments of salaries and wages can potentially lead to the politicization of the workers and the transformation of their collective action for the payment of salaries into action directed at the state.

In addition to sporadic firm-based actions, there has emerged a more collective form of labor militancy. Driven by opposition to a bill introduced by the conservative MPs in the parliament, tens of thousands of workers across the nation were mobilized in 1999, voicing their anger at a policy designed to further their disempowerment. On June 8, the *Majlis* approved an amendment to the existing labor law exempting all workplaces employing three workers or fewer from the terms of the law for a period of six years.[18] The amendment made employers of small enterprises free from the responsibility to provide their workers with health insurance and unemployment insurance. No limit to the length of the working day or the working week, no minimum wage, no pregnancy leave, and no statutory holidays for the workers of exempted workplaces; employers were allowed to lay off or fire workers without any notice and without any compensatory pay. They were made completely exempt from all of the expenses and regulations stipulated by the labor law of the Islamic Republic.

The bill passed by the *Majlis* in June 1999 was the result of a long process of intense lobbying, maneuvering, and factional struggle between the MPs belonging to different political factions of the state and various influential groups in the society. The proposal to overhaul the labor law led to intense behind-the-scenes lobbying, open confrontations in the press and organized protest on different occasions. It became a site for the rise of factional conflict within the state, intensifying the tension within its ranks. It led to a further deepening of the divide between those still adhering to the earlier populist platform of the Islamic state and those seeking to free the hands of Iran's traditional bazaar-based bourgeoisie, and the proponents of free market capitalism. The traditional Left tendency and its institutions waged an organized campaign against the overhaul, while the Islamic Right and its forces defended the plan.

The national opposition to the plan was organized and led by *Kaneh-e Karegar* (House of Labor), the sole existing national labor organization, an organization controlled by the traditional Left tendency and associates of President Khatami and Khatami's administration. Celebrating May Day, the House of Labor waged demonstrations and rallies across the country, protesting the possible passing of the amendment in the *Majlis* on May 1, 1999. The May Day rally and demonstrations were organized in Tehran, Khouzestan, and other provinces.

Despite the lack of independent workers' institutions, and the leadership of the national protest by an institution set up by the state, the attack on workers' rights inspired more activism, leading to a further politicization of the wage earners. It unleashed a latent energy and awakened the sense of collectivism repressed by twenty years of surveillance, coercion, and systemic assault. Seeds of a new awakening were planted in the process. This was the first instance in nearly two decades of collective expression on the part of the workers against an economic law passed by the state. The overwhelming support of the rank and file of wage earners for the call for the May

Day rally in Tehran and other cities reflected the readiness of the wage earners for a new wave of activism. Similar to the developments within the student movement, the factional divide within the state gave rise to new movements for change, leading to a potential for the politicization of the wage earners and the development of new forms of collective voice and demands for an independent workers' institution.[19]

The 1999 May Day rallies were, in some sense, the prelude to a new beginning in the labor movement. The continuing economic crisis, the widening political division of the state, and the cumulative impact of the reform movement, could potentially lead to the emergence of a labor movement independent of the House of Labor and the state. Facing the prolonged economic and political crises, the House of Labor, similar to the state-sponsored student groups, is prone to internal developments, divisions and breakups, and transformations. Losing control of the movement of wage earners by the House of Labor might result in further collective action and attempts for the creation of independent workers' institutions.

After twenty years of private struggle and retreat to personal survival, amidst the continuing state repression, signs of the emergence of the wage earners as an independent force with a group interest in the movement for reform and civil society are appearing. The inability of public and private enterprises to pay their employees is fueling new sentiments for collective action. The Interior Ministry banned a planned workers' demonstration outside the social security offices in Tehran and elsewhere to protest against nonpayment of unemployment benefits that had been scheduled for December 18, 1999. Originally requested by the Islamic Labor Councils, the protest was called off after the announcement by the Interior Ministry. But in Tehran and a few other cities, workers defied the ban, stepped outside the control of the Islamic Labor Councils, and protested the nonpayment of their salaries.[20] There were a number of protests by the oil workers in Tehran, Abadan, Ahvaaz, and Ramhormoz, and the textile workers in the province of Mazandaran, in the first weeks of the year 2000.

The protest movement has been spreading to different industries. The state is increasingly held responsible for the economic crisis. It must find a solution. The inability to do so leads to further politicization of the wage earners, their return to collective struggle, and the metamorphosis of the movement for reform.

APPENDIX A

STRUCTURAL ADJUSTMENT, EXCHANGE RATE LIBERALIZATION, WAGE EARNERS' STANDARD OF LIVING

Iran had followed a fixed exchange rate regime of seventy rials per dollar since 1955. Following the path of many developing nations and viewing the exchange rate as a tool for industrialization and meeting other domestic economic goals, the state established an elaborate multiple exchange rate system, using differential pricing for various categories of imported goods and domestic production. While the official rate was used for primary state projects and necessities, other rates were based on the priorities of the specific sectors or lines of economic activity.[21]

The war with Iraq, the bombing of oil fields and refineries, and the decline in Iran's supply of hard currency in the years after the revolution led to the development of a parallel black market and the establishment of rates far above the official exchange rate in the 1980s. The rising demand for foreign currency during the war and the limited and fluctuating foreign currency receipts from oil exports (Iran's primary source of foreign currency) resulted in an acute foreign exchange shortage, and a pervasive speculative frenzy in currency markets.

Moving toward the gradual liberalization of the foreign exchange market in 1989, the state officially terminated the long-existing multiple exchange rate system and reduced all rates to four categories of official, preferred, competitive, and floating. The continuation of the policy eventually led to a further overhaul of the system and the establishment of one single rate determined by supply and demand.[22] A single (floating) exchange rate regime was finally established in 1993, the last year of the First Plan.[23] A nonofficial/free market was allowed to coexist with the official foreign exchange market. The foreign exchange shortage and the inability of the state to deliver a sufficient supply of foreign currency at its single floating rate transformed the unofficial foreign exchange market into a lucrative site for speculative investment. The result was a continuous long-term decline in the value of the national currency in the free market. The central bank's objective was a gradual closing of the gap between the rates in the two markets.

The liberalization of the currency market resulted in the long-term (though fluctuating) decline in the value of the national currency and an increasing dollarization of the economy. The free market price of the dollar increased by more than one hundred times (or 10,000 percent) from 70 rials in 1978 (the year before the revolution) to 72,000 rials in May 1995. The state was forced to retreat. A fixed exchange rate regime at 3,000 rials per dollar was imposed by the central bank in May 1995.[24]

The sustained appreciation of the dollar created a lasting frenzy in the foreign exchange market and stimulated (along with other factors) the transfer of resources from (already weak) productive investment to short-term speculative investment in the dollar. The steady loss in the market value of the rial led to rising prices of most domestically produced and imported consumer goods, and a chronic supply-pushed inflation. The effect of currency liberalization in prices was not coincidental. Being dependent on the import of machinery and semi-finished goods, industrial production and capital accumulation were constrained by the availability of cheap imported capital goods (see the section on the international division of labor). The increase in the foreign exchange rate reduced capital imports and created shortages of necessary parts and materials.

Foreign exchange–generated bottlenecks resulted in simultaneous declines in output (growth) and rising prices. In addition to affecting domestic production, the depreciation of the national currency also resulted in increased prices of imported consumer goods. The simultaneous privatization and liberalization of foreign trade led to the allocation of scarce resources (foreign currency) to lucrative luxury goods imports, further depriving wage earners of their potential access to affordable articles of consumption, and to meeting their basic needs.

The unprecedented capital gains from speculative investment in the currency market led to yet further accumulation of wealth in the hands of a few, and the reprocessing of this wealth in other speculative ventures, including the housing market in a later period. Housing prices and rentals increased by proportions never experienced before, leading to monthly rents that surpassed the incomes of average wage earners in Tehran and other major cities. The psychological impact of the sustained increase in the relative value of the dollar produced further speculative price increases in the market for both tradable and nontradable goods. Retailers of even the most basic nontradable goods increased their prices with every increase in the value of the dollar. The result was the vicious cycle of daily price hikes and constant erosion of the purchasing power of fixed-income wage earners. According to published state statistics, while prices increased on an average by almost 50 percent per year during the 1989–1993 period, average wages and salaries only rose by 12–17 percent.

The effect of currency market liberalization on the standard of living of wage earners was further compounded by SAP's attack on the partial rationing of basic needs and state subsidies, and the "rationalization" of the price system. By 1993, a number of staples including butter, chicken, eggs, soap, and laundry detergent were removed from the system of rationing. In addition to removing specific commodities from the system, the state began a new policy of changing the pricing of rationed commodities in 1993. Accordingly, prices of rationed staples were determined on the basis of the conversion of full cost of imports (import price) at a new exchange rate of 1,750 rials per dollar (an increase of 2,400 percent from seventy rials per dollar).[25] The result was a further increase in the number of people living in poverty.

Defining the poverty line as access to "normal food intake," research has shown a marked increase in the percentage of population living below the poverty line after 1989, the first year of SAP.[26] In 1989, 45 percent and 52 percent of families in urban and rural areas lived below the poverty line respectively. The share of the population living in poverty increased by 29.3 percent and 23.3 percent in urban and rural areas respectively in 1994. The appreciation of the prices of staples also forced changes in the consumption behavior of the population, leading to their declining nutritional intake. In most cases, the daily intake of bread (continuing to enjoy high state subsidies) replaced the consumption of red meat, chicken, rice, and other nutritious food.[27] Meat was gradually elevated to a luxury item for many Iranians.[28]

This was the general condition of many wage earners when Khatami was inaugurated as Iran's president.

APPENDIX B

PARTIAL LIST OF COLLECTIVE ACTION AGAINST THE NONPAYMENT OF WAGES AND SALARIES (DECEMBER 1998–DECEMBER 1999)

December 1998—A number of workers of Jika'beh Factory waged a protest in front of the provincial office of the province of Gilan by the

Caspian Sea. The agency also reported protests by "many groups" from "various factories" in the city of Kashan in December 1998.[29]

December 1998—The workers at Cheet-e Karaj textile factory assembled in front of the gate of the factory to protest the nonpayment of their salary.

January 1999—A group of three hundred employees of Jamkou Factory assembled in front of Tehran's provincial governor's office to protest the nonpayment of wages and salaries in the preceding ten months. "We are hungry," said a worker. "We feel ashamed before our families" said another worker. A worker in slippers, unable to buy shoes, lamented about his wife's illness and need for surgery. He owes 145,000 tomans to the hospital.[30]

Workers of Javaherian Factory (manufacturing furnaces) waged a sitdown strike in front of the factory to protest the nonpayment of their salaries.

January 1999—A number of workers of Nakhkar Company assembled in front of the Ministry of Labor and Social Services in protest against the nonpayment of their salaries for eleven months.

March 1999—Four days before the New Year, the workers of a company providing medical services in Tabriz waged a sit-in in front of Razi Hospital in protest against the nonpayment of their salaries. The workers were paid neither their salaries nor their New Year bonus.[31]

A total of two thousand workers of Jahan Textiles Factory (belonging to the Mostazefan Foundation) assembled to protest the nonpayment of two hundred million tomans of their overdue wages and bonuses.

April 1999—Workers at a large smelting works in central Iran went on strike in protest against at the nonpayment of their salaries.[32]

Textile workers in Mazandaran protested the nonpayment of salaries by holding demonstrations in the main streets of the provincial capital Ghaem Shahr.[33]

April 1999—Workers locked out by Pars Iran textile plant on Lakan highway in Rasht protested against management in front of the provincial labor offices. Some of these workers had as many as twenty years of service in this factory.[34]

June 1999—Workers in the Naghshiran machine-made carpet factory, in Shahr-e Alborz, who had received no salaries or bonuses for three months, staged a sit-in in front of this plant on June 19, 1999. The security forces were brought in to break up the sit-in.[35]

Workers of Abadan Municipality went on strike, protesting the nonpayment of salaries. They staged a demonstration in front of the local governor's offices to express their anger and dispersed after the authorities promised to follow up on their demands.[36]

June 1999—Most factories in Khouzestan province had not paid any salaries to their workers for three to five months. The factories include tube manufacturers of Khouzestan, Koushan Factory, an agricultural plant, Pars Hospital, and a shut-down metal plant.[37]

July 1999—A number of ancillary employees of Abhar Hospital waged a two-hour work stoppage in protest against the nonpayment of their wages for three months.[38]

July 1999—Two hundred employees of Farsa Construction and Material Plant in Savjebalagh stopped work in protest against the lack of payment of salaries and bonuses for over six months. They walked twelve kilometers between the plant and Savjehbalagh and held a rally in front of the offices of the local governor. Farsa Construction and Material plant is run under the authority of the state-owned Bank of Industry and Mining.[39]

October 1999—Seven hundred workers gathered outside Eelam Municipality protesting the nonpayment of salaries in September and October. The protesting workers had previously written an open letter complaining, "We can't tolerate hunger any more," and had staged a demonstration on October 10, demanding payment of their wages.[40]

December 1999—Workers of a domestic appliance factory in Hashtgerd near Karaj demonstrated outside the headquarters of the company in Tehran against the nonpayment of their salaries for ten months.[41]

CHAPTER EIGHT

State, Economy, and Civil Society—Part II

Economic Decline, Divided State, and Policy Retreat: The Triumph of New Liberalism

The inauguration of Mohammad Khatami to Iran's presidency coincided with an economic slowdown, the deepening of the decline in the wage earners' standard of living, increased unemployment, unplanned inventory buildup, and other signs of economic decline.[1] Iran's factories operated at 50 percent capacity in 1998.[2] The number of enterprises unable to meet their payrolls was on the rise.[3] Thousands of wage earners were owed months of unpaid wages and salaries across the nation by 1999. Workers at 450 establishments were reported as not having been paid wages for between two and eleven months. Most plants suffered from archaic and internationally noncompetitive machinery and equipment. Lack of funds (foreign exchange) and the presence of old machinery led to plant closures.

Six hundred textile factories were shut down during the 1996–1999 period. Nearly five thousand textile plants remained, all with aging machinery, thirty years old on the average.[4] Most textile factories under the cover and control of *Bonyad-e Mostazefan* (Mostazefan Foundation) incurred losses in 1998. Eight were in a crisis condition, their closure anticipated, which would cause the loss of 8,000 jobs. One of the eight companies agreed to sell its machinery for twenty rials per kilo, while the dollar was exchanged in the free market for seven thousand rials. The company did not find a customer. Given the general price level, one could not even buy a stick of chewing gum with twenty rials.[5]

By 1999, twenty years after the revolution, the Iranian economy manifested a widening gap between the rich and the poor and an increasing impoverishment of the wage earners.[6] The economy had nearly collapsed and the state had lost its ability to boost production and reverse the entrenched process of marginalization of wage earners. Both working and nonworking wage earners (retirees and those receiving pensions) were rapidly falling into the abyss of poverty and disenfranchisement.

The average monthly income of those receiving pensions from the Office of Social Security was reported to be around 320,000 rials a month in 1997. This was while the director of the Office of Social Security reported monthly incomes of 850,000 rials and 450,000 rials as the "poverty line" and "survival line" respectively for five hundred Iranian cities. Thus, on the average, pensioners received incomes below the survival line, or on the "death line."[7] Half of the employees of the Ministry of Education lived below the "poverty line" or on the "death line." Four hundred fifty thousand of the ministry's employees received less than 500,000 rials a month and 38 percent of the nation's teachers earned 300,000 rials a month.[8]

The severity of the economic problem of the country had become an undeniable reality. State officials and influential figures lamented the country's "economic illness"—unemployment, inflation, and the plight of the working poor. The misfortunes of the wage earners and the deepening economic crisis became the subject of a factional struggle for domination in the period after the election of Mohammad Khatami. The shrinking standard of living of wage earners was a weapon used in the battle for hegemony. The earlier managers of economic decline and those with entrenched positions in the state and a fortified economic base engaged in a war of words, intentional economic mismanagement, and economic obstruction to preserve their power and gain hegemony in the state.

A type of populism, much like the economic populism of the early years of the Islamic Republic, emerged in the rhetoric and public pronouncements of all factions of the state. All factions posed as defenders of wage earners and the poor in their public statements, and all blamed others for the deepening misfortunes of the poor. But, while the economy was increasingly becoming a site of factional struggle and competition for power, the crisis remained and the standard of living of the wage earners further deteriorated.

The economy and its ills were used by the conservatives in their battle against "political development," the central tenet of Mohammad Khatami's platform for reform. "Political development," Khatami's all-encompassing phrase for the government of law, civil society, pluralism, and participation, became a subject of attack by all opponents of reform. They accused Khatami and his administration of neglecting "economic development" while focusing on "political development." Political development and the project of reform were presented to the public as the main cause of economic disorganization and the impoverishment of wage earners.

Rebuffing the president and his social agenda, Ayatollah Yazdi said in his Friday prayer sermon at Tehran University on July 3, 1998, "Inflation and economic pressures are the most important problems of the country. . . . The question of political development ranks fourth or fifth."[9] Mohammad Reza Bahonar, an influential conservative MP from Tehran, reiterated the same criticism in an address to a group of merchants from the bazaar. Attacking the supporters of civil society, Bahonar said, "Those who speak of pluralism, liberalism, secularism, political development, and reconciliation with the U.S., are all entirely the same. The discussion of civil society and pluralism belong to the nineteenth century and its epoch is over."[10]

Similarly, a July 4 article in *Resalat,* the important conservative daily affiliated with the conservative faction of the state, articulated the concept of "anti-economics," accusing the government of neglecting economic difficulties while addressing relatively "trivial" issues of political development and civil society. Following the basic theme of Yazdi's Friday prayer sermon at Tehran University, the daily stated:

> Focusing on political development is suspect when we have not yet achieved economic development. . . . It appears that some individuals and groups related to the government are addressing less important issues instead of dealing with the fundamental pains of the society. . . . The responsibility of the state policy makers is to set priorities for solving problems and plan for resolving these problems in accordance with the priorities and the common concerns of the society. . . . Political development is nothing new. This requirement exists in the essence of Islam. Essentially, those forces that enjoy ideological richness do not worry about political development.[11]

While the conservatives blamed the president's project of "political development" for the country's economic ailments, many supporters of Mohammad Khatami and those within the "May 23 Coalition" focused their criticisms on Hashemi Rafsanjani and the eight years of economic liberalization and structural adjustment during his tenure. Ali Akbar Mohtashami, member of the *Majma'-e Ruhaniyun-e Mobarez* (Militant Clerics League), blamed the policies of Rafsanjani and his party, the *Kargozaran,* as the main cause of Iran's economic difficulties. "*Kargozaran*'s Structural Adjustment and privatization," said Mohtashami, "reached a deadlock in that period [eight years]. Today, they obstruct Khatami's program and prevent [the realization of] justice and regulation of the economy."[12] With the further deepening of the crisis, the criticism of Rafsanjani grew within the ranks of President Khatami's supporters.

And in an unusually open statement, Fa'ezeh Rafsanjani, the ex-president's daughter and an MP from Tehran, responded to the mounting criticism of economic policy during her father's tenure. The Tehran MP blamed the new administration for the rising unemployment and the erosion of wage earners' standard of living. She charged that her father's critics were not dealing with Khatami's "lack of policy and direction." Here, for the first time, the split within Khatami's May 23 coalition was brought into the open. The president's "Economic Revitalization Program," said Fa'ezeh Rafsanjani, "is a bunch of economic definitions. How is it possible to run a country without a plan? Investment is stagnant. Reconstruction is forgotten. This is because Khatami has departed from the Second [Development] Plan. . . . This is the result of running a country without a plan for two years. Unemployment was 13% during the administration of Hashemi. It is now 30%."[13]

And the battle continued while the economy further plummeted and a larger section of the population sank into poverty and economic marginalization. The struggle for hegemony intensified. Reformers were jailed. Critical papers were banned. Students openly challenged the Islamic state. And President Khatami and his team of economic and political advisors presented the "Economic Revitalization Program," and the "Third Plan" as the macro solutions to Iran's mounting economic problems.

FACTIONAL DIVIDE AND THE MOVEMENT FROM WELFARE STATE TO STRUCTURAL ADJUSTMENT

In the course of its development, three distinct tendencies emerged within the Islamic Republic, competing both for a dominant position within the state and for power of the ultimate determinant of economic policy. Distinguished from the left wing of the clergy by its belief in private property and its support of the privatization of public enterprises, the group known as the Traditional Right Tendency (TRT) has been an opponent of state regulation of the economy. Rooted in the bazaar and representing the interests of the class of traditional merchants, the TRT has advocated free trade and the nonintervention of the state in economic affairs. Politically, the TRT has been the home to the most fundamentalist Moslems and members of the clergy, and a staunch advocate of the absolute and unconditional rights of the supreme leader.

The actual implementation of privatization policy was achieved under the presidency of Hashemi Rafsanjani and his associates in what has been known as *Kargozaran-e Sazandegi* (executives of construction). *Kargozaran* was the main force behind the privatization of public enterprises, the reduction of state subsidies, the move toward the liberalization of the foreign exchange market, and the promotion of an export-led growth strategy and other essential components of the neoliberal package. They advocated the fusion to the world economy as both the short-term and long-term solution to Iran's structural economic problems, and promoted free trade, the use of foreign resources (productive and loan capital), and the integration of Iran into the world economy based on its areas of "comparative advantage."

The Traditional Islamic Left Tendency (TLT) has been the principle opponent of privatization efforts of the past decade and an advocate of a mixed economy and a quasi welfare state in Iran.

The early economic policies of the Islamic Republic were designed and executed during the tenure of Mir Hossein Moosavi as the Islamic Republic's second prime minister. Advocating a quasi Keynesian/welfare state, Moosavi and associates in what was to become known as the TLT, were the dominant forces behind the earlier populist policies of the Islamic Republic. Backed by Ayatollah Khomeini, they successfully fought for state control of foreign trade despite fierce opposition from those who later became the buttresses of the conservatives of the TRT. A persistent advocate of a vague notion of Islamic social justice, the TLT opposed an uncontrolled market economy. While in power in the first decade of the Islamic Republic, it instituted an elaborate system of state subsidies, price controls, and other economic regulations. State involvement in the economy increased during the eight years of war with Iraq through the enactment of macroeconomic planning, a broad program of income redistribution, and the establishment of consumption subsidies and rationing. By the early eighties, design and control of production, distribution, and pricing were, to a large extent, in the hands of the state.[14]

The economic policies of the first decade of the Islamic Republic were the realization of the economic principles and perspectives institutionalized in the constitution. A broad economic framework was outlined in Article 44 of the Constitution of the Islamic Republic.

> The economic system of the Islamic Republic of Iran shall be based on public, private and cooperative sectors with sound planning.
>
> The public sector shall include all major industries, parent industries, foreign trade, mining enterprises, banking, insurance, supply of electric power, damming and irrigation system, radio, television, post, telegraph, telephone, aviation, navigation, roads, railway and the like which shall be considered as public property and shall be under the control of the government . . .

Article 44 created a constitutional framework for an economy organized around the state sector, with the private sector playing a subsidiary role in both production and distribution of commodities. The article, in conjunction with other clauses of the constitution, laid out the foundation for the creation of a comprehensive system of state capitalism with a central role for the state in both ownership of the means of production and the monitoring and control of market activities. The provision took away from the bazaar and the merchant bourgeoisie its primary channel for economic profiteering. The debate around Article 44 led to the surfacing of the silent tendencies within the Islamic state and resulted in the eventual separation of the more populist forces (TLT) from those rooted in the bazaar (TRT).

Led by the objective of "preventing foreign economic domination over the country's economy"[15] and forced by the requirements of the war economy and the shortage of hard currency, the Islamic Republic practiced severe control over the international flow of commodities and capital during the first decade of its life. Through the use of a strict trade policy the state prohibited or restricted the import of a large number of (consumer) goods. The inflow of foreign loan capital (international borrowing) and productive capital (direct foreign investment) were banned. The Islamic Republic also changed its trading partners, moving closer to Japan, western Europe, and other developing nations, distancing itself from the "Great Satan"—the United States.

The eight-year war with Iraq left a devastated economy, a defeated dream, a bankrupt government, and a system on the verge of losing its legitimacy. The peace with Iraq and death of Ayatollah Khomeini were historic events that resulted in a series of fundamental and determining changes and transformations in the Islamic Republic. The loss of the central pillar of the Islamic state—the incontrovertible and charismatic Ayatollah Khomeini—and the acceptance of defeat in the war with Iraq were the beginning of the process of questioning of the Islamic Republic from within the ranks of the state and its loyalists. The sphere of economics was not excluded from these questionings and changes. Factional battles for change and domination over the future course of the Islamic Republic began on the economic front.

By the end of the war, a new tendency showed signs of emergence. The *Kargozaran,* formed around Hashemi Rafsanjani, advocated similar policies to those of the TRT but with the promise of rationalizing the system of industrial production and distribution. Led by Rafsanjani, the tendency became an ideological magnet for technocrats and opponents of the earlier populist policies of the state, advocating the implementation of neoliberalism: trade and exchange rate liberalization, removal of state subsidies and price controls, etc. The *Kargozaran* became the main force behind the implementation of the World Bank–sponsored structural adjustment policy (SAP) in the period after the war with Iraq.

The termination of the war with Iraq produced the opportunity for a strategic break from the earlier welfare state and the move toward neoliberalism and the SAP by the pro-market forces within the state. Contrary to the earlier years, the postwar policies were, at least partially, guided by a desire to "rationalize" Iran's position in the world market. The implementation of the SAP was an indication of the readiness of a section of the ruling clique in the Islamic Republic to retreat from earlier hopes of building a populist and "independent" capitalist economy. Iran was now to become a rational member of the international economic community.

The design and implementation of the SAP was, on one hand, a reflection of the desire of a part (now the leading part) of the state to rationalize the country's position in the world economy and remove the structural obstacles to its further integration into the world market. On the other hand, the SAP was a policy requirement of the World Bank and a condition for its support for Iran in loan negotiations with private lenders.[16] The need to rebuild the war-torn economy and revitalize Iran's badly damaged industrial base were the pragmatic factors behind the policy switch in the postwar years. Given the general scarcity of hard currency and the large reconstruction expenses after the war, international borrowing became a priority. The old taboos against foreign borrowing were now discarded. Like most other developing countries, Iran was drawn to negotiating conditional loan arrangements with the World Bank.

The attack on the wartime quasi welfare state was brought about by a coalition of the TRT and the *Kargozaran*. Hashemi Rafsanjani was elected the first president after the war. Constitutional amendments were made, the position of the prime minister was eliminated, and the TLT was defeated in the parliamentary election. The war had produced a deep-rooted sense of social fatigue. Tired of the violence of the war, shortages of basic necessities caused by the war economy, and standing in long queues for milk, soap, eggs, and all the staples of life, the citizens were psychologically prepared for change. They were prepared for a change in the rhetoric of the state and a change in its policies. Tired of the old, they were ready to embrace a new promise of immediate gratification. Thus came the new national project for the "reconstruction" of the economy and a reversal of Iran's overall economic policies of the war period. The voters embraced the new project and defeated in the parliamentary election those more directly in charge of the government during the war. All of this paved the way for the development of a new policy consensus between the office of the president and the TRT, the new majority in the Parliament. Leaving behind their political differences, the two tendencies united in liberalizing different primary markets, ending the state monopoly in international trade, launching a privatization program, and reducing state subsidies.[17]

The new policy, the transformation of the state's role in the regulation and management of the economy, was formulated by Iran's First Plan (1989–1993). A comprehensive SAP was unleashed in 1989.[18] During the five years between 1989 and 1993, the state privatized foreign trade and moved toward the deregulation of domestic markets. Subsidies were gradually reduced and eliminated, and the shares of a number of state-owned institutions were floated on the stock market. Following the general framework of the SAP, the state pursued the liberalization of the foreign exchange market and the gradual phasing out of multiple pricing of exchange rates.[19]

The implementation of the SAP transformed the economic platform of the Islamic Republic.

THE GOVERNMENT OF REFORM AND THE INSTITUTIONALIZATION OF STRUCTURAL ADJUSTMENT

Mohammad Khatami's campaign for the presidency in 1997 included no specific economic scheme and program. Economics was, by and large, excluded from the campaign. What Khatami had achieved was a loose coalition of diverse forces with competing and conflicting economic programs and interests around a platform of political reform. Apart from millions of embattled wage earners, Khatami's coalition included the *Kargozaran* and almost all organizations and individuals within the TLT. The coalition thus included both supporters of free market capitalism and advocates of a statist approach to the economy. The diversity and tension in Khatami's coalition was later reflected in his administration and choice of key ministers. While the Ministry of Economics and Finance was put in the hands of the TLT and the believers in state regulation of the economy, the powerful central bank and planning organization were left to the *Kargozaran* and advocates of structural adjustment and market liberalization. And for the Ministry of Commerce, a minister was chosen with affiliations with the TRT, favoring trade liberalization and export-led industrialization.

Khatami's selected team of economic advisors, experts, and administrators were a collage of people with diverse and competing ideas and perspectives. It was with this team that Khatami announced his economic revitalization program to the nation in early August 1998. The plan was a compromise between two conflicting outlooks on the economy, development, social justice, and other related issues. The coexistence of these polarized views resulted in structural contradictions and inconsistencies throughout the program, weakening its ability to be a plan for economic revitalization and a way out of the crisis of the Iranian economy even in the longer run.

Echoing President Khatami's eclecticism, the economic revitalization program was a collage of perspectives and policies both from those opposing the World Bank (a symbol of foreign economic domination) and those who fully endorsed the bank's policies. The program was the result of a tenuous coexistence between groups such as the *Kargozaran* and the Organization of the Mojahedeen of Islamic Revolution, a pillar of the TLT.

Following the Left perspective, the economic revitalization plan was framed by a minimalist notion of social justice (distributive justice) and an economic perspective reminiscent of the earlier years of the Islamic Republic. It saw the market as the main force behind the unjust distribution of economic resources and economic instability. An important responsibility of the state was thus, according to this perspective, active intervention in the market through income redistribution schemes, subsidies for the poor, and other, similar mechanisms to remedy this inherent problem.

While adhering to a "social approach" to the economy, the program committed itself to the eradication of poverty through interventionist state policy and subsidized pricing of basic necessities, including drugs and certain staple foodstuff. The economic revitalization program called for the protection of the poor as a "universal right," and proposed "creating a workable social security system in order to protect the low-income sections of the population. This protection, as indicated in the constitution, must be regarded a universal right . . . members of the society must know that . . . those under protection are, in fact, obtaining their right."[20]

But in addition to and in spite of the interventionist and populist tenet, the program also called for opposite policies regarding economic stability and growth. It argued for the need to eliminate state intervention in the economy, balancing the budget, deregulation, leaving price determination to the market, and a host of other policies leading to the continuation of the eight years of the SAP of the Rafsanjani administration. Thus, while on one hand the program proposed policies that led to strengthening the role of the state in the economy, it laid out the grounds to empower market forces and eliminate the state's role in the economy. And, given the underlying tension and inconsistency in the president's economic revitalization program, the overall orientation and the dominant tenet appeared to be toward the implementation of a revised and more pragmatic SAP, and gradual liberalization in key areas including the foreign exchange market, foreign investment, and others.

The policy of exchange rate liberalization continued under President Khatami, and finally, in June 1999, the exchange rate with the dollar nearly reached the feared and speculated milepost of one thousand tomans. Although the early architects of the SAP during Hashemi Rafsanjani's tenure had been forced to intervene in the market and stop the nosing down of the national currency in May 1995 when the exchange rate reached seven hundred tomans per dollar, there was no sign of such intervention in the summer of 1999. The taboos were broken. People had become accustomed to swallowing the gradual decline in the value of their money. And exchange rate liberalization, a fundamental tenet of the SAP, proceeded without an obstacle. A similar situation emerged with respect to the state's attitude toward direct foreign investment and foreign borrowing. The Islamic Republic, once a staunch opponent of foreign investment, was now eager to make its market a suitable site for profitable foreign investment.

In a public address explaining his economic revitalization program, President Khatami emphasized the need to promote investment in manufacturing, including direct foreign investment. His program proposed the "attraction of foreign capital," while "guaranteeing foreign capitals' principle and profits," and facilitating the issuing of permits for investment in Iran.[21] And to create jobs, the program proposed "using the financial resources of the private sector, foreign credit and investment, and protecting and securing investment."[22]

The economic blueprint of President Khatami repeated the old hopes to "increase the share of Iran's economy [in the world market], and elevate its position in international trade and the world economy." Trapped in the confines of a single-commodity export and envying the success of South Korea, Brazil, and others in the export market, the president's program aspired for an elevated position in the world economy. Not able to produce and supply even for the noncompetitive local market, hurt by old and expensive machinery, and facing high excess capacity due to the lack of parts and material, Iranian industry was expected to triumph in the world export market, elevating Iran's position in the world economy. "Exports of goods and services are among the priorities of the country's economic policy," declared the program with a hope to "increase nonoil exports." This was to be achieved through deregulation, market liberalization, securing the principle and profits of capital (including foreign capital), and a host of other neoliberal policies.

A year after the announcement of the economic revitalization program, the factional battle around economic policy in Mohammad Khatami's coalition was finally resolved with the victory of the promarket forces. On September 17, 1999, the president presented the Third Development Plan to the parliament. And for the first time in Iran's modern history, the government proposed a large-scale privatization of the railways, tobacco, tea and sugar, the post, and telecommunications and other services that had been provided by the public sector from their inception. Trapped in the abyss of capital and foreign exchange shortage, the plan hoped to encourage foreign investment in Iran by launching a comprehensive privatization policy and other components of the SAP.

The third plan marked a new beginning in Iran's economic history. The five-year plan presented by the government was an ambitious plan to restructure the relationship between the market and the state in Iran. It represented the most comprehensive privatization plan in the history of Iran's industrialization. It set a new precedent.

Privatization and the emphasis on deregulation, foreign investment, and increasing (non-oil) exports made the plan a classical example of an SAP in developing countries. Through the third plan, Mohammad Khatami finalized the liberalization program launched by his predecessor, Hashemi Rafsanjani, marking a complete reversal of the original ideals and populist platform of the Islamic Republic and the policies of the traditional Left tendency. The Third Development Plan was, perhaps, a final defeat of the TLT and the victory of the Right in economic policy making. Twenty years of factional struggle between populism and a welfare state on one hand and market pragmatism on the other were brought to an end.

CHAPTER NINE

Oil, International Division of Labor, and the Structural Crisis of the Iranian Economy: A Political Economy Analysis

The economic revitalization program and the third plan cited dependence on oil exports as the main economic ailment of Iran, thereby identifying the expansion of non-oil exports as the solution to the current economic crisis. What will be the outcome of the third plan and the SAP in Iran? Will the plan resolve Iran's economic crisis and reverse the decline in the wage earners' standard of living? Will Iran succeed in securing sufficient foreign productive and loan capital to satisfy the economy's thirst for capital and cure its deepening crisis? Will it succeed in diversifying the composition of production and exports, changing the country's historic dependence on oil exports?

In what follows, I will present an assessment of the feasibility of Iran's success in the export markets and the possibility of an immediate rescue from the current crisis. I will argue that the current crisis is rooted in the coexistence of two types of international division of labor from the past: the earlier, colonial international division of labor, and that created by the experience of industrialization in the 1960s and '70s. The coexistence of these forms of international division of labor has led to structural crisis tendencies. The current economic crisis is the realization of these crisis tendencies triggered by various factors including fluctuations in the international price of oil and various social and economic policies of the Iranian state.[1]

STAGES OF THE INTERNATIONALIZATION (GLOBALIZATION) OF CAPITALIST ECONOMY, AND THE INTERNATIONAL DIVISION OF LABOR

The following section is an attempt to map the forms and stages of the spatial expansion of the capitalist relations of production and the consequent changes in the international division of labor (IDL). Following the theory of the internationalization of capital, it is argued here that the process of internationalization (globalization) has involved three general historical stages.[2] The first stage of the internationalization of capitalist relations of production was materialized in the form of the international exchange of capitalistically produced commodities (international trade). The globalization of capitalism at this stage was marked by the spatial expansion of the capitalist relations of production in precapitalist societies through the international exchange of manufactures. In this earlier stage of the internationalization process, the precapitalist countries were assigned the role of specializing in the production and export of primary goods, including minerals (oil, copper, etc.) and agricultural goods (basic foodstuffs), in return for importing industrial and manufactured goods from advanced capitalist countries. Historically, this coincided with the phase of colonialism and the colonial IDL.

The true realization of the internationalization of capitalism occurred through the spatial mobility of money and productive capital. But this further spatial mobility of other forms of capital was only achieved at a certain stage in the development of capitalism. The creation of credit money and share capital, and a consequent deepening of the centralization of capital, were the historical prerequisites for the spatial mobility of all forms of capital, leading to what is now known as "globalization"—the internationalization of production, exchange, and finance. What started with the internationalization of exchange was completed by the internationalization of production in the last decades of the twentieth century.

The internationalization of production and the integrated use of multiple sites for single production processes itself occurred in progressive phases. Early internationalization of production occurred through the spatial movement of a part of a single production process to a foreign site. This phase of international production coincided with the strategy of import-substitution industrialization (ISI). The early phase of the internationalization of production was the result of the intercourse between seemingly contradictory forces. On one hand, local (national) capitalist production and industrialization were sought by the capital recipient nation states (developing countries). The domestic production of imported manufactures was viewed by the ex-colonies as an escape from the colonial international division of labor. On the other hand, the partial dispersion of production and investment to foreign sites was a prelude to the full internationalization of production and the realization of the international character of capital.

Here, the internationalization of capitalist relations of production entered a new phase with the import of productive capital and the setting up of assembly lines in developing countries. A new IDL emerged, substituting for the earlier, colonial version in many developing countries.[3] The structure of production in developing (industrializing) countries changed. A new regime of accumulation emerged, one in which, for the most part, capital accumulation was not possible without the import of productive capital, machines, and semi-finished goods.

The need to generate adequate hard currency to finance the import of intermediate and capital goods developed into one of the most endemic problems of the IDL associated with this stage of internationalization. In most cases, balance of payments deficits escalated, reaching incurable levels. But, contrary to the period of the importation of the means of consumption (the colonial IDL), import controls could not be used as a solution to the payments deficit. A reduction in imports of intermediate and capital goods (through any means) in this case was a prelude to a drastic decline in industrial output and economic activities in general, giving rise to a crisis of accumulation.

Unable to cut or reduce this wave of new imports, most ISI economies had no choice but to borrow money capital from the surplus capitalist economies.[4] Such an outcome was (partially) avoided when the developing country could generate sufficient foreign currency through exporting other commodities. For most developing nations, given their entrapment in the colonial IDL, raw materials and foodstuffs were the only exportable commodities and the only sources of foreign exchange. But, due to the instability of the markets for raw materials and their low income and price elasticity, reliance on this source of foreign exchange further intensified the vulnerability of the economy and its crisis tendencies. As a result, borrowing in international money markets often became the only practical solution to this growing contradiction, leading to the accumulation of foreign debt as the characteristic feature of ISI economies. Debt crisis became an imminent tendency and the specific form of the realization of the crisis tendencies of developing nations.

The phase of import-substitution industrialization was the early stage in the process of the internationalization of production. Some developing countries, having started their industrialization through ISI, began the deepening of this strategy after an initial stage of successful domestic production of imported light consumer goods. Through state intervention in pricing and allocation of resources, countries such as South Korea, Brazil, Mexico, and others went beyond the earlier stage of ISI and initiated the domestic production of heavy industry, including shipbuilding, machine building, and others. Following this state-guided strategy, they weakened the reliance of industrial production on the imports of productive capital and entered a new stage in their industrialization.

At the same time, the internationalization of capital accelerated in the 1970s and the 1980s and assumed qualitatively new dimensions. The computer revolution and advancements in the communications and telecommunications technologies, and reduction in transportation costs led to an increasing internationalization of production and finance and a move toward the more complete integration of the world market through an unprecedented spatial mobility of capital and resources. The internationalization of production was carried out through direct investment, outsourcing and subcontracting, joint ventures, strategic alliances, etc.

With these developments, a transformation also occurred in the international organization of production. As opposed to ISI, the new spatial expansion of capital did not require production for the local market of the capital-importing nation. Capital-importing countries were now production sites used as platforms for exports to other markets in the world. Space ceased to be a constraint to international accumulation. A technological and material condition suitable for a new international division of labor was in the making.

South Korea and a small number of other "newly industrializing countries" succeeded in entering this new IDL and benefiting from the new geography of production. Using the influx of transnational capital, they acquired a higher degree of industrialization and an increasing share of the world exports market. But, while the newly industrializing countries benefited from this new arrangement, a large number of developing countries remained deprived of capital and technology and in search of success in the world export market. A deadly competition emerged for a secure position in the new international division of labor. Export-led growth became the new religion of economic policy making for the developing countries wishing to gain a new position in the changing international division of labor.

Iran's third plan and the economic program of President Khatami are the reflections of this aspiration.

IRAN, INTERNATIONAL DIVISION OF LABOR, AND STRUCTURAL CRISIS

In 1979, along with the victory of the Islamic Republic, Iran inherited a structure of industrial production that was the product of the coexistence of two international division of labors from two earlier stages of the internationalization of capitalism. On one hand, reliance on oil production and exports was a heritage of the early stage of the internationalization of capital and the IDL corresponding to that stage. On the other hand, the existence of a variety of automobile, electronics, and other assembly-line industries reflected Iran's entry into a new stage and the creation of a new economic structure. Iran's general entry to this stage in its historical development began with the Shah's White Revolution in 1962.

Reliance on oil was not a new phenomenon. But industry and its structure of production were indeed a new development for Iran. The economy had moved out of its traditional mode, gaining a semi-industrial and semi-modern structure. What had occurred was the establishment of new factories, the increasing share of industrial production in total output, and other signs of economic modernization (not modernism). But because the structure of industry was dependent on imports of machinery and other capital goods, industrial production and accumulation was not possible without an uninterrupted importation of these commodities.

As in many similar cases, the promotion of import substitution in Iran during the 1960s and '70s produced contradictory outcomes. On one hand, the process of industrialization accelerated and Iran entered the ranks of developing capitalist economies. Many new industries were established and a host of previously imported consumer goods were manufactured (assembled) domestically. On the other hand, along with Iran's industrialization (capitalist development), its position in the IDL was also changed to one of supplying oil in return for an increasing amount of productive capital. The composition of imports changed, and Iran's demand for capital and intermediate goods accelerated in the 1960s and '70s. The relative share of consumer goods declined steadily throughout the years after the launching of the ISI program, while the share of intermediate and capital goods rose (Table 9.1). The absolute growth of intermediate and capital goods imports reached their peak in 1974 due to a rapid rise in oil prices (Table 9.2). The same pattern was observed in the relative growth of capital and intermediate goods prior to 1978 (the year of the outbreak of the anti-Shah movement).[5]

Oil exports continued to be the largest contributor and the main source of financing for Iran's imports.[6] Thanks to the remarkable success of OPEC and the sharp rise in the price of oil, Iran was able to avert the crisis of IDL and continue financing its ISI program. However, the situation drastically changed with the outbreak of the anti-Shah movement in 1978 and the seizure of power by the Islamic Republic in February 1979. The spread of nationwide strikes in the oil sector and other industries resulted in a sharp decline in production in both oil and other industries in 1978. Total imports were reduced by 34 percent while imports of intermediate and capital goods declined by 54 percent together.

The year 1978 was the beginning of the realization of the crisis tendencies of the Iranian economy. The political shock in 1978–1979 and the war with Iraq in 1980 led to a dramatic decline in both the import of capital goods and domestic output. For most of the 1980s, capital goods imports remained well below their peak in 1977 (Table 9.1). The positive growth rates of capital and intermediate goods imports in the 1970s were turned into negative growth for most of the 1980s.

With the 1979 revolution and the political and social developments in the country, Iran entered a new phase in its economic development. The revolution and the eight-year war with Iraq resulted in a freezing of the process of industrialization. The process that had been fueled with high oil prices and the import of productive capital was halted. For a ten-year period (and to a lesser extent in later years) Iran's industry remained outside of the world's technological progress and capital fusion. Capital flight in the early years of the revolution, the lack of inflow of foreign productive capital, war and its absorption of scarce resources (including foreign exchange), and other social and political developments resulted in a halt in the processes of modernization and industrialization, as well as development.

The eight-year war with Iraq and the state of emergency in the country masked the underlying crisis tendencies of the economy. The termination of the war in 1989 removed the mask. Iran had inherited an outmoded, dysfunctional, noncompetitive, and bankrupt industry. The war was ended and reconstruction began. But there was no longer an unlimited oil revenue available to the state. Nor was there any noticeable import of productive capital and technology (foreign direct investment). There were idle and old industries, old technology, and an industrial structure starved for new capital.

The reconstruction of Iran's industries required a long period of conscious and rational state guidance and planning and a large expenditure of resources—resources that could only be obtained from oil exports, inflow of productive capital (direct foreign investment), or foreign borrowing. None actually occurred. The period of historic decline in oil prices had already begun.[7] For Iran alone, it was not possible to affect international oil prices and bring about sufficient increases in oil prices to raise the foreign exchange revenue needed for industrial reconstruction. The old international division of labor that was once a source of industrial vitality had now become an obstacle to economic survival and modernization. Iran was now clearly a hostage to its position in the international division of labor.

On the other hand, despite the state's change of policy toward direct foreign investment and borrowing in international markets, Iran was unable to gain access to international sources of productive or loan capital in the postwar years. From the point of view of transnational corporations and owners of productive capital, Iran no longer appeared to be a suitable site for investment. Political risk, a hostile state, internal social and political instability, and many other noneconomic issues have been impeding the influx of FDI to Iran.

The Islamic Republic, once a staunch opponent of foreign investment, became eager to make all possible compromises to make its market a suitable site for profitable foreign investment. Ten years after the war, Iran passed unusually friendly laws regarding FDI. In 1998, the Ministry of Foreign Affairs drafted a bill for the attraction of foreign investment to Iran. According to the bill foreign investors that form joint ventures in Iran are tax exempt for a period of between six and twelve years. The joint venture is also exempt from the payment of all duties and direct charges during the same period.

In addition, foreign investors are exempt from commercial duties (tariffs) upon entering Iran.[8] And, in a public address explaining his economic revitalization plan, President Khatami emphasized promoting investment in manufacturing, including direct foreign investment. His plan proposed the "attraction of foreign capital," while "guaranteeing foreign capitals' principle and profits," and facilitating the issuing of permits for FDI in Iran.[9]

But FDI has remained negligible. Iran continues to suffer from a lack of capital and technology. In competition with other developing nations who follow internationally accepted political and social norms and practices, Iran's possibility of success on the road to absorbing foreign productive capital seems unlikely. The political battle between the factions of the Islamic Republic and Iran's archaic political structure, and the potential social instability resulting from that conflict, seem to be stronger than the state's friendly new pronouncements. Capital seems to be continuing to shy away from Iran. Many other nations have now emerged with economic and political conditions superior to those of Iran; they are more suitable potential recipients of transnational capital seeking to maximize its global profit. What made Iran attractive to foreign capital in the 1960s and '70s has ceased to be, removed by the very existence of the Islamic Republic.

Iran's attempt to gain access to international money markets has not been successful. Here too, political factors have played important role. Blocked by the United States in its influential role in the World Bank, IMF, and other international financial institutions, Iran has not been successful in opening its frontiers to international loan capital and financing from these agencies. Despite entirely retreating from its earlier opposition to foreign borrowing, Iran's thirst for foreign loan capital remains unsatisfied. The hostility between the Islamic Republic and the United States serves as an obstacle impeding the influx of loan capital to Iran.

The implementation of a structural adjustment policy in 1989, deregulation, privatization, and other related policies were guided by the need for economic reconstruction and the state's new understanding of its relations with the world economy, as the prerequisites for acceptability in soliciting and receiving foreign capital. In some way, implementing the SAP was a (policy) prerequisite for entering a new international division of labor—one based in "openness," "outward orientation," and export-led growth. It was expected, at least theoretically, that deregulation and the implementation of other policy components of the SAP (recommended by the team of World Bank economists for Iran) would prepare the ground for Iran's exit from the confines of the old IDL-single commodity export, and import-substitution industrialization.

Nearly a decade later, the economic blueprint of the new president repeated the same hopes to "increase the share of Iran's economy [in the world market], and elevating its position in international trade and the world economy." Success in resolving the current crisis rests on a set of diverse and interrelated factors that seem beyond the control of the current administration in Iran. Fundamentally, the resolution of the crisis depends on the ability of the Islamic Republic to change Iran's economic structure and alter its position in the international division of labor, thus removing the current structural crisis tendencies. This, among other things, requires the universal revamping of the machinery and capital goods found in most ISI industries established some three decades earlier, and the creation of new industries with an influx of new and internationally competitive technology, as embodied in new capital goods.

The role played by the oil industry in the 1970s is a part of Iran's past. Even with occasional increases in the international price of oil, oil-generated hard currency will not suffice to meet the expanding needs of economic restructuring. The influx of money and productive capital will depend, to a large extent, on Iran's future political and social stability, its international image, and its economic competitiveness.

Despite the victory of the Right in economic policy determination, the factional struggle for hegemony and the control of the state remains. The Islamic Republic remains a divided state, infested with conflicts, tensions, and contradictions that are rooted in its constitution, its ideological and political heritage, and the combination of forces and social groups that have comprised the Islamic state in the past two decades. The achievement of political reform and success in changing Iran's international political image are central to the ability of the Islamic Republic to transform its economy. Thus, political reform remains an essential ingredient to Iran's success in attracting needed capital.

The resolution of the constitutional tension between the *faghih* and the republic is the precondition for the success of reform. Iran must either be a republic or a state under the unconditional rule of the *faghih*.

DATA APPENDIX

TABLE 9.1
Distribution of Imports

Year	*M*	*CM*	*IM*	*KM*	*IM/M*	*KM/M*	*CM/M*
1959	544.2	164.6	267.5	112.1	49.15	20.59	30.24
1960	688.3	196.6	324.6	167.1	47.2	24.3	28.6
1961	616.6	156.9	329.9	129.8	53.5	21.1	25.4
1962	547.6	119.5	313.2	114.9	57.2	21.0	21.8
1963	513.5	124	285.1	104.4	55.5	20.3	24.1
1964	742.3	171.9	408	162.4	55.0	21.9	23.2
1965	898.4	157.2	518.2	223	57.7	24.8	17.5
1966	963.7	144.8	558.2	260.7	57.9	27.1	15.0
1967	1190.3	150	711	329.3	59.7	27.7	12.6
1968	1389.2	156.4	856.5	376.3	61.7	27.1	11.3
1969	1542.7	168.2	987.3	387.2	64.0	25.1	10.9
1970	1676.6	217.1	1068.5	391	63.7	23.3	12.9
1971	2060.9	241.7	1336.3	482.9	64.8	23.4	11.7
1972	2570	332	1596	642	62.1	25.0	12.9
1973	3737	557	2274	906	60.9	24.2	14.9
1974	6614	1017	4266	1331	64.5	20.1	15.4
1975	11696	1995	6212	3489	53.1	29.8	17.1
1976	12766	2250	6713	3803	52.6	29.8	17.6
1977	14626	2697	7910	4019	54.1	27.5	18.4
1978	10372	2114	5350	2908	51.6	28.0	20.4
1979	9695	2559	5301	1835	54.7	18.9	26.4
1980	10844	2899	6207	1738	57.2	16.0	26.7
1981	13515	3141	8225	2149	60.9	15.9	23.2
1982	11845	2676	6861	2308	57.9	19.5	22.6
1983	18103	2911	10840	4352	59.9	24.0	16.1
1984	14494	2317	8310	3867	57.3	26.7	16.0
1985	11408	1576	7411	2421	65.0	21.2	13.8
1986	9355	1695	5461	2199	58.4	23.5	18.1
1987	9369	1662	5498	2209	58.7	23.6	17.7
1988	8177	1479	4829	1869	59.1	22.9	18.1
1989	12807	2344	7548	2915	58.9	22.8	18.3
1990	18722	2505	11854	4363	63.3	23.3	13.4
1991	29677	3441	16325	9911	55.0	33.4	11.6
1992	29870	3141	18195	8212	60.9	27.5	10.5
1993	20037	2233	12567	5085	62.7	25.4	11.1

M = Imports (million dollars)
CM = Import of Consumer Goods (million dollars)
IM = Import of Intermediate Goods (million dollars)
KM = Import of Capital Goods (million dollars)

TABLE 9.2
Growth Rates of Imports

Year	*GIM*	*5Yav*	*GKM*	*5Yav*	*GCM*	
1959						
1960	21.3		21.3		19.4	
1961	1.6	5.4	1.6	5.4	–20.2	–10.1
1962	–5.1		–5.1		–23.8	
1963	–9.0		–9.0		3.8	
1964	43.1		43.1		38.6	
1965	27.0	17.8	27.0	17.8	–8.6	4.7
1966	7.7		7.7		–7.9	
1967	27.4		27.4		3.6	
1968	20.5		20.5		4.3	
1969	15.3		15.3		7.5	
1970	8.2	17.6	8.2	17.6	29.1	17.2
1971	25.1		25.1		11.3	
1972	19.4		19.4		37.4	
1973	42.5		42.5		67.8	
1974	87.6		87.6		82.6	
1975	45.6	37.7	45.6	37.7	96.2	52.0
1976	8.1		8.1		12.8	
1977	17.8		17.8		19.9	
1978	–32.4		–32.4		–21.6	
1979	–0.9		–0.9		21.1	
1980	17.1		17.1		13.3	
1981	32.5		32.5		8.3	
1982	–16.6		–16.6		–14.8	
1983	58.0	–4.4	58.0	–4.4	8.8	–5.3
1984	–23.3		–23.3		–20.4	
1985	–10.8		–10.8		–32.0	
1986	–26.3		–26.3		7.6	
1987	0.7		0.7		–1.9	
1988	–12.2		–12.2		–11.0	
1989	56.3		56.3		58.5	
1990	57.0		57.0		6.9	
1991	37.7	21.1	37.7	21.1	37.4	8.6
1992	11.5		11.5		–8.7	
1993	–30.9		–30.9		–28.9	

GIM = yearly growth of intermediate goods imports (%)
GKM = yearly growth of capital goods imports (%)
GCM = yearly growth of consumer goods imports (%)
5Yav = five year average

CHAPTER TEN

The Great Debate: A Republic or *Velayat-e Faghih?*

The responsibility of the Assembly of Experts is to discover the *mojtahed* [expert in Islamic jurisprudence] who is chosen by the twelfth Imam. The Council does not elect the *faghih* [Leader] on behalf of the people. God appoints the Leader.

—Hojatoleslam Ferdosi Fard

Following the orders of the *faghih* is mandatory. The law that is issued by the *faghih* is not his own. It is from God. We all must act according to God's law. The Imam or the great leader of the revolution approves the six members of the Guardian Council. Even if the 270 members of the Parliament pass a law, the law will be worthless if [the 6 members of the Guardian Council] reject it.

—Ayatollah Khaza'li

The devil is tempting some people to impose limits for the *faghih*. Consciously or unconsciously, these are mischievous acts that hurt Islam and attack the roots of the government. The rights of the *faghih* are the same as the rights of prophets.

—Mohammad Nategh Nouri

We cannot proceed in the New World by having two or three people making decisions for the country. "Republic"

> means the government of the people. . . . We have the *"velayat-e faghih"* mentioned in our constitution. But this does not mean the *faghih* runs everything. In that case, the "republic" will be meaningless. The authority and responsibilities of the *faghih* are specified in the constitution.
>
> —Ayatollah Montazeri

> The leader is not an institution above the law in the Islamic Republic. . . . The law has specified his authority, responsibilities, and the conditions for his removal.
>
> —Abdollah Nouri

The Islamic Republic is entrapped in an unprecedented crisis. It is divided, unable to rule as a united body—as a state. The presidential victory of Mohammad Khatami in 1997 and the emergence of a movement for reform from within the state brought to the open the Islamic Republic's political and ideological divide. A seemingly united state was splintered into fighting factions, each accusing the others of "betraying Islam," and "weakening the revolution." Established practices and policies were questioned. Haunted by the battle between the proponents and opponents of civil society, and the debate around the role and authority of *velayat-e faghih*, the Islamic Republic has lost its moral authority and the grounds on which it ruled for twenty years. Two decades after its inception, the Islamic Republic is shaken by a battle about the role of religion in organizing a modern society, and the relationship between Islam and the concepts of republic and democracy. Tensions have surfaced, conflicts deepened, and the mask of unity has been removed. The *faghih* is questioned. The Islamic state entered an internal war, and became divided over the role of Islam in organizing the state! It lost its ideological authority. Challenged on the streets by youths and ordinary people, the Islamic state entered the new millennium faced with a profound crisis from within—an identity crisis. It is being asked to abandon the absolute authority of Islam in organizing the cultural and social/political structure of the state—become an Islamic state without Islam as its ideology!

The following is the pathology of a crisis in the making. It is a study of the battle between the republic and the *faghih* within the state, and the future of the Islamic Republic as an Islamic state.

THE FIRST BATTLE: FROM THE DRAFT OF THE CONSTITUTION TO THE CONSTITUTION OF THE ISLAMIC REPUBLIC OF IRAN

The state's political divide and the debate on the relationship between the *faghih* and the republic, and the role of religion in organizing the state, emerged as early as the inception of the new state. The Islamic Republic came to power with the final downfall of the Shah on February 11, 1979. From its inception, the state was divided into multiple and parallel centers of power, conflicting ideologies and platforms, and internal conflicts. It represented diverse social and class interests, modern and premodern, pro-West and anti-West, pro-republic and antirepublic. It included representatives of the traditional merchant class of the bazaar in the clergy, those believing in vague notions of "Islamic justice" through the state's regulation of the (modern) economy, and more modern and pro-West individuals with Islamic-nationalist ideas.[1] It was a divided state—a dual state. Embattled from within, it was embroiled in the competition for hegemony between the *Dolat-e Movaghat* (provisional government), composed of leading non-clergy Islamic-nationalist figures and headed by a known reformer, Mehdi Bazargan, and *Shora-ye Enghelab* (Council of Revolution), which was more directly influenced by Iran's leading clergy. It was this division that led to the first constitutional battle between the supporters of the "republic" and proponents of *velayat-e faghih*.

In commissioning the provisional government of Prime Minister Mehdi Bazargan to draft the Constitution of the Islamic Republic of Iran, Ayatollah Khomeini laid the groundwork for structuring the future of Iran by a committee of prominent non-clergy religious-nationalist figures.[2] A draft of the constitution, modeled after the constitutions of the European democracies, institutionalizing a primarily secular state with minimal influence from Islam, was prepared and delivered for review to Ayatollah Khomeini and the council of revolution.[3] With some revisions in articles about economics, the Council of Revolution approved the draft of the constitution. The phrase "according to Islamic principles" was added to many of its articles.[4] Reviewed by Ayatollah Khomeini, with suggestions for minor changes—none related to the structure of the state—the draft of the Constitution of the Islamic Republic of Iran was approved by the leader of the Islamic Republic in early 1979.

The approved draft proposed a state that primarily followed the structure of Western democracies, with no reference to the controversial principle of the *velayat-e faghih* and the rule of the clergy. It institutionalized the structure of the state, and the relations between the state and its citizens, with no special role assigned to the clergy. The separation of the church (religion) from the state was maintained. The draft proposed a republic (an Islamic republic) with the highest authority granted to the president elected by popular vote. No individual or group was granted a position of privilege or a special status; the state was structured around commonly accepted democratic principles. Islamic principles and values played only a marginal role in the constitution.[5] Even the parliament was called *Majlis-e Shora-ye Melli* (the National Assembly), later changed to *Majlis-e Shora-ye Eslami* (the Islamic Assembly) by the Assembly for the Final Preparation of the Constitution of the Islamic Republic of Iran. The draft of the constitution proposed:

> Article 15—The right to govern belongs to all citizens and must be used in the benefit of all. No person or group of people can monopolize this God given right, or use it in their own personal or group interest.
>
> Article 16—The branches of the state that stem from this right to national sovereignty include the Executive Branch, the Judiciary, and the Legislative Branch. These branches must always remain independent of one another, their relations established by the President according to the law.
>
> Article 75—The President is the highest authority of the nation with regards to domestic and international affairs, and the execution of the constitution. The President is responsible for the coordination of the relations between the branches of the state and heading the Executive Branch.
>
> Article 93—The President is the Commander-in-Chief of the Staff.[6]

The most direct reference to Islam and its role in the state was made in articles 142 and 146 through the provision regarding the Guardian Council. Even there, the composition of the council guaranteed the dominance of the non-clergy members, facilitating decision making without the control of the clergy. Of its eleven members, only five were to be from the clergy. The decisions of the council required approval by two-thirds of its members.[7]

The draft of the constitution was presented for review and approval to the Assembly for the Final Preparation of the Constitution of the Islamic Republic of Iran (a substitute for the Constituent Assembly).[8] The assembly included seventy-three members elected by the public on July 20, 1979. Of the seventy-three members, forty-eight were from the clergy. It was presided over by Ayatollah Montazeri, its sessions run and led by Ayatollah Beheshti, the deputy president of the assembly.

The assembly proceeded with drafting, discussing, and approving an entirely new constitution, putting aside the draft of the Constitution of the Islamic Republic already approved by the Council of Revolution and Ayatollah Khomeini himself. It transformed the authority of the elected president and instilled *velayat-e faghih* as the highest authority of the state. It ended the separation of church from state and created a tenuous state structure embodying the concept of the "republic" while granting an unchallenged power and authority to the supreme leader, a clergyman not elected by the citizens.[9] The *faghih* was given a power over and above that of the president and all other elected officials. The Islamic Republic became a true theocratic state, to be governed by Islamic jurisprudence.

A coup d' êtat was accomplished by the clergy in the assembly. The advocates of the republic were marginalized. The project for a modern state and a republic was defeated from its inception.

The assembly constrained and severely weakened the democratic tenets of the state structure in the draft of the constitution, but nevertheless, it retained within the constitution the concept of the republic, and parliamentary democracy. The coexistence of the republic and the *faghih* in the constitution manifested, on one hand, the fundamental tension between the advocates of modern ideas of the state and those whose ideas were based on Islamic jurisprudence within the Islamic Republic. On the other hand, it reflected the tensions of a traditional society on the verge of modernization (and perhaps the path to modernity). The 1979 constitution reflected the complexity of the social forces sharing the state and the unwillingness of the citizens to abandon the political project of building a republic. After all, the 1979 revolution was a revolt against the Shah's dictatorship, a monumental collective action for democracy. Thus, the coup against the republic in the assembly had to preserve, at least partially, what it had set out to destroy. The republic remained. But it was overridden by the *faghih*.

Although Ayatollah Khomeini himself had theorized the government of the *faghih* in his *Hokoomat-e Eslami* (Islamic government) in 1970, he declined to enforce the concept of *velayat-e faghih* before the inauguration of the assembly.[10] Indeed, Ayatollah Khomeini insisted in the use of the term *republic,* proposing an "Islamic

Republic" against the wishes of those wanting to create an "Islamic government." Given the relative significance of influential non-clergy nationalist-religious figures among his early associates and supporters, putting forth his own model of the state was not seen to be advisable by the leader of the Islamic Republic during and immediately after the revolution.[11] The provisional government of Prime Minister Mehdi Bazargan was dominated by the republican tendency.[12] Ayatollah Khomeini's silence was a strategic move to fend off Bazargan and the advocates of a "democratic republic" in his camp.[13] But this compromise position was changed when the assembly was inaugurated on August 19, 1979. In a special message to the assembly, the leader said the following about the constitution and its mission:

> [T]he constitution and other laws in this republic must be one hundred percent based on Islam. It will be a violation of the republic and people's vote, if even one article conflicts with Islamic decrees. Thus, any suggestion by an MP [member of the parliament, or the *Majlis*] or a group of MPs that deviates from Islam will be rejected. . . .
>
> Determining whether or not [a suggestion] conflicts with Islam is solely the province of *foghaha-e ozma* (grand Jurisconsult, the clergy members of the assembly). Thanks to God there is a group of them in this assembly. Thus, since this is a matter for experts, the intervention of other respected MPs in this *ejtehad* (exegesis of divine law) . . . is an intervention in other people's expertise without having the necessary qualifications. . . .
>
> I recommend with much emphasis, that if some MPs lean toward Western or Eastern schools of thoughts, or are influenced by devious thought, they should not include their tendencies in the constitution and separate their devious path from that of this law. . . .
>
> Islamic theologians present in this assembly must clearly express their view if they see an article in the draft of the constitution or a suggestion that deviates from Islam. They must not be afraid of the brawl by *gharbzadeh-ha* (those under influence of Western culture) writers and journalists.[14]

The message by Ayatollah Khomeini was a call for departure from the basic tenets of the draft of the constitution. The Ayatollah was openly calling for the dominance of the clergy in determining the future of the nation. Lines of demarcation were drawn. The critics of the clergy were refuted as *gharbzadeh,* under the influence of Western culture. They were later to be called the agents of "cultural invasion" and "enemies of the state." The non-clergy representatives of the people, those elected by popular vote, were asked to "separate their devious path" from the constitution. The stage was set for a showdown in the assembly.

A fierce battle was waged. The proponents of the republic were defeated.[15] The draft of the constitution was substantially transformed. The republic was separated from its democratic tenets. An autocratic state was institutionalized, one modeled after Ayatollah Khomeini's *Hokoomat-e Eslami*.[16] Thus, Article 5 of the constitution (a new article not included in the draft) declared:[17]

> The authority to command and lead the people shall be a just, virtuous, abreast of the times, brave, organizer, and judicious *faghih* accepted by the majority of people as their leader during the absence of *Hazrat Vali-Yi-Asr* (the absent Imam), may the Almighty lead his advent come to pass soon . . .

The three branches of the state were no longer to be coordinated by the elected president of the nation. Instead, they were to "operate under the supervision of *velayat-e amr va emamat-e ommat* (the leadership of the *faghih*) . . . and their relationship established by the president."[18] The president was made "next in rank to the leader," stripped of all the power granted to him/her by the draft of the constitution.[19] The *Majlis* no longer chose the members of the Guardian Council. The *faghih* was given the sole power to appoint the "theologians and canonists, members of the Guardian Council." He was to "appoint the highest ranking official of the judicial branch," thus enjoying a controlling power over the judiciary. The eligibility of candidates for the presidency was to be first confirmed by the Guardian Council (now handpicked by the leader) prior to the elections and endorsed by the leader for the first term of the presidency. The leader was given powers above all the democratic institutions envisioned in the draft of the constitution.[20] The constitutional thrust toward a republic received its first major setback.

THE SECOND BATTLE: THE 1989 AMENDMENTS AND THE ASSAULT ON THE REPUBLIC

Ayatollah Khomeini passed away on June 3, 1999. Prior to the leader's death, on April 27, 1989, a committee to amend the Constitution of the Islamic Republic of Iran began deliberations. On the day after the Ayatollah's death, an announcement by the Assembly of Experts made Hojatoleslam Said Ali Khamenei the next supreme leader of the Islamic Republic. A lower-ranking clergyman, now called Ayatollah Khamenei, became the grand *faghih*. Meanwhile, significant changes to the constitution were being made. Steps were being taken toward the further weakening of the republic and the total empowerment of the supreme leader. The 1989 amendments further eroded the remaining democratic tenets of the constitution, fortifying the social and political power of the clergy, and creating a political structure based on the absolute and unchallenged authority of an individual *faghih*.

The change of focus from the 1979 draft of the constitution to the 1989 amendments mirrors the battle over the de-secularization of the Iranian revolution and the power struggle that led to the absolute hegemony of the antirepublican forces and the empowerment of the architects of the state based on Islamic decrees. The original draft of the constitution was solely based on the concept of the republic and people's vote without any trace of *velayat-e faghih* (the rule of the Islamic Jurisconsult). The 1979 constitution incorporated *velayat-e faghih*, and the amendments replaced it with *velayat-e motlaghe faghih*. Article 57 of the 1979 constitution was amended. The president's authority to establish the relationship between the branches of the state was eliminated. The branches were to solely "operate under the supervision of *velayat-e motlagheh amr va emamat-e ommat* [absolute and unconditional rule of the *faghih*] and according to the future articles of this law."[21] All shadows of doubt about the unquestionable rule of the *faghih* were removed. Article 110 gave the supreme leader the authority to "determine overall policies of the Islamic Republic of Iran after consultation with the Expediency Council of the Islamic Republic" and to "regulate the relationship between the three branches of the government." It left in the hands of the leader the Islamic Republic National Broadcasting Agency, the only radio and television service in the nation.[22] The supreme leader was given the power of an unquestionable dictator.

Ten years after introducing the concept of the *faghih* and undermining the republican basis of the constitution in a coup d' état–like maneuver, a new meeting by the influential clergy debated the power of the supreme leader. This did not come about without a battle. By 1989, new tendencies and lines of demarcation had developed within the ranks of the clergy. The early republicans of the Freedom Movement and those associated with Mehdi Bazargan and the provisional government were isolated and scorned. New divisions were in the making within the state, this time in the ranks of the clergy. The debates in the Committee to Amend the Constitution of the Islamic Republic of Iran were in some sense the anticipation of the political divide that would develop in the late 1990s. This was a dress rehearsal for more open conflicts, which would surface after the presidential victory of Mohammad Khatami in May 1997.

The inauguration of the Committee to Amend the Constitution of the Islamic Republic of Iran in 1989, nearly a month before Ayatollah Khomeini's death, was not accidental. On March 29, 1989, Ayatollah Montazeri, the handpicked heir of Ayatollah Khomeini, resigned as the heir-designate. The resignation of Montazeri was preceded by a series of conflicts and tensions between the two Grand Ayatollahs and their followers. The climax of the rising divide between the two leaders occurred after the mass execution of political prisoners that followed the signing of UN Resolution 598 by the Islamic Republic on July 18, 1998.[23]

The war with Iraq had ended. A period of rising domestic tension was anticipated. The opposition had to be annihilated. Even those in the prisons of the Islamic Republic were considered a potential threat. They had to be silenced. Thus, on July 19, 1988, the day after signing the peace accord with Iraq, a massacre began in Iran's main prisons. Between 5,000 and 12,000 inmates were executed.[24] On August 31, 1988, in a letter to Ayatollah Khomeini, Montazeri condemned the mass executions, calling them a "violation of fundamental principles of Islam." The tension escalated. The differences between Montazeri and Ayatollah Khomeini became public. Ayatollah Montazeri resigned, his resignation accepted by Ayatollah Khomeini. The leader of the revolution was left without an heir.

The tension between the two Ayatollahs, and the scorning of Ayatollah Montazeri, also led to other divisions among the clergy and their supporters. In addition, the termination of the war with Iraq and the "national unity" to fight against foreign aggression, led to the gradual surfacing of new factional divides within the state, divisions that had been quietly developing in the first decade of the revolution. Political factions defined on the basis of economic, political, and cultural perspectives were being formed.

Earlier in 1988 the leftist elements within *Jame'eh-e Rouhaniat Mobarez* (JRM or the Militant Clergy Association) of Tehran, having obtained the permission of the revolution's leader, separated from that organization and formed an independent Islamic-Left grouping under the title of *Majma'-e Rohanioun-e Mobarez* (MRM or the Militant Clerics League). The two groups would later become the cornerstones of the traditional Right tendency and the traditional Left tendency, leading to fierce struggles in the aftermath of Mohammad Khatami's presidential victory. The old allies became adversaries. The clergy became divided.

Though it had not been formed as a political tendency yet, Hashemi Rafsanjani was to become the central figure of the emerging modern Right tendency, based on the neoliberal policies that would soon dismantle the Left-populist policies of the first ten years of the Islamic Republic. The unity that had helped the Islamic Republic to fight the war was rapidly eroding. Ayatollah Khomeini and other powerful figures of the state were aware of the emerging predicament. The Ayatollah's health had also been deteriorating for months. His death was near. A replacement for the Ayatollah had to be found to avoid a leadership vacuum amidst the rising political divide within the clergy. Open crisis was to be avoided. It was in this environment that the Committee to Amend the Constitution of the Islamic Republic began its work on April 27, 1989.

The committee had twenty-five members, twenty handpicked by Ayatollah Khomeini, the other five chosen by Parliament. More than fifteen of the twenty members appointed by Ayatollah Khomeini were from the known and influential clergy. Fourteen were appointed from the membership of the powerful Assembly of Experts. The clergy included powerful figures from all emerging tendencies within the state. The committee ended its work on July 11, 1989, nearly a month after the death of Ayatollah Khomeini.

To a large extent, the debate within the committee was a prelude to the open conflicts that surfaced later in the 1990s. Indeed, the positions adopted by various clergy in the debate anticipated their stands on the questions of civil society and *velayat-e faghih* in later years. Powerful members of the traditional Right tendency, including Ayatollahs Akbar Ali Akbar Meshkini, Mohammad Yazdi, and Azure Ghomi, defended the constitutional changes, while Moosavi Khoiniha and Abdollah Nouri criticized and questioned the amendments. Akbar Hashemi Rafsanjani and Ali Khamenei (the supreme leader) were also among the supporters of the constitutional amendments.[25]

The Committee to Amend the Constitution of the Islamic Republic of Iran succeeded in making the necessary changes and creating a compromise between the divided factions of the state. Finding the heir to Ayatollah Khomeini was a fundamental challenge for the system. Ayatollah Khomeini was a charismatic figure, accepted by all factions as their leader, followed and loved by many citizens. Feared, respected, and worshiped, Ayatollah Khomeini was able to ride above all factional divisions, resolve disputes, and make even the most powerful clergy follow his decrees. No other high-ranking clergyman had the prestige and charisma to fill the void after Ayatollah Khomeini's death. The Islamic Republic was to face a crisis of leadership.

A solution was found to the imminent crisis. Ayatollah Khomeini's heir would not be a high-ranking Ayatollah. Instead, a nonthreatening, well-liked, lower-rank cleric, Hojatoleslam Ali Khamenei, was chosen as the compromise candidate of all factions. The position of the *faghih* was strengthened in the constitution, the role of the clergy fortified, and a low-rank clergyman instilled as the leader. He was to command the respect and admiration enjoyed by Ayatollah Khomeini from the citizens. Not an ideologue or a powerful cleric, he would leave essential matters in the hands of the powerful mullahs in charge of the Islamic Republic. A figurehead had been appointed. The immediate crisis was resolved!

But the choice of a low-rank clergyman, a clergyman who was not *Marja'i Taghlid* (an authority on Islamic theological and canon law) was the end of *velayat-e faghih* as an institution genuinely respected and followed by all mullahs, a substitute of the absent Imam, and a leader of all Moslems. The institution of *velayat-e faghih* indeed died with the death of Ayatollah Khomeini. No one could replace him. The changes in the constitution in 1989 and the increased constitutional power of the *faghih* were legal actions to increase the political legitimacy of Khomeini's heir. They were clear signs of a crumbling institution in dire need of legitimacy and support. The legitimacy was to be created not by respect, but by fear, by the institutionalization of a figure above the law, one that should not be questioned. Despite the euphoria and victorious statements, the 1989 amendments were signs of the weaknesses of the Islamic Republic. The final constitutional assault on the republic reflected the weakness of a system unable to reproduce its legitimacy without force.

To pave the way for the appointment of Ali Khamenei to be the heir of Ayatollah Khomeini, another change in the constitution was required. The supreme leader had to be *Marja'i Taghlid* according to Article 109 of the 1979 constitution. Ali Khamenei was not even an Ayatollah when appointed supreme leader. He was, indeed, not a *Marja'i Taghlid*. Thus, the Committee to Amend the Constitution of the Islamic republic of Iran changed Article 109 and excluded the requirement of *Marja'i Taghlid* as one of the qualifications to be the supreme leader.[26]

Nearly a decade later, the compromise was openly broken. Ayatollah Montazeri, an architect of *velayat-e faghih* in the 1979 constitution spoke out against the supreme leader:

> We cannot proceed in the New World by having two or three people making decisions for the country. "Republic" means the government of the people. . . . We have the *"velayat-e faghih"* mentioned in our constitution. But this does not mean the *vali-e faghih* runs everything. In that case, the "republic" will be meaningless. *vali-e faghih*'s authority and responsibilities are specified in the constitution. [His] most important and main responsibility is to supervise society's affairs to make sure it does not deviate from the principles of Islam. . . . To have a monarchy-like court and luxurious billion-dollar trips do not suit *velayat-e faghih*. . . . [The *faghih*] cannot interfere in everything. The government must be independent [of the *faghih*] in the Islamic Republic. . . . We cannot run a country with multiple centers of power.

And openly challenging the leader, in his historic self-defense against charges of weakening the Islamic Republic, Abdollah Nouri said, "The leader is not an institution above the law in the Islamic Republic. . . . The law has specified his authority, responsibilities, and the conditions for his removal."[27] Distinguishing between the authority of Ayatollah Khomeini and his heir, Ayatollah Ali Khameniei, Nouri stated:

> The leader of the revolution is the person the revolution is identified with. Basically, the revolutionary movement and its victory are not possible without him. . . . But those assuming leadership after him are the managers of the revolution. The revolutionary movement and its victory are possible without him. . . . The leader of the revolution gets his legitimacy from the revolution itself and not from the political system. . . . The extra-law authority and rights of the leader are justifiable and stem from the nature of the revolutionary current. . . . Although *velayat-e faghih* is mentioned in religious texts, the political/state concept of *velayat-e faghih* in the form mentioned in the constitution is from the Imam [Ayatollah Khomeini]. Imam's leadership in the society did not stem from *velayat-e faghih*. That is, the society reached *velayat-e faghih* through the Imam and not the opposite. . . . In

> these conditions it is possible to assume special rights for the leader and the founder of the revolution under emergency circumstances and during the revolution.[28]

Nouri's defense and his statements about *velayat-e faghih* were a clear indication of the death of *velayat-e faghih* as such in the minds of many veterans of the revolution and devotees of the Islamic Republic after the loss of Ayatollah Khomeini. All those replacing the Imam were the managers of the society and must function according to the law, Nouri declared. Nouri's declaration was the rejection of the claims of other influential clergy who earlier had said:

> *Motlagheh* [the new adjective added to the *velayat-e faghih* in the 1988 constitutional amendments] means that . . . the leader shall be allowed to intervene directly if he decides to do so in the future just as Imam used to do. Imam [Khomeini] would tell us abruptly to appoint a minister, or allow a minister to do something without the consent of the parliament, or take money from somewhere and put it elsewhere. All these decisions will find a basis in the Constitution by interjecting the word *motlagheh*.[29]

This was proclaimed by Akbar Hashemi Rafsanjani during the amendment of the constitution in 1989. The developments after the death of Ayatollah Khomeini proved the indefensibility of this claim. Nouri's defense was its direct refutation. It was the sign of the growing crisis of *velayat-e faghih*.

THE NEW BATTLE: THE RISE OF "RELIGIOUS INTELLIGENTSIA" AND A NEW CHALLENGE TO THE ISLAMIC STATE

A new specter has been haunting the Islamic Republic. Organized around the movement of "religious intelligentsia," an increasing number of thinkers and activists among both the clergy and the non-clergy Moslems have opened a formidable front, fighting to reform the Islamic Republic through a discourse around "religious pluralism," "diversity," "nonsectarianism," and "the democratic religious state." A battle between the republic and *velayat-e faghih* has reemerged, fueling the confrontations between *bonyad garayan-e mazhabi* (religious fundamentalists) and *degar andishan-e mazhabi* (religious intelligentsia).

Central to this movement were the writings and teachings of Abdolkarim Soroush. An architect of the Islamicization of universities and the annihilation of the independent student movement in the 1980s, Abdolkarim Soroush was an important and influential ideologue of the Islamic Republic in its formative years. A staunch anti-Marxist, he shaped the new state's ideological battle against its secular Left and Marxist opposition. A member of *Setad-e Enghelab-e Farhangi* (Cultural Revolution Staff), he guided the Islamicization of the curriculum, and helped the institution of *gozinesh*—screening applicants and selecting students based on religious and political criteria—and the general transformation of universities into monolithic centers for ideological training of students. During the first decade of the Islamic Republic, Abdolkarim Soroush was an instrumental figure in combating pluralism, diversity, and independent thinking.

Now, two decades after the revolution, Soroush has become an ideological magnet of the "Islamic intelligentsia" movement, a guru to many young Moslems disillusioned by the old practices of the Islamic state, and an "enemy of the state." Physically attacked by *Ansar-e Hezbollah,* barred from lecturing and holding classes at Tehran University, harassed, and threatened with death, Soroush has become a symbol of resistance and the struggle for change to a growing number of Moslem students, activists, journalists, and writers. Once an ideological architect of Islamic violence, Soroush became an advocate of religious pluralism, rationality, and rights.

Abolkarim Soroush and his contributions were fundamentally transformed during the 1990s. Beginning in 1988 with the publication of the monthly *Kian,* Soroush and his associates launched a systemic critique of the "official reading" of Islam and religion. Soroush became an intellectual leader in challenging the philosophy of the Islamic state, its practices, and its compatibility with modernity and democracy. Through his articles in *Kian* and lectures in universities across the nation, Soroush popularized the ideas of religious pluralism, tolerance, and the benefits of modern rationality among thousands of devoted students. A new cadre of Moslem intelligentsia was trained. The popular and imprisoned journalists Akbar Ganji, Mashallah Shamsolvaezin, Hamid-Reza Jalaeipour, and many other critics of the state are among Soroush's students and followers.[30]

Through his courses in philosophy of religion, logic, and others, scores of young and zealous Moslems have become acquainted with the discourse of modernity, slowly distancing themselves from the *ghara'at-e rasmi as deen* (the official reading of religion), joining the movement for fusing religion with rationality, tradition with modernity. Relatively few in the beginning, they grew in number in the

1990s, surged after the election of Mohammad Khatami, penetrated the press, founded new magazines and newspapers, and imposed a new discourse on the Islamic state. They became a movement, a force the Islamic Republic had to reckon with.[31] They challenged the foundations of the religious state from within.[32]

In the 1990s Soroush's writings and teachings became the symbol of the struggle for democracy by the emerging Moslem intelligentsia. Articulating his idea of democracy, Abdolkarim Soroush separated democratic and nondemocratic states on the basis of "the degree to which they are based on collective rationality . . . and respect for human rights."[33] A precondition for a democratic religious state was, argued Soroush, "to make religious understanding fluid and flexible and highlight the role of 'rationality'—not individual rationality, but collective rationality that stems from everyone's participation and the application of the human experience." But such collective rationality, according to Soroush, was not possible "unless through democratic means."[34] Elsewhere Soroush distinguished between *hokoomat-e deeni* (religious state) and *hokoomat-e faghih* (religious-jurisprudence state), the former being based on people's "inner faith" and "religious experience" and not "external practice," the latter being organized by enforcing on people their "religious duties."[35] A religious state "obliges itself to create an atmosphere that defends believers' free and conscious faith and religious experience," argued Soroush.

Soroush challenged the Islamic Republic's imposition of jurisprudence decrees as a way of creating a religious society. Religious beliefs cannot be mandated, he argued. Such beliefs are private matters, stemming from the religious person's "inner soul and religious experiences." In many cases, "the external practice of the believer and nonbeliever are the same." The "[democratic] religious state (from the perspective that it is religious) is principally and foremost based on faith and religious belief, and secondarily based on the external practice of believers." The external appearance of a society, argued Soroush, " is, by no means, the reflection of its religiousness or the lack of. It is possible to create a secular or religious jurisprudence state and give society a particular appearance by legislating laws. But not a society based on faith. Because *inner faith* is the essence and what strengthens religion. State is neither responsible for nor able to create dislike about it."[36]

Soroush defined the role and responsibilities of a (democratic) religious state as fulfilling citizens' "primary needs like health, housing, food, security, and others" and "secondary needs like art, religion, and spirituality." A religious state is a government of a society of believers, argued Soroush. The state must satisfy people's primary needs, helping them attend their softer secondary needs.[37] This cannot be achieved without "a rational theory of the state."[38]

By the late 1990s the movement for religious reform had been fortified by other influential theorists, challenging the foundations of the Islamic state. Mohsen Kadivar, a clergyman, a loyal member of the Islamic Republic, jailed for expressing a view other than the "official reading," had become a new teacher and theoretical guide for reform minded Moslems. A young cleric, articulate, learned, and a researcher in the theory of the state in Shiite Islam, Kadivar became the authority for Moslems seeking the reforming of the Islamic Republic based on the teachings of Islam and Islamic theologians. Handsome, always smiling, calm, and thoughtful looking, Kadivar represented a new image of the clergy and the theologians to many young Moslems disillusioned with the Islamic Republic and its past history. He became an icon. He was thus tried, charged with insulting Islam and the Islamic state, and sentencd to two and one-half years in jail.

Mohsen Kadivar articulated nine types of states or theories of state in Shiite Islam. The nine are categorized based on the type of legitimacy they claim. The first four receive their legitimacy directly from God, while the rest gain their legitimacy from god and the people.[39] Thus, Kadivar concluded that since "there is no blueprint for the management of society in the time of the occultation [of the last Imam] . . . state must not see itself as having a special mission from God. Upon accepting the lack of a blueprint in the time of occultation, no one will have a special mission and authority to guide the society. . . . Great problems will arise if a person or a group conceive of having such a mission."[40] Kadivar arrived at the need for pluralism, term limits for rulers, and a democratic state as a response to the absence of a *ma'soom* (the infallible Imam).

Kadivar's work was originally popularized through his series on Islam and the state in the short-lived weekly *Rah-e No* (New Way). Licensed and managed by Akbar Ganji, a bold investigative journalist and a vocal critic of the antireform forces within the state, *Rah-e No* ceased publication half a year after its inception. Ganji was later charged with weakening the Islamic state and incarcerated in April 2000.

Though brief in life, *Rah-e No* made important contributions to the discourse of religion and the state. It was in *Rah-e No* that, for the first time, I became more formally acquainted with Mohammad

Mojtahed Shabestari's modernist views on Islam and the state. A middle-aged cleric, teacher of theology and philosophy at Tehran University, Mohammad Mojtahed Shabestari has challenged the Islamic Republic and its dominant political philosophy by focusing on the incapability of religion to organize a modern society. Gentle, noncontroversial, and subdued, Shabestari presents a sober and profound challenge to the foundations of the Islamic Republic. Scholar in religious enlightenment, theologian, and university lecturer, Shabestari has mounted an assault on the "religious state," rejecting it as a useful concept in a modern society.

Religion is unfit to organize a modern society, argues Shabestari. Contrary to Kadivar, Shabestari's principal opposition to the concept of religious state is independent of *ma'soom* and his absence. No distinction is made between democratic and nondemocratic religious states. The sole question is the ability of religion to provide useful guides and mechanisms for organizing a modern society. Mojtahed Shabestari's answer is negative. Speaking of the "crisis and chronic weaknesses in the official reading of religion" in Iran, Shabestari attributes the crisis to the "unfounded" and "irrational" claim that "Islam as a religion . . . possesses such political, economic, social, and legal systems based on religious jurisprudence that are suitable for all epochs." Not only has Islam failed to prove this claim, indeed "no religion can have such systems."[41]

Questioning the "traditional readings of religion," as "a collection of information and knowledge sent by God" to be used as the "foundations of social organization," Shabestari characterizes the religious society based on this reading as one "without the practical ability for creating a democratic society."[42] A state based on the traditional reading is, by nature, antidemocratic—it violates people's human rights. Based on the principles of human rights, argues Shabestari, "people are equal irrespective of their views. This is in conflict with the religious decrees. . . . The new perspective on human rights is a philosophical perspective. In this perspective the humanity of people comes before their views. How can we imply a philosophical perspective from a religious text?"[43]

Articulating the privatization of religion, Mojtahed Shabestari has assigned religion the role of guiding people's personal lives, and not the collective rationality of a modern society. Religions lack such capabilities. "We need to clearly express to people that we need science and scientific management in order to build a modern social life. There is no other way. . . . In the past, we did not clearly express to Moslem people how far we could go by suing religious teachings."[44] Religious teachings, the revelations of our prophets, and the world view they present reflect their own time. They are thus of a limited use for a modern society. "The prophet is a person chosen in a specific historical condition. . . . We have one thousand and four hundred years of distance from the time of the prophet. We are aware of this distance and cannot let go of this awareness. We must relate to the time of the prophet and his message from the very place we are today."[45]

Moslems have evolved in the past 150 years, argues Mohammad Mojtahed Shabestari. They have chosen "a new way of living which is starkly different from their past." They have chosen a way of living expressed in concepts such as "progress," and "development" and "conscious and methodic intervention in the environment and in human and social relations and realities for the all-rounded development of human life." This new way of life cannot be managed "with the old language of religious legitimacy. . . . A person seeking development can also be a believer in God, but cannot speak of religious progress and development."[46]

Velayat-e Faghih *and the Republic: A Reinterpretation by the "Religious Intelligentsia"*

Challenging the concept of the "religious state" ultimately meant a critique and rejection of both *velayat-e faghih* and the rule of the clergy. Soroush stated:

> State, is essentially, an extrareligious jurisprudence, and even an extrareligious (discourse and anthropological) concept. It must be analyzed within religious and nonreligious jurisprudence realms. The discussion of *"velayat-e faghih"* also follows this rule.[47]
>
> In these conditions Shiites, like other rational people, think of a rational way of administrating the society. Referring to people's votes is the rational theory of today. In this view, the chosen person is no longer a *ma'soom* or superior to all people. The rule about kindness and appointment by the Prophet no longer has a place. What is involved is only the interest of the society of Moslems. . . . The only way before us is accepting a rational theory about the state.[48]

Hassan Yousefi Ashkevari, a cleric and theologian, now in prison for expressing his interpretation of Islam, liberty, and the state called the creation of a state ruled by the clergy a deviation from the promises of the revolution, a deception of the people:

> The formation of the Islamic Republic with relatively monopoly rule of the clergy . . . is contrary to the original promise of the leaders of the revolution. . . . What was promised was that the clergy would be involved in their own business, and at the most, have a supervisory role. But, the administration of society, state, and political rule will be conducted according to the existing norm in the political systems (or so to say, the democratic systems) in the world. . . . A state based on Islamic jurisprudence is one in which all decisions in the judiciary, legislative, and executive branches are made within the framework of Islamic law. . . . The natural consequence [of this] . . . is the state of the clergy. . . . The state based on Islamic jurisprudence is the state of a sect. It is because the laws of the sect of Shiites must govern the state.[49]

Abdolkarim Soroush characterized the government of the clergy as a state based on "a fascist reading of religion," creating a "religious dictatorship" with "a speaker, religious jurisprudence, theoretician, philosopher, judge, press, and army."[50] Soroush, Akbar Ganji, Mohsen Kadivar, and many others called for the direct election of the leader with a term limit and continuous supervision. Akbar Ganji stated, "We think the election of the leader with term limits not only does not conflict with rationality and the Islamic divine law, it is also more consistent with democracy."[51] Released after eighteen months of imprisonment, Mohsen Kadivar said to a German daily on August 20, 2000, "*velayat-e faghih* must be abolished if we wish to have democracy [in Iran]." This was the demand of thousands of youth in July1999 when they shouted, "Death to the dictator."[52]

The battle between the republic and the *faghih* continues.

Conclusions

These lines are being written at a time when the reform movement in Iran is experiencing a setback. Some of the gains of the movement have been taken away by the opponents of change. The reformist press is being assaulted, and journalists and writers are in jail. The official advocates of change, those within the "May 23 movement," seem to have lost the upper hand and the courage and will to continue the battle for change. They are in disarray and crisis. The conservatives seem to be gaining momentum. Is this the end of reform in Iran?

Indeed, the future cannot be predicted with perfect accuracy. But my analysis and discussion of social movements, the crisis of legitimacy of the Islamic Republic, and the changing international conditions all indicate the improbability of a return to the pre-1997 period in Iran. Despite the current setbacks, Iran is experiencing one of the most dynamic periods of its recent history. Change is occurring in all spheres of life.

The Islamic Republic is being made to retreat from its earlier economic, political, and cultural designs. The globalization of economic relations and the dominance of the neoliberal paradigm are forcing the state to retreat from its earlier welfare/Keynesian model and its aspirations of de-linking from the world economy. Contrary to the first decade of the revolution, the current dominant economic discourse is that of the speedy inclusion in the world market and the global network of capital. The proponents of reform and civil society view the restructuring of the state as the solution to Iran's economic ills and a precondition for its political reform. The Islamic

Republic is expediently trying to return to prerevolution economic relations. It is privatizing state property, liberalizing international trade and investment, seeking loan capital in international money markets, and molding an economy modeled after the prescriptions of the World Bank and other leading international lending institutions. What was once scorned is now embraced with eagerness.

Culturally, the project of creating a society based on Islamic values and codes of conduct is being defeated by the children of the Islamic Republic, the youths with no memory of the old cultural paradigm, the generation born and raised under the Islamic state. Two decades of violent enforcement of Islamic values has led to the emergence of a powerful grassroots movement for the right to live a free life. All attempts to isolate Iranian youth from the increasing flow of global information have failed. A generation of young Iranians is emerging under the influence of the globally dominant youth culture. The Islamic state is most seriously challenged by its own creation—the children of the Islamic Republic.

Cultural "deviance" is becoming a norm. All that was condemned, scorned, and banned is becoming dominant. Premarital sex, the use of homemade alcohol, and all other cultural nightmares of the Islamic Republic are becoming dominant. The Islamic dress code is increasingly challenged and put aside by the young women in the streets of Tehran and other major urban areas. Headscarves are pushed back and loud lipsticks give sensuous color to the faces of the rebellious young women. Men and women stroll on the streets holding hands. The cultural project of the Islamic state is defeated. It is becoming history.

The early model of the Islamic state has been abandoned by many of its original supporters. A new political model is being constructed. Political Islam is defeated.

Reform is a slow and painful process. It is tenuous, actualized by the participation of heterogeneous social actors and classes with nonconforming interests and goals. It encompasses those seeking change to rationalize and secure their continued domination of others, and those who see reform as a road to freedom from domination. It includes the exploited and the exploiter, the poor and the rich, the powerful and the powerless. The process of reform is riddled with tension, distrust, agony, betrayal, defeat, and victory.

The reform movement in Iran includes segments of the state and those repressed for twenty-one years by the state. It encompasses youths hostile to the Islamic project and the anti-secular Moslems. It includes the propertied classes, and the poor and those working two or three jobs to sustain a meager standard of living. Reform is actualized by the participation of women wishing to rid themselves of all forms of Islamic social and cultural control and domination, and the secular forces (including the secular Left) seeking a breathing space and a move toward the complete de-Islamicization of politics. The future of reform depends on the balance of power between defenders of the old order, the official movement for reform, and the broad coalition of ordinary people, intellectuals, and the activists who seek a radical (albeit gradual) transformation of the existing order.

Reform and repression are alternative methods used by states facing a crisis of legitimacy. Reformers seek to strengthen the state legitimacy through inclusion, tolerance, and pluralism. The supporters of the old order adhere to repression, cling to power through the process of elimination. They fear change, wage war against the proponents of reform, eliminate old comrades, use violence, and terrorize others. Reformers are assaulted in Iran, defenders of rights are assassinated, newspapers are shut down, but the movement remains.

Reform is occurring amidst the imprisonment of the reformers, violence, and the threat of bloodshed. Despite the possibility of violence, the return to the old order seems unlikely. The awakened ordinary people cannot be tamed by the use of the old methods of fear and intimidation. The old order has been rejected. Change must occur. Collective action is the order of the day. The children of the Islamic Republic, the "deviant" youth with lipsticks, Western-looking outfits, and non-Islamic conduct, cannot be contained. They are out to create a new reality—freedom from religious control and domination, freedom to live, freedom to be deviant. Their movement is a celebration of deviance. It is a celebration of the right to live a free life. They seek the secularization of the state. Their support for the reformers within the state is a means toward achieving their final freedom from religious domination and the theocratic state. Their alliance with the Islamic reform movement is tenuous and unstable. They seek unconstrained reform. They want freedom. Not intimidated by the old guard, not contained by the limited horizons of the official reform movement, ordinary people are putting an end to the project of the Islamic state. The final chapter of the Islamic Republic is being written. A new Iran is in the making.

Postscript

MTV Utopia vs the Islamic Utopia

The world was shocked by the emergence of a new image of Iran in February 1997, an image born with the presidential victory of Mohammad Khatami and the widespread eruption of movements for rights. Angry proclamations against the West were replaced with a plea for the "dialogue of civilizations." Burning the U.S. flag was scorned and abandoned by those who occupied the U.S. embassy in 1980. An official movement for reform emerged, while grassroots movements for rights challenged the dominant political culture and sought to create a new identity for Iran and Iranians. A new discourse became dominant—the discourse of rights and civil society.

But, the road to a new identity and image proved to be turbulent, bumpy, and hazardous. The protectors of the old order fortified their position, built new trenches, fought tooth and nail to preserve their waning power, and assaulted the gains of the movement for reform. They shutdown the reformist press, jailed outspoken journalists, attacked student dormitories, and made all efforts to turn back the wheels and recreate the Islamic Republic's earlier political and social mosaic. The reformist-dominated Parliament was intimidated, and its decisions revoked by the Guardian Council. It was ordered by the *faghih* to abandon its responsibilities as an independent elected body when it chose to discuss and revise the conservative Press Law. Khatami's vocal supporters were arrested, jailed, tortured, and accused of plotting to "overthrow the system." Old loyalists of the Islamic Republic filled its dungeons. They became targets of torture, forced recantation. The conservative assault weakened the movement, created divisions within its ranks, revealed its incapability to utilize the unleashed energy of millions of young people and working men and women to institutionalize reform. It failed to protect its own cadres against the conservatives. The movement was dealt a heavy blow. Its ranks were divided. While some became more vocal and questioned the overall rationality of the religious regime, others retreated from their earlier demands, and attempted to contain the energy of the grassroots movements for rights. Mohammad Khatami's earlier call for a civil society in Iran was replaced with an advocacy of "religious democracy." As the conservatives continued their assault, calling the official reform movement non-Islamic, Khatami increased his emphasis on Islam and Islamic values.

The conservatives aimed at weakening, demoralizing, and paralyzing the movement for reform. They prepared for the next presidential election, sought a defeat or total submission of Mohammad Khatami and his close allies. And the world was anxiously watching, wishing for the continuation of the journey that began on May 23, 1979—the journey to reform. On June 8, 2001, the Iranians returned to the voting stations and re-elected Mohammad Khatami as Iran's president for another four years. Khatami emerged victorious against his opponents. The conservatives were, once again, rejected by the voters. Reform was endorsed in a public referendum. But the obstacles to reform remained.

Far from the jubilant and euphoric public mood that dominated the 1997 presidential election, the general mood in Iran was somber, hesitant, more thoughtful, and even ambivalent in June 2001. The nation was silent. It was reflecting. The electorate had gained political maturity. Trained by a burgeoning reformist press and a new cadre of political journalist and writers, and educated by the unraveling of the internal conflicts and contradictions of the Islamic Republic, it was quietly planning for the future. Despite the ineptness of the official reform movement, the electorate endorsed Khatami against the conservatives, voted for change, and used Mohammad Khatami to defeat the opponents of change. Once again, they revealed the fragility and weakness of the Islamic state and the inability of the Islamic Republic to materialize its original project.

Despite setbacks and systematic assault from the conservatives, the events between the two presidential elections revealed an undeniable new reality in Iran—the strength of the grassroots movements and collective action for cultural and social transformation. In spite of their control of the organs of power, the conservatives in the state seem unable to halt the process of change. Increasingly, the Islamic Republic resembles an ideological regime no longer able to enforce its world view, an empty political shell, and a state losing the last vestiges of its legitimacy.

Twenty two years ago, the founders of the Islamic Republic launched an ambitious social project. They wished to construct an Islamic utopia on earth. The utopia was to be defined in opposition to the West and the East. It had its own vision of politics, economics, and culture. Twenty two years later, the Islamic Utopia is all but degenerated and defeated. It is defeated by forces beyond its control.

Economically, the utopia was to build a welfare state, take care of the downtrodden and the economically disenfranchised, turn Iran to an example of a prosperous paradise on earth. Now, twenty two years later, it faces a seemingly irresolvable crisis of poverty, unemployment, and the widening of the income gap between the haves and the have-nots.

Politically, the Islamic utopia created an unsustainable and irrational mix of parliamentary democracy and the absolute rule of the *faghih*. But, the collage of modem politics and Islamic theocracy failed to create the stability required in the utopia. With the death of Ayatollah Khomeini, the *faghih* lost legitimacy. It became a power despised by people, ridiculed in popular joke, and defaced in street graffiti. And finally in July 1999, the loud cry of "Death to the Dictator" by the children of the Islamic Republic closed the last chapter to the state's political utopia. The *faghih* was the subject of popular anger in a week of mass protest in more than 20 cities across the nation.

But, more significant than its economic and political failure, the Islamic utopia is degenerated in the cultural sphere. It is facing a defeat to the children of the Islamic Republic—the generation that was hoped and trained to be the future of a new Islamic Utopia on earth, and its guardian against the Satanic West's cultural invasion. It has become a degenerated and dysfunctional hell. Its future guardians embrace the satanic West, long for its forbidden fruit, wish to escape the Islamic paradise for a life of sin and decadence in the scorned West. They are the crusaders of change, warriors of a different utopia—the MTV utopia.

The Islamic Republic fought for 22 years to defeat the West's "cultural invasion." It tried to create a utopia based on Islamic virtues, cultural, and social codes of conduct. It tried, at least in the sphere of cultural production, to defeat the global capitalist utopia. It failed. It used force, coercion, torture, imprisonment, stoning, rape, and all that was possible to mold a population based on its model of Islamic (non-Western, non-American, non-global capitalist) values. It celebrated mourning and death, and criminalized basic human feelings of love and joy. But it is losing the battle against the culture of globalization. The Islamic utopia is defeated by an assembly of seductive, powerful, and attractive material and cultural products: the MTV, satellite dishes, internet, Hollywood, and all that is "decedent."

Against the celebration of death, a movement for the right to live a free life has emerged: a movement for the celebration of life. Defying the eyes of surveillance of the state, openly confronting the state with the symbols of "cultural invasion," the children of the Islamic Republic are loudly announcing the defeat of the "Islamic utopia" of Iran. Armed with the weapon of cultural deviance, they are humiliating the state, defeating its utopia, capturing trenches, forcing the crusaders of Islam to retreat. The movement has no leaders and followers. It cannot be defeated. A return to the earlier days of the Islamic Republic is not possible.

Notes

CHAPTER 1. EMERGING SOCIAL MOVEMENTS, VICTORIES, AND SETBACKS IN THE BATTLE FOR RIGHTS

1. "I have emphasized the separation of religion from the state," declared Hashem Aghajari, a leading reformer and religious intellectual to a group of university students. "We must be careful not to lead religion collide with the institution of power. Otherwise, religion will be an instrument of repression." *Hayat-e No,* September 5, 2000.

2. The seizure of Ayatollah Montazeri's residence and Hosseinieh was compared to the takeover of the U.S. embassy by the "Students Following Imam's Line" in 1980.

3. On October 21, 1997, at a student rally in front of Tehran University, Heshmatollah Tabarzadi, leader of the left-leaning and radical student organization and journal *Payam-e Daneshjoo* (Voice of Students), demanded a constitutional amendment and the direct and democratic election of the *faghih* for a limited term by the citizens. This was the first public demand for a constitutional change in the power of *velayat-e faghih*. The Ansar-e Hezbollah attacked following the speech, the office of *Payam-e Danshjoo* was ransacked, and Tabarzadi and his staff were severely injured and hospitalized. *Payam-e Danshjoo* was closed down and never published again.

4. Habibollah Payman, "From the Discourse of the Revolution to the Discourse of May 23," *Donya-ye Sokhan* 84 (1999): 21–28.

5. Quoted by the prosecutor from Kadivar's newspaper interviews and articles in February 1999. In his defense, Kadivar accused the prosecutor of intentionally excluding other statements from his interviews, presenting a picture contrary to his intention.

6. Ibid.

7. Quoted in *Asr-e Ma,* 29 July 1998.

8. Associated Press, August 21, 2000.

9. Mostafa Tanha, "Achilles' Heels of the May 23 Movement," *Nameh,* April 1999.

10. "Our patience has reached its limits and we can no more tolerate any further disturbances," wrote twenty high-ranking commanders of the *Pasdaran* in a letter to the president during the July 1999 student uprising.

11. Joe Foweraker, *Theorizing Social Movements* (London: Pluto Press,1995); Alain Touraine, "Beyond Social Movements," in Stanford L. Lyman, *Social Movements: Critique, Concepts, and Case Studies* (New York: New York University Press, 1995).

12. Andre Gorz, *Farewell to the Working Class* (Boston: South End Press, 1982); Ernesto Laclau and Chantal Mouffe, *Hegemony and Socialist Strategy: Towards a Radical Democratic Politics* (London: Verso, 1985); Alberto Melucci, "The Symbolic Challenge of Contemporary Movements," *Social Research* 52, 4 (Winter1985); Claus Offe, "New Social Movements: Challenging the Boundaries of Institutional Politics," *Social Research* 52, 4 (Winter 1985); Alain Touraine, *The Voice and the Eye: An Analysis of Social Movements* (Cambridge: Cambridge University Press,1985).

13. Charles Tilly, "Repertoires of Contention in America and Britain," in Mayer Zald and John McCarthy, eds., *Social Movements in an Organizational Society* (New Brunswick: Transaction,1979); Charles Tilly, "From Interaction to Outcomes in Social Movements," in Marco Giugni, Doug McAdam, and Charles Tilly, eds., *How Social Movements Matter* (Minneapolis: University of Minnesota Press,1999).

14. Charles Tilly, "From Interaction to Outcomes in Social Movements," in Marco Giugni, Doug McAdam, and Charles Tilly, eds., *How Social Movements Matter* (Minneapolis: University of Minnesota Press,1999).

15. John Foran, "A Century of Revolution: Comparative, Historical, and Theoretical Perspectives on Social Movements in Iran," in John Foran, ed., *A Century of Revolution: Social Movements in Iran* (Minneapolis: University of Minnesota Press, 1994), 234.

CHAPTER 2. STATE AND THE SOCIALIZATION OF VIOLENCE

1. The scene in Tehran Airport has radically changed since the election of Mohammad Khatami. Gone are the bearded men in slippers. Passport control is reduced to one, with uniformed officers who even smile at times.

2. The street borders the south end of Tehran University and is named after the National Student Day in Iran.

CHAPTER 3. CHILDREN OF THE ISLAMIC REPUBLIC—PART I

1. *Farda-e No,* 27 June 1998.

2. *Iran Javan,* 26 June 1998.

3. *Omid Javan,* 29 June 1998.

4. *Khordad,* 26 December 1998.

5. *Khordad,* 3 December 1998.

CHAPTER 4. CHILDREN OF THE ISLAMIC REPUBLIC—PART II

1. In the years before the 1979 revolution, the student movement was a powerful social movement, embracing diverse social and political ideologies, including Marxism, nationalism, and different Islamic tendencies. The political tendencies within the student movement reflected the existing dissident political ideologies of the time. The student movement, to a large extent, was the site of actualization of the larger movement against the state.

In essence, all political organizations primarily recruited from universities and their leaderships were composed of intellectuals studying in prestigious institutions of higher education in Tehran and elsewhere. Except for the eruption of the mass rallies and strikes in the final months of the Shah's rule, the political movement against the Shah was primarily a movement embedded in universities. It was a movement of the students against dictatorship and the Shah's close ties with the United States. Though subsidiary to the main goal of the struggle against "imperialism" and "dictatorship," parts of the movement also carried some vague notions of social justice and equality. In many respects, apart from the short-lived burst of non-student opposition led by Ayatollah Khomeini in 1963, Iran's campuses were the primary sites where the Shah's rule was challenged in the 1960s and '70s.

2. It was the UCO from which emerged the "Islamic Students, Followers of Imam's Line"—the group that launched the takeover of the U.S. embassy in November 1979.

3. The above developments also led to the formation of independent Moslem student organizations such as *Jame'eh-ye Eslami-e Daneshjooyan* (Islamic Students Collective), *Anjoman-e Eslami-e Mostaghel-e Daneshjooyan-e Daneshgah-e Amir kabir* (Amir Kabir Independent Islamic Student Association).

4. "Student Movements: Rebirth or Continuation," *Gozaresh* 8, 89 (July 1998): 12–19.

5. Tabarzadi was released from prison in November 1999.

6. Tabarzadi began his activities through membership in the "Cultural Center of the Seventy Two Martyrs"—an organization created after the explosion in the headquarters of the Islamic Republic Party and the alleged death of seventy-two high-ranking party members in the early 1980s. Originally formed as a political alternative to the Left-leaning UCO, the union saw Ayatollah Beheshti as its organizational role model and Ayatollah Motahhari as its ideological and theoretical mentor. The group had close ties with the now supreme leader Ayatollah Khamenei during his presidency and with Hashemi Rafsanjani during his tenure as Speaker of Parliament. Earlier in its activities, the union invited influential members of the traditional Right tendency to speak in its educational camps. Habibollah Asgaroladi, Mohammad Reza Bahonar, Mohammadi Gilani, and other influential members of the IRT were among those invited to these camps.

7. *Hoviat-e Khish,* 1 May 1999.

8. The above statement was published in the final issue of the short-lived *Hoviat-e Khish,* 6 June 1999. The statement continued:

> Unfortunately, the current Leader [Ayatollah Khomeini] could not act according to his constitutional rights and responsibilities. And the Assembly of Experts that is responsible for supervising the Leader is engaged in praising and worshipping him instead of critiquing his performance in his ten-year rule. His failure to make firm decisions about gigantic foundations like Mostazafan Foundation . . . the widespread corruption in the judicial system due to the practices of the Chief of the Judiciary . . . the violence of the *Ansar* that appear to be supported by the Leader, the assassination of opponents [the serial killing of the writers and intellectuals in Winter 1998] by the Ministry of Intelligence whose minister was approved by the Leader . . . are clear cases that indicate the Leader of the system, to some extent, has declined to the level of the leader of a faction.

9. *Payam-e Daneshjoo,* 3 April 1995, cited in Hojjat Mortaji, *Political Factions in Contemporary Iran* (1999).

10. Criticizing sectarianism and the monopolization of power based on a specific reading of Islam, Tabarzadi said, "A group in society gives the state a sacred status and power, implying a divine status for the state, a person or group [within it]—a status granted by God. . . . In practice, this reading leads to the monopolization of power." He thus called for limiting "the

power of the *faghih* within the boundaries of the Constitution" (Speech by Tabarzadi on May 6, 1997, cited in the weekly *Aban* in two issues of the paper in November 1998).

11. *Payam-e Daneshjoo,* no. 4 (18 September 1995). Quoted from *Aban,* November 1998.

12. *Payam-e Daneshjoo,* no. 47 (29 February 1996). Quoted from *Aban,* November 1998.

13. *Payam-e Daneshjoo,* no. 41 (21 June 1995). Quoted from *Aban,* November 1998.

14. *Payam-e Daneshjoo,* no. 47 (21 June 1995). Quoted from *Aban,* November 1998.

15. *Payam-e Daneshjoo,* no. 47 (29 February 1996). Quoted from *Aban,* November 1998.

16. *Payam-e Daneshjoo* gained respect among many students for its criticism and for exposing the corruption of Hashemi Rafsanjani and his government. *Payam-e Daneshjoo* was the pioneer in challenging and exposing the results of neoliberalism in Iran. It argued against the privatization of public enterprises, and advocated the active role of the state in guiding the economy. Tabarzadi called for the termination of the Structural Adjustment Policy in Iran, while *Payam-e Daneshjoo* advocated state intervention to rescue the economy "that is damaged from the past and the imposed war." And "using state intervention," wrote the weekly, "we must gradually organize production and regulate foreign exchange and financial matters." Elsewhere, the group advocated strict state intervention to control prices and fight against "economic corruption." It called for the death penalty for charging high prices. The group supported the use of state subsidies for the underprivileged and regards subsidies as "injections that keep on its feet the weakened body of a large section of society. . . . Subsidies are [needed] for the survival of the poor."

17. The identity of Iranians is "being Iranian. . . . The mere citizenship of Iran can be the base for the distribution of power and wealth," argued Moradi.

18. These are names of places where decisive battles were waged between the Iran and Iraq during the war.

19. *Hoviat-e Khish,* 1 May 1999.

20. Ibid.

21. The agents of the Ministry of Intelligence in October 1998 murdered Hezb-e Mellat's secretary, Daryoush Forouhar, and his wife in their residence in Tehran.

22. The union organized a commemoration of the nationalist leader Mohammad Mossadegh on the anniversary of his death in June 1999.

23. *Aban,* 1 May 1999.

24. The paper had published a confession by a member of *Hezbollah* about the operation of the group, its command system, and the high-ranking members of the state (including the Leader) giving orders for violence to the group.

25. *Hoviat-e Khish,* 6 June 1999. "A Solution for Iran's Future Political Structure." Statement by the Islamic Union of Students and Alumni of Universities and Institutions of Higher Education.

CHAPTER 5. CHILDREN OF THE ISLAMIC REPUBLIC—PART III

1. *Tehran Times,* 18 June 1998.

2. *Doostan,* 1 June 1998.

3. *Jame'eh,* 11 June 1998.

4. A bill was introduced in the parliament by a group of conservative MPs requesting an increase in the voting age from fifteen to eighteen, a bill that was defeated by public outrage and active opposition by the critical press and the young.

The bill to increase the voting age became a subject of criticism in most of the liberal press in the country. And the young actively participated in the debate on the voting age. "If the age 18 is the age of maturity for girls, why then [according to the Islamic law] they are prepared to be married and make decisions about forming a family at the age nine? Is making a lifelong decision simpler than choosing a person to resolve the problems of a country?" wrote a young Iranian in *Aftab-e Emrooz* (Today's Sun). And, "Can anyone say that the youth were not wise when they joined the war front [with Iraq]," wrote Ali Omidi. See *Aftab-e Emrooz,* 3 August 1998.

5. The student support for the nationalist leader Mohammad Mossadegh has been a part of the reemergence of Mossadegh's popularity among intellectuals and reformist circles in the country. A specter is haunting Iran—the specter of Mossadegh. Twenty years of the Islamic Republic have given rise to a surge of interest in nationalism in opposition to Islam. Dr. Mossadegh, a hero of Iran's nationalists and a national symbol of patriotism and resistance against foreign domination has emerged out of the ashes of history and opposition by the Islamic state. His pictures decorate posters of independent organizations and student groups. The Freedom Movement used Mossadegh's picture on its posters in the city council elections. Different political groups and student organizations held memorials

for Mossadegh on the anniversary of his death on March 5, 1999. The Independent Student Society of Amir Kabir University organized a memorial at Mossadegh's tomb on that date. The National Organization of Students and Alumni of Iran joined others in commemorating Mossadegh at his tomb.

In a column in *Neshat,* Hamid Reza Jalaeipour wrote about "The Unfinished Project of the Rule of Law: From Mossadegh to Khatami." Jalaeipour's reopening of the issue seemed provocative and deliberate, representing a new boldness and courage by a movement that was gaining more momentum and capturing barricades from its opponents. On March 7, Hassan Yousefi Ashkevari, a liberal clergyman, wrote a column in *Neshat* titled "Kadivar and Mossadegh as a Moslem." The column defended Kadivar in his support for Mossadegh. Ashkevari wrote, "Is it possible to take away the national and human power and position of Mossadegh by using historical distortion and insult? Can you not see the humane image of Mossadegh is becoming more clear and known every day?" At a conference on the relationship between patriotism and religion, Ashkevari said, "Mossadegh's services [to the country] were unmatchable in the history of Iran. . . . Mossadegh conducted the cleanest election. . . . Moslems mix patriotism with religion as the ideological base for struggle against colonialism. . . . Patriotism as the [ideology of] return to our own culture is a historical necessity and does not conflict with religion."

"Who Is Afraid of Mossadegh?" was the headline of the March 9 issue of the weekly *Payam-e Hajar*. Carrying large pictures of Mossadegh and Ayatollah Taleghani on its front page, the weekly reproduced a speech about Mossadegh at his tomb by Ayatollah Taleghani. "Why Do They Attack Mosaddegh?" was the title of a column written by Ezatollah Sahabi in *Neshat* on March 15, 1989. *Sobh-e Emrooz,* too, carried a column titled "What is the Quarrel About?" by Mohammad Gorgani. Gorgani explained the attack on Mossadegh as a new tactic by the conservatives to discredit the May 23rd movement. In its March 16 issue, in a page-long article about Mossadegh, *Neshat* quoted Sadegh Zibakalam comparing Mossadegh with Gandhi, Mandela, and Nehru. *Khordad* continued the defense of Mossadegh through the publication of a long (page-long pieces in two days) interview with Mohammad Torkaman.

6. *Neshat,* 25 May 1999.

7. Ibid.

8. *Sobh-e Emrooz,* 25 May 1999.

9. Five days before the *Park-e Laleh* incident, many students and others attending a memorial for Mossadegh at his tomb in Ahmad'abad were violently attacked by a mob of men in black outfits while the Security Force stood by and made no effort to stop the violence. Many students were severely injured and hospitalized.

10. Students vowed to continue their protests until authorities met their demands. Also on May 26, an authorized gathering by the independent students of universities in Ghazvin was prevented from taking place. A number of students were arrested.

11. A complaint was filed against *Salam* by the Ministry of Intelligence for having published a classified document of the ministry's two days earlier—a document that revealed the awareness of Dori Najafabadi, the ousted minister of intelligence, of the scheme to kill and eliminate writers and intellectuals.

12. Fifty years earlier on December 7, three students were shot down by the Shah's guards at Tehran University. December 7 was declared the national Student Day and a day of protest against the Shah. In memory of these three martyrs on the path to freedom, and for the continuation of their bloody path! December 7 was coined by the secular anti-Shah student movement as the Student Day. For years, dissident students in Iran and abroad held meetings and rallies on December 7. With the victory of the Islamic Republic, the celebration of Student Day on December 7 was abandoned and replaced with Islamic commemorations and memorials.

13. *Tehran Times,* 13 July 1999.

14. From the *BBC News* Internet site.

15. The Iran Press Service (IPS), a Paris-based Internet group, reported that an informed source in Tehran had told the IPS "that during the SCNS President Khatami had insisted on the identification and resignation of all the officers responsible for the bloody attack and the dismantling of the *Ansar-e Hezbollah*."

16. Associated Press, September 9, 2000.

CHAPTER 6. A MOVEMENT FOR A FREE PRESS

1. *Tavana,* 14 June 1998. Cited in *Salam,* 3 June 1998.

2. *Azadi,* 11 July 1998.

3. *Tavana,* 14 July 1998, Cited in *Salam*.

4. And Akbar Velayati, the conservative foreign minister in the administration of Hashemi Rafsanjani declared, "Unfortunately, everyday more papers mushroom in the country. Some newspapers that have mushroomed in the past two years are attempting to erase the red lines." See *Hamshari,* 27 June 1998.

Ha'ezi Shirazi said, "Officials in charge of cultural affairs must prevent the publication of these journals." Ibid.

Ali Akbar Hosseini said, "It is interesting the Ministry of Health proudly announces the collection of fifty tons of spoiled chicken meat. But, the Ministry of Culture and Guidance sits silently before the publication of hundreds of tons of spoiled and harmful print material." Ibid.

5. *Jame'eh,* 16 June 1998.

6. *Arzesh-ha,* 14 June 1998.

7. *Kayhan,* 11 June 1998.

8. *Aban,* 13 June 1998.

9. Ibid.

10. *Mobin,* 13 June 1998.

11. *Tavana,* 14 June 1998.

12. *Aban,* 16 July 1998.

13. *Hamshari,* 13 July 1998.

14. *Hamshahri,* 1 August 1998.

15. Ayatollah Ibrahim Amini expressed similar views in the Friday prayer in Quom. Following the prayer, a group of 4,000 participants marched on the streets of Qom chanting slogans against the minister of Islamic guidance and the press. The protesters chanted, "The revolutionary *Majlis,* impeach, impeach," "Our minister of culture, resign, resign," and, "Death to mercenary newspapers." Finally, less than twenty-four hours after the speech by Ayatollah Yazdi and after only six issues of the paper, *Toos* was closed down by an order from the Tehran justice department.

16. *Abrar Eghtesadi,* 3 August 1998.

17. *Aban,* 19 September 1998.

18. *Payam-e Emrooz* (October 1998): 4.

19. Ibid.

20. The weekly *Aban* continued its independent and critical journalism as one of the last vestige of the free press. Knowing well the severe consequences of their activity, those in charge of *Aban* continued printing news and articles criticizing and exposing the judiciary, the Guardian Council, and those responsible for the death of the free press in Iran.

21. *Aban,* 3 October 1998.

22. *Salam,* 25 October 1998.

23. See the Interview in *Arzesh-ha,* 31 October 1998.

24. *Neshat,* 2 September 1999.

25. Though not taking a public stand challenging the illegal closure of critical press, Khatami confronted the rationale behind this action in a speech given to an assembly of artists on November 1. Indirectly challenging the accusation that *Toos* had endangered the nation's "national security" Khatami said: "Expression of ides does not endanger the society's security. Security is endangered when the legal avenues for the expression of ideas do not exist." See *Arzesh-ha,* 2 November 1998.

Addressing an audience of managing directors and editors-in-chief of the press on November 25, Khatami reiterated the same positions and once again warned the opponents of free press of the inevitability of "social explosion." "We can repress ideas only temporarily," said Khatami, but, "when repressed thoughts will go underground we must anticipate social explosion."

Challenging the illegal summary trial of the press in closed courts in recent months, Khatami repeatedly called for obeying the constitution and using "open trials with jury" to handle the alleged violations of the press. Here, more than any other occasion, Khatami sounded like an opposition leader inviting the press to stand up for their rights against state repression. "There is no doubt that all press violations must be dealt with in open trials with jury," said the president. "In case this does not occur" continued Khatami," all of us must oppose it. And in the first place, it is the press that must oppose this." Khatami also welcomed the criticism and scrutiny of the state by the press. "Unchallenged power leads to corruption," said Khatami. "All violations must be confronted as violations of law. Violations committed by the state must also be opposed." See *Hamshahri,* 26 November 1998.

26. *Iran Farda* (December 1998): 4.

27. *Iran Farda* (December 1998): 6.

28. *Iran News,* 26 December 1998.

29. *Khordad,* 26 December 1998.

30. *Khordad,* 6 January 1999.

31. *Sobh-e Emrooz,* 7 January 1999.

32. *Sobh-e Emrooz,* 7 January 1999.

33. *Iran News,* 10 January 1999.

34. *Khordad,* 10 January 1999.

35. *Khordad,* 13 February 1999.

36. Ibid.

37. *Aban,* 24 April 1999.

38. *Sobh,* Second half of April 1999.

39. Much has been written about Abdollah Nouri's defense of rights and civil society before the Special Court of the Clergy. The trial created a national hero. It turned Abdollah Nouri into the most respected member of the official reform movement in Iran. Nouri surpassed the president in popularity, gained the respect of the opponents of the Islamic Republic, and became a part of history.

40. *Khordad,* 22 April 1999.

CHAPTER 7. STATE, ECONOMY, AND CIVIL SOCIETY—PART I

1. Other than in the oil industry, (independent) trade unions were nearly nonexistent in the remainder of the economy.

2. My discussion of workers' actions and institutions in 1978 and 1979 are based on Asef Bayat's book *Workers and Revolution in Iran* (London: Zed Press, 1987).

3. See the following collection of articles: *Civil society and the Contemporary Iran* (Tehran: Nagsh va Negar press, 1998); *The Realization of Civil Society and the Islamic Revolution in Iran* (The Ministry of Culture and Islamic Guidance Press, 1997).

4. Class is defined here in terms of ownership and control of productive and financial assets.

5. The act of "participation" assumes the equality of power and willful action on the part of equal social agents. Subordinates do not participate in a social project with their superiors. They take part in the reproduction of the conditions of their subordination.

6. In 1998, Iran had three official exchange rates—around 5,700 rials to the dollar for travelers, 3,000 for exporters, and 1, 750 for state agencies importing "necessary goods and equipment."

7. *Sobh-e Emrooz,* 2 Februay 1999.

8. The judiciary reported this in early 1999. The daily *Khordad* reported of an unprecedented rise of usury, and issuing of bad checks in Qom. *Khordad,* 7 January 1999.

9. *Statistical Yearbook* (1996), 402.

10. Half of those who attempted suicide were younger than twenty-five. The rate of suicide was much higher among young women (between fourteen and forty-two) than men. The higher rate of suicide attempts among women can also be attributed to the severe social repression of women under the Islamic Republic.

11. *Pegah,* 28 July 1998.

12. The extreme censorship and the lack of published information about these events make the accurate analysis of the causes of these ruptures and public explosions a very difficult task. In April 1995, in a typical bread riot in Eslam Shahr, an impoverished suburb of Tehran, the residents poured into the streets in a spontaneous act of defiance and rage, and demanded an end to the rising utility prices and declining subsidies for basic necessities. The protesters were immediately attacked and gunned down by the state's armed forces. A curfew was imposed for two days. Houses were searched for protest leaders not arrested or killed during the ambush. Similar protests occurred in Arak, Najaf Abad, and Ghaem Shahr. They were all violently put down by the state.

13. The oil refinery workers in Tehran, Tabriz, Shiraz, and Esfahan went on a two-day warning strike on December 18 and 19, 1996. The striking workers demanded state recognition of collective bargaining in the refineries. Early the following year, on February 16, 1997, workers of the same refineries waged a strike to protest the arrest of hundreds of oil workers in Tehran during a picket in front of the Oil Ministry building the day before. Their homes were raided in search of protest leaders. More arrests were made later.

14. Due to the lack of materials and continued financial problems, the workers of Cheet-e Behshahr Textile Factory waged a job action and stopped working for the second time within a few months. *Islamic Republic News Agency* (IRNA) telex, 1 July 1999.

A number of fishermen in the Caspian Sea provinces protested their dire economic conditions, the government procurement policy, and the unfair prices paid for their catch. *Islamic Republic News Agency* telex, 31 January 1999.

After having held two hunger strikes, a number of workers of Abgin Factory in Ghazvi assembled and demanded a meeting with the company's manager to resolve pay and job classification problems. Two of the workers were arrested the day after the gathering. Other workers assembled in front of the main administration building and demanded the release of their co-workers. As a result of the pressure by protesting workers, the arrested workers were released. A number of others were interrogated afterward. *Iran Farda* (January 1999): 44.

A group of 1,500 workers from a number of factories in Kashan demonstrated in front of the governor's office in early January 1999. To calm the situation, the governor attempted to read a written statement to the protesting workers, but they refused to hear the governor, making him leave the scene. *Khordad,* 5 January 1999.

More than 1,000 oil workers gathered outside the provincial governor's offices in Abadan February 23, 1999, to demand a pay raise and an end to the expulsion of contract workers in Abadan refinery. Following this protest, sixteen oil workers were arrested in Abadan, Ahvaz, and Shiraz in April 1999. *Solidarity Campaign with Iranian Workers* (Internet Site), 1 (July 1999).

"Thousands" of unemployed youth and workers who couldn't get jobs in the agricultural /industrial complex in Shooshtar attacked the central building of this complex, breaking windows and smashing doors on April 18, 1999. Ibid.

Workers of Tehran Municipality, Section 4, demonstrated outside the council offices on April 22, 1999, protesting the outsourcing of part-time jobs to a private contractor.

Workers in Azmayesh Factory in Sarvdasht went on hunger strike on Monday, May 17 in protest against their dire economic conditions in contrast to the management of the company. *Khordad,* 24 May 24 1999.

Having been on strike for several months for the nonpayment of their salaries, workers in a textile factory in the town of Qahemshahr in the northern province of Mazandaran locked their boss in an office following a protest over plans to close the plant on March 9, 1999. Earlier, in November 1998, the workers attacked the previous director and threw him out of the factory. There have been other protests by the textile workers of the province of Mazandaran over the nonpayment of salaries in 1999.

15. *Solidarity Campaign* 1, Issue 1 (July 1999).

16. March 1999—Workers of Ghaemshahr Textiles factory reportedly assaulted the factory manger in his office in protest against the shutdown of machinery and the nonpayment of their salaries. The factory's previous manger was assaulted by the employees five months earlier for the same reason. The workers of Nakhkar Factory were assaulted by members of the Security Force while marching toward the Ministry of Labor in protest against the nonpayment of their salaries. "The workers have not been paid for fourteen months. They were not even paid the New Year bonus for 1998. . . . Two hundred workers decided to go to the Ministry of Labor to ask for an answer [to the situation]. The factory is located seven kilometers outside Tehran. We did not even have money to pay for the fare. So we walked. . . ."

Three hundred fifty workers of Alladin Corp. organized a picket line in front of the gates of the factory to protest the nonpayment of their salaries for the preceding two months. "I had a heart attack a while ago. I need to buy medicine. But, I have no money," said a picketing worker. "I have not paid the daycare for two months. I feel ashamed to go there today. I work twelve hours a day. The heavy smell of acid has made me ill. I want nothing but my back pay. Where can I go after Wednesday when they close the factory," said a worker with twenty-two years of work at the factory—a single mother with two children. "I have a wife and nine children. I did not have enough money to buy bread for them this morning. Tonight, I will not return home. I feel ashamed. There is no money to buy food for them," said another worker on the picket line. "Thirty years of work in the company. I spent my youth at this company. Who can I tell my pain? Thirty thousand tomans a month! Four children. Five hundred thousand tomans of debt. What shall I do?"

17. *Solidarity Campaign* 1, Issue 1 (July 1999).

18. Nearly 90 percent of all workplaces in Iran employ three employees or less. Close to 40 percent of the workforce works in these small establishments (workshops, retail stores, etc.).

19. And similar to the student movement, the deepening of the economic crisis and political division of the state also paved the way for the transformation of the workers and the Islamic Councils in different factories. Workers in the metal and steel sectors of Foolad Mobarakeh plant went on shrike on International Workers Day, May 1, 1999, in protest against lack of benefits, uncertainty regarding retirement, difficulty of their jobs, bad food, and the antiworker policies of the management. The strike ended in three days after a compromise was presented by management. Workers at a bakery in Isfahan protested the amendment to the labor law passed in the *Majlis* on June 8. They gathered outside the offices of the MP from Isfahan. *Solidarity Campaign* 1, Issue 1 (July 1999).

A protesting worker in Shiraz called the amendment "humiliating" to the workers and the president of the board of directors of Shiraz Coordinating Committee of Islamic Councils called it a violation of the "declaration of human rights" and a subject of protest by the International Labor Organization. *Islamic Republic News Agency* telex, 3 May 1999.

20. *Iranian Workers News* I, Issue 6 (January 2000).

21. In 1989, prior to the overhaul of the market, twelve different rates were identified in Iran. See Mohammad, Rafati, and Nader Mehregan, *Exchange Rate: From Multiple to a Single Rate* (Tehran: Business Studies and Surveys Institute, 1993), 88.

22. All rates were increased over time. By 1993 most commodities were removed from the official exchange rate category and, by and large, the floating and competitive rates became dominant in all categories of goods and services. Mohammad, Rafati, and Nader Mehregan, *Exchange Rate*.

23. Mohsen, Noorbakhsh, "Opening Presentation," *Report from the Third Seminar on Money and Exchange Rate Policies* (Tehran: Bank Markazi, 1993), 13.

24. See chapter 5 for the psychological impact of currency liberalization on ordinary people and their experiences in everyday life.

25. Abbas, Rahimi, "Commercial Policy and a Comparative Analysis of Poverty in Basic Goods," in *An Analysis of the Economics of Poverty* (Tehran: Business Studies and Surveys Institute, 1996), 84.

26. Ibid., 83–106; Abbas, Rahimi, "The Effect on Poverty Line of Eliminating Subsidies in Iran," *Mahnameh-e Barresiha-ye Bazargani* 81 (1996): 5–24; Ali Deeni Torkamani, "An Analysis of Food Poverty in Iran," in *An Analysis of the Economics of Poverty,* 53–82.

27. "The living style of workers today denotes a severe decline of their living standard. The quality of food of working families has come down severely, as is proved by abundant pieces of evidence. For example it is enough to have a look at workers' districts and ask the local butcher how many people have referred to him, to buy say between 100 and 150 tomans worth of meat, which would be about 100 grams at the current price. This piece of meat is certainly not for beefsteak or steak, but for 'Abgoosht' [soup] to feed a family of not fewer than five. It constitutes two meals for them. Here, the dry and spiritless figures come to life and get frightful." Maryam Mohseni, "Effects Of Economic Adjustment Plan on Status of Iranian Workers," *Farhang-e Tose'e,* nos. 34 and 35 (June-July 1998): 12–14

28. Ali, Deeni Torkamani (1996). It is important to note that the estimates of poverty outlined above do not include the cost of housing, medical care, and other highly inflationary essential goods. Housing expenses alone surpass the monthly income of many employed wage earners in Tehran and other large cities. On average, Iranians spent nearly 57 percent of their income on rent.

29. *Islamic Republic News Agency* (IRNA) telex, 16 March 1999.

30. *Khordad,* 19 January 1999.

31. *Islamic Republic News Agency* (IRNA) telex, 17 March 1999.

32. *Iran,* 19 April 1999.

33. *Solidarity Campaign* 1, Issue 1 (July 1999).

34. Ibid.

35. Ibid.

36. Ibid.

37. *Solidarity Campaign* 1, Issue 1 (July 1999).

38. *Islamic Republic News Agency* (IRNA) telex, 1 July 1999, 22 June 1999.

39. Ibid.

40. Ibid.

41. *Solidarity Campaign* 1, Issue 5 (December 1999).

CHAPTER 8. STATE, ECONOMY, AND CIVIL SOCIETY—PART II

1. In Khatami's first year in office (May 1997–May 1998) the following increases were recorded in the inventories of important industrial goods.

Commodity	*Increase in inventory %*
electronic radio and color TV	50
carpet	70
telephone receivers	50
batteries	45
machine-made rugs	51
blanket	900

2. Statement by the deputy minister of finance, Gharebaghian.

3. It was reported that workers in 450 establishments were not been paid for between two and eleven months by March 1999. The number of factories with financial problems in the province of Khorasan was on the rise. According to a report in January 1999, Lama Corporation, a producer of automobile parts, was among the troubled factories that had not paid its employees since September 1998 despite protest by its workers. On December 13, 1999, the *New York Times* reported that for nearly two months, the 7,500 workers who punched in every morning at Iran Tractor Manufacturing Co. found themselves with almost nothing to do. The assembly line was nearly shut down, starved of raw materials that the government could no longer afford to import due to the endemic foreign currency shortage. Tractor sales had plummeted; most customers were struggling to make ends meet. According to the daily, only the promise of a paycheck kept workers showing up, but the previous month most got just half of their $130 wage. Other newspapers in Iran printed similar reports.

4. *Akhbar-e Eghtesadi,* 21 September 1999.

5. *Khordad,* 1 January 1999.

6. Income Distribution by Percentiles for 1996

Income Percentiles	*Share in Income (%)*
1 poorest	1.4
2	3.1
3	3.3
4	3.9
5	5.1
6	6.9
7	10.2
8	12.1
9	14.2
10 richest	39.8

Source: From the research conducted by the *Majlis*.

	Share in Total Income
Poorest 60% of the population	23.7%
Richest 40% of the population	76.3%

	Share in Total Income
Poorest 50%	16.7%
Richest 10%	39.8%

Source: Ahmad Yousef, "Dr. IMF and the Ailing Economy of Iran," *Gozaresh* (November 1998): 58–67.

7. Four hundred eleven thousand people received retirement income from the National Pension Funds in 1996. The great majority of these pensioners received incomes either below the "survival line" or on the "death line." See Hooshang Tale'e, "'Poverty Line', 'Survival Line,' 'Death Line,'" *Gozaresh* 89 (July 1998): 51–53.

8. Taking into account the increasing number of unemployed and disguised unemployed creates yet a starker picture. According to the 1996 census data, there were 1,475,000 unemployed people seeking jobs in 1996. Adding to this number those who have given up looking for a job and the seasonally unemployed, we get a much larger number of people living at the "death line."

9. *Payam-e Azadi,* 4 July 1998.

10. *Aban,* 4 July 1998.

11. *Resalat,* 4 July 1998.

12. *Arzesh-ha,* 9 November 1998.

13. *Khordad,* 1 June 1999.

14. Akbar Kamijani and M. Ahmadvand, "An Analysis of the Theory and Practice of Privatization in Some Countries—a Study of the Iranian Experience," *Eghtesad va Modiriat* 31 (Winter 1996): 33–73.

15. Article 43, the Constitution of the Islamic Republic of Iran.

16. The association with the World Bank and the bank's role in the implementation of the SAP has been vehemently denied by the state.

17. Despite the change in economic policy, the state's policy regarding the nature and forms of response to people's opposition and reaction to their conditions of social, economic, and political disempowerment remained unchanged. The state has continued using official and unofficial organs of repression to prevent the formation of collective action in response to its policies.

18. The plan was designed by the Organization of Budget and Planning and approved by the parliament. It called for the privatization of large industries, the partial transfer of state responsibilities to the private sector,

and the removal of all forms of export restrictions. The plan proposed the reconsideration of the pricing of domestically produced goods, exports, and imports, and the reduction of state subsidies for education. It introduced the gradual pricing of electricity, water and fuel, and telephone and postal services according to their cost of production, gradual reduction in state payroll, and an end to the state monopoly in foreign trade.

19. Exchange rate is defined here as the local currency price of one unit of foreign currency (the dollar, for example). The rial is the official name of Iran's currency. But, the unit often used by the public, retailers, and the media is toman, an equivalent of ten rials.

20. *Hamshahri,* 9 August 1998.

21. *Hamshahri,* 10 August 1998.

22. *Hamshahri*, 8 August 1998.

CHAPTER 9. OIL, INTERNATIONAL DIVISION OF LABOR, AND THE CRISIS OF THE IRANIAN ECONOMY

1. The fluctuation in oil prices indeed leads to economic shocks and instability where oil exports account for nearly 80 percent of the country's hard currency receipts. But under special circumstances, such fluctuations result in a severe decline in industrial output and capital accumulation. Fluctuations in oil prices lead to an interruption in accumulation only if the structure of production relies on oil exports and the foreign exchange receipts from that export. Such is the case in Iran.

Crisis is avoided if, instead of production, the structure of consumption (imported consumer goods) depends on oil or any other single-commodity export. In such a case, what occurs is interruption and instability in the sphere of consumption rather than production, leading to a decline in the consumption of imported staples or luxury goods. Though catastrophic and damaging (to wage earners and the poor, in the case of subsidized staple imports) in some cases, consumption instability or austerity of this type (caused by a decline in imports) is, nevertheless, a problem outside the sphere of production with no or minimal impact on accumulation.

The negative impact on accumulation of fluctuations in the price of single-commodity export (oil) occurs when the structure of production depends on capital goods (machinery, tools) and semi-finished goods imports. Indeed, with the increasing internationalization of economic relations and the growing interdependence between different economies, such import reliance is becoming more common. But, in the case of Iran and many other developing nations, the dependence on the import of capital goods (productive capital) is a structural phenomenon, rooted in the specific position of the country in the international division of labor. It is that structural dependence on imports that makes accumulation a function of export price fluctuation and creates an inherent tendency toward crisis. The articulation of these crisis tendencies presupposes the study of the historical transformation in the international division of labor and the position of the country within it.

2. For the Theory of Internationalization of Capital see Christian Polloix, "The Internationalization of Capital and the Circuit of Social Capital, " in Hugo Radici (ed), *International Firms and Modern Imperialism* (Harmondsworth: Penguin, 1975); Patric Clawson, "The Internationalization of Capital and Capital Accumulation in Iran and Iraq," *Insurgent Sociologist* VII, no. 2 (1997); John Weeks, "Epochs of Capitalism and the Progressiveness of Capital Expansion," *Science & Society* XIIX, no. 4, (1985); Dick Bryan, *The Chase Across the Globe: International Accumulation and the Contradictions for Nation States* (Oxford: Westview Press, 1995).

3. Parts of the developing world, especially Africa, are still engaged in the international division of labor from the colonial period. This is despite the end to colonialism and that phase in human history.

4. In some cases, for example South Korea, the developing nations succeeded in moving to higher stages of ISI, locally producing capital goods and machinery, thus transforming the structure of production and reducing dependence of accumulation on the imports of productive capital. The success of the process of deepening import substitution and moving from domestic production of light consumer goods to durable consumer and capital goods depends on a host of local and international factors. Such possibilities are increasingly weakened with the advent of economic liberalization and the decline in the ability of developing countries to pursue national development policy. See Behzad Yaghmaian, "Globalization of the State: The Political Economy of Global Accumulation and Its Emerging Mode of Regulation," *Science and Society* 62, no. 2, (Summer 1998).

5. See Behzad Yaghmaian, "Internationalization of Capital and the Crisis of the Iranian Economy," *Review of Radical Political Economics* 20, no. 4 (1988).

Import of consumer goods increased at a significantly greater rate in the later 1970s, due mainly to the state's food import-promotion policy.

Iran officiated a comprehensive land reform policy in 1962. The land reform was pronounced completed in September 1971. Despite the conclusion of the reform, agriculture remained predominantly precapitalist and backward. Facing the backwardness of agriculture, the Shah's government began promoting and subsidizing the import of foodstuffs in an attempt to lower the cost of labor through cheapening the workers' means of subsistence, and thus enhancing the profitability of Iran's new import-substitution industries.

6. In 1972, oil exports financed 53 percent of the growth of total imports, while the contribution of the manufacturing sector was only 0.7 percent. Thus, despite the large inflow of productive capital and the accelerated growth of industrial output, the one-sidedness of the economy and its heavy reliance on revenues from oil exports persisted throughout the 1960s and '70s.

7. Cyrus Bina, *The Economics of Oil Crisis* (New York: St. Martin's Press, 1985).

8. *Jame'eh,* 29 June 1998.

9. *Hamshahri,* 10 August 1998.

CHAPTER 10. THE GREAT DEBATE

1. See the following for the analysis of the formation of the Islamic Republic. Ervand Abrahamian, *Iran Between the Two Revolutions* (Princeton: Princeton University Press, 1982); Fred Halliday, *Iran: Dictatorship and Development* (New York: Penguin, 1979); Mohsen Millani, *The Making of Iran's Islamic Revolution: From Monarchy to the Islamic Republic* (London: Westview Press, 1988).

2. Many in the first constitutional committee were affiliated with Barazrgan's *Nehzat-e Azadi* (Freedom Movement) and the late Mohammad Mossadegh's *Gebhe-e Melli* (National Front). The committee in charge of drafting the constitution consisted of prominent lawyers and national figures including Nasser Katouzian, Hassan Habibi, Ja'afari Langaroudi, Naser Minaji, Sadr Ha'j Said Javadi. It also included two others (Zavarreh-ee and Mohammad Khamenei) who participated only in the first meeting. Interview with Naser Minaji. Naser Minaji, "How was the Draft of the Constitution Prepared," *Iran Farda* 51 (February 1999).

3. The Council of Revolution had fifteen members. Eight were from the Freedom Movement.

4. Interview with Ezatollah Sahabi, "What Happened in the Council of Revolution," *Iran Farda* 51 (February 1999).

5. Islam was declared the official religion of the country. The president was to be a *Shiite.*

6. "The Text of the Draft of the Constitution," *Minutes of the Assembly for the Final Evaluation of the Constitution of the Islamic Republic of Iran, Volume 4* (Tehran: Cultural and Public Relations of the Parliament, 1985).

7. Article 142—To protect the constitution and maintain the consistency of the common laws with the constitution, a Guardian Council is set up with the following composition:

1. Five experts in Islamic jurisprudence and familiar with the predicaments and requirements of the time. They are chosen by *Majlis-e shora-ye melli* [parliament] from a list suggested by *marage'e ma'roof-e taghlid*.
2. Six experts in legal matters: three professors from the country's colleges of law, and three judges from the Supreme Court. They are chosen by *Majlis-e shora-ye melli* from the above two groups.

Article 146—The decisions of the Guardian Council are made by the vote of at least two-thirds of its members.

8. The meetings were held for a period of nearly three months between August 19 and November 15, 1979.

9. *Velayat-e faghih* was first introduced by a council member, Hassan Ayat, and endorsed by Ayatollah Montazeri and Ayatollah Beheshti.

10. Defining his Islamic government, Ayatollah Khomeini said in 1970:

> The fundamental difference between Islamic government, on one hand, and constitutional monarchies and republics on the other, is this: whereas the representatives of people or the monarch in such regimes engage in legislation, in Islam the legislative power and competence to establish laws belongs exclusively to God Almighty. The sacred legislator of Islam is the sole legislative power. (Ayatollah Khomeini, *Hokoomat-e Eslami,* cited in Hamid Hosseini, "Theocracy Versus Constitutionalism: Is Velayat-e Faghih Compatible with Democracy?" *Journal of Iranian Research and Analysis* [November 1999]: 90).

11. Ibrahim Yazdi, a close ally of the Ayatollah, reiterated this point in an interview in 1999.

> Ayatollah Khomeimi insisted on writing Islamic Republic instead of Islamic government. In a text I had written, he crossed out the Islamic government and wrote Islamic Republic. He in fact made the type of the [new] government clearer—a republic. (See Interview with Ibrahim Yazdi, "Behind the Scene of the Revolution in Paris," *Iran Farda* 51 [February 1999]: 22).

Ezatollah Sahabi reaffirmed this.

> I believe Ayatollah Khomeini did not view it advisable to raise the question of *velayat-e faghih* at that point (during the course of the revolution). My argument is based on the following. The Ayatollah's entourage was engaged in discussing the slogans of the revolution when Ayatollah Khomeini was in Paris. The slogans were independence, freedom, and the Islamic government. But, Ayatollah Khome-

ini told them to change the slogan to Islamic Republic, because the Islamic government had certain context and form that were not advisable then. (Interview by Ezatollah Sahabi, "What Happened in the Council of Revolution," *Iran Farda* 52 [March 1999]: 7–8).

12. From the outset, there were fundamental differences in their views of the state between the provisional government and others in the new state. As explained by Habibollah Asgaroladi, "They [the provisional government] had nationalistic views and the majority of the first Assembly of Experts did not accept these views. That is why they did not get [enough] votes. They put forth different views. They even had different views about the name of the republic. For example, the National Republic of Iran. . . . The draft of the constitution that was prepared by the provisional government had strong nationalistic tenets. But, what was approved was a different text." See Interview with Habibollah Asgaroladi, *Gozaresh* 93 (November 1998).

13. Immediately after the 1997 revolution, Mehdi Bazargan was a favorite politician among most common people, and well liked and respected within the ranks of the new state. Two years later, Bazargan was demoted, disliked, and scorned as a "liberal." An MP slapped him in the parliament. Bazargan's organization, the Freedom Movement became known as the hotbed of "liberalism" and a home to "dangerous liberals."

14. *Minutes, Volume 4* (1985), 319–321.

15. The following is a representative of the debate during the general discussion about the draft of the constitution in the assembly:

Mohammad Mehdi Rabbani Amlashi (clergy): "Is the separation of branches of the state desired? . . . I believe the position of *velayat* is both the executive branch and the judiciary in Islam. . . . He gives orders. Obeying him is a duty of all Moslems." Ibid., 62.

Ali Akbar Ghorashi (clergy): "If we include *velayat-e faghih* in the constitution and always remember the guardianship of the *faghih,* then following his orders will have to be incumbent on people. We must train the people in such a way that the orders of the government shall be incumbent on them." Ibid., 73.

Jalaloldin Farsi: "Government or the power to legislate belongs exclusively to God. Whoever claims the power to legislate is an apostate. . . . The power to legislate does not belong to people or the Moslem people. Thus, it cannot be granted to anyone or a group through elections. . . . We do not have a legislative person or institution in Islam. . . . We have the *faghih* or the canonist. Thus, we must have *Majlis-e faghihan* (the assembly of the canonists). What belongs to the people is not rights, but duty." Ibid., 77.

Mohammad Ali Moosavi Jazayeri (clergy): "I believe that we do not need a president. In case we needed a president, he must be the second highest ranking authority in the country." Ibid., 80.

Mir Abolfazl Moosavi Tabrizi (clergy): "I believe that the authority given to the President in the [draft of] constitution of the Islamic Republic does not coincide with the Islamic, Quoranic, human, and scientific principles." Ibid., 85.

Naser Makarem Shirazi (clergy): "I voted positively for *velayat-e faghih* from day one. I will do so till eternity. But, this is not the way to implement *velayat-e faghih*. . . . We must leave to the president the work of the nation if he is approved by the leader. . . . How can we give no authority to the president that is elected by the people and approved by the leader. . . . This article [Article 110] cannot be implemented. . . . This article of the constitution indicates that we [the clergy] control everything. This is the best excuse for the enemy. They will say that a group of clergy got together in the Assembly of Experts and drafted a law to fortify the basis of their rule. . . . I beg you not to do this. People may be silent today. But, they will reject this law tomorrow. . . . We approved the rule of the people in the earlier articles. Let us not make the rule of the people an empty slogan.

"The people of Iran endorsed the Islamic Republic by a 98 percent vote. They will choose their president according to this. But, given this article, it is not clear what the president's role is. . . .

"It is not right for the clergy to choose a president, while maintaining all the authority and power. . . . Are you saying that the president and the commander-in-chief must be two separate people forever? We must try to maintain the trust of the people. If we lose people's trust and loyalty, even the commander-in-chief cannot help." *Minutes, Volume 2* (1985), 114–116.

Hassan Ayat—"I am one of the serious defenders of this principle *[velayat-e faghih]*. Perhaps, the reason I accepted to become a member of this assembly was to do all in my capacity to help pass this. I do not see conceivable an Islamic state without this." Ibid., 1092.

Abolhossein Dastgheib—"*Imamat* and *velayat* mean that, based on the principle of kindness, God cannot leave humans without a guardian. Like the prophetic mission of the prophet, *imamat-e Imam* [the guardianship of the Imam] is also based on the principle of kindness. Similarly to the need to send decrees through prophets, it is for God to assign Imams. Imam means leader, supervisor, someone who guides people and takes charge of the people. . . . The appointment of Imam, the assignment of Imam. . . . This is the truth about *imamat*. . . . The prophetic mission might end with the prophet, but, in terms of *imamat,* God must assign a guardian for the people until eternity. . . . The government of God—the government of Imam and *vali-e amr,* is established when the majority of people want it. When the majority of people are ready to follow orders, the *vali-e amr* is required to step forward and take charge of the matters. . . . Government is the right of the just *faghih*." Ibid., 1158.

16. Article 2 of the draft defined the Islamic Republic as follows:

> The Islamic Republic is a monotheist system based on the genuine, dynamic, and revolutionary Islamic culture. It relies on the value

and greatness of humans, their responsibilities to themselves and the principle role of virtue in their development, the negation of all types of cultural, political, and economic prejudice and dominance. It is based on the necessity of applying the useful fruits of human culture and science toward the obligation to all divine teachings of Islam.

Article 2 of the 1979 constitution approved by the Assembly to Draft and Finalize the Constitution of the Islamic Republic of Iran declared:

The Islamic Republic is a system based on the faith in

1. the one God *[La-ilah-illal-lah]*, that he establishes the *sahri'at* [canon law] and that humans should resign to his will;
2. the divine revelations and their fundamental role in the interpretation of laws;
3. the resurrection and its role in the human perfection toward God;
4. the justice of God in creation and in establishing the canon law;
5. the uninterrupted *imamat* and leadership and its fundamental role in the continuity of the revolution of Islam;
6. nobility and sublime value of humans and their liberty and responsibility before God which ensure equity, justice and political, economic, social, and cultural independence as well as national unity and solidarity through
    a. uninterrupted administration of canon law by fully qualified religious jurisprudents on the basis of the Scripture [the Quran] and the traditions of the fourteen innocents for whom we invoke God's blessing;
    b. taking advantage of advanced human knowledge and experience and endeavoring to further advance them;
    c. denouncing oppression or being oppressed, dominance or being dominated.

17. Defending Article 5, Ayatollah Beheshti declared the following:

Nonideological societies are free of ideology. They believe solely in one principle—the principle of government through people's vote. But, there are other societies that are ideological. These are societies where people choose an ideology before anything else. From that moment, they in fact proclaim that all matters must be regarded within the framework of the ideology. . . . The Islamic Republic is such a society. It differs from a democratic republic (*Minutes, Volume 1* [1985], 380).

18. Article 57 of the Constitution of the Islamic Republic of Iran.

19. Article 113 of the Constitution of the Islamic Republic of Iran.

20. The *faghih* (supreme leader) was granted the following authority by Article 110 of the Constitution.

1. Appointment of theologians and canonists, members of the Guardian Council.
2. Appointment of the highest ranking official of the judicial branch.
3. In the capacity of the Commander of the Armed Forces, as follows:
    a. Appointment and dismissal of the chief of general staff.
    b. Appointment and dismissal of the commander-in-chief of the Revolutionary Guards Corps *[Pasdaran]*.
    c. Forming the Supreme Council of National Defense.
    d. Appointment of commanders-in-chief of three armed forces as proposed by the Supreme Defense Council.
    e. Declaring war and peace and mobilization of the armed forces as proposed by the Supreme Defense Council.
    f. Appointment of the president after having been elected by the people. The eligibility of the candidates for presidency as specified in the constitution shall be confirmed by the Guardian Council prior to the elections and endorsed by the leader for the first term of the presidency.
4. Pardoning convicts . . .

21. Article 57 after the 1989 amendment.

22. Article 110 as approved by the Committee to Amend the Constitution:

1. Determining the overall policies of the Islamic Republic of Iran after consultation with the Expediency Council of the Islamic Republic.
2. Monitoring the proper enforcement of the system's overall policies.
3. Calling a referendum.
4. Commander-in-chief of the armed forces.
5. Declaring war and peace and mobilizing forces.
6. Appointment, dismissal, and the acceptance of the resignation of:

a. Theologians of the Guardian Council.
b. The highest-ranking official of the judiciary branch.
c. The head of Islamic Republic National Broadcasting Agency.
d. Chief of the General Staff.
e. Commander-in-chief of the Revolutionary Guards Corps.
f. The Commander-in-chief of the armed and security forces.

7. Reconciling the differences and regulating the relationship between the three branches of the government.
8. Resolving through the Expediency Council of the Islamic Republic those problems of the system that cannot be solved through regular channels. . . .

23. See the excellent book by Ervand Abrahamins for the documentation of these executions. Ervand Abrahamian, *Torture Confessions: Prisons and Public Recantations in Modern Iran* (Berkeley: University of California Press, 1999).

24. Ibid.

25. Akbar Meshkini—"We think that without a problem the *faghih* must have *velayat motlagheh* (absolute and unconditional power to rule). We say that you need to interject a phrase in your law to indicate this. Do not limit the authority of the *faghih.*" See *Minutes of the Committee to Amend the Constitution, Volume 3* (Tehran: Cultural and Public Relations of the Parliament, 1990), 1630.

"This is the meaning of *motlagh:* The [authority] of the *faghih* will not be limited to articles 110, and 111. The *[faghih]* can interfere from above at all times, telling us what can and cannot be done." Ibid., 1632.

Ali Khamenei—(days before his promotion to *velayat-e faghih*): "I do not think adding [the word *motlagheh*] is a negation of the constitution." Ibid., 1638.

Abdollah Nouri—"We like to know whether the constitution will be enforced or *velayat-e motlagheh faghih?*" Ibid., 1631.

Moosavi Khoiniha—"This article implies that no other article [of the constitution] will have any stability. . . . It means that . . . *vali-e amr* can disrupt the constitution and the system of government we have claimed to have. . . . In fact you are voting for a principle that implies that in the system of Islamic Republic all matters are in the hand of *vali-e amr* and his *velayat* is the rule. It is absolute and unconditional. He can change anything and everything whenever he sees fit. . . . The understanding of the people of the world will be that we have one person in charge of everything. This person can change the constitution. . . . Dissolve the parliament sometimes. . . . For these reasons I do not agree with entering such an interpretation in the constitution." Ibid., 1633.

26. Article 109 declared the following qualifications of the leader.

1. Scientific ability and theological virtues essential for expounding various aspects of the Islamic theological and canon law.
2. Correct political and social insight, bravery, power, and adequate managerial capabilities for leadership. In case many share the above qualifications, a person shall be chosen with stronger insight in politics and [Islamic] jurisprudence.

27. Abdollah Nouri, Hemlock for Advocate of Reform: The Complete Text of Abdollah Nouri's Defense at the Special Court of the Clergy (Tehran: Tarh-e No Publishers, 1999), 24.

28. Ibid. p. 5051.

29. *Minutes of the Committee to Amend the Constitution, Volume 3* (1990), 1631.

30. Eighteen years after the cultural revolution, Soroush said the following in a meeting with Moslem students. See Abdolkaraim Soroush, "Fascist Reading of Religion," *Razdani and Roshanfekt-e Mazhabi* (Tehran: Sarat Cultural Institute, 1998).

> The call for the Islamicization of universities once again . . . is a witness to the failure of the clergy crying loudly that perhaps professors and students . . . are not in love with and subjugated to the clergy as much as they should be. . . . I have learned from experience and thinking that the Islamicization of universities is like making formulas for being in love or being a poet. The experience of love and poetry should tell everyone to what extent this is possible.

Three years earlier in a lecture at New York University, Soroush defended the cultural revolution and his role in removing the Marxist forces that had turned universities into armed camps.

31. Despite its general endorsement of pluralism, tolerance, etc., many differences existed between the leading figures in the movement. The interviews conducted by Hossein Yousefi Ashkevari with Mehdi Bazargan, Abdolkarim Soroush, Mohammad Mojtahed Shabestari, Ezatollah Sahabi, Habibollah Payman, and others provide a very useful guide to the issue. See Hossein Yousefi Ashkevari, *Review and Critique of the Current Islamic Movement: Religious Modernism* (Tehran: Ghasiden Press, 1999).

32. Responding to the widespread criticism of the "official reading" of Islam by those in Mohammad Khatami's camp, Ayatollah Mesbah Yazdi, an

influential theologian and an expert in Islamic political philosophy said, "Western democracy is based on people's vote. But, based our Islamic views, God's order is the criteria. . . . Today, some inside Iran speak of different readings of Islam. But, the reading of our Islamic people of Iran and the Islamic revolution is nothing but the rule of God. Our people will defend this view till the last drop of their blood."

33. Abdolkarim Soroush, "Democratic Religious State," speeches given in 1991 and 1992, published in *Fatter than Ideology* (Tehran: Sarat Cultural Institute, 1997), 279.

34. Ibid., 280.

35. Abdolkarim Soroush, "Analysis of the Concept of 'Religious State,'" speech delivered at the Conference on Religion and the State organized by the Association of Engineers on June 29, 1985, published in Abdolkarim Soroush, *Modara va Modiriat* (Tehran: Sarat Cultural Institute, 1997), 353–380.

36. Abdolkarim Soroush, *Modara va Modiriat,* 354–360.

37. Ibid., 372–373.

38. Abdolkarim Soroush, "Heartfelt Velayat and Political Velayat," *Kian* 8, no. 44 (November-January 1999): 10–20.

39. Mohsen Kadivar, *Theories of State in Shiite Jurisprudence* (Tehran: Nay Press, 1997); Mohsen Kadivar, *Hokoomat-e Vela-ee* (Government of Religious Jurisconsult) (Tehran, Nay Press, 1998).

40. Mohsen Kadivar, "A Round table on Religion, Tolerance, and Violence," *Kian* 8, no. 45 (February and March 1999): 12–13.

41. Mohammad Mojtahed Shabestari, "The Official Reading of Religion: Crises, and Solution," interview with Akbar Ganji in *Rah-e No* 1, no. 19 (September 1998): 18–22.

42. Mohammad Mojtahed Shabestari, "A Round Table on Religion, Tolerance, and Violence," *Kian* 8, no. 45 (February and March 1999): 9.

43. Ibid., 17–18.

44. Mohammad Mojtahed Shabestari, interview in Hossein Yousefi Ashkevari, *Review and Critique of the Current Islamic Movement: Religious Modernism* (Tehran: Shaaback, 1999).

45. Mohammad Mojtahed Shabestari, "A Round Table on Religion, Tolerance, and Violence," 14–15.

46. Mohammad Mojtahed Shabestari, "The Official Reading of Religion: Crises, and Solution," *Rah-e No* 1, no. 19 (September 1998): 18–22.

47. Abdolkarim Soroush, *Modara va Modiriat,* 354.

48. Abdolkarim Soroush, "Heartfelt Velayat and Political Velayat," 20.

49. Hassan Yousefi Ashkevari, "Seminary and the State: Twenty Years after Merger," *Neshat* (2 May 1999), 6.

50. Abdolkarim Soroush, "Fascist Reading of Religion," in Abdolkarim Soroush, *Razdani va Roshanfekr-e Mazhabi* (Tehran: Sarat Cultural Institute, 1998), 80–81.

51. Akbar Ganji, "The Leadership, Direct Election, with Limited Term and Continuous Supervision," *Rah-e No,* no. 20 (September 1999).

52. *Iran Emrooz* online.

Selected Bibliography

BOOKS

Abrahamian, Ervand. *Iran Between the Two Revolutions*. Princeton: Princeton University Press, 1982.

———. *Torture Confessions: Prisons and Public Recantations in Modern Iran*. Berkeley: University of California Press, 1999.

Bayat, Assef. *Workers and Revolution in Iran*. London: Zed Press, 1987.

Bryan, Dick. *The Chase across the Globe: International Accumulation and the Contradictions for Nation States*. Oxford: Westview Press, 1995.

Foweraker, Joe. *Theorizing Social Movements*. London: Pluto Press, 1995.

Ganji, Akbar. *Taarik Kaneh-e Ashbah* (Ghosts' Darkroom). Tehran: Tarh-e No, 1999.

Gorz, Andre. *Farewell to the Working Class*. Boston: South End Press, 1982.

Halliday, Fred. *Iran: Dictatorship and Development*. New York: Penguin, 1979.

Kadivar, Mohsen. *Nazarieh-ha-ye Dolat dar Fegh-e Shieh* (Theories of State in Shiite Jurisprudence). Tehran: Nay Press, 1997.

———. *hokoomat-e vela-ee* (Government of Religious Jurisconsult). Tehran: Nay Press, 1998.

Laclau, Erriesto, and Chantal Mouffe. *Hegemony and Socialist Strategy: Towards a Radical Democratic Politics*. London: Verso, 1985.

Millani, Mohsen. *The Making of Iran's Islamic Revolution: From Monarchy to the Islamic Republic*. London: Westview Press, 1988.

Mojtahed Shabestari, Mohammad. *Eiman va Azadi* (Faith and Freedom). Tehran: Tarh-e No, 1999.

———. *Hermenotic, Ketab, va Sonnat* (Hermeneutic, The Scripture, and The Tradition). Tehran: Tarh-e No, 1998.

Mortaji, Hojjat. *Jennah-ha-ye Siasi dar Iran-e* Emrooz (Political Factions in Contemporary Iran). Tehran: Naghsh VA Negar Publications, 1999.

Nouri, Abdollah. *Shokaran-e Eslah: Defa'iat-e Abdollah Nouri* (Hemlock for Advocate of Reform: The Complete Text of Abdollah Nouri's Defense at the Special Court of the Clergy). Tehran: Tarh-e No, 1999.

Soroush, Abdolkarim. *Farbehtar as Eidehology* (Fatter than Ideology). Tehran: Sarat Cultural Institute, 1997.

———. *Eidehology-e Sheitani* (Satanic Ideology). Tehran: Sarat Cultural Institute, 1994.

———. *Modara va Modiriat*. Tehran: Sarat Cultural Institute, 1997.

———. *Razdani and Roshanfekt-e Mazhabi*. Tehran: Sarat Cultural Institute, 1998.

Touraine, Alain. *The Voice and the Eye: An Analysis ofSocial Movements*. Cambridge: Cambridge University Press, 1985.

Yousefi Ashkevari, Hossein. *Naghd va Barresi-yeh Gonbesh-e Eslami-ye Waser: No garaee-ye Deeni* (Review and Critique of the Current Islamic Movement: Religious Modernism). Tehran: Ghasiden Press, 1999.

DOCUMENTS

Soorat-e Mashrooh-e Mozakerat-e majles-e barresi-e Nahaee-e Ghanoon-e Asasi-e *Jomhoori-e Eslami-e Iran* (Minutes of the Assembly for the Final Evaluation of theConstitution of the Islamic Republic of Iran, Volumes 1–4) Tehran: Cultural and Public Relations of the Parliament, 1985.

Soorat-e Mashrooh-e Mozakerat-e Shora-ye Baznegari-e Ghanoon-e Asasi-e Jomhoori-e *Eslami-e Iran* (Minutes of the Committee to Amend the Constitution, Volume 4). Tehran: Cultural and Public Relations of the Parliament, 1990.

INTERVIEWS

Asgaroladi, Habibollah. "Jam'iat Mo'talefeh: Four Decades of open and Hidden Influence," *Gozaresh* 93 (1998): 13–21.

Mojtahed Shabestari, Mohammad. "The Official Reading of Religion: Crises, and Solution," *Rah-e No* 1, no. 19 (September 1998): 18–22.

———. "A Round Table on Religion, Tolerance, and Violence," *Kian* 8, no. 45 (February and March 1999): 9.

Mlojahat Shabestari, Mohammad, and Molisen Kadivar. "Religion, Tolerance, and Violence," 45 *Kian* (February 1999): 6–19.

Payman, Habibollah. "From the Discourse of the Revolution to the Discourse of May 23rd," *Donya-ye Sokhan* 84 (1999): 21–28.

Sahabi, Ezatollah. "What Happened in the Council of Revolution," *Iran Farda* 51 (February 1999).

Soroush, Abdolkarim. "Heartfelt Velayat and Political Velayat," *Kian* 8, no. 44 (November-January 1999): 10–20.

———. "Religiousness, Tolerance, and Civility," *Kian* 45 (February 1999): 20–37.

Yazdi, Ibrahim. "Behind the Scene of the Revolution in Paris," *Iran Farda* 51 (February 1999): 22.

———. "The Untold Stories of the Revolution and After," *Gozaresh* 91 (1998): 12–20.

ARTICLES

Clawson, Patrick. "The Internationalization of Capital and Capital Accumulation in Iran and Iraq," *Insurgent Sociologist* VII, no. 2 (1997).

Foran, John. "A Century of Revolution: Comparative, Historical, and Theoretical Perspectives on Social Movements in Iran." In John Foran (ed.), *A Century of Revolution: Social Movements in Iran* (Minneapolis: University of Minnesota Press, 1994).

Melucci, Albert. "The Symbolic Challenge of Contemporary Movements," *Social Research* 52, 4 (Winter 1985).

Nikfar, Mohammad. "Human Rights and Citizen's Rights, " *Negah No* 39 (Summer 1998): 23–36.

Offe, Claus. "New Social Movements: Challenging the Boundaries of Institutional Politics," *Social Research* 52, 4 (Winter 1985).

Polloix, Christian. "The Internationalization of Capital and the Circuit of Social Capital." In Hugo Radici (ed.), *International Firms and Modern Imperialism* (Harmondsworth: Penguin, 1975).

Tilly, Charles. "From Interaction to Outcomes in Social Movements." In Marco Giugni, Doug McAdam, and Charles Tilly (eds.), *How Social Movements Matter* (Minneapolis: University of Minnesota Press, 1999).

———. "Repertoires of Contention in America and Britain." In Mayer Zald and John McCarthy (eds.), *Social Movements in an Organizational Society* (New Brunswick: Transaction, 1979).

Touraine, Alain. "Beyond Social Movements." In Stanford L. Lyman, *Social Movements: Critique, Concepts, and Case Studies* (New York: New York University Press, 1995).

Weeks, John. "Epochs of Capitalism and the Progressiveness of Capital Expansion," *Science & Society* XIIX, no. 4 (1985).

Yaghmaian, Behzad. "Globalization of the State: The Political Economy of Global Accumulation and Its Emerging Mode of Regulation," *Science and Society* 62, no. 2 (Summer 1998).

———. "Internationalization of Capital and the Crisis of the Iranian Economy," *Review of Radical Political Economics* 20, no. 4 (1988).

INDEX

Ansar-e Hezbollah, 14, 31, 52, 54, 83, 94, 97, 98, 100–2, 104, 107, 111, 134, 218, 233n, 236n, 240n
Approbatory supervision, 96, 100
Assembly of Experts, 96–97, 205, 211, 214, 236n, 254n, 255n
Ayatollah Khamenei, 9, 16, 105, 108, 211–12, 214–15, 239n, 252n, 258n
Ayatollah Khomeini, 11, 27, 75–76, 79, 84, 86, 101, 107, 139, 207, 209, 211, 213–15, 217, 233n, 235n, 236n, 153n
Ayatollah Montazeri, 11, 205, 208, 213, 216, 233n, 253n

Basij, 52, 54, 67, 68, 83, 106, 111, 121–22, 128, 135
Behnood, Masood, 141

Civil society, 4–5, 9, 11–12, 15, 18, 21, 32, 47, 77, 79, 81, 86, 88, 95–96, 117–18, 120–25, 128–31, 139–49, 171, 175, 181, 183, 206, 214, 226, 230, 243
Committees: factory, 147; neighborhood, 144
Council of Revolution, 12, 207, 209
Crisis: economic, 5, 23, 172–73, 175, 182, 193, 246n; political, 3, 139
Cultural Invasion, 41, 43, 48, 50, 64, 66, 121, 139, 210
Cultural Revolution, 74, 75, 78, 79, 102, 104, 218, 259

Eskandari, Parvaneh, 31
Exchange rate, 149–53, 156, 176–78, 187, 190, 246n, 250n
Export-led growth, 185, 197, 200

Football, 49–54
Forouhar, Daryoush, 31, 237n
Free press, 4, 13, 18, 24, 37, 81, 85, 117–21, 124–31, 135–40, 240n–243n

Ganji, Akbar, 126, 132, 136, 141, 260–61
Guardian Council, 22, 96, 100, 120, 205–6, 211, 241n, 253n, 257n

Hajjarian, Saeed, 38, 135, 138
Hashemi Rafsanjani, 15, 19, 76, 77, 80, 84, 129, 135, 155, 184–90, 192, 214, 217, 236n, 240n

Import-substitution industrialization, 195, 196, 200, 201
International division of labor, 5, 193, 195, 196, 199, 251

Internationalization of capital, 194–97, 251n–252n
Islamic Councils, 144, 145, 147, 172, 246
Islamic: left tendency, 80, 146, 185; right tendency, 122, 174
Islamic jurisprudence, 209, 223, 253n

Jalaeipour, Hamid-Reza, 120, 122, 126, 218, 239n
Jame'eh, 18, 120–25, 128, 129, 238n, 241n

Kadivar, Mohsen, 12, 132, 220–23, 133n, 239n, 260n, 263
Kargozaran, 15–16, 120, 184–89
Khatami, Mohammad, 5, 9–16, 20, 51, 72, 81, 85, 87, 93–99, 102–3, 108–10, 114–15, 117–18, 120, 122–23, 126, 130, 133, 135, 145–46, 172, 178, 181–84, 189, 191–92, 197, 200, 213–14, 218, 229–30, 234n, 239n, 240n, 242n, 248n, 259n

May 23rd movement, 114–15, 225, 239
Modernity, 7, 73, 74, 92, 209, 218; postmodern, 19, 113; postmodernity, 19, 37, 58
Modernization, 7, 73, 197, 199, 209
Mohajerani Ata', 115, 136, 137
Mojtahed Shabestari, Mohammad, 6, 219–22, 259–60n, 265
Mokhtari, Mohammd, 31–33
Mossadegh, Mohammad, 87, 99, 238n, 239n, 252n
Movement for Joy, 4, 17, 37, 47, 48, 91, 98

Nabavi, Behzad 16
Nabavi, Ibrahim, 126–27, 137, 141
Neoliberalism, 5, 15, 80, 187, 237
Non-oil exports, 191, 193
Nouri, Abdollah 13, 16, 17, 21, 38, 51, 94–95, 135, 138–40, 214, 216, 217, 243n

Oil, 5, 23, 75, 176, 191, 192–94, 197–99, 201, 243n, 244n, 245n, 250n, 252n; exports, 176, 191, 198, 250n, 251n, 252n, 253n

Pasdaran, 13–14, 121, 122, 126, 135, 136, 144, 234n, 257n
Pluralism, 3, 6, 8, 19, 21, 77, 79, 81, 84, 119, 121, 183, 217, 218, 220, 227
Political development, 18, 96, 146, 143, 184, 199
Political divide, 5–6, 9, 10, 12, 13, 79, 105, 175, 207, 213, 214, 246n
Pouyandeh, Ja'far, 2, 31–32
Privatization, 7, 14–15, 79–80, 150, 172, 184–85, 188, 192, 201, 221, 237n, 249n
Provisional government, 207, 210, 213, 254n

Religious democracy, 230
Religious intelligentsia, 6, 79, 217, 22, 233n

Sahabi, Ezatollah, 124, 132–33, 239n, 252n, 253n, 259n
Shamsolvaezin, Mashallah, 120, 125, 126, 129, 139, 141, 218
Social movements, 3, 4, 7, 16, 17, 23–25, 48, 94, 131, 148, 225, 234n; new, 2, 3, 17, 24, 47, 117, 118, 234n
Soroush abdolkarim 5, 79, 217–20, 222–23, 259n–261n, 264–65
Student movement: Islamic, 74–76, 82, 105; old Islamic, 76–77; new Islamic, 105; new, 4, 21, 82, 92, 94, 96, 98, 101–4, 108, 112

Tabarzadi, Heshmatollah, 76, 82–90, 96–97, 112, 114, 137, 233n, 236n, 237n
Traditional left tendency, 185, 186, 189, 191, 214
Traditional right tendency, 96, 185–86, 214, 236n

Unity Consolidation Office (UCO,) 4, 73, 75–83, 87, 95, 104–6, 109–10, 113–14
Utopia: MTV, 229–32; Islamic, 229–32

Velayat-e faghih, 5, 9, 11, 20, 60, 82, 84, 85, 86, 97, 122, 205, 206, 207, 208, 209, 212, 214, 215, 217, 222, 223, 233n, 253n, 254n, 255n, 258n; motlagheh-e faghih, 84, 85; motlagheh-e fardi, 84, 85

Women's movement, 23
Workers' Councils, 143, 145, 147

Yousefi Ashkevari, Hassan, 22–23, 239n, 259n, 269n, 264